Also available at all good book stores

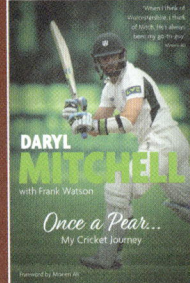

9781801502023

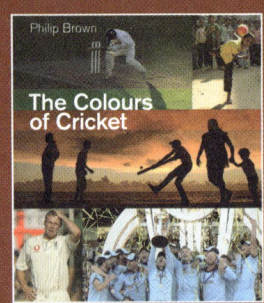

9781785319952

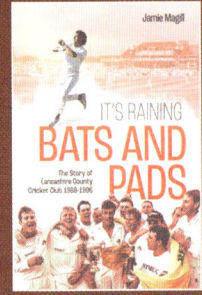

9781801500678

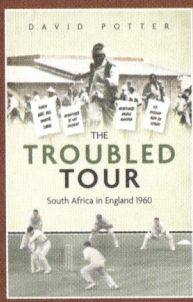

9781801502009

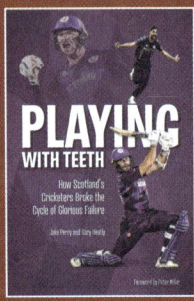

9781801501217

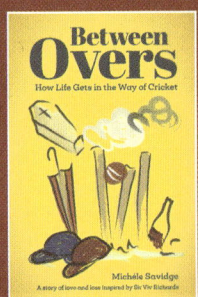

9781801500715

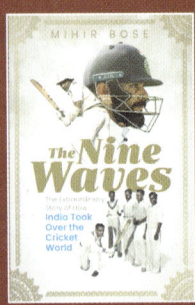

9781801501040

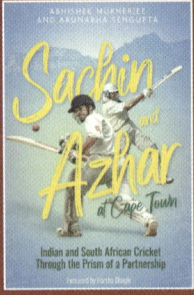

9781785318191

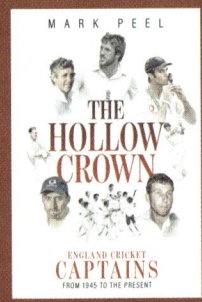

9781785316630

Swallows and Hawke

Richard Parry and André Odendaal

SWALLOWS AND HAWKE

English Cricket Tours, the MCC
and the Making of South Africa
1888-1968

First published by Pitch Publishing, 2022

Pitch Publishing
9 Donnington Park,
85 Birdham Road,
Chichester,
West Sussex,
PO20 7AJ
www.pitchpublishing.co.uk
info@pitchpublishing.co.uk

A CIP catalogue record is available for this book
from the British Library.

ISBN 978 1 80150 134 7

Typesetting and origination by Pitch Publishing
Printed and bound in India by Replika Press Pvt. Ltd.

Contents

To Krom Hendricks, Frank Roro, Basil D'Oliveira, and all those thousands of black players including Ebony Rainford Brent and Azeem Rafiq who fought racism and the exclusionist cricket establishments which denied them the opportunity to fully achieve their potential in the game they loved. May this book support the eradication of discrimination on grounds of race, gender and class wherever cricket is played.

Foreword by Peter Hain

SWALLOWS RE-AWAKENS my earliest cricketing memories hearing of Compton's legendary triple hundred and watching the 1964/65 tourists at Berea Park with my brother Tom, and it reminds me of how the South African Security Police confiscated my pencil cricket scoresheets suspecting that Sobers, Hall and May were coded revolutionaries.

The intense on-field struggle between white South Africa and their oldest sporting rivals reinforced the soft power of empire. Racial segregation and inequality were the bedrock of South African sport and society; white advantage depended on excluding the black majority. After Black Lives Matter, it is self-evident that what happens on the pitch reflects what happens beyond it. *Swallows* explains how politics shaped sport and how sport and particularly these tours reinforced the power of the racist state, and introduces black and women's cricket and the history of resistance to the apartheid state. Fifteen cricket tours, echoed to the thump, not just of leather on willow, but to the jackhammers wielded by millions of black mineworkers. Gold enriched British mining magnates while empire supported South Africa's evolution from segregation to apartheid, ignoring the oppression of the black population. Eventually, MCC foundered between its loyal player, the black South African Basil D'Oliveira, and his persecutor, the white South African government. *Swallows* provides an essential window into today's struggles over race and power including Yorkshire's disgraceful treatment of Azeem Rafiq.

Lord Peter Hain spent his childhood in South Africa and is a former British anti-apartheid leader and Cabinet minister. He is co-author with André Odendaal of *Pitch Battles, sport, racism and resistance*.

Foreword by Stephen Chalke

I HAVE LEARNED so much reading this book – about the development of cricket in South Africa and about the forces that led to the creation of the apartheid system. The authors' ambitious approach, viewing it all through the prism of 15 English cricket tours, weaves the two strands together to telling effect. In South Africa the sport and the racial politics can never be wholly separated.

The early South African performances were dreadful, but inside 20 years their cricket had taken a giant leap forward. The tale of their first victory over England … well, you would be pushed to make up the thrilling climax. I was on the edge of my chair reading it. And, as I found out as I read on, it was far from the only game with such a gripping ending.

Cricket, however, is only one part of this story. The authors describe in horrific detail how South Africa turned itself into a brutal police state, enforcing rigid laws of racial separation, and how the English tourists were for the most part cocooned in a bubble of privilege.

The book ends, as the 80-year history of these tours ends, with the D'Oliveira Affair, and here the superb research skills of the authors have come up with a real plum, unearthing minutes of Lord's meetings that were thought to have been destroyed. As with so much in this most original book, the authors have added to our understanding – and not just of cricket's history.

Stephen Chalke is the author of *Summer's Crown: The Story of Cricket's County Championship* and founding publisher of Fairfield Books.

Acknowledgements

WHEN WE write history, even if we're not actually standing on the shoulders of giants, we gain inspiration and influence from many directions. This is particularly true when the narrative veers off the well-trodden path and the echo of leather on willow meets the creaking of wagon wheels and the cacophony of jackhammers deep in the earth.

Our efforts to reconstruct the impact and significance of the MCC's relationship with this corner of the empire are indebted to all those historians who seek to transform South Africa's understanding of its past, built on structural racism and extreme economic inequality, into the foundation for a new inclusive and equal society.

Swallows and Hawke is a book about cricket, reliving the compelling nature of an on-field rivalry over 80 years. The duel between England and South Africa may not have been as noisy as the Ashes, but it was fought with no less intensity or ferocity. Each of the seven Test series in South Africa between 1922 and 1965 went down to the wire; every Test counted, there were no dead rubbers. *Swallows* explores the visceral application of skill and power, of temperament and intelligence, and of strategy and decision-making in the unfolding of matches.

It describes how, off the field, the experience of the cricketers lifted the veil on the political economy of the golden heart of empire. They played to against whites-only teams before segregated crowds and watched watched 'dances' performed by black workers secured in mining compounds. Lord Harris and other grandees were the masters of both the players and the miners, directing simultaneously the operations of MCC and the South African mining industry.

It is a truism that politics and capital controlled cricket but to challenge the barriers of race, class and gender we need to understand who decides who plays, under what conditions, and in what circumstances. In the tradition of Rowland Bowen, Mike Marquese, Ramachandra Guha and Derek Birley, *Swallows and Hawke* is intended to point towards new possibilities for researching and writing post-colonial histories of English cricket.

The significance of historical transformation in South Africa's road to democracy has inspired the building of a solid foundation of new writing on South African cricket and on its history. André Odendaal's work, especially the multi-volume *History of South African Cricket Retold*, with Krish Reddy, Christopher Merrett and Jonty Winch, lift the lid on apartheid's cricketing past and provides the evidence, analysis and statistics for an understanding of South Africa's real story.

A complementary series of narratives has interwoven class, race and gender with political process and South African cricket. This book builds on essays contained in *Empire and Cricket, 1884–1914*, and *Cricket and Society, 1914–1971*, presided over by Bruce Murray, who sadly passed away in 2019. They were shaped by South African and British-based writers including Goolam Vahed, Ashwin Desai, Richard Parry, Jonty Winch, Dale Slater, Bernard Hall, Geoff Levett, Keith Booth, Albert Grundlingh, Heinrich Schultze, Rafaelle Nicholson, Patrick Ferriday and Jon Gemmill.

Swallows and Hawke concludes with a new analysis of the Basil D'Oliveira crisis, which ends the sequence of English cricket tours to South Africa – if not the close relationship between the English cricketing establishment and the apartheid regime. Peter Oborne's empathetic approach to D'Oliveira and forensic analysis of the machinations in Pretoria and at Lord's over the tour rejuvenated a perennial issue and additional important contributions have been made by Bruce Murray, Rob Steen, Mike Brearley, Stephen Chalke and Peter Hain, who has described his own role in the successful

Stop the Seventy Tour direct action protests, which dramatically ruptured the age-old colonial partnership. The current focus on racism in cricket, within the broader focus of the Black Lives Matter campaign against racism in sport, has demonstrated the overwhelming significance of this issue and the distance still to go to achieve resolution.

This book argues that the ideological, political and economic partnership between Lord Harris and MCC shared a mantra of 'mines, empire and cricket' with the South African establishment. This set the framework within which the fifteen tours and the D'Oliveira crisis was managed. The MCC stuck rigorously to its strategic policy of accommodating and conciliating the South African regime between 1906 and 1968. An MCC 'war cabinet' with the formal sanction of the MCC committee managed the crisis itself.

The authors would like to thank two of the key figures who were active on and off the field in the latter years and who generously shared their time and experiences. In 2017, a few months before he passed away, Doug Insole vividly described the intensity of the 1956/57 series and spoke guardedly about his role as chairman of selectors. In 2020, with the Covid-19 pandemic in full swing, Mike Brearley cast a wise eye over his youthful memories of South Africa in 1964/65, his key role in the challenge to MCC in 1968 and shared his perspectives on the D'Oliveira non-selection/selection. The authors are very grateful to both for their courtesy and for bringing to life otherwise sterile documentation.

But the documentation provided an important if surprisingly little examined source. Despite the fountains of ink splashing over the D'Oliveira imbroglio, a common belief that crucial committee meeting minutes were missing has gone relatively unchallenged. Thanks are due to the Lord's librarian, Neil Robinson, and Robert Curphey, who is responsible for the MCC archives, for their helpfulness and efficiency in granting access to the committee records, which, through both omission and commission, tell a nuanced and compelling story.

The authors would like to thank Maurice Nettley and David Allison who provided important assistance in accessing, reviewing and teasing out the significance of some of these events. David also provided key details given his role in the action itself.

The history of the various English tours relies in part on the players' own accounts, some of which were published in the British press including *Cricket*, the *Cricket Field*, *The Sportsman*, and the *Westminster Gazette*, as well as numerous usually ghosted autobiographies and biographies.

Balancing this, the South African press, trading on the huge public interest that these relatively rare tours elicited, provided passionate and often partisan, if generally well-informed, coverage. Newspapers are vital for any contemporaneous understanding and thanks are due to the staffs of the National Library of South Africa (Cape Town), the British Library in London, the William Cullen Library at the University of the Witwatersrand, and the archives of the Western Cape.

No book is an island, and the authors would like to thank profusely their wholly informal 'panel' of critics who patiently read early chapter drafts. They provided invaluable and detailed input as the manuscript began to take shape. Occasionally combative, usually polite, but always supportive contributions came from Stephen Chalke, Patrick Ferriday, Bernard Hall, Geoff Levett, Graham Mouat, Maurice Nettley, Dale Slater, Jonty Winch, Christopher Merrett, Mogamad Allie and John Young. They helped us avoid many errors and sent us off on the scent of new enquiries. Any responsibility for errors or omissions due to ignorance or lack of space remain ours alone.

Over the years Cricket South Africa has embraced the rewriting of the old, skewed apartheid cricket histories, and we see this work as a further contribution to that project, too. Andre wishes to thank successive CSA CEO's and Boards and Max Jordaan, the executive with whom he has co-ordinated the history project, for their support in maintaining the writing momentum.

The authors would also like to thank Jane Camillin, Gareth Davis, Graham Hales, Duncan Olner, Dean Rockett and the team at Pitch Publishing for their excellent work, not only in producing this volume, but for playing a leading role in the regeneration in sports publishing generally and cricket in particular. Their crowded awards shelf is testament to their understanding of the interrelationship between sport and the society in which it is played, and they have helped us explore what it is that we need to know, to know cricket.

Finally, the stresses and strains of the last two years have been universal. The authors would like to thank their families, Helen and Carolyn (Richard) and Zohra, Rehana, Adam and Nadia (André). You put up with us and gave us perspective when the pandemic threatened to turn the world upside down.

South Africa

c. 1910

To Livingstone, Salisbury

RHODESIA

Bulawayo

BECHUANALAND

TRANSVAAL

GERMAN SOUTH WEST AFRICA

Middleburg

Pretoria

Johannesburg

Benoni

Potchefstroom

Vereeniging

Lourenço Marques

SWAZI-LAND

Vaal River

Bethlehem

Newcastle

ORANGE FREE STATE

Kimberley

Blomfontein

Ladysmith

NATAL

Orange River

Eshowe

Tugela River

CAPE PROVINCE

BASU-TOLAND

Pietermaritzburg

De Aar

Durban

Queenstown

Graaff-Reinet

Cradock

Matjesfontein

Kingwilliamstown

East London

Worcester

Uitenhage

Grahamstown

Paarl

Robertson

Oudtshoorn

Port Elizabeth

Cape Town

Mossel Bay

Cape of Good Hope

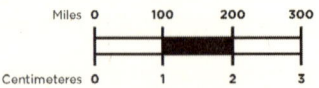

Approximate Scale

Miles   0   100   200   300

Centimeteres   0   1   2   3

Introduction

Summer Swallows

FOR COUNTLESS millennia, swallows have chased the sun between England and the Cape. The origins of this annual aeronautical odyssey are mysterious, but who would not want to fly south to escape the damp grey British winter?

The swallows glided and swooped on rivers of air, snatching insects on the wing, surviving storms, predators and exhaustion. Below them, 14 bands of English cricketers braved the witches' cauldron of the Bay of Biscay and the rolling menace of the Skeleton Coast (the 15th arrived by air in 1964). At last, drawn into the summer embrace of Table Bay, they stared up at the huge flat-topped timeless monolith, shaped by South Africa's strident geology, a stunning gateway to another world.

South Africa is defined by its physicality. Flying north-east from the Cape Peninsula our swallows encounter the twisted and jagged granite mountains, a monstrous staircase into the interior enclosing vineyards, wheat fields and then a featureless plateau of scrubland and desert. At last, having forded the Orange and Vaal rivers, they reach the Highveld and its beating golden heart.

Climate determines Africa's eclectic botanic and animal cargo, and its diverse and complex human presence. The freezing Benguela current scythes north from the Southern Ocean, chilling the toes of paddlers on Clifton beach, up the west coast to the seal and penguin playgrounds and Namibia's moisture-free skeleton desert.

17

From the north-east, the warm Mozambique current sweeps down the continent's lush green southern coastline. It collides with the Benguela at what mariners called the Cape of Storms and later, with an eye on marketing, what came to be known as the Cape of Good Hope. The Cape was Janus-faced from the beginning.

This dichotomy of climate and geology created an Eden for the earliest humans. The San and Khoikhoi ('men of men') left carvings in the Blombos Caves around 100,000 years ago. These hunter-gatherers had the country to themselves until, in the historical flicker of an eye, the great southward migrations of Bantu-speaking ironworkers and cattle keepers arrived at the Great Fish River. Centuries later from the north-west came the seaborne invasions of sharp-nosed and bellicose Europeans.

Six centuries ago, Europe embarked on a great wave of globalisation, based on new navigational techniques which allowed ships to sail south by heading west. Bartolomeu Dias set sail from Lisbon in 1487 via the Azores, was blown round the Cape of Storms and landed at Mossel Bay, where the first English cricket tourists arrived 401 years later before embarking on their great adventure. Dias received a chillier welcome than the cricketers would do and reacted to a fusillade of stones from the local Khoi by shooting one dead with a crossbow. Ten years later, Vasco da Gama swept out like a yoyo on a string almost touching the Brazil coast before swinging back on the westerlies to the Cape. Like Dias he landed at Mossel Bay and outstayed his welcome. The dispute was over water, cannons were fired and blood again shed. It was not an auspicious start. Da Gama fled east as the Khoi diligently destroyed the *padrao* (stone cross) the Portuguese had left to mark their landing.

Two hundred years later, the mercantilist Dutch set up a 'refreshment station', which soon became a depot for the East African and Asian branches of the global slave trade. In 1795, the British seized the Cape from the distracted Dutch to protect the empire in India. After a brief hiatus involving a non-cricketing French Emperor, the British retook the Cape in 1806. This was the first date from which, according to the magisterial *Cricket and Conquest*, cricket was definitively played at the Cape.[1]

The vegetable garden and slave lodge at Table Bay became a military enclave pushing out into the hinterland and intermingling with and displacing the indigenous populations. As in Galle, Bombay and Bridgetown, forts were built facing the internal threat with their backs to the sea. For two centuries, the settlers hunted the San peoples almost to extinction and forced the remnants into the desert interior. The next hundred-year war began on the Cape frontier in 1779 against the Xhosa. For at least 60 years the sides were evenly balanced and the outcome in doubt. By the 1830s, the Dutch pastoralists, chafing under oppressive British rule, ineffective military tactics, and incomprehensible race relations embarked on an event which would define their identity in Afrikaner mythology. This continental land-grab known as the Great Trek set up independent Boer Republics in the Transvaal and Orange Free State.

The struggle over land, water and cattle on the Eastern Cape Frontier was waged between an African population which had been used to absorbing invading cultures and an imperial establishment anxious to create a colonial buffer between the Fish and Kei rivers and whose greed for land and resources made conquest the long-term goal. The balance of diplomatic manoeuvrings, a British scorched earth policy and savage skirmishes, was not irrevocably settled in favour of Europe until after the tragedy of the great Xhosa cattle killing of 1856. This was a last-ditch response by the starving Xhosa to the depredations of the war and its aftermath. The seer Nongqawuse fatally predicted that killing all livestock would resurrect the ancestors and drive the British into the sea. Xhosa power was finally broken and while African military resistance continued sporadically for another 50 years, the war had been won.

Cricket was the main form of recreation for the military and playing cricket reflected an ease in the foreign environment and

---

1   André Odendaal, Krish Reddy, Christopher Merrett, and Jonty Winch, *Cricket and Conquest, 1795–1914*, (Cape Town, HSRC, 2016) 17

the transplantation of a culture suggestive of permanence. But it also suggested an overconfidence in colonial power. On Christmas Day 1850, during the bitter eighth frontier war, the entire male population at Auckland military village was occupied in a cricket match. Xayimpi, a local Xhosa chief, strolled in with his warriors. On a given signal they attacked and only nine of the white males escaped.[2]

The discovery of diamonds at Kimberley in 1867 turned Southern Africa from a backward nuisance into an economic asset. Britain suddenly recognised their liability had become an asset and developed a pro-active policy for a confederation of the British colonies (the Cape and Natal), and the independent Afrikaner Republics (Orange Free State and South African Republic).

It was a false start. The Zulu defeated the redcoats at the battle of Isandlwana in 1879, Lord Carnarvon's Confederation strategy failed, and the Afrikaners on the Highveld won back their independence in 1881 after the Battle of Majuba Hill. The tide of empire had run into the buffers. Then, at the Berlin Conference of 1884, with a self-confidence and arrogance which could only be described as delusional, the great powers crowded around an almost empty map spread across the conference table armed with rulers and determined the lives of the Africans forever.

C.L.R. James asked what do they know of cricket who only cricket know? For him, cricket could only be understood within the cultural, social, economic and political environment in which it developed and was nurtured.[3] His insight has sharpened our understanding of the game, but to reverse his concept, how does cricket impact on the political and social evolution of society itself?

As Tolstoy famously said, historians end up answering questions no one has bothered to ask.[4] Between 1888 and 1968, English cricket

---

2   The Xhosa never targeted or killed women and children. Noel Mostert, *Frontiers*, (London: Jonathan Cape, 1992) 1034-1035

3   C.L.R. James, *Beyond a Boundary*, (London: Serpent's Tail, 1994)

4   Bill Nasson, *History Matters: Selected Writings 1970–2016*, (Cape Town: Penguin, 2016) 216

tours to South Africa illuminated, reinforced and on occasion shaped the nature of South African society and its relationship with the wider world. Throughout this period, English cultural exoticism marched in lockstep with South African exceptionalism, a sporting and political double helix of cricket, imperial power, institutionalised racism and colonial resistance. English cricket tours provided an opportunity for the English cricketing establishment to play an active role in South Africa's evolution from colonialism to republicanism and from segregation to apartheid. International sport in turn had a direct impact on the operation of Britain's empire.

This book charts this roller coaster relationship on and off the cricket field. Understanding the impact of England's cricket tours to South Africa illuminates not only international cricket, but imperialism and South Africa's racist political development and resistance as well.

After 1867, diamonds provided an economic lifeline to a dying imperial fringe. In Kimberley, diamond diggers inspired by a cricket obsessive, William Ling, used the town's cricketing ambitions to advertise it as the booming centre of the empire, though its 20-year spell in the imperial sun was rudely eclipsed by the discovery of vast gold deposits on the Witwatersrand in 1886. Within four years, from a few ramshackle farm buildings, Johannesburg had overtaken Kimberley in size and population.

English cricket needed fresh touring markets; South Africa's mines needed investment and labour. Within two years of its discovery, gold fever propelled the first English cricketing adventurers south. Prospectors, fortune seekers and adventurers flooded to the Witwatersrand with heads full of dreams and barroom gossip. For the capitalists, the political struggles in the 1870s and 1880s were about the creation of an orderly labour market and infrastructure – the beginnings of an alliance between what was termed Gold and Maize, namely agricultural and mining capital. Communications were vital and the race for rail created significant competition between the ports – Cape Town, Port Elizabeth, and Durban. In the lead up to Union, A.K. Soga, editor of *Izwi Labantu,* warned that the grand design for a capitalist-dominated South Africa, controlled by Rand magnates based on cheap labour, would create a glorious country for 'corporate pythons and political puff-adders, forced labour and commercial despotism, but no fit place for freemen to live in'.[5]

The struggle over labour formed the backdrop to competition between the various political entities. Twenty years before Union in 1910, English cricket tours helped build unity to ensure that the resources of the subcontinent were not lost to the empire. Major Warton, who managed the first English tour, was, the *Natal Mercury* commented, 'a most practical federationist'.[6] The 15 cricket tours between 1888 and 1965 were a barometer of the stresses and strains of empire as South Africa and its political economy evolved from colonialism to republicanism, from farming and mining to industrialisation, and from segregation to apartheid.

The career of Lord George Harris highlights the connection between cricket, empire and the profitability of the mines. Harris had been England's cricket captain in Australia and in its inaugural home Test in 1880 at The Oval. From 1885, he was Conservative under-secretary of state for India and for war, governor of Bombay from 1890 to 1895, and president of the MCC in 1895. A close associate of Cecil Rhodes, he was also chairman of Rhodes' Consolidated Goldfields from 1899 to 1929 and of the South African Gold Trust. In 1904, he was in South Africa helping design the cheap migrant labour policy and presiding over a cricket match between Consolidated Goldfields and the Cornerhouse mining group. He served as MCC treasurer from 1916 to 1932, and *Barclays World of Cricket* concluded, 'No man has exercised so strong an influence on the cricket world for so long.'[7]

He shared the arrogance of his class and reigned 'as though English cricket were part of his patrimony'. According to Benny Green, he was a 'bigot who always proclaimed his own rectitude

5   André Odendaal, *Vukani Bantu! The Beginnings of Black Protest Politics in South Africa to 1912*, (Cape Town: David Philip, 1984)

6   *Natal Mercury*, 13/2/1889

7   E.W. Swanton (ed.), *Barclays World of Cricket*, (London: Guild Publishing, 1986) 50

with absolute certainty ... a moral imbecile ... without the faintest hint of self-delusion'.[8]

No South Africans of power and influence from Cecil Rhodes and Paul Kruger in the 1890s, through to Hendrik Verwoerd and John Vorster in the 1960s were untouched by the cricketing swallows. Emissaries of empire, the English cricketers walked the corridors, pavilions and verandas of power. They played cards in jail with the Jameson Raiders, had coffee in silence with President Kruger, sipped gin with Sir Hercules Robinson, drank tea with Jan Smuts, imperialist and apologist for segregation and posed for photographs with the architects of apartheid.

Cricket has been described as a typically English compromise between religious manifestation and an instrument of policy, a vaporous hinterland where ethics and biceps merged into a third entity, an exquisite refinement of that other Victorian concept, the white man's burden.[9] For the tourists, this meant advertising and reinforcing empire, maintaining class and racial barriers as well as spreading cricket. Draped in principles like a man in three overcoats, cricket inevitably struggled to meet all its unrealistic ideological aspirations.

Class was at the heart of the English game, though race could trump class as the stories of Ranjitsinhji and Duleepsinhji, non-English 'outliers', demonstrate. The differentiation between amateurs and professionals was not determined by the receipt of direct or indirect rewards from the game but by the amateurs' class background, public school education and social and political authoritarianism. The military-inspired touring balance between a public-school amateur officer class and the working-class professional 'men' was exacerbated on tour.

The amateurs stayed at gentlemen's clubs, associating only with their class equivalents. The professionals travelled separately sleeping

---

8   Benny Green (ed.), *The Wisden Papers, 1888–1946*, (London: Stanley Paul, 1989) 119

9   Benny Green (ed.), *Wisden Anthology, 1864–1900* (London: Queen Anne Press, 1979) 5

in inferior hotels. They identified with working men, their fellow professionals whatever their colour, as their association with 'Krom' Hendricks, C.J. Nicholls and the Malay community in Cape Town, demonstrated.[10] They were almost universally acclaimed. Johnny Briggs, George Lohmann, Albert Trott, Wilfred Rhodes, Jack Hobbs, Bert Strudwick, Frank Woolley, Sydney Barnes, Maurice Tate, Eddie Paynter, Denis Compton and Johnny Wardle achieved legendary status in the South African imagination.

The MCC establishment was the tip of the class pyramid which reflected only a tiny minority of cricketers in the UK. This distorted its impact and made it impervious to change. The D'Oliveira affair was fought with the weapons of the 19th century. This was mirrored by an even smaller cricketing establishment in South Africa where a small handful of powerful clubs, Wanderers, Collegians, Western Province, Ramblers and a few others effectively shaped establishment cricket, while ensuring the exclusion of black cricketers.

Cricket was played with huge enthusiasm by thousands of players from every population group at a level equivalent to the establishment game. Black cricketers, including the legendary 'Krom' Hendricks, only had one opportunity, in 1892, to take on the English tourists.

Likewise, only a single women's tour (in 1960/61) took place in the 80 years even though women had played cricket in South Africa from the 1880s. Gender discrimination in sport reflected the broader society where women were systematically excluded from economic opportunities and deprived of the vote until 1930 when the franchise was extended to reinforce a racial stranglehold over political power. But sport provided an opportunity for women to control an area of their cultural lives even if limited resources meant this was often an adjunct to male sporting dominance.

Class in South Africa trod a minefield across racial, gender and linguistic groups. White South Africa had a clear class structure too, strongly indicated by its schools. To play international cricket was a

---

10   Jonty Winch and Richard Parry, *Too Black to Wear Whites*, (Cape Town: Penguin, 2020) 14-16

financial risk, and to make the grade a player needed the resources to allow them to play unpaid and the elite school environment – modelled on the boys' public school ethos in Britain – to make this a possibility. Test players were inevitably middle-class Anglophones from these elite boys' schools. This in part reflected the assumptions and prejudices of the selectors. In 1956/57, the 15 South African players selected came from 12 schools. Only Peter Heine was an Afrikaans speaker and attended a non-elite school. He complained that his accent inevitably led to his dropping down the batting order. In 1964/65, 18 players came from only 11 schools, and only Harry Bromfield from Observatory Boys High School came from a non-elite school. It was a ridiculously small world.

Many English professionals had already sampled the country or returned (like single swallows) to coach in schools and clubs. The first, H.H. Webster, arrived in Port Elizabeth in 1881 and was followed by hundreds of English professionals, including the young tyros Sydney Barnes, Wally Hammond and Jim Laker cutting their teeth in the coaching nets and on club wickets. In a country where the only South African 'professionals' were black 'net bowlers', English professionals shaped white South African cricket, though only very rarely did they stray into black cricket. Just as they did in laying the foundations of the English game, professionals developed white South Africa's batting and bowling skills, its tactics and ethos, and the cultural commitment to and love of the game. In times of crisis, some such as Harry Lee and Ken Palmer found themselves in the English Test side.

The amateurs were less popular outside the social elite and gentlemen's clubs. The autocratic Aubrey Smith upset the locals by flagrant sharp practice and Walter Read was briefly jailed when his financial speculation turned sour. Lord Hawke's legendary arrogance and his relentless drive to win won him no friends. Peter May, Trevor Bailey and Mike Smith were all accused of negative cricket and Johnny Douglas managed to upset an entire town.

For the players, South Africa was the most exciting of all tours. The world view of African colonialism was learned from 100 years of fascination with African 'exploration', the narratives of Speke and

Burton, Livingstone, Stanley, hunters like Frederick Selous, and novelists like Rider Haggard describing ever threatening predators, wily and hostile locals, and undreamed of riches. The first tours were a succession of hazards to life and limb, blinding lights and bumping pitches. But as the roads and railways developed, the tourists were no longer pioneers, but sank gently into their comfort zone, inhabiting a luxurious and glamorous world and experiencing a controlled and sanitised evocation of South African life.

After the first floundering steps by South Africa's Victorian cricketing novices, the cricket was often compelling and always hard fought. After losing all four 'Test' series before the Anglo-Boer War by a knockout, South Africa cricket regrouped around Abe Bailey and the mining industry. The googly bowlers briefly dominated the cricketing world and shattered (temporarily) the self-esteem of MCC's Plum Warner and 'Shrimp' Leveson Gower. South Africa and MCC seized the chance to legitimise their relationship within the ICC. But almost before the ink was dry, the avenging angel Sydney Barnes appeared, ball encircled in his prehensile fingers, spreading South African despond across the Test grounds of England and South Africa as if to herald the road to war.

Cricket eventually resumed but in a new world, less sepia-toned and more reddened by the intensity of struggles over labour which formed the backdrop to the increased intensity on the pitch.

A real Test rivalry required evenly matched teams fighting to the end of meaningful contests. If one ignores the essentially exhibition matches before 1902, then the playing record of MCC in South Africa looked at series by series was surprisingly even. When the players stepped on to the pitch for the fifth Test, the result of the series was still at stake in every one of the seven home rubbers from 1922/23 and only once was a series won by more than one Test. This contrasts significantly with Ashes contests in Australia when only twice in ten rubbers was the issue still in doubt when the final Test began. The first was the amazing series of 1936/37 when Australia clawed back from a 2-0 deficit to win 3-2 against Gubby Allen's MCC, and the 1962/63 series where the last two Tests were hard fought draws and the series shared 1-1. The rest were walkovers often decided after three Tests.

Series wins often depended on exceptional and heroic performances. The rivalry between Sydney Barnes and Herby Taylor drove them to sublime heights where both were playing on a sporting Valhalla only faintly visible to those toiling in the Test foothills below. Events on the pitch were given added spice by the conditions; by wickets often unfamiliar to the tourists and more so to the South Africans, at least until the grass era began; by a regular series of selection blunders which came close to cricketing sabotage; and by the rigours of this most physically demanding of tours.

The Tests in turn demanded much of the spectators, often crowded into full grounds, suffering the heat, glare and dust. Slow Test cricket could be compelling. Peter May's 1956/57 tourists played cricket which would have been soporific in a funeral parlour, yet the tension could have been cut with a knife when Hugh Tayfield dragged South Africa back from 2-0 down with two to play.

The English cricketers toured a racially divided country and shared the white dominant class perspective that cricket was self-evidently a 'white man's game'. This book inevitably reflects the era so when it refers to 'South African cricket', it describes 'official' whites-only cricket under the control of the South African Cricket Association (SACA) which ignored which ignored the abundance of cricket talent among players of African, 'coloured' and Indian origin and the myriad matches and tournaments played everywhere throughout the period.

This cast a long shadow. Cricket learned in mission schools in the eastern Cape, in the Malay communities of freed slaves and immigrants in Cape Town, the cosmopolitan mix of early Kimberley, the indentured or immigrant Indian populations in Natal, and the flourishing African cricket communities on the Witwatersrand, matched the standard of 'establishment' or 'white' cricket from the 1880s. These cricketers were proficient at administration and fundraising, operating for the first half of the period through the South African Coloured Cricket Board, known as the 'Barnato

Board'. The board embraced the principle of 'non-racialism', stating in its constitution that it 'does not recognise any distinction amongst the various sporting peoples of South Africa whether by Creed, Nationality or otherwise'.[11] Cricket diverged along ethnic lines in the 1930s and 1940s, until 1947 when the South African Cricket Board of Control (SACBOC) created a new 'inter-race' framework which returned to the old 'Barnato' non-racial principle.

Regular competitions took place between the main Cape centres from the 1880s and Austin Ngcumbe, Ebrahim Ariefdien, Lamarah Samsodien, Armien and Krom Hendricks, Robert Grendon and many others showed that when given the opportunity, black players were more than capable of holding their own against the best white players. Non-establishment cricketers (in fact only one element defined by whites as 'Cape Malays') had a single opportunity against the professionals among Walter Read's tourists in 1892. It is one of the tragedies of South African cricket that the English tourists showed so little interest in and concern for cricket played by other communities. The tourists brought their own prejudices, but these were reinforced by both their hosts and MCC establishment which prevented them from experiencing real South African conditions and recognising the wider African game.

Black players continued to perform at a high level throughout the 20th century despite the vastly inferior conditions and opportunities. Their players, performances and talents went unrecognised and unmeasured by the white political establishment. This was not accidental. Since the 1890s, cricket had been a bastion of white supremacy. Black players were excluded, and black cricket systematically unreported and ignored. As the Truth and Reconciliation Commission put it a century later, 'The story of apartheid is … the story of the systematic elimination of thousands of voices that should have been part of the nation's memory.'[12] The Transformation Project is busy reversing this process, re-inserting those excluded into the history of the new South Africa.

---

11 André Odendaal, Krish Reddy and Christopher Merrett, *Divided Country: The History of South African Cricket Retold 1914–1950s*, (Cape Town: HSRC, 2018) 3

12 Truth and Reconciliation Commission, *Final Report*, 201

Women's cricket too is taking its rightful place in the cricketing framework. The *Cape Times* in 1889 reported that 'women's cricket is not a novelty but in fact a daily occurrence … It is now admitted, if it were ever questioned, that ladies are not naturally incapable of playing cricket or any other game played by men.'[13] This book tells the story of the only English women's cricket tour to South Africa in this period but also seeks to celebrate the generations of women who ignored the taboos to nurture the game over 130 years.[14]

This book traces the 15 English cricket tours to South Africa which took place in four distinct eras: four tours look place before the Anglo-Boer War when the scramble for Africa's resources drove the country into war; three came before the First World War when Union was built on white supremacy; four were during the interwar period riven by labour relations and the rise of Afrikaner nationalism; and finally the four tours between 1948 and 1965 when the triumph of white nationalism constructed the apartheid edifice on the bedrock of colonial segregation.

The cricket takes centre stage, but it is presented in the context of the evolution of the South African apartheid system, African resistance and the perspectives and engagement of MCC. The MCC never challenged the abusive operation of the savage racist regime with whom they shared 'ties of blood' even after the expulsion of South Africa from the ICC in 1961. They toured in 1965, during a highpoint of apartheid repression and social engineering, reinforcing their support for the regime, seen as 'keeping politics out of sport'.

The 16th tour due in 1968/69 never got on the plane. The epilogue of this book draws on the MCC archives, to show how MCC's reactionary institutional culture lay behind its mendacious and manipulative betrayal of Basil D'Oliveira, orchestrated by a leadership cabal mandated by the membership and directed by ex-Conservative prime minister Sir Alec Douglas-Home and treasurer Gubby Allen.

---

13 *Cape Times*, 11/1/1889
14 See Odendaal, Reddy, Merrett and Winch, *Cricket and Conquest* and Odendaal, Reddy and Merrett, *Divided Country*

The partnership between the English establishment and the South African political elite was almost timeless. George Allsop and Algy Frames ran the South African side for more than 50 years; lords Harris and Hawke and Plum Warner played key roles for MCC over six decades. Wally Hammond was a player or spectator on every tour to South Africa between 1927 and 1965. He socialised with Sir Aubrey Smith, captain of the first tour, in Hollywood, handed over flowers to the Broederbond on the 100th anniversary re-enactment of the Great Trek in Pretoria in 1938, and coached Mike Brearley in Durban on the final MCC tour in 1965.

It is time now to follow the generations of English cricketers in Africa, reinforcing the values and sharing the profits of empire, and riding the apartheid train. For the players, the imperial mission is subsidiary to the game, and we can feel their awe, joy and pain, celebrate their efforts, triumphs and appreciate the intensity of a cricketing rivalry which brought out the best and sometimes the worst in the contestants.

Ranged against them on the pitch are cricketers from South Africa's small colonial governing class fighting heroically and skilfully for their country (and determinedly unconscious of the ghosts of legions of excluded black South Africans and cricketers). Off the pitch, black strikers, mineworkers, pass resistors, bus boycotters and political activists struggle against the power of the South African state to remake the world their way, knowing that time is on their side.

Every year, the swallows arrive, like the English cricketers around November, skimming through reed beds and nesting under eaves. They cover the 6,000 miles in 27 days, surfing the air currents for more than 200 miles a day. The record for a Union Castle line coal steamer, when Warton's team first groped through the Deptford fog, was 17 days.

We cannot know why the swallows make their astonishing journey, what delight they feel in South Africa's ageless beauty or what joy in the purity of the air and the clarity of the light. The swallows are temporary sojourners, who do not build or defend their territory. But they change the summer sky. Let the games begin.

PART 1:
OPENINGS

Tour 1: 1888-89
Inscribing cricket on the South African landscape

Johannesburg

Vaal River

Orange River

Kimberley

Pietermaritzburg

Durban

Graaff-Reinet

East London

Oudtshoorn

Kingwilliamstown

Grahamstown

Cape Town   Mossel Bay   Port Elizabeth

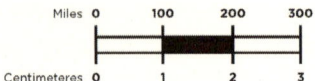

Approximate Scale

Miles	0	100	200	300

Centimeteres	0	1	2	3

1

Adventures: Aubrey Smith 1888/89

TIMING IS everything, in life and in cricket. December 1888 was Southern Africa's moment. The geopolitical plates of the empire were spinning. The Battle of Majuba Hill in 1881 had ended direct control by Britain over the Transvaal and put back the cause of the federalists on the subcontinent. But five years later gold was discovered on an unprecedented scale and Britain's citizens led the ravenous wolf pack descending on the independent Boer Republic of the Transvaal. Cricket had a role to play in keeping the subcontinent within the imperial embrace.

A cricket tour of Southern Africa, even by the standards of the risk-addicted late 19th century, was a mad sporting idea, perhaps the maddest since 1859 when George Parr's North American cricket tourists were cast adrift on a storm-tossed north Atlantic with a broken jib. A tour required financial commitment, extraordinary organisation, personal bravery, and an ox-wagon load of luck. Distances, scheduling constraints, climate, limited transport infrastructure, physical perils, political difficulties, (questionable) quality of the opposition, playing conditions, day-to-day logistics and infrastructure, and not least the financial adventure, should have deterred any sane would-be enthusiast. But this was an age characterised by overconfidence, arrogance, ignorance and a relish for risk.

The mail steamships traversed the oceans reliably and quickly carrying hundreds of thousands of passengers annually across the

Atlantic and to Australia. With the mineral discoveries, the prospects for a massive expansion of passenger activity between Britain and the South African ports inspired Sir Donald Currie, owner of the Castle Line, to use a cricket tour to South Africa to promote his ships.

Two men created the 1888/89 tour to South Africa. William 'Joey' Milton an old Marlburian, was the South African salesman and organiser. He was a Victorian super-hero: an England rugby international; captain of the Western Province, Cape Colony and South Africa cricket teams and president of the Western Province Cricket Club (WPCC). In 1890, he would become prime minister Cecil Rhodes' private secretary, his servant as head of the Civil Service, responsible for the first segregationist legislation, and a racist who excluded 'Krom' Hendricks from representative and professional cricket.

In 1888, Milton raised a £3,000 guarantee. The tour was on.

The hero behind the tour's delivery was Major Robert Gardner Warton. Warton had played for Essex and had been secretary of Milton's WPCC. In 1887, he returned to England with a heart condition, but fortified by an army pension, recruited and managed the touring party. He shepherded 13 cricketers around Southern Africa on a relentless timetable and tight budget, braving the immense distances, meeting the demands of the players and hosts, and even spending long days umpiring in the broiling sun. It was an astonishing achievement.

Previous foreign tours to Australia or the USA were primarily entrepreneurial, but in South Africa's case the profit imperative was partly balanced by the imperial mission to gather the scatterings of colonial South Africa into the imperial family, to advertise the country for investors and support the mining industry.

Warton's team needed to exhibit cricketing skills beyond the locals, but only enough to encourage and not overwhelm them. The team were ambassadors for empire and entertainers both on and off the pitch. It was a tall order. Warton engaged the 25-year-old C. Aubrey Smith as captain, supported by the even younger Monty Bowden and signed up Johnny Briggs, Maurice Read and Bobby

Abel, all previous Australian tourists, Frank Hearne from Kent and Somerset's A.J. Fothergill. Briggs, Harry Wood and Abel had all played Tests against the Australians in 1888, Frank Hearne had played for an England XI, and Smith had captained Shrewsbury's team against the Australians.

1.1 Aubrey Smith: An education in captaincy

Aubrey 'Round-the-Corner' Smith, the son of a Brighton doctor, was a fast-medium bowler, tall and broad-shouldered, and effective on matting wickets which suited the off cut and bounce he got from a high action. He was in demand as an 'amateur' who could hold his own at first-class level. In 1887/88, both Sydney and Melbourne invited a Shaw/Shrewsbury combination and Martin Bladen (Lord Hawke) respectively to tour. Smith captained the Shaw combination. He faced dust storms which blew acrid dust into every orifice; strikes of both players and officials; press criticisms of his ungraceful batting style; attacks on the 'shamateurs' and the enthusiastic attentions of various ladies. He managed all with aplomb.

As captain, he had already experienced the extremes. In Melbourne, the player strike meant a Smith-led victory by an innings and 456 runs to the complete indifference of the locals. Six months later, in a season so wet that not a single first-class hundred was scored in July, Smith captained Sussex against Surrey at The Oval. Monty Bowden hit 189 not out out of 698 and Surrey won by an innings and 485 runs. A record victory and a record defeat within the year.

The side was 'balanced' by amateurs who had the right class and social polish. Basil Grieve, the hon. Charles Coventry, Emile McMaster and Cameron Skinner were at best club cricketers but were the 'right sort' and could afford the trip. Skinner, 'an unreliable bat and an uncertain field', was there for his entertainment value. He was a member of the Lyric Club opened in London in 1888 by the grandees of international cricket tours, Lord Hawke, G.F. Vernon and Sir Timothy O'Brien and he specialized in scenes from

Shakespeare, musical interludes, and 'tableaux vivants.'[15] An even split of seven professionals and seven amateurs provided the social balance and adventurous if fallible performances on the field. They were drawn by gold fever and colonial adventures for the military inclined adrenaline-junkies. [16]

English amateurs, Warton discovered, were divided into 'shamateurs', who performed at a professional standard and needed to be remunerated accordingly, and amateurs who had sufficient resources to play without payment but whose cricket skills were incidental. The 'shamateur' Monty Bowden negotiated a deal, which included superior accommodation and 'well lighted' transportation, expenses and a fee (£100). Warton was also forced to hand over £125 to keep his 'shamateur' captain on board.[17]

The tour followed the money. 'Joey' Milton had negotiated guarantees with nine centres across the sub-continent.[18] The guarantee system meant the financial tail wagged the touring dog. Overall viability relied heavily on discounted travel from Sir Donald Currie's Castle Line and the Cape Railways under Sir James Sivewright.

Before they set sail Warton said his main objective was to strengthen colonial cricket. He expected to win and did not see matting wickets as a problem. The tour began a month earlier for professional Frank Hearne who was sent to coach the Cape cricketers. Hearne was welcomed by Harry Cadwallader of Kimberley's *Diamond Fields Advertiser* as a boost to local cricketers, but his rival scribe Charlie Finlason, writing as 'Daily Gossip' for the same town's *Daily Independent*, branded Hearne a 'spy' who would learn far more than he taught.[19] It was the first shot in a press war that was to dominate the tour.

---

15 Kevin Walmsley, 'A.C. Skinner revealed', *The Cricket Statistician*, issue 180, Winter 2017, 27-31

16 Charles Cox, *The Cricketing Record of Major Warton's Tour*, (London: Reprinted by J.M. McKenzie, 1987) 18

17 David Kynaston, *Bobby Abel*, (London: Secker and Warburg, 1982) 126-127

18 *Cape Times*, 15/9/1888

19 *Cricket*, 27/12/1888, 471

The team were excited to be escaping the murk and depression of the London streets. Bobby Abel was given a send-off in the Prince Albert pub with Tom Hayward's father on the piano. Sir Donald Currie hosted a farewell lunch on board the *Garth Castle*. The team's Surrey affiliations were reflected in chocolate and yellow colours and a Union Jack badge. As the hospitality flowed, Currie donated a cup for the best performance against the tourists. Aubrey Smith in his first speech of the tour described this as 'a pioneer team' which did not want to 'crush out the germs of cricket'. He commended the unity of professionals and amateurs working together 'showing an example to all sportsmen'.[20] Major Warton warned them of the task ahead. They would travel a remarkable 15,975 miles, including 2,218 by rail and 785 by coach and cart.

At last, the *Garth Castle* eased through the greasy waters of the East India Dock, away from the Whitechapel streets where the Ripper's hapless final victim, Mary Kelly, had been gruesomely dispatched just two weeks before. (The cricketer Montague Druitt, who earlier that season had bowled Bobby Abel, was suspected of being the Ripper. He drowned himself in the Thames in early December.)

On 23 November 1888, Warton's boys sailed from Dartmouth. The Bay of Biscay was choppy and when they arrived in Lisbon, the port was blanketed under a thick fog.

1.2 *The* Garth Castle *Minstrels*

As they left Europe behind, Aubrey Smith and the team 'blacked up' as the '*Garth Castle* Minstrels'. The musical theatre mixed slavery, racism, spiritualism, and the abiding popularity of the exoticism of Africa into an entertainment staple which was astonishingly popular. Seventy-five years later, Fred Trueman was to celebrate his 300th Test wicket by appearing on stage in *The Black and White Minstrel Show*.

The troupe performed in a semi-circle with Smith and Monty rattling bones and tambourines while exchanging jokes between

---

20 David Rayvern Allen, *Sir Aubrey*, (London: J.M. McKenzie, 2005) 68

songs and dances. The show was a huge success, particularly Smith's boss stump speech, traditionally full of outrageous pomposity and malapropisms.

Blackface perpetuated the Jim Crow stereotypes of the American south – with the clear emphasis of black inferiority through racist humour heavily based on white interpretations of slave lore. The bizarre spectacle of an English cricket team in black face pretending to be American slaves in colonial Africa reinforced white supremacist world views and entertained simultaneously. What the black waiting and kitchen staff must have thought can only be imagined.

On deck, a grand six-a-side cricket match was played, and Johnny Briggs walked away with the potato race. Then the Skeleton Coast treated them to a 35-degree roll which put an end to the entertainment. In Cape Town, the papers filled column yards about the strength of the tourists. At Newlands Cricket Ground, a score box was built to shield the pencillers from the 'maddening questioning crowd' and a grandstand constructed for 800 guests.

Cape Town was a diverse and stratified society. The social hierarchy, 50 years after the end of slavery at the Cape, encompassed Xhosa and Khoi migrants employed on public works, a predominantly Muslim ('Malay') working class descended from slaves, sailors and immigrants who inhabited the Bo-Kaap and District Six areas and well-heeled white colonials in the salubrious southern suburbs. At Newlands Cricket Ground, a small enclosure was built at the request of the Malay community.[21] It was here that the correspondent of the Transvaal's *Potchefstroom Budget* was shocked by two English professionals socialising with black female companions in plain sight.

Under Table Mountain, the long-running debate about poverty, the working class and urban blight in District Six had begun and was to continue until the nationalist government's forced removal policy in the 1960s saw the area bulldozed and its inhabitants scattered on the

---

21 *Cape Times*, 6/12/1888

windswept plains of the Cape Flats. Ratepayers in 1888 complained of 'sickness due to the smell as there is no drainage ... streets with no lights ... being killed by loafers in the absence of police protection'.[22]

The *Garth Castle* finally nosed into Table Bay around 3am on 14 December. Journalist Harry Cadwallader scrambled aboard the pilot boat, to be the first to greet the team. On reaching Table Bay, the Englishmen found themselves 'with a lovely view of Cape Town and Table Mountain rising sheer and square completely dwarfing the town ... when we got into dock we found a large crowd awaiting us – a large percentage being [Africans] and Malays ... the team were driven up in wagonettes drawn by white horses to their hotels – the amateurs to the Intercontinental and the professionals to The George'.[23]

Warton and Milton met to finalise the ambitious itinerary. Their self-confidence was a reminder that it was only four years since the whole continent had been parcelled out among the European powers at the Congress of Berlin although less than ten per cent was under European control. Budget constraints meant constant pressure to play and get to the next venue, which condemned them to endless gruelling days baking on a blinding cricket field or trying to sleep squeezed rattling and bouncing over dangerous and unpredictable tracks. Meeting the tight schedule of 19 matches over several thousand miles was to be a triumph of player resilience and management resourcefulness. And luck.

The team had a gentle practice session at Newlands, eagerly watched by the locals. The professionals were characteristically downbeat, with one telling the *Cape Times*, '[As] good a ground as this means there is good cricket about.' The amateurs attended an evening bazaar in aid of the Organ Fund. Skinner provided a recital and Smith sang 'Enniscorthy', a mournful 18th-century Irish ballad, which was already his signature tune. The next day, they had their first sight of 'that curious effect, the table-cloth over the mountain, a

---

22 *Cape Times*, 29/11/1888
23 Major Warton in *Cricket*, 24/1/1889, 1-2

clear sky above and a white cloud lying flat and bright upon the top and pouring down like a huge waterfall'.[24]

Cricket was the focus, but politics was the game. The biggest social event Cape Town had ever seen was attended by the governor, (the picaresque Sir Hercules Robinson), the prime minister (Sir Thomas Upington), and everyone who was anyone in Cape Society. Sir Thomas Upington called for a British protectorate to the Zambezi and did not see why they shouldn't go further north. As for the role of sport in politics, 'nothing has greater effect of binding colonies together than visits by teams such as this. The future of England depended on her colonies.' India had effectively financed Britain, while having its own economy destroyed, for more than two centuries.[25]

But an even greater source of wealth and power in the African hinterland might be about to tumble into the Queen's lap.

For Sir Hercules, cricket was, after racing, the most English of sports. He preferred sports where he had an animal between his legs rather than a cricket ball.[26] Aubrey Smith was not put out by Cape flummery. He recognised the significance of the first tour and foresaw regular visits in a few years. There was a far thicker link 'between us as subjects of Her Majesty than anyone realises at Home'. Major Warton drily reflected that Sir Thomas Upington had laid out a challenge for future visiting teams – not only to go as far as the Zambezi but to head off on a kind of circular tour via Khartoum.

1.3 Aubrey Smith at Newlands

'Newlands was a picture to be remembered with its surrounding mass of pines, overtopped by the great Table Mountain on one side, the new stand covered with red cloth standing out against green background. The picturesque effect given on our own grounds by the ladies' dresses being enhanced by the bright and varied colour of the many Malay women in their holiday attire.'[27]

---

24 *Ibid*
25 Shashi Tharoor, *Inglorious Empire*, (London: Penguin, 2018)
26 *Cape Times* 18/12/1888
27 *Daily Independent*, 16/1/1889

At midday on 21 December 1888, Johnny Briggs, the diminutive and charismatic Lancashire left-armer, bowled the first ball to Cape Town publisher W.H. 'Dicky' Richards of the Western Province XXII. Richards pushed it defensively to point and opened a new field of dreams in international sport. It is hard to imagine a sporting baptism in a grander setting.

Monty Bowden stood up to Briggs and Smith's right-arm medium and had two stumpings and an lbw appeal turned down before Richards eventually pushed the ball to mid-on for a single. Western Province were on the board. From 32/1 the locals collapsed to 36/7 before 'Joey' Milton cut Briggs through point, then smashed him over square leg and clubbed him into the Pavilion for the first six. After lunch he was caught by Bowden, having scored 36 out of 38 while he was at the wicket. Twenty-two batsmen meant cascades of wickets – nine to Briggs, eight to Fothergill, with five stumpings and two catches to Bowden.

The visitors faced the heat, intense glare and the express pace and hostility of Nicolaas Theunissen. His steepling bounce, raw pace and a loose mat laid on grass, smashed the batsmen in the ribs and on the knuckles, and with 22 in the field runs were as rare as molars on a duck. By close of play, Warton's men were 50/4 with a grimly determined Abel on 18, all in singles. The mat was re-stretched overnight, batting became easier and the tourists finished two runs behind on the first innings.

The second innings replayed the first: a small but significant opening partnership (21/1), followed by a collapse (25/7) and advantage to the tourists. Milton again collared Briggs, smashing him for six boundaries before Johnny gratefully grasped an uppish straight drive and Milton departed for 40 to a huge ovation. He ensured a target of 141, but sunstroke put him out of action for the remainder of the game and the next. Theunissen again worked the batsmen over. When Smith was bowled at 115/7 the game was in the balance, but Theunissen polished off the last three wickets and the Western Province XXII had won by 17 runs, a feat which, as Smith pointed out, Australian XXIIs had never achieved. Smith blamed the defeat on the impenetrable mass of fielders, English injuries, sunstroke and the relentless banquets.

1.4 Christmas Day and black cricket

On Christmas Day, the team drove to the Simon's Bay naval base. 'For the first ten miles the road was shaded by avenues of splendid oaks or tall pines, which scented the whole district. All along the road, the oleanders and plumbago are in full bloom, with here and there a huge magnolia. At Muizenberg, the road passes along the foot of the mountains rising sheer out of the sea. The white sands at Fish Hoek have all the appearance of snow, suitable for Christmas,' said Warton.[28]

'Here and there wherever a spare piece of ground could be got, we saw young blacks playing cricket; some with stumps and bails, others with empty paraffin can and stones for wickets – anything for a game of cricket … [O]n our return journey we saw a public ground at Mowbray literally covered with black men, eagerly contesting three or four cricket matches, while all around the ground under the trees sat hundreds of Malay and [African] women intensely interested in the cricket. It was a curious sight, even to a cricketer,' reflected Smith.[29]

On Boxing Day, the tourists faced a Cape Colony XV with Milton replaced by Charlie Finlason. Finlason was destined to have a huge impact on the pitch and in the press box. He was a talented cricketer, and his pro-colonial journalism was as combative and controversial as his bowling.

The tourists started well, reaching 86/2, but then Johnny Briggs was lbw to a ball which he claimed to have hit the cover off, Maurice Read was given out hit wicket to Ashley and Smith was stumped by Porter standing up to Theunissen. The tourists subsided to 122, with Theunissen claiming 7-51. The Colony XV managed a handy 37-run lead on the first innings thanks to a superb 46 from A.B.

---

28 Major Warton in *Cricket*, 24/1/1889
29 Aubrey Smith in *The Sportsman*, 23/1/1889

Tancred, who hit Briggs into the pond for six before being bowled by Basil Grieve's fast underarm. Three of the last four batsmen were all 'bowled Briggs 0', in a lemming-like panic which was to become a familiar tour motif. The tourists raised their game the second time round, with Smith leading from the front with 46 and set a target of 126.

1.5 Charlie Finlason in action

Charlie Finlason as a player and talented writer was able to bring a strong sense of immediacy to the action, writing in the *Daily Independent*:

'The Colony have 126 to make with 14 wickets in hand. Tancred and Cox set ... only 75 to get with all wickets intact. Wickets of the very best batsmen in the Colony for the most part. Men of renown ... all were smiling when Tancred played carelessly at a low long hop and was bowled. Cox went almost directly afterwards, then came catastrophe. W.H. Richards the Cape Town crack, Dunell, the Bay [Port Elizabeth] champion, Stewart the oft proclaimed best bat in the Colony, De Villiers, Grimmer all went in and came out without scoring. Five ducks' eggs all in a row!

'But hope did not desert the colonial supporters ... The sprinting Charlie Vintcent started with a huge skier which almost fell into the hands of a fielder ... Richards put up a ball when he had but 5 and Howe played on before he had scored. Twenty-nine still wanted, the tail reached, the bowling deadly, the fielding as close as a box and the crowd standing on their toes with excitement! What a time for a nervous batsman!

'Finlason and Vintcent began to run at once, ran indeed at the very ghost of a chance. The roars that accompanied each run demoralised the field, some overthrows took place, a snick for two, a boundary hit, some leg byes and the men still with 11 runs to make.

'The wily Briggs put a stop to all this happiness; Finlason was completely humbugged by an artful yorker on the leg stump. Even then there was still hope as Vintcent was still in. Alas for such hopes Theunissen placed the first ball back into the hands of the India-rubber Briggs, and then Charlie Vintcent retired from a spread-eagled wicket. No hope now for those 11 runs. Still people did hope

> against hope. Ashley spooned a catch to Briggs who missed it amid a terrible howl, but Porter was run out ... and the Englishmen ... won only by the skin of their teeth.'[30]

From Aubrey Smith's perspective victory was essential, 'In defeating the Combined Fifteen of the Colony, a side stronger than our first match, the effects of that [first] reverse are completely wiped out. Cricket in South Africa is far more developed than has hitherto been supposed at home.'

Nicolaas Theunissen, the Stellenbosch express who claimed 25 of the 40 English wickets in the two games, was in Smith's view 'a dangerous bowler on a matting wicket, where he can get "work" on his fastest balls – and he has considerable variety of pace'. In the second game, Theunissen claimed 70 per cent of the 20 available wickets at 14-114, while Briggs took 42 per cent of the Colony's 28 available wickets at 12-106. 'Joey' Milton, facing considerable debts for the new ground, was delighted with a profit of £400.[31]

As the lights of Cape Town glimmered on the water, a grand farewell ball on the *Roslin Castle* proved the event of the season. Once the exhausted dancers had staggered to their carriages, the *Roslin* cast off for Port Elizabeth (PE). As Algoa Bay this was the destination for the 1820 Settlers, imported to serve as a buffer against the Xhosa on the eastern frontier, and the port of entry for the Cape Mounted Rifles in King William's Town. In PE, Warton's tourists shared a stage decorated with Union Jacks and a large portrait of W.G. Grace, already a god-like figure on the periphery of empire.

Owen Dunell's Port Elizabeth XXII won the toss and the locals totalled a challenging 193. They might have managed more if Briggs had not rolled over the last four wickets in four balls (first three bowled and last man stumped). In reply, Bertie Rose-Innes, cutting the ball both ways off the mat, had the tourists stumbling to a humiliating 24/6 and only a battling 58 from Harry Wood dragged

---

30 *Daily Independent*, 3/1/1889
31 *Sportsman*, 31/1/1889

them to 127. Even so, Maurice Read's half century in the second innings was not enough to prevent a second loss, this time by 55 runs.

After three losses against odds, they had to find a way to score against packed fields. Not even the exceptional Johnny Briggs could win these games on his own. He would be ever present, playing in every game, and bowled right through 18 of his 38 innings in the field.

Aubrey Smith, perhaps seeking to draw attention away from the team's performance, suggested that their presence was 'to have so great an effect on the cricket of the Cape not only amongst the white population but even amongst the black ... I think it is not only the case here but wherever you go in the colonies it is cricket which binds men together in the cause of sport and I hope it will always be so.'[32]

This was the only time black cricketers were mentioned in a speech by an England captain for 75 years. It was ignored by the locals. Smith was on safer ground when he promised 'a succession of visits to this country and return visits of South African cricketers to England (cheers) ... although it is very kind of you to invite us out every evening, I think when playing cricket [hospitality] ought to have its limits.'

1.6 Travails

Hospitality over, they steamed to Mossel Bay with team colours flying, even if their tails were between their legs. They regretfully declined an oyster supper on arrival and embarked in small swaying two-person 'Cape carts' for an epic journey through the Outeniqua mountains to Oudtshoorn. It was moonless, pitch black and only one of the carts had a flickering light weakly illuminating flashes of rock and plenty of sheer emptiness as the carts laboured upwards a wheel turn at a time. Bugle calls kept them in touch. Abel and Fothergill in the last cart veered off the road, inches from disaster. After interminable bone-shaking terror they reached the Great Brak River and wolfed down duck and chicken legs at the Temperance Hotel. Bobby Abel implored Smith to wait until daybreak before

---

32 *Daily Independent*, 10/1/1889

proceeding further, 'It's better to be killed at once than to be frightened to death by degrees.' The team were quickly unmovable, curled up in corners and under tables. At first light they were on the road again.

Another steep climb through mountains thickly decorated with yellowwood and ironwood and a 400-foot sheer drop brought them through the Montagu Pass drenched in the clouds. Down the other side they spotted hawks and inspected ostriches. The Sundays River was in flood, but they plunged in. The carts stuck fast as the horses struggled desperately and eventually reached the far bank greeted by a cheering crowd. Bobby Abel arrived last as usual, but a frontiersman's brandy flask cheered him up considerably. 'Mr Smith,' he shouted, 'this is ripping, and I don't care tuppence for any river in this country.'[33]

The tour was a travelling trading and cultural exhibition designed to showcase South Africa and its resources. Oudtshoorn was the global centre of the ostrich feather industry, the essential ingredient of late-19th century fashion. High-quality feathers were worth more than their weight in gold. Oudtshoorn was also the base of Jack van Reenen, big hitting batsman and president of Western Province CC in its early years.

The game against a South Western Districts XXII was predictable. The opposition featured substantially built farmers with long black beards, looking (according to Smith) like Old Testament prophets. Divine inspiration was sadly absent. They found themselves 16 down for 29 before recovering to 53 all out. While there was some improvement in the second innings, the tourists won by an innings and 80 runs, thanks to Harry Wood's 85. Intense local interest was not limited to the white population. The lower end of the field was segregated and roped off for black spectators, for whom, unusually, a refreshment booth was provided. The black population supported the visitors.[34]

---

33 *Cricket*, 21/1/1889
34 *Cape Times* 3/1/1889

Next came the precipitous Swartberg Pass, even more terrifying than the Outeniquas, with sheer drops on either side of the hairpins. Many preferred to walk. They spent a day 'along the most dismal road' it had ever been Warton's fate to travel on, 'some 30 miles of bleak desert; small salt bushes and mimosa shrubs alone relieved the monotony of sand and stones; and six hours of jolt, jolt, jolt, at a miserable pace dragged by lame horses.' At last, they met the train for the onward trip to Kimberley and slept dreaming of lush outfields and a gentle drizzle.

Kimberley's modern existence began with the discovery of the 'Eureka' diamond in 1866. By 1870, the volcanic diamondiferous pipe on De Beers farm was the largest man-made hole on earth. Africans as well as whites poured into Kimberley digging out endless tons of blue earth to convert their share of the mineral bonanza into guns. While numerous profitable finds made prospectors and buyers rich, the real money flowed with the setting up of a Stock Exchange in 1881 and Cecil John Rhodes' consolidation of thousands of claims into the De Beers monopoly.

Africans dug and whites sifted for the stone which would make their fortunes. Black diggers finding stones were the scourge of the white industry. The Kimberley Magistrates Court was devoted to illicit diamond-buying (IDB), which usually took place in the dead of night. To counter IDB, Kimberley installed electric lighting before London. Jack swallowed a stone weighing 68 carats and worth an estimated £150. 'I came here to work like everyone else,' he told the court, '… and I wanted something too.'[35] The monopolistic industry created a compound system which imprisoned African workers in enclosures fenced and roofed with fine mesh. Insanitary and crowded conditions meant the Rhodes-controlled De Beers compound had an annual mortality rate of more than ten per cent. Rhodes' crony, Dr Leander Starr Jameson, was the medical officer and ignored a smallpox epidemic which ravaged the De Beers compound in 1885.

---

35   Richard Parry, 'Diamonds, Cricket and Major Warton: Cricket in Kimberley 1885 to 1889', *Cricket Lore* vol. 3 issue 6

Some 1,838 black miners died in 1888 out of a total black male population of 11,814.[36]

Cricket was a large part of the cultural baggage of British adventurers in the northern Cape. By 1871, thanks to the enthusiasm of the prospector, editor, professional firebrand and cricket tragic, William Ling, the first games were under way.[37] The game flourished in the red dust and for the next 20 years cricket became the main cultural activity in the town apart from the bars and flophouses. It rooted its peculiar values in the dusty veld, provided an intangible linkage to England and briefly advertised the town as the cutting edge of 'progress' in the sleepy Cape Colony.

The English XI were about to face new challenges. The informal competition for the 'warmest welcome' was driven by Kimberley's desperate struggle to convince the world of the viability of the town. Kimberley had a week to milk the imperial spotlight and slow the breakneck rush of prospectors to the richer pickings of the goldmines.

Warton's tourists were met by a large crowd at 4.30am. Their week's programme included a promenade and photography session, a visit to the mines, smoking concerts, a pyrotechnic display, a lavish banquet at the Kimberley Club (amateurs only), dinners and public balls. And six consecutive days of cricket from Monday to Saturday. If the endless round of social events hampered the visitors on the field, well Kimberley had to match the wins in Cape Town and Port Elizabeth.

1.7 Labour, tragedy and scandal

The visitors' programme started with a visit to the 'Big Hole' and the De Beers compound. Just six months previously on 11 July 1888, the De Beers night shift had been trapped by a fire that swept through both main shafts. A total of 178 Africans and 25 Europeans lost their lives, but the tragedy was hushed up and hardly reported beyond Kimberley.

---

36 *Cape Times*, 29/1/1889

37 Richard Parry, 'Diamonds, Cricket and William Ling', *Cricket Lore* vol. 3 issue 4

> During the cricket week, a rockfall at De Beers mine killed three black workers and a dynamite explosion killed a black worker and wounded an overseer. The following week, eight Africans cut holes in the compound wall and escaped over the roof. Two were caught, charged with the criminal offense of absenting themselves from their master's employ without leave and sentenced to a month's hard labour – a free month's work for De Beers.[38]
>
> Half a century later, Aubrey Smith told Bill Edrich that he had had to charm the local authorities who discovered a player trying to smuggle out a large diamond. The player was not identified.[39]

The town had been whipped into a frenzy by Charlie Finlason, Kimberley's all-rounder on the pitch and cheerleader off it. He was a vehement critic of English class-based hypocrisy and a 'South Africa first' patriot anxious to advertise Kimberley's pioneering spirit over the lackadaisical and complacent snobbery which he thought defined Cape Town.

Warton, hoping to reduce the glare on the Eclectics ground, had wired a request for the matting to be (as Finlason put it) 'dyed a nice green tint to look like the velvety turf of England'. Kimberley's reply was robust, 'Very sorry, no green dye available on the diamond fields but we can manage a brilliant sky blue.'[40]

All cricket in South Africa was played on matting, but no two mat surfaces were the same. Mat was laid on grass in Cape Town and Port Elizabeth, and on rolled earth, gravel and cinders away from the coast. The Kimberley match was played on brick-red soil, the colour of a cricket ball with the shine knocked off it, patched with white sand spread by wind, the surface rolled until hard as asphalt and studded with sharp stones. The straw-coloured matting threw up a glare which made the eyes water. Johnny Briggs took one look and asked, 'Do we have to play cricket on that?'

---

38 *Diamond Fields Advertiser*, 19/1/1889
39 Bill Edrich, *Cricketing Days*, (London: Stanley Paul, 1950) 95
40 *Cape Times*, 17/1/1889

They did. Nearly 5,000 spectators, more than half the town's white male population, crammed into the ground decorated with flowers and ribbons. A.B. Tancred lost the toss and Smith batted. Despite the alien conditions, most of the English XI, apart from Read and Smith, played the quick and bouncy pitch with ease.[41]

Finlason was as idiosyncratic and as talented a cricketer as he was a journalist. He was an incessant talker and bowled with an unusual slinging action beginning with his wrist somewhere behind his heels. He normally bowled at fast medium pace, but once an over or so threw up a 'moon ball', which could turn sharply but often had the close fielders jumping for cover.

Bobby Abel was England's best professional batsman after Arthur Shrewsbury, with a decisiveness of stroke and a high backlift which generated his power of shot. He showed composure, concentration and at 5ft 5in a remarkable ability to stay on top of the high bounce on an exploding surface while accumulating runs against the packed 18-man field.[42] Bowden made 31 before being caught by Finlason to the disappointment of the spectators. Briggs clowned around, pretending to run and to dismiss himself off a bump ball, but soon lunged at a Finlason moon-ball and was stumped. A 41-run partnership for the eighth wicket between the amateurs, Emile McMaster and Basil Grieve, took the visitors to a respectable 177.

Kimberley's first five wickets fell for 44, until Charlie Vintcent cut loose, in what Warton, who was umpiring, described as 'scorching heat throwing up insupportable glare from the matting'.[43] Vintcent was South Africa's 100 yards record holder, lightning fast between the wickets and innovative with the bat. Despite the heat, he ran three fives in the innings, one of which the tourists were sure had ended in a run out. When Major Warton at square leg gave Hickson not out, Bowden kicked one of the stumps halfway down the pitch. Eventually, Vintcent was given out lbw but only after completing two leg byes.

41 *Cape Times*, 21/1/1889
42 *Daily Independent*, 15/1/1889
43 *Cricket*, 21/2/1889

His 87 would be the highest score against a touring side until Frank Hearne scored 94 for the Cape Colony XIII against Lord Hawke's team in 1896. Vintcent was one of two South African representative cricketers with only one eye. 'Buster' Nupen was the other.

A cameo from Alfred Hill, the 'Slogger of Kimberley', ended controversially. Bowden appealed for a stumping when Hill was in his ground, threw the ball up and when Hill left the crease, thinking he was out, Monty ran him out. Charlie Finlason dipped his quill in venom to describe the action. Warton's team faced a deficit of 48 and Finlason ran through them with his exotic mixture, taking 6-25. Only Bowden resisted with a dogged 27 and with 34 to get to win in the last innings, Kimberley was a racing certainty. Before the match started, the hon. Charles Coventry had picked up £500 to £10 for a Kimberley win.[44]

With the betting frenzy in the pavilion, Kimberley's nerve almost failed them. Finlason and Tancred were run out and seven wickets were down for 15 before a tea break gave everyone a chance to compose themselves or hedge their bets. To frantic cheers, Hickson and Howe finally saw Kimberley home by ten wickets.

The tourists were exhausted by travel, entertainment, playing against odds and demanding and alien conditions. 'You have a hot sun in Kimberley and a dry climate,' Smith said, 'We found our mouths like limekilns and our tongues like hearthrugs.'[45]

The following day, the tourists ventured blinking into the savage sun to face a Cape Colony XV. Theunissen reminded the tourists of his speed and hostility. He hit Hearne and Wood with deliveries that reared off a length and several batsmen were caught at short leg. Wood went to hospital before continuing his innings and a fighting 29 from Bobby Abel was needed to save England from total humiliation. Theunissen's analysis of 5-37 in 31 overs restricted them to 91, their second sub-100 total of the week. They were jeered by the spectators.

44 *Cape Times*, 21/1/1889

45 Allen, *Sir Aubrey*, 80

The Cape Colony XV were comfortably poised on 139/11 in reply when Finlason joined Bobby Klinck and ran the fielders ragged, putting on 73 for the 12th wicket. Klinck made 81 in a powerful display of hitting. Finlason combined unlimited confidence, speed between the wickets, crude technique and obstinate defence, making 47 before Klinck was run out by a direct hit from Smith. The Colony was 176 runs ahead. Monty Bowden and Bobby Abel fought back, but ultimately Kimberley claimed a second win.

Finlason praised the intensity which the tourists brought to the game. Their ground fielding was 'a revelation ... they are on springs and field with an élan never found in a colonial team'.[46] But their intensity veered into sharp practice. Umpires were hustled, and malicious appeals were common. Bowden's behaviour in kicking a stump down the pitch, his sleight of hand to run out Hill and his petulance when hit by Theunissen were not well received.[47] Initially sympathetic to the challenges of playing against odds in unfamiliar conditions, Finlason decided the tourists were cheats and 'squealers'.[48]

His rival, Harry Cadwallader, writing in the *Diamond Fields Advertiser*, slammed these 'discourteous and churlish comments' by a writer of 'contemptible scurrility and babyish lampooning'.[49] Charlie Finlason never shirked a fight. 'I trust the addle headed goose will take this timely hint,' he said. '... His wild abuse of me is a sort of hogwash emanation from a muddy brain and an enlarged liver.'[50]

The final banquet at Pirates Club started well. The Kimberley mayor hoped that Johnny Briggs with his 'jovial smile and aldermanic appearance' would come back as their local professional. Warton too managed to remain light-hearted. They had played three games not two and the last game was Kimberley hospitality versus sleep. He shrewdly added that Kimberley had reaped a bonanza. The first day

46 *Daily Independent*, 18/1/1889

47 *Ibid*

48 Jonty Winch, *England's Youngest Captain*, (Windsor: Windsor Publications, 2003) 100

49 *Daily Independent*, 22/1/1889

50 *Daily Independent*, 21/1/1889

alone contributed a gate of £616 and the total gate for the week was in the region of £1,600. A huge windfall of £500 would be shared among the three main clubs – Kimberley, Pirates and Eclectics.[51]

1.8 'Cricket is a rotten game'

Aubrey Smith made his frustrations evident. 'I suppose you want me to say something about cricket', he said. 'It is the rottenest of all games. After travelling 6,000 miles to make five runs in four innings I do not know of a more rotten game.' He accepted defeat, 'as all Englishmen know how to do', but warned 'wait until we meet you again'.[52]

Darny Haarhof, a prominent local businessman, said he was 'not at all satisfied' with the way the English cricket team were referred to by 'Gossip' (Finlason) in the *Daily Independent*. The English applauded and shouted, 'Quite right.' His toast to the press pointedly omitted the *Independent*. Warton regretted that the issue had been raised. Finlason blamed Harry Cadwallader, 'the journalistic flunkey of the South African press'. The *Free State Express*, which had its own political priorities, thought 'Gossip's' 'truthful criticisms' upset the English team and 'they were even more chagrined when he backed up his words by bowling them out and running up a big score'.[53]

Despite this melodrama, Charlie Finlason managed a chat with 'quiet little Bobby Abel' who described the hardship of playing six days cricket in baking heat and against odds. 'You see,' Abel said, 'where the skill comes in is in placing the ball through fielders and you can't place the ball through a 22-man field. You just shut your eyes and hit.' In Bobby's opinion, uneven cricket was not cricket and 'you would learn so much more with equal sides'. He thought that South Africa would be beaten by the better county sides but were stronger than the Parsees from India.[54]

---

51 *Diamond Fields Advertiser*, 26/1/1889
52 *Cape Times*, 24/1/1889
53 *Cape Times*, 9/2/1889
54 *Daily Independent*, 26/1/1989

The players couldn't wait to reach the next destination. By January 1889, fortunes were being made on the Witwatersrand as the gold was stripped from the outcrops, land prices along the line of the gold reef boomed and trading on the stock market reached hysterical proportions. The Transvaal Republic asserted its independence under president Paul Kruger. Amid the mayhem, they collected taxes and retained control through a dynamite monopoly, which controlled the operation of the mines and a restrictive railway policy, which prohibited a rail link from the south until an outlet to the sea through non-British-controlled Delagoa Bay was built.

Kruger's rail ban condemned visitors to wedging into 'Buffalo Bill's coach', three to a seat with shoulders overlapping, shins and seats in contact and eight men including the two drivers outside with 6,000lb of luggage. 'How we hated our neighbours whose elbows were continually finding our ribs; how we abused those behind for grinding our backs with their knees. How hopelessly and mournfully we endeavoured to court sleep and with what shouts of joy we hailed each outspan,' lamented Smith.[55]

The unending scrubland broken only by the odd melancholy animal skeleton made for monotonous scenery. Johnny Briggs had a huge catapult but could only find Cape sparrows and meerkats. The coach stuck fast in a stream at Klerksdorp, and they set off on foot until the vehicle was finally dragged out of the mud. Four hours' sleep on the first night became three on the second.

When they arrived at the Johannesburg Club, they had travelled 300 miles in 60 hours sardined into a boiling, bouncing box. But they were energised by the smell of blasting cordite amid a sea of tents, and corrugated iron stores with mine-heads stretching out in every direction. Their hosts took them to Jumpers mine where they were shown 'Banket' rock formation in which the gold was found. Aubrey Smith was absent, already negotiating his post-tour career as a Johannesburg stockbroker.

---

55 *Sportsman*, 27/2/1889

The party explored the underground workings by candlelight, saw the extraction process and explored the black workers' compound. The miners on night shift were 'lounging around', cooking maize meal and 'inhaling copious whiffs of dagga smoke'.[56]

Warton was inhaling cigar smoke at his next social venue – the Stock Exchange. 'At 10am the secretary enters the rostrum and then the howling, screaming, excited mass of brokers raises pandemonium.'[57] The dramatic speed of 'progress' on the Rand was exemplified by the development of The Wanderers cricket ground. President Kruger had been persuaded to grant the lease for the ground and act as club patron. Jacob Swart constructed a venue in six months, clearing and levelling the ground and building a pavilion despite the summer rains.

Spectators were charged three guineas for a week in the pavilion and the Johannesburg XXII readily agreed to the tourists' request for a dark green mat. Briggs, Smith and Fothergill dismissed the locals for 138. After the Kimberley humiliation, Smith decided to lead from the front and opened the batting as well as the bowling. But the tourists foundered against James Wishart (35-21-24-5) and George Cooley (36-19-35-5). They avoided the compulsory follow-on by a single run. The bowlers steamrollered the XXII for 58 in the second innings. Briggs claimed 9-19 and Smith, bowling like a man possessed, 10-25. Sixteen batsmen were either bowled or LBW. It was game on with 137 to get. Abel was dropped on one and the day ended with Warton's team secure on 76/0. The local nine-man attack could not shake the openers and the following day they completed a ten-wicket win.

In the first innings the XXII's fielding had surpassed expectations, and the bowling of Cooley and Wishart was surprisingly effective.[58] In the second innings numerous chances were grassed. It is seldom that a score of 60 in the first innings translates into a second innings

56   *Daily Independent* 1/2/1889
57   *Cricket* 21/3/1889
58   Cox, *Major Warton's Tour*, 76

total of 137 for no wicket. In terms of runs per wicket these were the lowest and highest scores of the tour.

The tourists' first innings failure followed the fearsome journey and a gruelling session in the heat. The turnaround came after a Sunday off, when the team had a chance to regroup. It allowed Smith to channel his frustrations into leadership by example. His ten wickets were taken at a rate of one every seven balls. He was on a hat-trick four times in his 17 overs, and snapped the off stump of Fleischer, top scorer in the first innings. He inspired the rest of the team, and Abel and Hearne stepped up when it mattered.

Not only had the match been turned on its head, but so had the tour in this single innings. But what caused this turnaround? Johannesburg was a town where fortunes were made daily and anything that could attract a bet did so. The game was the backdrop to frenzied betting. It was alleged that the XXII had taken every bet against themselves that they could find.

Cecil Rhodes bet £5 at 9/1 that Abel and Frank Hearne would win without losing a wicket. The winnings were shared between them. Abel's innings was worth nearly £200 and the professionals also received a gold nugget with a rough diamond set in it. Finlason was delighted by the English performance against his Johannesburg enemy.[59] But the result hinged on a scoring error which had allowed the English to avoid the follow-on.

The following day Warton's men returned to The Wanderers to face a Transvaal XV. Bobby Abel continued in a batting bubble until a catch at silly point finally dismissed him for a remarkable 114 in five hours. It was England's first hundred in South Africa. He was shouldered off to receive the plaudits of the ladies as the band launched into 'See the Conquering Hero Comes'. The innings ended with a merry 48-run last-wicket partnership between Coventry and Fothergill. Amateurs could not receive cash, so Coventry was motivated by J.B. Robinson's offer of a mine share, valued at £70, offered for the highest amateur score. Fothergill supported Coventry

---

59 *Daily Independent* 2/2/1889

for long enough for the latter to claim the prize and received £20 for his efforts.

George Cooley took 4-73 in 36 overs, adding to his 54 overs in the previous game. Tragically his exertions were to prove fatal. He caught a cold, then a lung infection and in these pre-antibiotic days, he sadly passed away. When Transvaal batted, a huge dust storm made the pitch invisible from the pavilion and the matting disappeared under a coating of red sand. Faced with a deficit of 130 runs, the second innings was a familiar procession and the tourists won by an innings and 42 runs.[60]

1.9 Johnny the Lionheart

Johnny Briggs's efforts over these two intense weeks showed his stamina and strength of character as well as his skill. England's wins depended on his performances during an era of four-ball overs. In the two losing games in Kimberley, his figures had been 133 overs, 58 maidens, 203 runs and 19 wickets – an average of 10.7 per wicket at an economy rate of 1.5 per over. His equivalent figures in the winning games in Johannesburg were 119.4 overs, 67 maidens, 189 runs and 29 wickets – averaging 6.5 and conceding 1.6 runs per over.

Johannesburg's *Diggers News* described facing him, 'First you get a ball breaking from your leg, then comes one looking just about the right length for a slog, and you are tempted and get out to it, and find by some unaccountable means the ball pitches much shorter than you anticipate and shoots under your bat ... and you look round and find your stumps down ... the style of delivery is never changed; you can get no intimation from that twinkling eye and good-humoured mouth ... hit him over the pavilion and he will laugh with you, and the next ball will raise your bails.'[61]

As the *Natal Mercury* explained, knowing what Briggs did, did not make him any easier to play. He turned the ball both ways and disguised his dramatic changes of pace. He relied principally on variation and studied batsmen's weaknesses. He deliberately sent down loose balls. He was a clever dissembler up to all sorts of tricks

---

60 Cox, *Major Warton's Tour*, 85-9
61 *Standard and Diggers News* 14/2/1889; *Dimond Fields Advertiser*, 11/3/1889

and antics and raised many a laugh in trying to get rid of a batsman. He took liberties which would not be permitted in a man of lesser ability.[62] It is hard not to imagine a 19th-century Shane Warne.

Asked for the secret of his bowling, Briggs swore he didn't know it himself.

South Africa, said Warton, was a land of surprises. The players were astonished by the two-year-old 'toddler town' with a population of 20,000, fine streets and handsome buildings. They visited three mines and spent their mornings in the Stock Exchange delightedly following the bull market where a little information went a long way. If the cricketers were obsessed with the exchange, the brokers were getting through business as fast as possible to get to the cricket. By the time that Smith's report on the first game of the tour appeared in *The Sportsman* during England's February freeze, he and Monty Bowden were registered members of the Johannesburg Stock Exchange.[63]

Natal was a separate British colony with a population of 30,000 whites, 60,000 indentured Indians working on the sugar plantations, and around 400,000 Zulus. Whites were continually frustrated by 'work-shy' Africans who preferred an independent existence to labouring at derisory wages. The government's key problem was to force them out through stringent taxation and labour regulation. Natal's divide and rule strategy to control Zululand to the north rested on maximum force to crush any perceived resistance to taxation as the fates of traditional leaders Langalibalele in the 1870s, Dinizulu in the 1890s, and finally the Bambatha Rebellion in 1906 demonstrated.

The team may have hoped the worst of the travelling was behind them. The professionals took the shorter route via Harrismith and the amateurs the longer northern route to see the battlefields at Majuba Hill and Laing's Nek. The former clambered aboard their coach at 5am on the Saturday and reached Harrismith on the Sunday night.

62 *Natal Mercury*, 16/1/1889
63 *Cape Times*, 16/2/1889

On Monday morning, they found themselves marooned in the middle of a flooded river until hauled out by a span of oxen.

The amateurs started eight hours late on Saturday and had to travel through the night. During a savage electric storm, they discovered one of the drivers was paralytically drunk and the other asleep and they had to take over the reins of the ten-horse coach. On Sunday afternoon, they ascended Laing's Nek, and 'gaunt and drear' Majuba Hill towering away to the right with Colley's grave and those of the fallen. Warton found it incredible that in 1881 the red coats could have been dislodged by a handful of Boers. Colley had taken the hill for no apparent purpose, failed to spot the Boers on the slopes until too late and had not secured his defences.

After this reminder of British vulnerability, the amateurs drove, in Warton's words, 'Up and down steep hills, strewn with large boulders over which we bumped mercilessly, until our heads and every joint of our bodies ached ... the last 33 miles taking eight hours'. The coach passed ox wagons heading to Johannesburg from Durban carrying tram rails, Pommery champagne and Worcestershire sauce. At last, in a heavy thunderstorm the amateurs fell into a railway carriage, arriving in Pietermaritzburg on Tuesday hours before the start. The *Natal Mercury* heralded the visitors, 'Chosen from a population of 34 million, our champions represent 34 000 ... let the best players win.'[64]

Awaiting the team in Pietermaritzburg, therefore, were the army – the 64th Staffordshire and the Inniskilling Dragoons – and George 'Happy Jack' Ulyett to join the party. Ulyett was a veteran of five Australian tours, had played in the first-ever Test and was a front-rank batsman, fast-medium bowler and outstanding fielder. More significantly, his lively and humorous personality provided a shot in the arm for Warton's weary travellers.

The Pietermaritzburg skipper insisted on playing XXII instead of XVIII players. In cool, damp conditions, Briggs claimed 11-34 as the home side subsided to 92 all out. In reply, tight bowling limited the tourists to 164. Despite rain delays, the home side failed to bat

---

64 *Natal Mercury*, 13/2/1889

out for a draw. Basil Grieve's fast underarm had a rare outing and his 5-10 in 11 overs were his best figures on the tour.

The cool weather continued against a Natal XV. The tourists managed 176. Orthodox left-armer Gustav Kempis turned the ball sharply and young policeman Peter Madden's raw pace and eccentric action proved troublesome. Even J.T. Henderson, doyen of Natal cricket, admitted that Madden threw 'but only occasionally when he was anxious to get rid of a particularly sticking batsman'.[65] Batting for 35 minutes in poor light, Natal were six wickets down for seven runs at stumps. When Don Davey was bowled by Smith the next day, they were drowning at 8/8. They eventually conceded a lead of 91, followed on and lost by an innings and ten runs. Luck and the umpires were not on their side. Major Warton later admitted that his lbw decision against Natal's star batsman, Frank Crawford, was a 'shocker'.

When the governor referred to the team as 'good companions', Smith retorted that if they lost, they were 'about as objectionable a set of fellows … as could be found … and they cordially hated the game of cricket'.[66] Airy thoughts about 'balance' and the duty to encourage the local game had been crushed by four losses and Kimberley. Now only victories would do.

The visitors' train switch-backed through the lush spectacular landscape of the Valley of a Thousand Hills to Durban. They were welcomed by a volley of railway fog signals and delighted to see grass on the outfield for the game against a Durban XVIII, but it was long and thick. Monty Bowden took the aerial route and smashed a couple of huge sixes off Madden, one of which lodged in a tree. Cameron Skinner scored his only run of the tour before running himself out trying to steal another. Thanks to a ninth-wicket partnership between Coventry and Fothergill, the visitors made 187.

Briggs's achilles heel was discovered. He could not cope with the extreme humidity. Durban responded with 127, including a fighting

65 M.W. Luckin, *The History of South African Cricket*, (Johannesburg: W.E. Hortor and Co, 1915) 99

66 *Sportsman*, 20/3/1889

22 not out from Madden and a stylish 17 from Don Davey. Skinner, confidence running high, clutched E.C. Davey's lofted drive, his only catch of the tour. Rivalry with Pietermaritzburg was satisfied when Durban, unlike the uplanders, avoided the follow-on. In the second innings, Kempis demolished Abel's stumps for the second time in the match and did the same to Read, Grieve and Coventry. His 5-32 and Madden's 4-35 dismissed the tourists for 68. With Durban chasing 129, Johnny Briggs rallied, telling the team, 'My soul is in arms and eager for the fray.' Durban started well and looked like having the edge. Briggs removed the foundations when he snatched five wickets for four runs, but Bob Christison counter-attacked, and the pendulum swung towards the locals until he was caught for 31. With four wickets in hand, 35 to win and 15 minutes left, the home side shut up shop to earn the tourists' first draw of the tour.[67]

Durban had the largest natural harbour on the sub-continent, but like most South African ports it was protected by a sandbar. Known as Annabella's bar after a famous wreck of the 1860s, ships anchored in the outer bay while passengers and goods were ferried by lighters. Pier extensions had failed, and it was not until 1904 that the Bar was defeated by a fleet of 15 dredgers. Warton's team had two options for embarkation from a lighter on to a moving ship – a semi-dignified ascent by ladder or a less heroic basket hoist. Most scrambled up on rope ladders. Bobby Abel tried a dozen unsuccessful ladder ascents to the guffaws and unsolicited advice of his team-mates, before accepting the ignominy of the basket with elder citizens Maurice Read and Jack Ulyett.

They arrived in East London 20 hours later and following another basket offload, transferred by train to King William's Town (KWT). They were travelling and playing cricket in the Eastern Cape, which for 100 years had seen endless sporadic but bitter warfare between colonial interlopers, the British army and the Xhosa peoples. Only the social collapse during a final disastrous famine among the Xhosa brought the sequence to an end in 1878.

---

67 *Ibid*

Many Africans were among the 2,000-strong crowd at the Eastern Cape military HQ. The King William's Town Africans, captained by Nathaniel Umhalla, had won the African version of the Colony's Champion Bat competition and often defeated their white KWT counterparts.[68] Nathaniel was a son of paramount chief Mhala, who was convicted of a war plot during the cattle killing of 1856 on evidence, which William Porter, Cape Attorney General, suggested was 'scarcely conclusive'.[69] While Mhala languished as one in a long line of African leaders imprisoned on Robben Island, his son learnt his cricket across the bay at Zonnebloem College for African chiefs.[70]

No African players were considered for the Cape Mounted Rifles XXII, whose ineptitude scraped the bottom of the cricketing barrel. Briggs took their first four wickets without a run on the board and ended up with the other-worldly figures of 15 wickets for four runs off 22.3 overs. He was slightly more profligate in the second innings with 12-19, taking his figures for the match to a ridiculous 27 wickets for 23 runs. In the return fixture, Ulyett smashed three sixes in a chanceless 103, and the tourists won by an innings and 95 runs. These games had no pretence to genuine competition, but supposedly strengthened troop morale on the frontiers of the empire.

At the City Lords ground in Grahamstown, nestling in a bowl of hills and part of the scene of a famous battle in 1819, Bobby Abel carried his bat for 126 not out from a team total of 256. Giddy smashed 45 in the Grahamstown XXII reply, as the fielders staggered around in a dust storm, but another innings defeat swiftly followed. Next came a 300-mile rail trip, via Port Elizabeth, to the old Boer town of Graaff-Reinet, scene of the infamous Slachter's Nek rebellion[71], to play a Midland Districts XXII. They clattered through 150 miles

68 Richard Parry, 'Black Cricketers, White Politicians and the Origins of Segregation at the Cape' in Bruce Murray and Goolam Vahed (eds), *Empire and Cricket*, (Pretoria: UNISA, 2009) 24-26

69 Mostert, *Frontiers*, 1229

70 Janet Hodgson and Theresa Edelmann, *Zonnebloem College and the Genesis of an African Intelligentsia, 1857–1933*, (Cape Town: African Lives, 2018) 2, 3, 118

71 Mostert, *Frontiers*, 403-406

of the 'dismal and monotonous' Great Karoo ('place of thirst' in the Khoi tongue) where animals lying on the rails proved the only diversion, eventually arriving at the 'gem of the desert', an oasis with an abundance of trees, a river and almost encircled by mountains.

The town had been built in the 1770s, as the Dutch trek-boers (nomadic herders) settled on farms called *Vergenoegd* (far enough) or *Slegtgenoegd* (bad enough). They fought a vicious 30-year war with the San peoples, whose hunting lands they had appropriated, exterminating thousands in a colonial genocide. The remainder amalgamated with the local Khoi peoples or headed deep into the Kalahari Desert. Despite periodic rebellions against authority in distant Cape Town, Graaff-Reinet became the centre of the South African wool industry, which explained the early advent of the railway in 1879 and the cricketers a decade later. The place was more memorable than the game. The ball came through like 'greased lightning', off the mat laid on antheap, cinder, and cement, while the glare rivalled Kimberley. A patient innings by Abel and a spectacular collapse to 12/18 in the second innings produced the usual innings defeat.

Warton's team returned to Port Elizabeth a toughened, seasoned and more confident XI. The match against an Eastern Province XV was a warm-up for the representative game against a South African XI. Potential South Africa XI players Rose-Innes, Jackson, Giddy, Dunell and Stewart batted well before Arnold Fothergill took 7-19 in a sustained and aggressive spell and Abel's technique and patience ensured a comfortable win by eight wickets. The phoney war was over. Now Warton's men would be pitted against the best players in the subcontinent on, at last, equal terms.

Warton's team selected itself with McMaster and Skinner on the bench. The South African XI tried to balance regional as well as cricketing priorities: a surprise pick being the teenage Okey Ochse from the Free State who had not faced the tourists. Their match-winner, Nic Theunissen, was refused leave to play by his Stellenbosch theology professors.

The South Africans took the field in olive-green caps with a yellow 'SA' monogram embroidered by the wife of Owen Dunell,

South Africa's captain. Dunell, who had played for Oxford University in the 1877 FA Cup Final, won the toss and batted. But the side described as having no tail proved to have almost no body. In Briggs's second over, Rose-Innes lost his off stump to a 'snorter'. Philip Hutchinson was bowled first ball. Tancred and Vintcent defended resolutely, but South Africa had to wait ten overs before recording what history would later declare to be their first Test run.[72]

Three slip catches by Bobby Abel reduced the home side to 17/5 and confirmed the worst fears of the South African batsmen, promotors and caterers. Tancred and Dunell, the best South African batsmen on display, staged a recovery until Tancred was beaten by a fast Smith in-swinger and bowled for 29 at 58/6. Smith, bowling with speed and hostility, ended with 5-19 as South Africa were rolled over for 84. Dunell was left on 26 not out.

Bobby Abel, excited at facing only 11 fielders for the first time on the tour, smashed the first ball of the innings from Gus Kempis to the leg boundary for four. But the South Africans exerted some pressure. Kempis got George Ulyett and Maurice Read, reducing the tourists to 14/2. Bobby Abel dropped anchor until caught by Milton for 46. The English were only three runs ahead with two wickets left at 87/8. Two runs later, Fred Smith fluffed a stumping chance from Grieve to howls from around the ground.

Getting rid of the English tail had proved a stumbling block all tour. Coventry hit out to take the total to 103 and was replaced by the dangerous Fothergill, a wolf in sheep's clothing at number 11. After a nasty crack on the finger, he smashed four fours and a huge driven six off Rose-Innes. When Milton had him caught for 32, the English had a lead of 64.

South Africa batted steadily to overhaul the deficit with three wickets down, but Tancred was fooled by Briggs's dip and caught and bowled for his second 29 of the match. The dangerous Milton slogged a quick 19 before he was caught by Bowden. In this team of 'amateurs', South African-born Tancred played the colonial role,

---

72 Cox, *Major Warton's Tour*, 176-184

canny and focused, while Milton was the archetypal upper-class English amateur, playing country house cricket. A more judicious approach on Milton's part might have created a more challenging target than the 66 England required to win. South Africa's first Test match ended in an eight-wicket defeat.

This was the tourists' 17th match. Fit, travel- and battle-hardened, they had not lost since Kimberley – ten wins ago. Unlike the 'home' team they were experienced in local conditions and had played on all varieties of matting and underlays. They knew what they were capable of, how to exploit local conditions, the quality of the opposition, and had a winning habit and the confidence to match.

The South Africans by contrast were weekend amateurs with no experience of three-day cricket. They had never played together and only a few had played at PE. With minimal time for preparation, there was no chance of assessing the conditions or their resources. They had done remarkably well in their first Test.

Finally, the show swung north for a return against Kimberley. They had not lost since their previous visit. Their captain stayed behind. His mystery 'fever' may have been a diplomatic means to avoid Kimberley where he had not gone down well in the press furore. The locals insisted on the same glare-inducing beige mat and 18 players and escaped with a draw to maintain an unbeaten record against the tourists. James Logan, the self-styled 'Chief of Matjiesfontein', made his first tour appearance.[73] He was to be a central figure for the next decade.

Smith had apparently not recovered from enteric fever and Monty Bowden as the only amateur with first-class cricket experience became, at 23, England's youngest captain in the second Test in Cape Town. The Western Province match-winners, Theunissen and Ashley, were back, and Milton replaced Dunell as captain. Bowden won the toss and batted. The fearsome Theunissen, who had terrorised the pink and perspiring English batsmen two months before, now found a different team from the hesitant outfit who had

---

73 *DFA*, 22/3/1889

been flummoxed by 22 fielders. Bobby Abel anchored the innings as he had held the tour together and was seventh out for 120 hitting out tiredly at Ashley. The left-armer finished with 7-95 in an England total of 292.[74]

It would be charitable to draw a veil over the rest of the match, remembering a reasonably closely fought first day and a masterful performance from Abel. But the history of cricketing car crashes has its own ghoulish fascination. The record number of enthusiasts who flooded through the gates next day hoping for a South African fightback had little idea what an extraordinary morning's cricket was in store.

After a quiet start, Briggs seized South Africa's fragile batting by the throat. Demonstrating total control, he bowled Hutchinson for three (11/3), Dunell for four (19/4), and Milton with a 'magnificent ball' for seven (31/5). Richards broke the sequence by nicking to Abel off Fothergill for a duck and then it was all Briggs. Vintcent and Fred Smith bowled Briggs, Theunissen lbw Briggs, and finally, after Tancred had steered him for four through fine leg, Briggs demolished Ashley's stumps. South Africa were all out for 47 in less than an hour and a half, Johnny finishing with figures of 19.1-11-17-7.

Tancred had carried his bat for 26, an oasis of calm amid the mayhem. This was a remarkable achievement among the clatter of wickets. But until the ninth wicket fell, Tancred played Briggs primarily from the non-striker's end. Should he have tried earlier to protect the bottom half of the order?

Trailing by 245, South Africa's prospects looked hopeless as they followed on. Briggs, the cherub turned avenging angel, again slaughtered South Africa's representatives in front of 4,000 stunned spectators. Sixteen South African wickets had fallen for 65 runs between the start of play and lunch. Briggs bowled every batsman except Rose-Innes, who had managed to run himself out off the first ball of the innings without facing a ball, and Dunell, who got out to Fothergill. Briggs owned the South Africans. They were all out for 43.

---

74 Cox, *Major Warton's Tour*, 195-201

Briggs bowled 58 deliveries in the innings, conceding 11 runs, several of which came from misfields, and the only ball to go for more than a single was an overthrow for two. His second-innings figures were 14.2-5-11-8, and his match figures were 33.3 overs, 16 maidens, 28 runs and 15 wickets, still a record in a single day of Test cricket.

So how do we explain this massacre by an innings and 202 runs, still the worst trouncing (in terms of innings defeats) by England against South Africa? Port Elizabeth had suggested that despite the gulf in experience, South Africa could at least put up a fight. Newlands was a different proposition. And Briggs was the X-factor. As a tactical cricketer, his ability to exploit the surfaces he bowled on was unparalleled. On hard, high-bouncing wickets, Briggs had relied on orthodox left-arm style with subtle variations of pace and length, but at Newlands, slower with a lower bounce, he bowled a little quicker with the ball drifting in with the arm from off to leg, sharp turn from leg and a devastating faster ball. His control, reputation and personality paralysed the opposition. His fellow professionals said he had never bowled better in his life. He destroyed and dismantled the defensive technique of any batsmen at the other end of the mat, sometimes even before a ball was bowled.

After a final unofficial match, the English tourists headed back to the *Garth Castle* for presentations and farewells. The professionals received £20 bonuses for 'their social qualities and gentlemanly behaviour' (of course they were not actually 'gentlemen'). Tancred, Theunissen and Gobo Ashley scooped the batting and bowling awards – gold watches not cash to avoid offending amateur sensibilities.

The final annihilation obscured South Africa's earlier successes and their fighting efforts in the first Test and created a climate of inferiority. The tour had severely tested the stamina of the tourists, who had no respite from an endless round of baking days, sandstorms, long alcoholic evenings, endless packing and bouncing across the veld. They had covered 15,975 miles, 13,003 by steamer, 2,218 by rail and 785 (painfully) by coach and cart. They were away for 146 days, 41 on board ship, 25 in coaches, carts or trains and spent 51 days in the field.

Net profits outstripped the Warton guarantees, and the excess was shared between local clubs to pay for improvements and build facilities. Warton had his future secured in Rhodes' employ. Bowden's showmanship and keeping skills were eye-openers, Briggs was a force of nature with the ball and in the field, and Abel showed why he was one of the world's best batsmen.

The significance of the matches was not lost on either set of players. Of the colonial players, their fielding was often brilliant. The bowling was much better than the batting, with Theunissen their star fast bowler and Ashley a model of consistency. The batsmen, apart from Tancred and Dunell, showed understandable nerves before large crowds.

As Bobby Abel pointed out, playing against odds reduced the quality of the cricket on display. Batting was more difficult with packed fields; bowling took longer and was more exhausting. The talent gulf was widened by the experience gap and by the tourists' greater familiarity with South African conditions than the locals.

1.10 Farewell

Aubrey Smith already had the stage uppermost in his thoughts, 'The curtain was going down and the play over, would the audience applaud (yes) ... hoped those who had looked on the play had seen something which will live in the memory ... Those on stage would look back on the tour with a feeling of gratitude and pleasure.'[75]

Bowden and Smith waved goodbye as the tug escorted their colleagues out of Table Bay. Their thoughts turned to the riches of the Rand, but the outcrop mining bubble burst and their stockbroking business failed. Monty Bowden met a sad end and was buried in a coffin made out of whisky cases near 'Old Umtali'. Aubrey Smith begged his fare home and reinvented himself as a professional on the stage. Hollywood would call later. The long theatrical nights on the tour had not been wasted.

75 *Cape Times*, 27/3/1889

For South Africa, the purpose of the tour was to place the region in the spotlight. As Cadwallader put it, 'Among the tourists were one or two men gifted with brains and money ... and no doubt have transmitted accurate information on the state of affairs here and in the Transvaal and the prospects which await South African development'.[76] Two decades later, when South Africa joined the Imperial Cricket Conference, the two representative matches gained Test status, creating an imperial back story. Cricket did not take place in a neutral bubble. The status of these early games demonstrated cricket's place in the tool kit of empire.

---

76 *Diamond Fields Advertiser, 22/3/1889*

2

Speculations: W.W. Read 1891/92

WARTON'S BOYS had driven a cricketing circus through the scrapes and bumps of a first tour with panache and no little steel. The adventure would be remembered for the subcontinent's celebration of colonialism on the global stage and for Johnny Briggs, as huge in cricketing status as he was small in stature. But it also made a profit and piqued the commercial rather than educational interests as the *Cape Times* politely put it.[77]

Two years was a long time in Africa and by the time the next venture under Edwin 'Daddy' Ash and his captain, Walter Read, arrived, Warton's days seemed long ago. Monty Bowden's 126 not out had won the first Currie Cup challenge in April 1890 for Transvaal over Kimberley, but neither he nor Aubrey Smith were around to play in the return fixture in which a seven-day match the 'most magnificent game ever contested in South Africa … such a crowing, swaggering, and persistent drunkenness by Kimberley supporters' was won by Charlie Finlason's unbeaten 154 for Kimberley,

Bowden and Smith's dreams may have foundered on personal differences, but the mining industry came face to face with realities. By 1890, the gold bearing reef had to be chased deeper into the earth. But gold extracted from below 120 feet had not oxidised and could not be recovered through the standard process. The mine stamps fell

---

77 *Cape Times*, 27/11/1891

silent. It took 18 months for the MacArthur-Forrest cyanide process to solve the technical problem, and it would be much longer before payable gold was produced. The stock market collapsed, and three banks shut their doors. President Kruger, alarmed at the powder keg smouldering in his back garden, travelled to The Wanderers to be met by 10,000 'starving, hopeless young men' and was forced to beat a hasty retreat to the chief of police's house. [78]

Kimberley was anxious to exploit its comparative advantage. The Australians offered to stop off on their way home from England in 1890 but were too expensive. James Lillywhite proposed bringing a team in 1890/91. Kimberley demanded W.G. Grace, Arthur Shrewsbury and George Lohmann and offered to guarantee £600. To Kimberley's annoyance, Milton's Western Province vetoed the offer, citing the financial crisis and state of South African cricket. [79]

2.1 Edwin Ash's rugby tourists

The South African Rugby Football Board (set up in 1889) had invited a British rugby team managed by Edwin Ash to tour in 1891. The team included ten internationals. The tourists won all 20 games and conceded only a single try. The rugby tourists developed patterns of play, which the colonial opposition, like the cricketers, coming together on an ad hoc basis, could not match.

Following the fiasco of the twin tours to Australia in 1887/88, Arthur Shrewsbury considered that cricket was 'practically done' in the colonies, 'It will not pay ... if we take out a representative team ... the Colonists naturally get tired of seeing their own team defeated ... if we send out a weak team, they will not pay to watch them.' [80]

Despite the depression, 'Daddy' Ash's rugby team (costs guaranteed by Cecil Rhodes) suggested that another cricket tour

---

78   Thelma Gutsche, *Old Gold*, (Cape Town: Howard Timmins, 1966) 57
79   *Cape Times*, 1/9/1890
80   *Ibid*

might be profitable. Ash signed up Surrey's 'shamateur' assistant secretary, Walter Read, as captain for £350 plus expenses (triple what Smith had received), as well as the Australian captain Billy Murdoch and opening bowler J.J. Ferris. In late November 1891, there were three English teams on tour. Lord Hawke's amateurs were in North America, Lord Sheffield's side was on the way to Australia with Grace, Abel, Briggs, Lohmann and Maurice Read on board. W.G. Grace had a £3,000 contract. He was the magic ingredient and would quadruple the gate wherever he played. And who else could be a more plausible Neptune as they crossed the line?

Walter Read, Ferris, Murdoch and Fred 'Nutty' Martin had all played in the last Ashes Test at The Oval in 1890. Martin, bowling left-arm and spinning it at almost medium pace, took 12 wickets on debut, a performance enhanced by George Lohmann bowling from the other end. His record was to stand until Bob Massie. George Brann, a football international, was the only real amateur on board. The 'balance' was wrong. Too few amateurs meant the team was too strong on the pitch and lacked social cachet for the snobbish colonial establishment. Nor were they entertainers. They were not averse to the odd song, but did not aspire to the theatrical heights of Smith, Bowden, and Skinner. There was no blacking up for Minstrel shows on board the *Dunnottar Castle*.

The *Dunnottar* took on 420 tons of coal in Madeira and that evening held an informal smoker with Read, Ash, Joe Leaney, Vic Barton and George Ayres warbling for the amusement of the company. They beat the ship's officers at cricket and won most of the prizes at sports day, with Brann pipping the ship's doctor in the half mile despite the latter's experience in keeping his footing round corners on a pitching deck. William Chatterton won the sprint, the walking half mile and Walter Read the shot put.

They arrived in Table Bay on 8 December to be met by Milton and Frank Hearne. A few days later they were formally welcomed by the governor, Sir Henry Loch. Walter Read dutifully assured them that there was more than just a sporting purpose. His Australian tours had 'done more to create friendly feeling between the colonies and mother country than political movements could possibly attain'.[81]

But this was mainly business, and it was up to the promoters to maximise the returns. With the backing of the Cape establishment, and a guarantee of 75 per cent of the profits from each of the venues, Ash was confident, but the high fees paid to Read, Ferris and Murdoch put a premium on attracting large gates. Tour finances were built on the vagaries of weather, performances and variables such as the tension of the mat. Up-front investment was needed but uncertainty meant distinctions between loans and investments were left deliberately ambiguous. The consequences would be significant.

On a glorious Saturday, Walter Read won the toss against a Western Province XVIII before 3,000 spectators, with bunting streaming above the newly erected stands and marquees. The East Yorkshire band ran through its repertoire and Frank Hearne, who had remained in the Cape as player, coach and groundsman, had prepared the wicket. His brother, Alec, opened the batting with William Chatterton , the Derbyshire pro. Unlike the cat and mouse opening of the first tour, Chatterton glided Vollie van der Byl's first ball through the slips and the pair raised the first 50 in 70 minutes.

Chatterton dominated a tidy local attack and was last out for 83 in a total of 200. Ferris charged in and claimed 6-19 in 22.1 overs in the local reply. With a 55-run lead, Read's batsmen were strangled by a 15-year-old slow left-arm bowler, Murray Bisset (later South Africa's wicketkeeper and captain), who took 4-60 in 45 overs. Read declared 201 ahead with less than three hours to play and the match petered out into a draw.

The second match against a Cape Colony XV was played over the Christmas period with an eye on the Boxing Day gate. Read again won the toss and thanks to a rapid 45 from George Brann and an excellent 6-58 from the big-spinning Irvine Grimmer, deputy manager of De Beers in Kimberley, the English innings closed for 180.

---

81 *Cape Times*, 21/12/1891

2.2 Christmas

James Logan led a Christmas trip through the Constantia Nek Pass to the fishing village of Hout Bay in the shadows of Chapman's Peak. A swim was followed by a climb and a picnic lunch in a sylvan glade. The team returned in its class components – the amateurs were entertained by Herbert Castens, showcasing his banjo skills, and the professionals dined in the sergeant's mess of the East Yorkshires. On Christmas Day, two pews were reserved for the team at a choral service at St George's Cathedral, and all assembled for roast beef, plum pudding and brandy sauce at the Queen's Hotel in Sea Point.

Boxing Day was a scorcher with an enormous crowd of 6,000 people jamming all vantage points. Despite resuming at 73/6, the Colony XV didn't disappoint their supporters. Castens put on 71 with Van der Byl, then Milton, bristling with aggression, drove consecutive fours off Dick Pougher to pass the English total. Castens was clean bowled by Martin for 49 and the innings closed for 197, a lead of 17. Read's team responded as they were to do all tour. Alec Hearne and Chatterton patiently accumulated enough runs to make a loss impossible. On the third day, Grimmer trapped the obdurate Chatterton for 37 and Alec Hearne, the young Kent pro 'who had played as correct an exhibition as any onlooker would wish to see', was out to a brilliant running catch by Mills at long on for 91. Brann hit his second 45 of the tour in 31 minutes and Read declared with the Colony needing 202 and three and a half hours to get them. Despite some adventurous hitting the Colony were 59 runs short with four wickets in hand at the close. Read's safety-first tactics appeared designed to attract a full gate but not risk a loss. It was an uneasy balance.

Read's party steamed out of Cape Town station and into the night. 'Table Mountain with its cloudy summit loomed up towards the sky in its blackness and hurled out the south-easter as a parting reminiscence of its power, whilst the southern cross stood out … bright and clear in bold relief with its myriads of stars around,' said

Edwin Ash, in his report to *The Sportsman*.[82] Next morning the sun rose over the train as it wound up through the Hex River Pass, 'lighting it up with tints of purple and gold'.

2.3 Matjiesfontein and Imperial Federation

They stopped at Matjiesfontein to spend a day at James Logan's oasis and health resort on the line to Kimberley. Logan, the self-described 'Laird of Matjiesfontein', had appointed himself patron of the tour.

'J.D. Logan's resources for entertainment seem unlimitable,' commented the well-lunched *Cape Times* reporter, 'and [he] had compelled the azure vault of cloudless skies to shower down upon this wilderness the many varieties of amusement for both body and mind.' The team gave a brief coaching session then took on the locals at lawn tennis and football. Olive Schreiner, celebrated author of *The Story of an African Farm*, and sister of William Schreiner, politician and future supporter of African land rights, was a Matjiesfontein resident. She was also Logan's whist partner.

Logan aimed to 'bind sympathies and affections of colony and mother country in still closer Union'. He hoped England would abandon free trade radicalism and protect colonial interests from one-sided competition from the United States. This fiscal theme was unusual for these occasions which tended to focus on the ties of empire and the healthy and manly sport of cricket. The depth of the depression had brought economics to the fore.

Another guest argued, 'The day was not far distant where they would hail not only South African federation, but imperial federation ... every part of the Queen's dominions would receive equal treatment. Sleepy Downing Street with its blunders and red tape would be relegated to limbo as each would have a voice in the domestic and foreign policy of empire.'[83]

The team set off the following morning for Port Elizabeth. By midnight they had reached De Aar where the turn of the year was

---

82 *Sportsman*, 28/1/1892
83 *Cape Times*, 21/12/1891

rung in with glasses to absent friends. The next day they found themselves in a new green landscape with winding streams and valleys, and the ostrich farms showing off the magnificent birds. Prickly pears, aloes, wild fruit trees and wildflowers contrasted with the dull red sand and mountain stone of the Karoo.

They puffed into Port Elizabeth station with the ocean running right up to the walls. The St George's Ground pavilion was festively dressed, and the wicket was mat on turf but much slower than in Cape Town. Whether it was the strong glare, the pace of the wicket or the hospitality, Read's team were ambushed for 74 by the Port Elizabeth XXII's formidable young opening bowlers, Dante Parkin (right hand) and Dick Crage (left hand), who kept the batsmen under constant pressure. Crage took 6-41, bowling five of his victims. The XXII started brightly until Ferris ripped through the heart of the home side with 9-43, and they collapsed in a heap for 78. With honours even, a smoking concert with 500 people tested the team's singing, partly redeemed by a stellar performance from George Brann. The next day a boating trip on the Zwartkops river almost ended in disaster when a boat sprang a leak as the 'river police' – sharks – circled. The boat made it back at record speed for a reviving lunch of oysters, brown bread and stout.

The matting was stretched tighter on the second day. On a quicker surface, an excellent 72 from Chatterton left the home side needing the now standard 202 with a day to bat. The Test bowlers Ferris (8-14) and Fred Martin (8-48) destroyed any thought of resistance and Port Elizabeth finished 109 runs short to hand the tourists their first win of the tour. In each of the first three games played, the colonials batted second and failed to chase over 200 to win, although twice Read had failed to provide sufficient time to bowl them out.

In the next match against Milton's Cape Colony XV, Walter Read applied meaty pulls to anything slightly short, before holing out to mid-off for 67 out of 246. If the batting was starting to learn the mysteries of the mat, the bowlers had fully mastered the conditions, carrying, as the *Eastern Province Herald* put it, 'a great deal in their heads which they did not neglect to use … no analysis can describe the unplayable character of ball after ball'. Despite Frank Hearne's 37, the Colony XV could not avoid an innings defeat.

Harry Wood, as the only returner from Smith's previous tour, must have spent much of the long train journey to Kimberley telling tales. While Kimberley was looking forward to the tourists, the previous air of febrile excitement was absent. The lure of the gold mines had scattered the victorious 1889 Kimberley team, including Charlie Finlason, around the Rand.

The Eclectics' red sand still played like concrete and the cloudless sky produced foot-baking heat. Irvine Grimmer batted first on what for the tourists was an extraordinarily fast wicket. But the quality of the tourists' bowling told despite the skating rink-like qualities of the outfield ringed by large aloes. Jack Coghlan, through a 'perfect display of sound defence and judicious hitting', made 38 out of 124. In reply Murdoch made a lively 64 and Chatterton accumulated 80 as the fielders and the wicketkeeper grassed, or more accurately, grounded, numerous chances. The tourists led by 94 and Ferris and Martin were unstoppable in a win by an innings and 20 runs.

The tourists visited the blue ground wash-up, where the diamonds were extracted and they handled the diamonds – worth £50,000 – on display. George Brann reported on the visit to the labour compound where black workers were imprisoned in a huge enclosure, watched tribal dances, tried out the convict station's cell and inspected the searching sheds where Africans stripped after their shifts.[84]

Against another Cape Colony XV, Read sent the opposition in on a wet mat. Tommy Routledge (47) put on 50 with Jack Coghlan before being brilliantly caught by Chatterton on the boundary, and the Colony finished on 142. Murdoch's 77 featured all the shots until Vollie van der Byl stopped the rot with 4-12 in 17 five-ball overs. The English led by close to 100 runs and the locals were rolled over to lose by an innings and 15. The bowling of Ferris and Martin was quite beyond the capacity of the batsmen, 'most of whom could not play and would not try to hit' in the words of Edwin Ash to *The Sportsman*.

---

84 *Cricket Field*, 7/5/1892

The diamond pin for the best score of the week was presented to William Chatterton for his 80.

President Kruger's desire for a railway line to the sea outside British control remained a cornerstone of his foreign policy. This forced the tourists onto coaches at the border. 'Words cannot express the feeling of relief when after the last span of 42 hours without a rest we finally sighted the Rand'[85]

A.B. Tancred, ex-Kimberley and comfortably South Africa's best batsmen, won the toss and took strike for the Johannesburg XVIII. The locals were a mixture of South Africa's past (Tancred, Fred Smith, P.H. De Villiers and Charlie Finlason) and its future ('Barberton' Halliwell and a precocious 15-year-old, Jimmy Sinclair).

Read had a 8-1 off-side field for Ferris and Martin, the fashion of the day before Grace's 270-degree batting presented new challenges and Ranji's leg glance inaugurated the Golden Age. Tancred patiently defended for 46 in four hours as wickets tumbled around him. Jimmy Sinclair smashed his second ball from Martin for four before being caught at mid-on and Abe Bailey ended on 16 not out in a total of 156.

The gap in class was illustrated by Ferris's first-day figures – 55 overs, 36 maidens, 44 runs and 12 wickets. His endurance was remarkable given the harshness of the conditions. His second-innings figures were almost identical to his first – 55-36-53-8. Martin's figures were hardly less noteworthy with 46-18-63-5 and 46-18-60-7 respectively. This marathon of 550 and 460 balls respectively at a run rate of not much more than one run per over must have stretched their physical resources to the limit. Read had other quality bowlers available but was relentlessly determined to keep the opposition on the rack.

2.4 John James Ferris

Batsmen throughout Southern Africa were in awe of Ferris's length and ability to deceive through his pace variations. He was identified at various times as a fast and a slow-medium bowler. One of his most destructive attributes was his unusual action.

---

85 *Sportsman*, 24/2/1892

Cricket described how, 'Ferris the left-hander starts his long run with his bowling hand close to his leg, when he has got three or four yards he brings both hands together almost on a dead level with his chin and looks as though he is kissing the tips of his fingers to the crowd. Down goes the hand again and another trot of four yards and he brings his hands together above his head, and just as you wonder when he is really going to bowl, his arm disappears behind his back and appears with extreme rapidity to deliver the ball.'[86]

Tancred had Alec Hearne taken at slip and Murdoch 'magnificently caught' by Halliwell with only four on the board. When Halliwell stumped Read off Pieter De Villiers, they were 13/3. Halliwell then caught Brann off Sinclair's second ball (4/29), but a solid partnership between the other two Hearnes in the side, Jack (50) and George (56), gave the tourists a 33-run lead. Eight batsmen made double figures in the locals' second innings, and England were left to chase 129 in three hours against an 18-man field. At 34/3 with Read and Murdoch back in the pavilion, the excitement was intense, but to the hosts' dismay several dropped catches and error-ridden ground fielding gave the Sussex hitter George Brann and Dick Pougher the momentum they needed for an undefeated partnership of 95 and a comfortable seven-wicket win. It was hard to avoid a feeling of déjà vu given the highly suspicious capitulation in the same game on the previous tour.

If the Johannesburg game had been challenging, the Transvaal XV game showed the locals' determination to make life difficult for Read's men. Tancred won the toss again and Transvaal inched to a 'pitiful' 118/11 by the end of a day in which 112 overs were bowled. But Transvaal had seen out the day's play, a rare event, and a tactical transformation the following day saw 'Barberton' Halliwell and the tail smash the bowling around the Wanderers. Halliwell ended on 43 not out, with five fours, as the innings closed for a competitive 159. Ferris had figures of 36-23-36-2 when a foot injury finally ended his spell. He had bowled more than 700 deliveries in three days.

---

86 *Cricket*, 17/9/1891

'Nutty' Martin soldiered on to complete an exhausting analysis of 60-34-76-4.

Pougher and Brann continued where they had left off. Pougher took on J.H.D. Piton's underarm lobs, lofting him over the rope at square leg for the tourists' first six of the trip. Ferris came in at 172/7 batting with a runner and Brann lifted Finlason for a six over his head. Eventually Brann was caught and bowled Finlason for 142 with 17 fours and three sixes out of a total of 283. He had won the match with the bat, as he had to do given that Ferris (foot), Martin and George Hearne (both unwell) could take no further part in the game. Jack Hearne seized his chance. He bowled Tancred second ball and Transvaal collapsed to 19/7, with Hearne taking all seven wickets for eight runs. The tourists easily knocked off the 22 required.

The team visited the May Consolidated mine and amid the cacophony of crushing stamps, the extraction process was explained. After dancing the night away with the elite of Johannesburg society, a bleary-eyed band were packed into the coach for Pretoria, 50 miles north-east of Johannesburg, and the capital of the Transvaal Republic. Ash and Read were granted an audience with President Kruger but Kruger had little interest in the English or cricket and their invitation to the Pretoria XXII match was received in stony silence.

The ground lay in a hollow surrounded by weeping willows and fig, orange, peach, pomegranate and apple trees. Jack Hearne took 10-6 and Ferris 10-31 out of a total of 41. Only at the fall of the 20th wicket did Howlett's strike for six indicate any resistance. The reserves, Leaney and Ayres, passed this total without losing a wicket and the tourists won by an innings and 29 runs. The lack of interest cost the local guarantors £157.

They rolled back to Johannesburg through clouds of red dust to take on a Transvaal XVIII. The crowd jeered the locals for their inaccurate throwing and slapdash fielding. William Chatterton by contrast fielded 'like a cat in wait for a mouse'. Murdoch made 63 'by quiet but very stylish cricket', and the veteran Pieter De Villiers claimed 5-56 in 42 overs. The tourists led by 47 on the first innings.

It was assumed that the English would score quick runs to set Transvaal a challenging target, but Read saw no reason to please the crowd. Murdoch and Chatterton prodded and stonewalled their way to 153/2 in a marathon 125 overs. Chatterton's 49 not out was achieved at a rate of one run every seven balls. It was an epically brainless performance.

Read applied his formula to the letter. He declared 200 ahead with three hours left to bat. Rain mercifully cut proceedings short after Tancred relieved his feelings by smashing Ferris out of the ground. Read's bloody-mindedness was suicidal for the financial health of the tour. His central concern was to win, without risking defeat. This was not the spirit of cricket and its unpopularity with the crowds would come back to haunt Read at the end of the tour.

The amateur issue generated significant heat as South Africa sought to emulate the class elitism of British society. *The Star* attacked Transvaal players Halliwell, Wimble, Klinck and Amesbury, who had claimed expenses for playing despite allegedly being employed by May Consolidated. Abe Bailey on behalf of management had arranged paid leave of absence for the players, but Halliwell had also allegedly claimed £26 in expenses, including a £16 coach fare from Barberton. 'Unsportsmanlike in the extreme,' thundered *The Star*. 'Most cricketers would see the honour of being selected an ample return for any small out-of-pocket expenses.' If the claim was allowed, then 'in future matches they may see their names figuring in the scores with the "Mr" omitted'.[87]

But the editor had got it wrong. Halliwell had given up lucrative employment in the Cape to play and had not taken up any appointment. His expenses claim was made several weeks earlier when the Union agreed expenses could be paid without loss of amateur status. The spat was not quite over. The general manager of May Consolidated unsuccessfully demanded compensation for employing substitutes at £1 per day for the four players. Halliwell's £16 travel claim from Barberton was refused.

---

87 *The Star*, 15/2/1892

The saga of Major Warton's journey from Johannesburg to Pietermaritzburg had already passed into legend. This time Ash and the professionals had company in the form of Harry Rickards' comedy and variety troupe. But lashing rain soon mired the coach, packed inside and out with passengers and luggage, in the deepening mud. The track turned into a river and the horses were up to their knees in water. They were forced to stop at the way station near the Bushman's Spruit which was unprepared to be confronted by 27 drenched and hungry travellers. Food was in short supply and they slept on a small patch of floor.

> ### 2.5 Homesick? Just hungry and thirsty
>
> William Chatterton was later asked whether he had had any longing to be back in England. He replied, 'Only once and then I would have given anything to be in a country where you can get something to eat if you can pay for it. We were landed for nine hours at the side of a spruit and were ravenously hungry and thirsty as we had nothing with us … we sent back to the last outspan and got brandy and bad mealies which we couldn't eat try as we might … it was not safe to drink the river water and neat brandy wouldn't do at all.'[88]

They provided their own increasingly lively entertainment. Alec Hearne opened proceedings with a violin solo, Vic Barton contributed 'Love's Old Sweet Song' accompanied by cornet and violin, and Rickards and his troupe provided the comedy. Next morning, they were pulled across the torrent. Nine hours of slow travelling brought them to the next river – the Sandspruit. The bank was swarming with produce wagons and coaches, which were dragged across with the occupants putting all their weight against the rushing stream.

The rail head was still two hours away and the road so bad that the coach was forced to jolt unhappily across the open veld. Finally, they reached the station, and stared exhaustedly out of the train

---

88 Interview with William Chatterton. Chats on the *Cricket Field*, 10/6/1893

windows at the British disasters of Majuba Hill and Laing's Nek. They arrived in Pietermaritzburg 13 hours later.[89]

The amateurs had fared even worse. George Brann described how the 50-hour journey took five days without a wash or a change of clothes. Threats and bribes were necessary at every step to keep the show on the road, commandeering wagons and oxen, as well as shelter from the reluctant Dutch locals. 'Water, water everywhere, but not a dram of whisky,' he complained.[90] The wiry J.J. Ferris had been piggybacked across the Bushman's Spruit by an African who at the half-way mark said he would drop him in the torrent unless he doubled the fee. The locals refused all inducements to carry Murdoch and the other heavyweight amateurs.[91]

2.6 Billy Murdoch makes himself comfortable

At one stop Ferris and Murdoch were offered a room with only one bed. Ferris suggested Murdoch try it first. The frame collapsed and Murdoch's head was wedged in the ironwork of the bedstead. It was quite a work of art to get him out, according to Ferris, and an even greater work of art to prop up the bed again so it became usable. The next night, Murdoch, Read and Ferris had the luxury of sleeping on a table, while the rest slept on the floor.[92]

With the amateurs still floundering downstream, George Hearne became the first professional to captain a touring team in South Africa against a Pietermaritzburg XVIII. The town had made a huge effort for its biggest social event for three years. Natal always sought to out-England England. The governor, Sir Charles Mitchell, arrived with his entourage just like royalty at precisely three o'clock. To their consternation, the amateurs had not yet arrived, but the professionals gave them three hearty cheers.

---

89 *Sportsman*, 24/3/1892

90 Interview with George Brann, Chats on the *Cricket Field*, 7 May 1892

91 Interview with J.J. Ferris, Chats on the *Cricket Field*, 29 July 1893

92 *Ibid*

Pietermaritzburg agreed to bat first, so that if the amateurs arrived by the next day they could play. Even without Ferris, the home team struggled to 116. The tourists then profited from several missed chances and made 251 with fifties from Alec Hearne and Harry Wood. The English won by ten wickets, the last rites witnessed by the amateurs who arrived just in time to play in (and lose) an exhibition game.

After a night's sleep on the train to Durban, the professionals happily settled into the Marine Hotel overlooking Durban Bay. The mosquitoes were happy too. Fred Martin became their instant best friend. The Durban XVIII scrambled to 90, worth more given the grassy outfield, and Peter Madden, the youthful terror with a dubious action on Smith's tour, opened the bowling. Chatterton cracked him hard to leg, relieving the umpire of his hat but Madden with the wind at his back bowled at his fastest. The tourists were reduced to 38/6. Chatterton was hit several times and his yelps of pain were audible in the stands. He gritted his teeth, got in line and carried his bat for 38 out of 134. Madden had figures of 8-39. The locals then subsided to 'Mosquito' Martin's 10-37. Read's comatose batsmen took 47 five-ball overs to score the 30 needed to win the game, with Chatterton again not out on 22.

Governor Sir Charles Mitchell apparently having few other calls on his time watched the game and attended the post-match banquet. He claimed to be the only one among them who could remember the generation of cricketers who used to play in white top hats. In replying, Read insisted they had done their utmost to play the game as it should be played and up to the present time, he was pleased to say the team had not met with a reverse.

The team reluctantly left the delights of Durban for King William's Town via East London.

This was the 'social' leg of the tour, with the quality of cricket low and banquets and smokers high. Arriving in 'King' to play a Border District XXII, the tourists found matting stretched over turf in Cape Town style. Ferris's fast deliveries captured 16-23 out of a batting total of 59. England found themselves 4/3 in reply before

Murdoch appealed against the light. Read's XI were all out for 109, with only Dick Pougher (44) able to cope with conditions. Border's nerves had settled and they set a target of 106 in 90 minutes. Read ignored it and they tamely played out time, ending on 48/2 in 43 overs. Another travesty against the spirit of the game maintained Read's unbeaten record.

Then came the 80-mile trip from King William's Town to Grahamstown in two-wheeled Cape carts drawn by six-in-hand horses with long whips popping. The track passed through 'Pluto's Vale' with hills towering on each side covered with cactus and abundant wildflowers. The cricketers in true Victorian style hurled a fusillade of rocks at the baboons and enjoyed their stampede up the rocky sides. After pitching and jolting for 12 long hours, they made it over the mountains into Grahamstown, the 'city of the saints', stuffed with churches and schools.

Read lost the toss and the Albany XXII subsided for 69 to Ferris and Jack Hearne. Read's team again gave their opponents a view of their soft batting underbelly, making 78 in a mind-numbing 82 overs. The locals did slightly better the second time round and with 69 to win, rain drew a veil over the game with the tourists on 27/0.

Back in Port Elizabeth, the visitors were put in against an Eastern Province XVIII and their old adversaries Dante Parkin and Dick Crage. Previously they had been rolled over for 74, but this time they managed 77, Parkin snatching 5-27 and Crage 5-43. Pougher's 27 was the only score in double figures. The home team could not take advantage, Ferris and Hearne demolishing them for 50, and while Eastern Province improved in the second innings they lost limply by 66 runs.

Following a 'second to none' send-off, the team steamed north to Bloemfontein on an ultra-slow mail train whose coaches were too heavy for the engine. Eventually they arrived at 2.30am to find a raucous welcome awaiting the first British sports team to visit the Orange Free State. The team spent two out of three days fielding in the hottest and harshest conditions so far on a ground which had been completed only a month before. The corrugated iron roofs of the town reflected a blinding glare into the faces of the players.

George Brann sprained his ankle coming down the pavilion steps, ending his tour as a result. The locals batted first in front of President Reitz. J.W. Hopwood compiled an excellent 32 out of 142. The tourists replied with 162. Charles Fichardt batted 'beautifully' for a chanceless 54 not out in the second innings and the match fizzled out into another draw.

2.7 Charles Fichardt's mind games and nationalist politics

Fichardt spent his innings playing cat and mouse or *schrikmakery* with the British, taunting them into presenting him with overthrows. His challenging performance had a political flavour. Despite his enthusiasm for cricket, Fichardt was an Afrikaner republican of virulently anti-British sentiments and no shrinking violet. He would later serve as a Boer captain in the Republican Scouts commanded by the 'bittereinder' (fight to the end) General Hertzog in the South African War. He was a member of the National Convention and the deputation to the UK which secured Union based on a racially based constitution and joined Hertzog to found the National Party.

Twenty-eight hours on the train and another 2.30am arrival brought them to Kimberley and what would have been the first 'Test' had Kimberley not failed to raise the £250 guarantee. Irvine Grimmer led a replacement Griqualand West XXII. He challenged Read to go for a win, declaring at 158 ahead with two and half hours left to bat. As he almost certainly knew, he had the wrong man. Chatterton's 33 not out ensured the draw and another diamond pin for the player.

Hard times meant that the hospitality was much diminished. At the Diamond Fields Club, smoker Walter Read reprised his old standard 'Knocked em in the Old Kent Road' and regretted that the representative match against 11 players had collapsed.

'Everyone on the team had been looking forward to a huge picnic and getting up their averages,' said Read.[93] They would soon have their opportunity.

The final overland trip of 650 miles to Cape Town seemed interminable. The Western Province XV had no hesitation in batting before a meagre crowd. Cripps made 32 and 22, many scored with a 'peculiar glancing stroke to leg' (which suggests that Ranji may not have been the only player to develop this method of dealing with the off-side obsessed character of the English game).[94] In the second innings, Pougher sent Cripps' leg bail 20 yards behind him as if to make a point about his cricketing ethics. When they batted, Chatterton with 77 and Walter Read with 49 ensured a 60-run lead on the first innings, and even by Read's glacial standards they had more than enough time to chase the 48 runs required.[95]

Finally, they were to play a representative game, 11 versus 11. South Africa's team was selected by Western Province as the host province. William Milton included six Western Province players. Tancred, Davey and Grimmer were unable to take part and they lacked a fast bowler like Nic Theunissen, despite having an even better speedster hiding in plain sight.

After three tough months on the road, playing 19 matches against odds, the team were travel-weary, battle-hardened and unbeaten. They knew their game, had a simple strategy to avoid losing, and their bowlers were too strong for any batting line-up on matting. J.J. Ferris did not need the Johnny Briggs box of tricks. Relentless length bowling, significant movement and a surprise fast dipping 'yorker' were enough. Read's batsmen were now familiar with matting wickets laid on all surfaces. Chatterton had been a barnacle at the top of the order and even when he was eventually prised out, someone else would come to the party. Read was confident of beating Lord Sheffield's Australian tourists, Grace and all, on matting.

---

93 *Daily Independent*, 9/3/1892
94 *Cape Times*, 18/3/1892
95 *Sportsman*, 12/4/1892

The South Africans, on the other hand, were an untried combination, unknown to each other and the absentees denied them leadership, experience and stability under pressure. The public, according to the *Cape Times*, anticipated a 'rapid ripping out of the wickets' by the English bowlers, followed by 'leviathan scoring' by the batsmen. A few optimists hoped for a relatively close match, but no one thought the South Africans stood a chance.

Milton batted first but had included three non-Western Province batsmen (Fichardt, Halliwell and Wimble) in the top six. These three were unfamiliar with the Newlands matting on grass and had only a few hours to practice before the game. It was left to the local players – Frank Hearne, Cripps and Milton – to save the innings from total ignominy. Ferris took 6-54 in South Africa's first innings total of 97.

The spectators sat back waiting for the tourist run fest, but the intensity of the South African performance took them by surprise. Dante Parkin captured the Hearne brothers and Murdoch with only 33 on the board and Mills trapped the wall-like Chatterton for 48. The English batsmen played in free style against 11 opponents, but Charles Fichardt reminded spectators of Johnny Briggs at extra cover and the South African team showed an unexpected zest and dash before a surprised and appreciative crowd.

The tourists finished the first day 13 runs ahead on the first innings with five wickets in hand, teasing the local optimists. Wicketkeeper Harry Wood, who had risen to the occasion on Warton's tour, came in at 144/6. He hit his only first-class hundred, 134 not out in a total of 369, adding 71 with Read for the seventh wicket, 65 with Ferris for the eighth and 71 with Jack Hearne for the ninth. The 'batting leviathan' had arrived late and extinguished South African hopes. In South Africa's second innings, Fichardt ran himself out for ten, trying to complete a risky third, perhaps undone by his own *schrikmakery*. Milton played an over-ambitious shot when well set on 16 and Frank Hearne top-scored with 23 out of 83. Read's tourists had triumphed by an innings and 189 runs.

The apparently indestructible Ferris's final spell of the tour read 25-16-37-7. But this magnificent physical and mental effort emptied the formidable tank of this great bowler. He proved a failure at Gloucestershire and by 1895 had lost his action, his pace and his bite. Little was heard of him until the outbreak of the South African War when he joined the Uitlander-supported Imperial Light Horse. He took ten wickets in a scratch match in Natal, but he had, as *Wisden* put it, 'outlived his fame' and in November 1900 sadly died of epilepsy in a Durban tramcar, in his 34th year.[96]

Warton and Ash had been interested in the black cricket taking place in the shadows of white privilege. Ash noticed, 'The natives are very fond of our national game for it was quite a frequent sight to see batches of them playing on the beach taking part in practice and matches,' and there were well-organised and thriving black cricket leagues in Cape Town, Port Elizabeth and Kimberley. England's racism had taken a particularly virulent turn in the 1880s and the new ideology of 'scientific' racism dominated establishment thinking. Racism underpinned Rhodes' political alliance with J.H. Hofmeyr in the early 1890s and his strategy to force cheap black labour into the economy to meet the increasing demands of mining, agriculture and railways.

The ideology of race was the property of the amateurs. The professionals in Walter Read's party happily engaged with their fellow professionals. Frank Hearne, the first high-profile professional to arrive at the Cape in 1888, quickly developed a close relationship with Malays who like the English professionals made a living as net bowlers, groundsmen and caretakers. Smith's professionals were spotted in the Malay enclosure chatting with locals, and on the 1891 tour the professionals in Read's party attended a 'Malay wedding feast' a couple of days after their arrival at the Cape.

The following day, the professionals went to a Malay match at the Cape Town CC ground. *The Sportsman* noted, 'They seem to have a fair amount of knowledge of the game, the bowling and fielding

---

96 *The Owl*, 23/11/1900

reminded one of the Parsees. The bowlers go in for pace ... pelting as hard as possible at the wickets. They have a fair knowledge of batting ... but lack judgement in making runs.'[97]

The Test ended an hour into the third day and local reports suggested that an 'unofficial' exhibition game was hastily arranged between Abdol Burns, president of the Malay Union Club, and the professionals with the agreement of the WPCC to fill the gap. In fact, the fixture had been organised some time before to build on the achievements of the Cape Town Malay team, which had engaged in an epic encounter with the Malay community from Kimberley.[98]

2.8 Abdol Burns, Ebrahim Ariefdien and the 'Malay community'

The Cape's 'coloured' community included descendants of East Asian Muslim and Madagascan slaves, local Khoikhoi, Europeans, and mixed-race Christians, including labour from St Helena, sharing a common language (Afrikaans), and living in the Bo-Kaap, District Six, Woodstock, Claremont and Wynberg. These communities were referred to by whites as Malays, a designation that infuriated black cricketers such as 'Krom' Hendricks and Robert Grendon who identified with the dominant culture, pushing back against the evolving climate of segregation.

Community cohered around mosque, church, cricket and rugby. While there was no formal sports colour bar, by the 1880s the community increasingly organised their own sports. Despite massively inferior resources and facilities, Malay cricket was comparable in strength and organisation to establishment cricket.

Abdol Burns, the 'Scots-Malay' president of the Cape Town Union Club, organised a national tournament in 1890 and Cape Town hosted black teams from Johannesburg, Port Elizabeth, Kimberley and the local Union and Claremont clubs, winning in an exciting final at Newlands umpired by Frank Hearne.

---

97 *Sportsman*, 5/1/1892

98 For more details see Winch and Parry, *Too Black to Wear Whites*, Chapters 1 and 2

The next tournament was held in Uitenhage at Easter 1891, when Ebrahim Ariefdien, the Cape Town captain, achieved almost certainly the most remarkable bowling performance ever in a representative game. Ariefdien bowled the first Port Elizabeth batsman first ball, then bowled the rest, taking all ten for 18 in nine overs. Not satisfied with this, he made 54 as an opening batsman, and then in the Port Elizabeth second innings he took a hat-trick with his first three balls. In the end, Kimberley proved too strong in the final thanks to a hundred from Robert Grendon, part Irish and part Herero.

In early 1892, the tournament was held in Kimberley and amid intense excitement 'Krom' Hendricks and Ebrahim Ariefdien defied both the home team and the hometown umpires, bringing the gleaming Glover Cup back to Cape Town.[99]

The professionals (excluding 'shamateurs' Read, Murdoch and Ferris), captained by George Hearne, met a South African Malay XVIII, the only time before South Africa's isolation that a 'white' touring team played against players considered to be 'non-white'. The Malay team was massively popular within the community and added thousands to the gate. But the amateurs ignored the game – the race divide might have been crossed by the professionals, but the class line was not.

Armien Hendricks won the toss and thousands of spectators watched Lamarah Samsodien's outstanding 55 out of a total of 113, the highest individual score against the tourists. Samsodien 'cracked the bowlers for threes and fours to the great glee of the majority of the spectators'. He hit Jack Hearne, who had taken 162 wickets on the tour at an average of 6.5, for ten in an over before being caught at the wicket, returning to an ovation.

When England batted, 'Krom' Hendricks bowled at his fastest. Jack Hearne, who made 67, saw his off stump cartwheel when he tried to drive a fast one. Harry Wood retired hurt thanks to a bouncer from the same bowler and the innings closed for 176. Armien Hendricks claimed the wickets in figures of 25-8-50-4, but it was the pace and

---

99 *Ibid*

accuracy of 'Krom' Hendricks who finished with 23-7-29-1 that was the focus of attention. Pougher and Martin bowled the Malays out for 70 in their second innings, and the eight needed for victory were quickly knocked off.

2.9 Hendricks, George Hearne's tie and Brockwell's handkerchief

George Hearne, interviewed in the *Cricket Field*, said a Malay called 'Krom' Hendricks was the fastest bowler he had met in South Africa, 'He was very fast and … we didn't like facing him at all. Wood asked me to think of his fingers, and I told him to get double figures and then get out … Brockwell disappeared into Cape Town on business and did not come back until after the game cheerily waving his handkerchief.

'I was in a long time with Jack Hearne. We exasperated Hendricks by telling him we had heard he was a fast bowler but were surprised he was only medium. This made him bowl faster and off-target which is what we wanted. After the match we were surrounded by the Malays and one of them begged for a bit of my necktie which was in the team's colours. I cut off a piece and pinned it to his coat and he said afterwards it would be buried with him.'[100]

'Krom' Hendricks generated immense speed and power effortlessly off a relatively short run, perhaps in the style of a right-handed Wasim Akram. A year later, William Chatterton agreed that much might be made of Spofforth as the world's greatest bowler, yet 'the very finest bowler he ever met was a South African black, Hendricks. The memory of this man's pace from the pitch, his quick swing away, alternating with a fine break back, stirred a cold and critical nature to enthusiasm.'

He went on, 'The Malays ought to have a future … they are exceedingly earnest in their desire to play the game properly, and the bowlers try to make better use of the ball. The worst of it is

---

100 *Cricket Field*, 25/11/1893

that the colonials will not play against them, so they do not get the opportunity of measuring themselves against others.'[101]

Abdol Burns wrote to the *Cape Times* to thank the professionals for the chance to play against them and asking for access to decent practice facilities. 'Straight Tip' replied, condemning the Malay 'impudence' and regretted the 'indecent' encouragement they received to take part in matches with senior players, 'they will ask for the Cathedral next for their singing clubs to practice'. 'Son of Japhet' suggested that his 'little brother Straight Tip' become a Moslem then he might have a chance of making the highest single score against the tourists, 'Which is the sore point when you knock all the padding out of it.'[102]

This bittersweet moment might have opened the gates of opportunity. Instead it gave way to the massive sadness of South African cricket history, driven by the ostracism of South Africa's great fast bowling hero, 'Krom' Hendricks, who was vetoed by Rhodes at national level, banned by the colonial establishment from its representative matches and prevented by the Western Province Cricket Union (WPCU) from plying his trade as a professional in league matches on grounds of race. The WPCU labelled him as Malay but never attempted to establish what his background was. The result was not only a tragedy for Hendricks and the many thousands of black cricketers who lost the chance to be citizens of, and to represent, their country. It was also a tragedy for South African cricket, which lost the chance of nurturing the talents of many thousands of skilled and enthusiastic players and fielding a representative South African side.

Read's team was undefeated with 14 wins and seven draws and, he said, only once – in Johannesburg – was the outcome ever in doubt. On his return, Read expressed pride in the performances of the team, particularly Ferris and Chatterton, and his unbeaten record. For Read, only results counted. For the spectators, a contest was what mattered.

---

101 William Chatterton, *Cricket Field*, 10/6/1893
102 *Cape Times* 25/3/1892; *Cape Argus*, 25/3/1892

If Read had had a more flexible strategy, a tactical imagination, and a willingness to take risks he could have significantly increased his gates.[103] Somehow, he did not recognise the harm his arrogant obsession caused to his own pocket.

Admittedly, he was hamstrung by playing against 15, 18 or 22 players as English batsmen threaded the ball through massed ranks of fielders and bowlers faced an endless procession of batting incompetents. Spectators were the losers and the gates reflected this. Viewed through modern eyes, the tourists and their opponents maintained an astonishingly high over rate of above 25 five-ball overs per hour. When local sides were in the field captains needed to orchestrate 15, 18 or 22 fielders who were not used to playing with each other or playing with more than 11 fielders. Even when Harry Wood was putting South Africa to the sword in the Test match, the bowlers managed 119 completed overs in under five hours. To do this required set fields with limited changes, long bowling spells and short run-ups, a large proportion of defensive shots and no 'gardening'.

If over rates were lightning quick, scoring rates were funereal. In the Test match, when the English faced 11 men, they scored at over three runs per five-ball over. Against odds despite differing quality among the attacks, the number of fielders was a good indicator of the scoring rate. Against 22 the English managed 1.48 runs per over; with 18 in the field they managed 1.71; and against 15 1.93. Trying to score runs against such fields must have been a hugely frustrating experience. Against the Transvaal XVIII, for example, the English second innings consumed 125 overs in scoring 153/2 with Chatterton 49 not out.

The visitors became experts at running between the wickets in contrast to the South Africans. 'Some of our men had no more sense of backing up than a cow and lounged on their bats as if not setting out to run again until judgement day,' 'Stroller' commented in Johannesburg, continuing that Murdoch 'although looking as if he

---

103 *Sportsman* 12/5/1892

could take a 20-yard start and lose, could give our sprinters a good many pounds and a beating between the sticks'.[104]

The financial experience of the early matches raised great expectations. But the tour was a gamble given the depression and by focusing on avoiding defeat, Read cooked his financial goose.

2.10 Funding the Tour – Logan v Read and Ash in the Cape Supreme Court

The financial problem for Edwin Ash and Walter Read began when Donald Currie was unable to subsidise the trip as the depression squeezed his Castle Line margins. The pair owed £900 in travel costs on arrival before they had any income at all. They set up a partnership with Edwin Bridgett, whose wife would pay a surety of £750. She somehow managed to hold on to her money and 'the bounder' Bridgett was sent packing before the first game.

Desperate to find a replacement, Ash and Read verbally offered James Logan 40 per cent of the profits for an investment of £1,000. Logan testified that he advanced the money 'in the interests of cricket', but declined a share of profits as he 'did not wish to make money out of sport', apart from a 'small turn of 7-8 per cent interest'. Read claimed that Logan had spoken of a dividend and said he did not mind losing £300-£400.

It was soon clear that the tour was a financial failure. Logan's money was gone. Read and Ash professed to be 'shocked' when Logan demanded the return of his 'loan' during the Cape Town Test. Logan asked Read to dinner, Read pleaded a prior engagement, and Ash gave Logan the slip. When Logan caught him, Ash, who 'appeared very much afraid of Read', started to cry, saying, 'Don't blame me, I told Read you would never stand for it.'

Amateurs Read, Murdoch, and Ferris shared at least £750, sufficient to turn any potential profit into a significant loss, while the professionals received £100 each. When chief justice Sir Thomas Upington expressed surprise, Sir Henry Juta responded to laughter, 'They were paid for the loss of their time.'

---

104 *The Star*, 15/2/1892

In the end, Logan's cronyism and familiarity with the courts, (where he had just won a major case regarding his railway catering monopoly), ensured a ruling in his favour. Despite the ambivalence of his position until it was clear the tour would lose money, Upington decided that the benefit of the doubt lay with the lender. He was awarded his outlay of £750 and costs.[105]

Edwin Ash and Walter Read were in jail when the *Dunnottar Castle* was due to sail, possibly the only other instance of an English touring captain being incarcerated until footballer Bobby Moore's unfortunate experience in the Mexico World Cup of 1970. Logan had issued writs of arrest, used to prevent debtors disappearing like rats up the mailship's bowlines. Ash and Read were not released until they found the security to meet Logan's claim. Their ship remained at anchor with the cricketing establishment who had travelled out by tug to wave them off partying on board. Eventually, several hours late, after Jack Richards guaranteed their return, the embarrassed pair were rowed out to the vessel. Read's autobiography simply said, 'In the winter of this year [1891] I captained a team out to South Africa.' No further comment was necessary.[106]

105 *Cape Times*, 7/3/1893

106 W.W. Read, *Annals of Cricket*, (London: Sampson, Low, Marston and Co, 1896) 184

Ambassadors for the imperial game. C. Aubrey Smith's first English XI. In Kimberley, 1889.
Back: J. Briggs, M. Read, [Simpson, Cape Town], H. Wood, A.J. Fothergill Seated: B.A.F. Grieve, M.P.
Bowden, Major R. Gardner Warton, C.A. Smith (captain), E. McMaster Front: Hon. C.J. Coventry, R.
Abel, F. Hearne

South Africa's first whites-only Test team, 1889. Back: A R Innes, A B Tancred, C E Finlason, C H
Vintcent, F W Smith. Middle: C Deare (Umpire) P Hutchinson, O R Dunell, W H Milton. Front: A E
Ochse, R B Stewart, G A Kempis

Digging for the stone. The Diamond Mines in Kimberley 1893 which formed the basis of Cecil Rhodes' fortune

The 'Imperial Tourist', Lord Hawke sold cricket and empire, though his patrician values and personality did not endear him to the locals. In his first South African tour in 1895/96, he is third from the left in the middle row. The controversial James D. Logan is seated on his right with his hands on Sammy Woods' shoulders

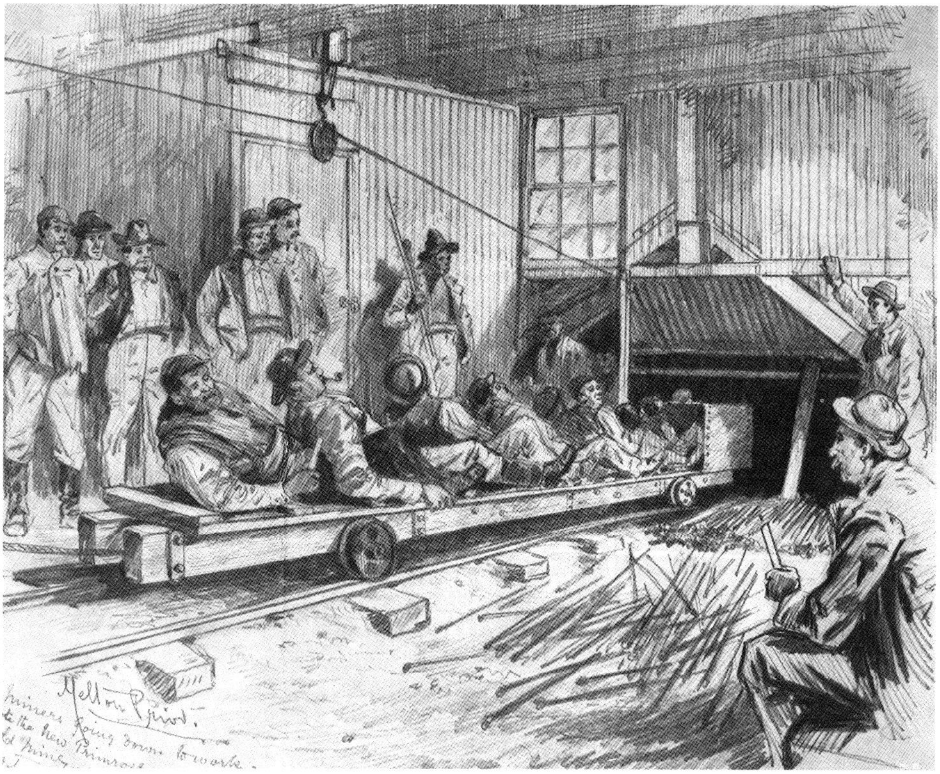

Fighting for the lifeblood of the empire and braving a death rate of about 10% per annum in the first years of the gold mines, black miners begin their shift at the Primrose Gold Mine, 1896

Women's cricket was well established in South Africa by the turn of the century. Pioneer Women's Cricket Club, Port Elizabeth, 1902

Larger than life, both on and off the field. English all-rounder, Albert Trott

The empire, gold, and cricket. The Consolidated Gold Fields and Corner House cricket teams, at The Wanderers, 1904. Lord Harris is sixth from the left in the front row. To his left are the mine magnate Julius Werner of Werner Beit and Co and South Africa's premier all-rounder, G. Aubrey Faulkner (captain of the Corner House XI). Ernest 'Barberton' Halliwell is on the far right of the middle row

South Africa's remarkable first series win. The South African XI which played in all five Tests v MCC in 1905/06. Back row: B. Malraison (scorer), A.D. Nourse, S.J. Snooke, A.E. Vogler. Middle row: L.J. Tancred, J.H. Sinclair, R.O. Schwarz, P.W. Sherwell (captain) W.A. Shalders, C.M. Hathorn. Front row: G.A. Faulkner, G.C. White

Plum Warner and Percy Sherwell, with black spectators in the background before the final Test at Newlands 1906

Every spare inch taken and spilling across the boundary ropes: the crowd in front of the pavilion, Newlands Test 1906.

'Dave' Nourse, the South African Cricket Association's hero in its first Test win.

THE SOUTH AFRICAN NATIVE AND COLOURED PEOPLE'S DELEGATES IN LONDON, 1909.

The names of the Delegates shown in this photograph are as follows : In the front row, from left to right—Mr. Matt. J. Fredericks, General Secretary of the African Political Organisation ; Dr. A. Abdurahman, President of the African Political Organisation ; the Hon. W. P. Schreiner, K.C., C.M.G., M.L.A., Ex-Prime Minister of the Cape Colony ; the Rev. Dr. W. B. Rubusana, Ph.D., President of the South African Native Convention ; and Mr. Tengo-Jabavu, Editor of " Imvo" and President of the King William's Town Native Association. In the back row, from right to left, are Mr. D. J. Lenders (Kimberley), Vice-President of the African Political Organisation ; Mr. Daniel Dwanya, Agent-at-Law and Representative of the South African Native Convention ; Mr. J. Gerrans, representing Bechuanaland Protectorate ; and Mr. Thos. M. Mapikela, General Secretary of the Orange River Colony Native Congress.

Opposing the betrayal of the black population under Union.

The fearsome and single-minded Sydney Barnes, perhaps the best bowler ever whose personal duel with Herby Taylor took cricket to a sporting Valhalla seldom matched.

Mining and cricket: Lord Harris of the Corner House Group and MCC strolls with Hubert 'Nummy' Deane, South African touring captain (1929)

A portrait of two characters. Nummy Deane and Herby Taylor

3

Politics: Lord Hawke 1895/96

WALTER READ'S tour had been underwhelming. Economic depression, financial incompetence, the superiority of the team's bowling, a win-at-all-costs mindset driving a rigid and negative strategy and a lacklustre social presence contributed to its unpopularity. South African cricket was ill equipped to handle a team of full-time professionals on the pitch, nor could professional tours connect with the complex social and political landscape. The snobbish South African establishment had wanted amateurs who reflected their class aspirations. Lord Hawke's tour in 1895/96 met this requirement and was composed primarily of amateurs of varying standards and paid for in advance. It was not dependent on 'gates' and marched straight into the hottest political moment of the decade – the Jameson Raid debacle.

Lord Hawke was a classic imperial 'divide and ruler' drawing an indelible class line between amateur and professional. By introducing winter pay for his Yorkshire professionals, he created a settled labour aristocracy which owed him an almost feudal loyalty. As part of this class war, he sought to dismantle Yorkshire's working-class drinking culture. Left-arm spinner Robert Peel was his most famous victim. Hawke claimed Peel bore him no ill will. Peel allegedly remarked, 'Lord Hawke put his arm around me and helped me out of the ground – and first-class cricket. What a gentleman!'[107]

---

107 Benny Green, *A History of Cricket*, (London: Barrie and Jenkins, 1988) 139

C.B. Fry described the main moving figures behind Hawke's tour as James Logan, a Scottish cricket enthusiast who had risen from railway porter to hold a catering monopoly on Cape railways; Lord Hawke, a Yorkshire peer who devoted himself to taking the best teams abroad; George Lohmann, England's best bowler who was staying with Logan at the Cape for his health; and K.S. Ranjitsinhji a Rajput Heir Apparent who was not considered for racial reasons, and was replaced by Fry himself.[108]

In 1891, the ex-porter, James Logan was granted a monopoly over the Cape railway catering system without a tender by his friend and public works minister, Sir James Sivewright. The outcry over nepotism was loud enough to force Cecil Rhodes, Cape prime minister since 1890, to resign briefly. But Logan retained vast profits from every meal at every station (including his signature 'superheated porridge').

3.1 Rhodes and the 1894 South African tour to Britain

In 1894, Rhodes was at the height of his power as Cape premier, controller of South Africa's diamond monopoly through De Beers, gold production through Consolidated Goldfields and the British South Africa Company which ran 'Rhodesia' as his personal fiefdom. As the new deep level gold mines came on stream, Rhodes recognised the strategic importance of a unified cricket tour from South Africa as a symbol of a strong South Africa within the empire. Rhodes and his allies' multifaceted racism lay behind the veto of the so-called Malay, 'Krom' Hendricks, the best bowler in the country.

Despite a series of adventures, including a battle between the players and cabbies at Sheffield Park, the tour was a financial failure. They earned less than £500 in gates in 24 matches and racked up expenses of £3,600. Stranded in Belfast the team called on Logan to bail them out. The press spent the tour bemoaning Hendricks' absence. Without him it was like watching an inferior version of themselves.[109]

---

108 C.B. Fry, *Life Worth Living*, (London: reprinted by the Pavilion Library, 1986) 105

109 Richard Parry, 'W G Grace, Cecil Rhodes and 1894 South African Cricket Tour' in *Cricket Lore*, vol 2 issue 2 38-42; Winch and Parry, *Too Black to Wear Whites*, Chapters 4 to 6

Political patronage could be bought on the playing fields of the empire. Logan persuaded Surrey to send George Lohmann to his Karoo railway resort to improve his lung condition. Lohmann, acting as his CEO, proposed a tour in 1895/96. James Logan effectively owned the subsequent tour, appearing in the official photograph seated next to Lord Hawke with his hands proprietorially on Sammy Woods' shoulders.[110]

Hawke had led amateur tours to India, the USA and Australia and was delighted to explore South Africa.[111] He was a proactive agent of an empire based on a rigid class structure run by Oxbridge Blues. South Africa was the most exciting of destinations by the mid-1890s. It was in the grip of gold fever and returns to UK investors were beginning to pay the costs of empire. Its natural beauty and hospitality were unmatched and there was less direct hostility to the English upper classes than elsewhere.

George Lohmann was both selector and secretary. Hawke and his team relied on Lohmann to nursemaid them off the pitch and win their games on it. As a predominantly amateur outfit, it was inevitably weak on bowlers. Football injuries restricted Sammy Woods, the Australian 'shamateur' who also played for Somerset, as a bowler, which left them reliant almost entirely on Lohmann. Despite his delicate health he bowled more than a third of all the overs delivered by the English and took 43 per cent of the wickets. Hawke characteristically had little compunction in running his prime asset into the ground, effectively ending Lohmann's career and almost certainly hastening his early demise. Lohmann's professional status and his own professionalism determined his fate.

Hawke's party included ten amateurs, all but two Oxford or Cambridge Blues, supported by four professionals. It was a team of characters sharing Hawke's ultra-autocratic views, the hot-headed Sir Tim O'Brien, the sclerotic Herbie Hewett, the devious Charles Wright, the versatile Sammy Woods who had played rugby for

---

110 Luckin, *History*, 522
111 *Cape Times*, 7/12/1895

England, cricket for Australia and football for Sussex, and the athletic Charles – C.B. – Fry. Ledger Hill, Hugh Bromley-Davenport, Christopher Heseltine and Audley Miller were the other amateurs. Harry Butt, the Sussex wicketkeeper, Teddy Tyler, Tom Hayward and Lohmann himself were the four professionals.

Lord Harris was determined to keep Ranjisinhji out of the England team on racial grounds and Hawke did not select Ranji despite his Cambridge background, princely status and stellar cricketing abilities. The controversy over Hendricks suggested, as Fry put it, that Ranji 'may have been unwelcome' in South Africa. Ranji himself was clearly aware that racism would block his selection and recommended Fry instead. Hawke shared colonial prejudices and the imperial establishment performed a 'reverse Hendricks' to keep the teams white. Had Ranji made the trip, discrimination against Hendricks and other black cricketers would have been harder to rationalise, and South Africa's cricketing and social history might have taken a different turn.

Lord Hawke's appointment would, the *Cape Times* reported, ensure 'the hallmark of proper conduct'. But proper conduct in practice meant little more than racism and authoritarian arrogance. Hawke and Hewett captained North and South respectively in the fine September drizzle at Scarborough shortly before embarking on the tour. They refused to begin play and were jeered by the large crowd. Hawke threatened to cancel the match and Hewett retired from the match because, 'As an amateur and a gentleman, he ought not in the face of insulting remarks go on with the game.'[112]

The team separated into two parties embarking a week apart. Wright, Woods, Fry, Hill, together with Miller, Heseltine, Bromley-Davenport and the professionals, sailed on the *Guelph*. The leadership party of Hawke, O'Brien and Hewett embarked on the *Moor* but suffered an exploded boiler and ate Christmas dinner at sea.

Sammy Woods took Charles Fry under his wing and taught him the basics of touring life, including a fracas with the local ferrymen

---

112 *Sportsman*, 6/9/1895

in Tenerife involving boat hooks, guavas and a pipe which Sammy pretended was a revolver.[113] Hill organised the onboard sports (Fry jumped 5ft 6in in the high jump) and social events. At St Helena, Harry Butt, the wicketkeeper grateful to be on dry land, hiked four miles each way to visit Napoleon's grave in the broiling sun.

Table Mountain hove into view at 6am on Sunday, 22 December and the *Guelph* was met by the mayor. Milton was 'indisposed' perhaps because of the absence of Lord Hawke. The next day the team set off up Table Mountain but turned back in the heat. Had they continued they might have witnessed a cricket match played on the top between two teams made up of black waterworks employees and enjoyed by a small but enthusiastic band of spectators. One black left-hander played shots through the leg-side with an ease and freedom 'which would have done credit to Ranji himself'.[114]

3.2 Fry's first impressions

Fry described Cape Town as more attractive at first sight than any other city. Its glory was the garden suburbs, strung along the railways with flowery names such as Wynberg and Rondebosch.

The Newlands ground was a delightful spot with an unpretentious pavilion on the edge of a pine wood flanking the side furthest from the mountain. The lower slopes in the near distance were covered with scrub oak, and long red avenues of gum trees separated gardens splashed with tall bushes of fuchsia and bougainvillea.

He remembered a canopy of dark blue, the moon shining down between the gum trees and the pop of champagne corks.[115]

Cape Town – the 'Tavern of the Seas' – was going through a periodic xenophobic panic which wasn't limited to black visitors, as was reported, 'In a general way the colony may hail arrival of any man with a white skin to allay fear of the browning of the country. It is possible however to buy even whites too dearly ... influx of hordes

---

113 Sammy Woods, *My Reminiscences*, (London: Chapman and Hall, 1925) 69-70
114 *Sportsman*, 7/1/1896
115 Fry, *Life Worth Living*, 107-8

of people possessing a thicker veneer of dirt than civilisation raises a serious economic question ... the influx of waste material from Europe and India is seriously aggravating traders in the Western districts through petty peddling.'[116]

The Malay community focused on sport as well as education and religion. 'Krom' Hendricks, described by Read's tourists as the fastest bowler in South Africa, was now in his prime but blocked purely on racial grounds from playing representative cricket. Milton and his allies decided that English professionals Smith and Street could play for the Cape colony despite no residential qualifications, but the Cape-born professional Hendricks could not.

The tourists, excluding the leadership trio marooned on the *Moor*, had several days to practise before the start of hostilities against a Western Province XV on Boxing Day. Despite an overcast sky and a south-easterly wind which blew dust into the eyes of 6,000 spectators crowded around the ropes, the scene was described by *The Sportsman* as 'almost worthy of Lord's or The Oval'. Charles Wright lost the toss and Western Province were quickly rolled over for 115 soon after lunch. But the visitors were still at sea with the bat. Middleton ripped out Woods, Fry and Hayward, and the innings was only saved from going down with all hands by Bromley-Davenport's 29, which allowed them to crawl to 79.

3.3 George Lohmann's game of spoof

When Lohmann, who had taken 7-17 in the Western Province first innings, emerged with half the team down for about 20, he was heckled with comments, including, 'A fine lot of cricketers you've brought out, why they couldn't tell the game from shinty.' When Lohmann was pinned in front by a straight one from Middleton and feigned surprise at the upraised finger, a spectator pointed out, 'I have seen these English pros play before, and rubbing the chest hard when you are caught in the slips off your hand, or pretending your thigh smarts when it has been snapped up off the inside edge, are rather old to me ... however I don't blame him for trying on a game of spoof.'

---

116 *Cape Times*, 4/12/1895

Western Province resumed in the sharp light of the second day. Milton was missed several times in making 23. Fry sent down 'rattling good and rank bad balls alike' and took five wickets in each innings. *The Sportsman,* official spokesman for the team, described his action as 'perfectly fair'. The locals disagreed.

Joseph Willoughby came on for the first time in the match with the tourists on 72/1 in their second knock. He bowled at pace and plundered 6-15 as the visitors imploded, losing their remaining nine wickets for 20 runs. They failed to reach 100 in either innings and lost by 74 runs in two days. Willoughby was chaired off to the disgust of the late-arriving Hawke.

On 29 December, Cecil Rhodes' co-conspirator Dr Leander Starr Jameson and 600 men invaded Kruger's republic. Rhodes and Jameson had intended to spark an uprising against Kruger's government. The Raid was plotted in detail by Rhodes, Jameson and John Hays Hammond, the United States mining expert with the tacit consent of the secretary for the colonies, Joseph Chamberlain. It had its roots in the restrictions on mining capital and the diversion of labour to Boer farms under the Kruger government. [117]

Kruger's commandos were fully informed as to Jameson's every step. He was carefully shepherded into an ambush. Far from avenging the British defeat at Majuba Hill as he had hoped, Jameson was forced into a humiliating surrender at Doornkop. Sixteen men died and the hon. Charles Coventry, who had played on Aubrey Smith's tour, was injured. Jameson was marched to jail in tears.[118]

In Cape Town, on the same day, Hawke and the team had a lunch invitation at Rhodes' Groote Schuur residence. Rhodes was 'unavoidably absent'. Three decades later, Hawke still remembered the quality of the Veuve Clicquot. Rhodes, Fry said, was locked in his 'palatial office' in Cape Town consoling himself with his own case of 'the widow'. A few days later he resigned the Cape premiership, this time for good.

---

117 *Cape Times,* 27/12/1895

118 Thomas Pakenham, *The Boer War,* (London: George Weidenfield and Nicholson, 1979) 5

The next day the tourists took on a Cape Colony XIII. After their failure in the first match, Hawke had plenty to say to the batsmen: his reward was a 'perfect' 73 from Hayward and a partnership of 233 between Fry (148) and Woods (89) out of 405, a record for an English team in South Africa. The Colony batting was wrecked by Hill's 5-3 in the first innings and Lohmann's 8-40 in the second. Frank Hearne's 94 showed some colonial resistance, but the match was lost by an innings and 125 runs.

After the match, the gentlemen amateurs attended a ball in the Cape Town Castle, while Rhodes' reform committee plotters in Johannesburg were rounded up, jailed and the ringleaders sentenced to death. Hawke's men, due to travel to Johannesburg, remained in Cape Town until they received a telegram from Abe Bailey a week later inviting them to Johannesburg, as Fry described it, 'as an antidote to the inflamed melancholy of that distant city'. The tourists were a second front in the phoney war against Kruger's Republic.

The train trip was delayed by an impenetrable swarm of locusts and suspicious burghers on the Transvaal border who shook down the tourists for 'duty' on their cricket bats (the naive Fry paid four times as much as the wily Wright). Sir Tim O'Brien and Hewett challenged the Boers, leading to a stand-off which Hawke finally resolved with the present of a couple of bats. On the team's arrival in Johannesburg, they discovered Bailey had been detained at President Kruger's pleasure.

Hawke did not underestimate the Transvaal XV and arranged to bat 12 men and field with 11. The Wanderers was full. A large profit was likely until the manager allegedly forgot to put the last day's takings in the safe and lost £179. Hawke batted and young Jimmy Sinclair took 7-60 out of 178 and followed it with 75, giving the locals a 15-run lead. The home team required 254 to win in under three hours. Rose-Innes hit four consecutive boundaries off Lohmann, and Routledge hammered the bowling to all parts before running himself out for 86. Time was called with the home team on 195/8.

The amateurs were highly visible, dining at the Rand Club, and filling boxes at the theatres and variety halls. The failed Jameson Raid was initially spun as a glorious imperial adventure but details soon emerged of ramshackle planning, drunken implementation and craven surrender. The South African Republic grabbed the moral high ground and General Cronje preached conciliation to his burgher commandos.

3.4 In Jameson's footsteps – Hawke's tourists at Doornkop

In a final challenge to Kruger's authorities, the team visited the site of Jameson's surrender less than two weeks earlier. On the way they were apprehended by the state mining commissioner and subjected to a full search, including the inside of their hats.

On reaching Doornkop, the scene of the ambush was strewn with the corpses of 22 horses in a state of decomposition. After a macabre picnic, the tourists hunted souvenirs. There were few bullet casings, so they wrenched the hooves off the dead animals. On their return, the Boer drivers abandoned the English and they were forced to quick march three miles in the sweltering heat dragging their bags and souvenirs to the station to catch the train to Natal.

The 56-hour train journey between the Transvaal and Natal did not repeat the perilous river crossings of previous tours though the slow haul around the base of 'unforgettable' Majuba Hill brought the usual imperial melancholy exacerbated by the fresh wounds of the Raid.

The match against the Maritzburg XV was 'one of the most phenomenal displays of cricket' seen in South Africa. The multi-talented Lieutenant Poore of the 7th Hussars, which had been posted from India, hit ten fours in his first 50 and did not give a chance until caught at the wicket for 112 at 182/2, the first century conceded by an English side in South Africa, in their 46th game. Charlie Hime contributed 62 out of 310 for a first innings lead of 81. In reply, the visitors struggled to 80/5 in their second innings, still 1 run behind, when Sir Tim O'Brien joined Fry. O'Brien crashed 118 with five sixes, Fry stroked 153 out of 433/9 and the match was drawn. The tourists and the South Africans had achieved their highest collective and individual scores against each other in the same match.

The teenage Natalian, 'Buck' Llewellyn, took 4-49 with his left-arm spin. 'We will have to take you back with us,' said Tom Hayward. 'We'll find you a job right enough in Surrey.' 'Yes,' answered the Zingari trundler, 'but I don't want to do Lohmann out of a job.' Surrey's loss was ultimately Hampshire's gain.

3.5 Smokers, polo ponies and Sammy Woods

There was, said Fry, 'a clash' between the hospitality of the 7th Hussars and the local reception committee. The latter laid on a smoker attended by 150 city dignitaries, but the visiting cricketers, to the disgust of the townsfolk, preferred to celebrate Poore's century in the congenial company of Prince Alexander, Queen Mary's brother, and the Hussars. Fry's excuse that they had arrived late was not corroborated but they offered no apology. According to Fry, Sammy Woods had made amends with his engaging baritone and battery of facial expressions. Once he was on stage the only question was whether he could ever be induced to come off it; Fry 'had never seen a less self-conscious performer nor one who so enjoyed his own interminable repertoire'.[119]

Six of the cricketers on foot challenged the Hussars mounted polo four. Fry allegedly outsprinted the ponies on several occasions and the cricketers won. Hubris told as they challenged the Johannesburg Polo Club a couple of weeks later and Fry spent much of the match sprawled on his back in the dust.

The team travelled to Durban to play a Natal XV and were socialised to within an inch of their lives. Advertisements for the game included concerts under the patronage of the tourists on three consecutive nights. During the first day's play with all eyes on the cricket, Dr Jameson was smuggled on the train from Johannesburg and to the port in Durban en route to his trial in England. He received a 15-month sentence and served a year.

Meanwhile, members of Jameson's auxiliary entertained the Durban locals with tales of derring-do. To add to the foment, an unknown species of huge red locusts arrived from the Cape. Like a

---

119 Fry, *Life Worth Living*, 116

plague, the beach and port were blanketed in locusts. Indian tenant farmers lost their entire crops having 'through great exertion driven the locusts from the land but having no more strength have given up and let the locusts have their fill and remain until all is gone'. A day of prayer was held reflecting on the biblical plagues as retribution for misdeeds.[120]

The tourists' familiar nemesis, Peter Madden, despite suffering from German measles, took a hat-trick in his seven-wicket haul in the first innings. Local fans rated Fry's deliveries as far more suspicious than Madden's. As Fry had been passed by the umpires at Lord's, in their view this vindicated Madden. Lieutenant Poore, the 'Grace of the Army', made a duck in the first innings but on the last day, when a draw seemed the only possible result, and playing 'with a confidence and certainty that only a master of the game could command' he cut and drove his way to 107 not out and led Natal to a storming nine-wicket victory with 20 minutes left.

The al fresco concert at Lord's after play was the off-field highlight. The Town Hall promenade concert attracted a smaller audience – around 600 – with the ubiquitous band of the 7th Hussars. The band sergeant brought the house down with his cornet solo of 'Star of Bethlehem'. But for all this, the press was scathing about the English amateurs. 'Those who encountered Warton's and Read's teams found them very good fellows, the reverse is true with Lord Hawke's combination,' complained the *Natal Mercury*. One of the amateurs 'growled and grumbled at everyone and generally made himself as nasty as he could. They all ... tried to bluff the umpire and take every advantage that they could.'

Before play in Durban, Hawke picked up a framed picture of Walter Read's team and proclaimed, 'Here are the beauties who came out last time – good old semi-amateurs.' Of course, the *Natal Mercury* commented, the present lot are 'genuine amateurs but if their conduct characterises gentlemen rather than professionals and semi-amateurs, then it is fervently to be hoped that South Africa will

---

120 *Natal Mercury*, 25/1/1896

not have inflicted on them another team of genuine amateurs. In the future, send us semi-amateurs and decent pros.'

3.6 Charles Wright and the ball trouble

In the *Mercury*'s view, it was 'natural that professionals should eke out their living by taking round bats and selling them on tour'. When, however, 'an amateur who wants Mr in front of his name and professes to play for the love of the game goes "smousing" with cricket balls, and wants to make a certain percentage profit, we begin to wonder where we are. It's not only that he sells them but it's the nasty way he does it.'

At the beginning of the Durban match, there was no ball ready. 'The amateur produced his wares and sold a ball that costs 7/6 here for 10s. He clamoured for his money and was eventually forced to refund 2s. It's not (W)right,' wrote the *Mercury*.[121]

After the Durban cacophony, the team set off for East London without Hewett, who had had enough and headed back to England. Then George Lohmann refused to board the tug which was to take them over the bar. The games against King William's Town ('King'), Grahamstown (Albany) and Cradock (Midlands) XXIIs were the usual flag-waving exhibitions. However, without Lohmann, 'King' led on the first innings by 91 runs, and only time stopped them scoring 65 to win in the fourth innings. It was a similar pattern against Albany who only needed to take three wickets to win with the English 55 runs behind. After two 'losing' draws, the tourists smashed 392 against the Midlands XXII in Cradock with a century for Ledger Hill and fifties for O'Brien, Bromley-Davenport, and even Hawke, but the locals hung on for a draw.

Lohmann rejoined them back in Port Elizabeth and took 26 wickets for 82 runs against a Port Elizabeth XVIII on a super slow and capricious pitch, which might have been created especially for him. Hawke's men scrambled to a seven-wicket win, breaking a winless sequence of seven games.

---

121 *Natal Mercury*, 30/1/1896

3.7 *A would-be murderer and a runaway horse*

The 'King' to Grahamstown route involved a two-day trip by Cape cart, bringing them face to face with black mambas and other local characters. Fry, dared by Woods to steal a tail feather from an ostrich, was forced to run for it and escaped by diving headfirst through a hole in the wire as the indignant bird kicked the fence hard enough to rattle it for 30 yards. Fry had been chased twice by a bull, and once by a stallion, but none had got as close as the would-be murderer to whom Sammy Woods then offered a bun.

What Woods failed to achieve on the ostrich farm was managed later in the tour at Logan's Matjiesfontein. Fry's 'unfriendly dun nag with a very light mouth' bolted after crashing into the wall of the station, as they galloped out of town. After a mile Fry, careering at breakneck speed, was alarmed to see that they were heading straight for a spruit running under the railway. Rather than risking a head-on collision with the railway bridge, he jumped. He was found by a rescue party, which included the horse's less than contrite owner. Diagnosed with a broken fibula, his cricketing contribution to the tour was at an end.[122]

Hawke must have been seriously concerned about the possibility of losing the first Test. His team were tired, Hewett had returned home presumably after a disagreement, and Tyler had been suffering with dysentery since his arrival. Hawke approached Major Poore to join the tourists. Poore was overruled by his superior officer and made to play for South Africa, perhaps fortunately for Hawke. Hawke's local reputation, already tainted by arrogance and sharp practice, would have been damaged beyond repair had Poore turned out for the visitors.

Lohmann's performance on the uniquely difficult Port Elizabeth wicket made Hawke's men favourites against a South African team missing Tancred, Alf Richards and George Rowe. The controversial Madden, who had a better strike rate and average against the tourists

---

122 Fry, *Life Worth Living*, 126-127

than all the selected bowlers, was merely a reserve. Lohmann took 7-38 in the first innings as a prelude to stunning figures of 9.4-5-7-8 in the second. South Africa's dismissal for 30 was beyond their worst nightmares. Tommy Routledge, who managed 22 and two, said Lohmann was unplayable. The turf over which the mat was laid was thicker than in Cape Town which meant he could do as he liked, and he did.[123] Lohmann's performance was statistically exceptional. But the inadequate and ill-prepared opposition made the game a travesty.

3.8 Hendricks, Halliwell and Milton

'Barberton' Halliwell, South Africa's world-class wicketkeeper and selector for the Johannesburg Test, had advocated the selection of 'Krom' Hendricks for the 1894 English tour, but he had been blocked by Milton and Rhodes. With Rhodes in disgrace following the Raid, Halliwell saw the chance to strengthen the bowling and reinforce Transvaal cricketing authority vis-à-vis Western Province by inviting Hendricks and Peter Madden to Johannesburg for trials before the next Test.

Western Province were outraged. Hendricks was a 'non-person' as far as they were concerned and Milton made sure he never made it to Johannesburg.[124] He created a smokescreen by blaming Halliwell for approaching the Cape Town professional, Bonnor Middleton, a fixture in the Test team, directly and not through the proper channels. Out of pure spite, Middleton was recalled to play in an 'important' league game during the Test, undercutting South Africa's chances of a successful challenge under Halliwell.

From Port Elizabeth, Hawke's men swung north again to play an Orange Free State XVI. The match ended in a tame draw and when the team approached the Rand their visit was again overshadowed by events. First, the dispute over players between the Transvaal and Western Cape simmered on and while the second Test had originally

---

123 Luckin, *History*, 521
124 *Cape Times*, 23/1/1896

been scheduled by Milton to begin on 22 February, Halliwell and the TCU moved the start date to 26 February.[125]

Johannesburg was suffering from a severe outbreak of dysentery and typhoid, but this was quickly forgotten when an engine shunted into ten railway trucks laden with 50 tons of dynamite. The subsequent explosion resulted in a crater 200 feet long, 60 feet wide and 50 feet deep, and destroyed the overcrowded Braamfontein tenements. Hundreds were estimated to have died and many victims were never identified.

The Wanderers, a few hundred yards away, was turned into a hospital and the skating rink became a morgue. President Kruger dashed to the Rand from Pretoria and wept openly when he saw the stricken relatives queuing to identify victims amid a long line of black coffins. Dr Hillier, who had been jailed for his role in the Jameson Raid, led a medical team, and Wanderers players, including Jimmy Sinclair, helped search the devastated area for victims.

As always in South Africa, the story had a political dimension. There had been a long-running dispute between the mining industry and government over the dynamite monopoly held by Edward Lippert. The monopoly effectively gave the government a stranglehold over gold production. The Chamber of Mines highlighted the public safety issue and pressed for free trade in high explosives and proper restrictions on carriage and storage. Kruger refused to give up this key element of his policy, but donated £25,000 to survivors in recognition of the calamitous human cost of his political strategy.

No cricket was possible in Johannesburg in the circumstances, and instead of the Test, the players headed north to face a makeshift Pretoria XV which included A.B. Tancred. Tancred's team led by seven runs on the first innings, but eventually subsided by five wickets. The ground was within sight of Pretoria jail where many of the Johannesburg Reform Committee were still in residence. They had been arrested at the Rand Club and, after stocking up on cigars and cigarettes and having a final drink, they were marched to

---

125 *Cape Times*, 20/2/1896

the Johannesburg jail where they cheered themselves up by playing cricket. After they were moved to Pretoria a couple of weeks later, crowds of Afrikaner locals surrounded their carriage, hooting and yelling.

A roster of prisoners' wives did the catering for the rebels and Jameson begged for insect powder. Lord Hawke, Sir Tim O'Brien and Charles Wright spent an evening visiting Frank Rhodes, George Farrar, Percy Fitzpatrick and Lionel Phillips. Hawke said he 'never partook of a merrier meal' although his pleasure might have reflected the £98 the visitors won at after dinner poker.[126] The reform committee leaders – John Hays Hammond, Frank Rhodes, George Farrar, Abe Bailey and Percy Fitzpatrick – were sentenced to death for high treason but eventually allowed to buy their freedom for £25,000 each. Cecil Rhodes and Albert Beit paid the Raid fines, worth hundreds of millions of pounds in today's money.

3.9 Fry, Hawke and President Kruger

Despite this volatile situation, an audience with President Kruger was arranged at his modest bungalow.

According to Fry, Kruger sat 'in his broadcloth frock coat, big head sunk in his shoulders on a short neck, long biblical face, quick cunning eyes in a frame of patriarchal beard … his wife behind him, hands crossed under her bosom like a reproachful landlady'. The team sat on wooden chairs in a semi-circle drinking sweet coffee and were introduced to Kruger by a young barrister.

Lord Hawke hoped that Kruger would find the visit of his cricket team to his capital of interest and that the people of the town would come to the match. Kruger grunted three words which sounded like 'no good here', while his interpreter told them that the 'president was very pleased to see them'. Sammy Woods, unafraid to step into the limelight, said he hoped the president was well as they had travelled a long way to see him. Kruger snorted in reply and the rest of their half hour was spent in silence.[127]

---

126 Lord Hawke, *Recollections and Reminiscences,* (London: Williams and Norgate, 1924) 151

127 Fry, *Life,* 113-115

Kruger, Sammy Woods commented, 'was not very hearty.' He did not welcome English invaders entertaining the English population, exploiting the wealth of the mines and bent on overthrowing his state. He would have been annoyed by their visit to his death row prisoners, and their failure to thank their hosts or offer condolences following the dynamite tragedy. Kruger's silent treatment of Hawke and his team challenged the self-possession of some of the most arrogant and superior visitors he was to have the misfortune to meet.

The English returned to The Wanderers to play a Test match, while doctors, nurses and undertakers continued to attend to casualties in the makeshift hospital in the pavilion. The South African XI was missing A.B. Tancred, who was a member of the legal defence team for the jailed reformers. Some of South Africa's best cricketers were less keen to spend time in Johannesburg. As Luckin's official record put it, 'Owing to disappointments, several players were brought in at the last minute.'

The team showed six changes from the demoralised XI in Port Elizabeth. Hawke won the toss on a fast wicket and lightning quick outfield against a threadbare attack of George Rowe, Jimmy Sinclair and the teenage debutant, 'Buck' Llewellyn. Despite Rowe's industrious 5-115 in 49 overs, Hayward's superb 122 and fifties from Fry, Bromley-Davenport, Wright and Hill took the tourists to a record score of 482. 'Krom' Hendricks meanwhile grabbed 7-6, including a hat-trick in a club match in Cape Town.

Lohmann did not open the English bowling and when he finally appeared, he bowled Poore with his first ball for 20 and picked up the rest of the wickets. Sinclair top-scored with 40 but otherwise only Llewellyn with 24 showed any resistance. Lohmann had taken 9-28, not on a pitch which gave him every assistance as in Port Elizabeth, but on a batsman's wicket where the tourists had already made close to 500. South Africa followed on, Routledge was caught in the slips before a run was scored, Sinclair was out to a doubtful catch for 29, and a determined 41 by Halliwell could not prevent the locals from being pulverised by an innings and 197 runs.

After Johannesburg's sensory overload, Hawke's team arrived in Kimberley's dusty backwater. De Beers took them on the usual tour of the Big Hole. Some discreet diamond purchases were made by the team's plutocrats, which did not include the impecunious Fry and Wright.

Black underground workers were subject to four-month contracts, paid 15s per week (fortnightly) and forced to buy their supplies at full price at the De Beers stores in the compounds. Even official sources recognised the reality of the recruiting process. As G.W. Barnes, Kimberley's 'Protector of Natives', noted, 'Labour agents may give it out that tobacco, coffee and brandy are available free. This liberality has not been experienced in the Kimberley compounds.'

Barnes had noted the exodus of labour in the *Blue Book on Native Affairs* at the end of 1895, 'Assaults and other harsh and cruel treatments have not altogether been absent and I have been forced to prosecute or take other measures regarding management … It is a fact that the natives are not treated as well as they might be, though it appears that orders have gone out from De Beers central office that the natives are not to be struck, but the striking still goes on, and that for the most trivial offences, and in some cases for pure accidents … such conduct is likely to injure the labour supply for as the natives leave the works they take with them the sting remaining in their hearts from the treatment they have undeservedly received.'[128]

The match against a Griqualand West XV turned out to be the hardest fought of the tour, in front of an excellent crowd on a grey sand surface fenced by aloes. Samuels (7-42) demolished the tourists in the first innings. Trailing by 49, Woods (63) and Hill (89) ground out a lead of 182, while George Glover, who 'had more catches dropped off him than is good for a man's peace of mind', took 6-75. Although Fry took six wickets, eight batsmen got into double figures and only Hayward's magnificent performance in the field kept the visitors in the game. Hawke's replacement of Lohmann

---

128 *Cape Times*, 14/4/1896

with Hill proved decisive. Two quick wickets and the tourists had won by 13 runs.

Hawke said in the post-match speeches that the team made up of young South African-born players had given them one of the best matches. Unlike the match against Grahamstown, he was pleased to say that he 'did not see one bit of funk in the Kimberley team'. He intended to present the Currie Cup for the best opposition to Kimberley.[129]

Cricket ran deeply in the blood of Kimberley, and the tussles between white players from Cape Town and Kimberley were mirrored by intense tournaments between combined teams of African, 'Malay' and 'coloured' cricketers where players such as Ebrahim Ariefdien, Lamarah Samsodien, Robert Grendon and 'Krom' Hendricks demonstrated that they would have significantly strengthened a South African team, if the racist state had not already slammed the door.[130] Black cricket was supported in Kimberley by the Glover family, of whom George played for South Africa in the third and final Test of the tour. The Glover sports and entertainment business was run out of the Pirates ground and the Cape black cricketers representing the main urban areas fought for the Glover Cup.

The curtain-raiser to the final stage of the tour consisted of a recreational game at Matjiesfontein between J.D. Logan's XI and Lord Hawke's XI and replete with practical jokes and kangaroo courts. Hawke preached his usual sermon on 'shamateurism'. Any player who accepted money for playing cricket was a professional. 'While he had the greatest respect for Dr [W.G.] Grace, he was neither more nor less than a professional,' he thundered.

The team train pulled into Cape Town station for the last time. After endless complaints about the meaninglessness of 'odds' games, Hawke's men were pleased to find themselves facing a Western Province XI. The batting shackles were loosened for Hayward (83) and Wright (68). Alf Richards responded with a 58 full of precision

---

129 *Cape Times*, 11/3/1896
130 Winch and Parry, *Too Black to Wear Whites*, 10-13

and power which saved the follow-on, but Western Province needed rain to save them.

The South African side for the third Test included Middleton and Willoughby, although Tancred was still occupied by legal matters in Pretoria. This time Hawke put the home side in and Lohmann bowled unchanged to take 7-42 in 24 overs. No batsman had the technique to deal with him for long and South Africa subsided to 115.

For the tourists, Ledger Hill made a match defining hundred, South Africa trailed by 150 on the first innings. As *Cricket* put it, 'only a vast amount of luck and a small earthquake in the middle of the pitch' could have saved them. There were no earthquakes. While the South African batsmen restricted Lohmann to one wicket in 23 overs in the second innings, Hill's bustling pace grabbed 4-8 and South Africa tumbled to their second straight innings defeat.

The English cricketers danced through the closing festivity of the tour with 'commendable determination' in the 'tropical heat'. At the farewell dinner on the *Pretoria*, Lord Hawke presented the Currie Cup to George Glover, captain of Kimberley, as Donald Currie shamelessly milked the occasion.[131]

South African cricket had to face a harsh reality. The lack of competitive cricket, given the distance between centres, meant they were ill-equipped to deal with conditions with which the tourists were already familiar. Only Sinclair and Halliwell made anything like decent scores in the representative matches. The talented Lieutenant Poore, who smote consecutive hundreds to rescue the locals in Maritzburg and destroyed the tourists in Durban, survived the tug o' war over his services, but he too became caught in Lohmann's iron grip and would soon be back in England.

3.10 Tom Hayward's judgement

Rowe and Middleton strengthened their reputations and Willoughby was unplayable in his first game but posed little threat thereafter. One wonders what might have happened had South Africa selected

---

131 *Cape Times*, 26/3/1896

players on merit. Tom Hayward was asked the best bowler he faced in South Africa, and replied, 'I thought that Hendricks bowled better than anyone else, but as, on account of his colour, he was not played in any of the matches on the last tour, it is difficult to say … But as a practice bowler, which is all I know of him, he was certainly very good and very fast indeed.'

Hendricks must have been outstanding for Hayward to single him out above the South African Test bowlers, and Hayward's endorsement may also have reflected his professional empathy with local Malay players.[132]

The tourists batted better than Read's team but faced fewer opponents: three of 22 (six on the previous tour) and most teams which had put out 18 previously put out 15 this time. While the overall standard of the opposition was a little higher, the gaps in the field were not so elusive. Runs were scored much faster, Fry, Hill and Hayward all averaged over 30, and the top four batsmen – Fry, Hill, Hayward and O'Brien – all made hundreds, Fry and Hill doing so twice. Fry topped the averages with 34.09, which highlighted Chatterton's feat in averaging 41 on the previous tour.

But the tour again belonged to a single great bowler. This time it was Lohmann who took a wicket every 18 balls. Briggs and Ferris, who had plenty more rabbits in their sights, had averaged 17 and 20 balls per wicket respectively. After carrying Hawke's team despite the toll on his health, Lohmann together with Hayward, Richardson and Abel challenged Surrey over Test match fees at The Oval. These had not changed since the 1880s and the amateurs received more than the professionals. Charles Alcock 'naturally refused to be dictated to by professional cricketers' and the great-hearted but increasingly ill Lohmann was forced to apologise for his 'rebellion'.[133] It was characteristic of the cruelty and injustice of the game's hierarchy.

132 *Cricket Field*, 20/8/1896, 362
133 *Cape Times*, 27/8/1896

4

Clouds: Lord Hawke 1898/99

WHEN LORD Hawke's planned tour of the West Indies fell victim to a hurricane, the 'Odysseus of Empire' was prevailed upon by James Logan to arrange another tour to South Africa in 1898/99. The autocrat was the son of a country parson ennobled following the deaths of two childless brothers. The great Yorkshireman, who invented a closed shop for Yorkshire-born players, was born in Lincolnshire. Being an imposter may have intensified his views though these, according to Benny Green, were 'uncorrupted by the slightest taint of cerebral function'.

If Lord Hawke was the visible side of British imperialism from South Africa's perspective, he was below Lord Harris in the cricketing pecking order. Harris, who cultivated English cricket between the 1890s and the 1930s, was his own personal patrimony. Harris captained Eton, Kent, and England, and was treasurer, president and chairman of key MCC sub-committees until 1929. He served as a Conservative minister from 1885, and governor of Bombay from 1890. Between 1899 and 1929, he was active as chairman of Consolidated Goldfields and focused on the central dilemma – how to secure an adequate black labour supply at less-than-subsistence wages.

At the centre of the cricketing world's web, he was also at the heart of the mining industry, which would drive imperialism from the 1890s. Benny Green described his 'wonderful gift for being brusque, rude and callous while remaining convinced he was the very model of an English gentleman'.[134]

In the 1890s, Harris had tried to keep the super-talented Ranji out of the England team but was thwarted in England by the selection system which gave the casting vote to the county hosting the Test. Lancashire, eager to thwart Harris and his county Kent, picked Sussex's Ranji in 1896. Ranji not only scored a century on debut but became the first player to make a hundred before lunch. Overseas it was a different matter and Ranji was again ignored by Hawke for his second South African tour. Back home for Australia's next tour, MCC set up a selection sub-committee with Hawke in the chair. Hawke opposed Ranji's selection but was trumped by W.G. Grace who insisted on selecting Ranji.

His behaviour in 1895/96 reinforced Benny Green's verdict that Hawke was 'one of the most spectacular noodles in the history of team sports making Lord Harris seem like Albert Einstein by comparison'.[135] He was out of his depth, bumbling through the political landscape of the Jameson Raid, floating on a cloud of ignorance and arrogance. Undaunted, Hawke was ready to again bestride the Southern African cricketing landscape. As he pronounced in his autobiography, 'On the cricket grounds of Empire is fostered the spirit of never knowing when you are beaten, of playing for your side and not yourself ... and of never giving up a game as lost ... the future of cricket and the Empire is ... inseparably connected.'

But South Africa had moved on and become considerably more dangerous. President Kruger had counselled patience when warned of Jameson's Raid plans, 'When the tortoise puts out its head, I will cut it off.' But Kruger did not simply cut off Jameson's head. He posted him back to the Queen and her embarrassed government. By the time Hawke had returned, a wretched Rhodes was revealed by public trial as the arch-plotter and arch-bungler. Rhodes had overestimated the willingness of British and other foreigners to support an uprising, had

134 Maryna Fraser and Alan Jeeves, *All that Glittered*, (Cape Town: Oxford University Press, 1977) 113

135 Benny Green, *The Wisden Papers*, (London: Stanley Paul, 1989) 119, 137

alienated his Afrikaner political power base and instructed Jameson to take the blame. The Jameson Raid disaster seemed politically unmanageable until a congratulatory telegram from the German Kaiser to Kruger was discovered and Jameson became a hero again, galloping his Stoke-on-Trent-manufactured porcelain black stallion across thousands of British mantelpieces.[136]

4.1 Hawke and Rhodes

A lunch guest told how Rhodes had brought out a collection of photographs of himself and asked his guest's wife to choose one. On seeing her choice, he beamed at her, 'You have chosen the same picture that pleased HM Queen Alexandra the most,' before autographing it.[137] It seemed hard to match this display until he repeated the scene for Hawke. 'His presentation of his portrait to me … was the crowning tribute to his wonderful career,' said Hawke.[138]

In 1895/96, Hawke brought a few 'socially acceptable' amateurs – like O'Brien and Hewett, who paid for their own wine – in contrast to 'shamateurs' like Wally Read or Aubrey Smith. But Hawke's team had been attacked for class arrogance. It was not easy to please the South African establishment torn between worshipping 'home' privilege and resenting imperial superiority. Hawke's previous team had been massively reliant on the already ill George Lohmann. He took 35 out of the 59 wickets to fall in the three Test matches and almost four times as many wickets as the next bowler, Bromley-Davenport, over the whole tour.

This time Hawke produced a team with seven amateurs and five professionals of whom three, Trott, Haigh and Cuttell, shared the wickets. Lohmann toured as manager. Johnny Tyldesley stiffened the batting and amateurs Plum Warner and Frank Mitchell contributed most of the runs.

---

136 Pakenham, *Boer War*, 22

137 Cape Times, *Sports and Sportsmen in South Africa*, (Cape Town: Cape Times, 1929) 8

138 Gibson, *England Captains*, 36

In November 1898, Sir Alfred Milner, South African high commissioner, was in England. Milner, an ex-chairman of the Inland Revenue, had been selected to pick up the pieces from the Jameson Raid. Milner was an advocate of a consolidated British empire run by a federal Greater Britain, with a grand imperial parliament. He tried to persuade the Colonial Office that Kruger's regime was a fatal threat to the empire. The colonial secretary, Joseph Chamberlain, careful to avoid blame, criticised 'local bunglers and schoolboy heroes'. Milner chose to construe this as a nod and a wink that local initiatives might drive the region into a necessary war.

Milner 'worked up to a crisis', thwarting Kruger's proposed resolution of the franchise issue. He sent a lengthy dispatch comparing the British in the Transvaal to disenfranchised Greek 'Helots'. British public opinion began to shift but not all agreed with Milner's warmongering. The compromised Rhodes, whom Sir James Sivewright had once found in his bathroom shaking his fist at a portrait of Kruger, now called the latter a splendid old man 'who had defended his wicket against all comers'.[139]

Hawke's team sailed out of Southampton on the SS *Scot* as the band played 'Life on the Ocean Wave' with an enthusiasm which suggested they had been enjoying themselves onshore. The voyage was uneventful. With a Hawkesian lack of imagination, Hawke's team turned out for the fancy dress ball as 'a cricket team'. Hawke presented first prize to a lady who had come dressed as 'The Road to Ruin'.

On arrival in Table Bay, the team were met by James Logan and George Lohmann, several English professionals, including Fred Tate and Sydney Barnes, and a batch of bandwagon-jumping politicians. As Cape Town's satirical *The Owl* pointed out, they were welcomed by the premier, William Schreiner, flattered by the mayor and patted on the back by the president of the cricket union. 'It does an immense amount of good to our local cricket and makes us feel that we are of

139 Pakenham, *Boer War*, 58

some account in the cricketing world ... English teams are the oasis in the desert of South African sport.'[140]

William Schreiner, prime minister of the Cape, clambered on board sweeping 'all political differences aside in his desire to welcome' them. *The Owl* made the obvious connection, 'Without classifying Lord Hawke and his Merry Men as political agitators it does look a little peculiar that as soon as he invades the country... the clarions of war sound throughout the land ... It is perhaps a question for Oom [Uncle] Paul [Kruger] and his secret detectives to consider what subtle link there is between Hawke's teams, Mr Rhodes, Dr Jameson, the Uitlanders of Johannesburg and war scares'[141] Hawke, with characteristic obtuseness, wrote that while the first tour had been clouded by the political considerations of the Jameson Raid, there were no 'adverse external influences' in respect of the second tour.

Hotels were required; the amateurs were accommodated in the Royal and the professionals in the Fountain, the latter being full of bookies who, Schofield Haigh complained, 'Shouted the odds all day and a good proportion of the night.' On Christmas Eve, Hawke won the toss against a Western Province XIII. 'Bonnor' Middleton, whom Cape Town CC had bought out of the army, was playing against his second English touring team. He had taken 7-50 off 23 overs in the first innings of the previous tour and captured 7-54 in 30 overs this time. Hawke's men subsided to 141 and 140. Western Province failed by 25 runs to chase 133, Haigh took 5-14 and the tourists had won their opening game for the first time. Plum Warner noticed in the crowd, 'Malays, many of whom are engaged as bowlers by the clubs. Some of them bowl quite well and their keenness is beyond a doubt.'[142]

Christmas Day found Hawke and his team in the governor-general's pew in the cathedral after which he maintained class

---

140 *The Owl*, 23/12/1898

141 *The Owl*, 30/12/1898

142 Plum Warner, *Cricket in Many Climes*, (London: Heinemann, 1900) 192

protocols in gift giving. A south-easterly wind ruined the Hout Bay picnic. The sandstorm was strong enough to send their driver's fez over the parade ground and out to sea.

Hawke noted that there had been a 'great deal of unpleasantness' based on jealousies between territories. Further, he added, 'We were [not] a commercial movement, a thing against which I have invariably set my face in all my tours ... all amateurs simply had their hotel and travelling free and paid for their own drinks and washing.'[143]

The Western Province team for the second game was due to include the English professionals but a pay dispute intervened. The professionals coaching at the Cape – Jack Brown, Frank Hearne, Fred Tate and Sydney Barnes – saw no reason to play for free given their impact on the gate.[144]

The Western Province Cricket Union was no more inclined to pay them the £5 demanded than Surrey had been to concede a pay increase to Lohmann and his colleagues in 1896. Hawke, always keen to thrash poor sides rather than risk defeat, didn't want to play against the professionals anyway. Public sympathy was with them, and the crowds stayed away.

Without the professionals, 'Bonnor' Middleton and George Rowe shared 19 wickets between them, but Hawke's team won by 106 runs thanks to 12 wickets from Trott. Sydney Barnes would have to wait until 1913, when he returned as a member of Johnny Douglas' MCC, to showcase his skills on matting wickets. [145]

The Owl reported the fractious mood, 'It would be amazing if not so painful ... the amount of trouble which the English team seem to have brought on South African cricketing circles. Practically all the centres are at loggerheads.'[146] Natal and Kimberley fought with Logan over the guarantee, with Natal pulling out altogether. The Free State also declined, so Hawke's tour was limited to the Cape and the Transvaal, hardly a vehicle for bringing all four territories

---

143 Hawke, *Reminiscences*, 155
144 *The Owl*, 6/1/1899
145 *Sportsman*, 23/1/1899
146 *The Owl*, 13/1/1899

together. Logan was blamed for encouraging internal bickering over resources.[147]

On leaving Cape Town, the team zigzagged on the narrow-gauge railway for seven hundred miles through mountain ranges to De Aar in the northern Cape then doubled back to Graaff-Reinet. The Karoo was dry, dusty and featureless, the sleeping cars cramped and airless, and the heat intense. The last hundred miles took eight and a half painful hours. The match against a Midlands XXII, some of whom had ridden 60 miles to play, began a few hours after their arrival. Albert Trott bounced off the train like Tigger and mesmerised the opposing batsmen, taking 12-38 and 8-26 in an eight-wicket win.

Next stop was a Port Elizabeth XV, mat laid on grass and famed as the 'most difficult' wicket in South Africa. 'Alberto' again won the game on his own with 15 out of the 28 wickets to fall and a display of huge hitting in his 84, the first 50 of the tour. The fifth game had been scheduled as the first of three Tests, but a dispute between the Cape and Transvaal caused South Africa's replacement by a Cape Colony XI. 'Until the jealousy between centres is ended,' Warner said, 'cricket can never flourish in South Africa.'[148] The scent of war was everywhere in the air.

Warner was delighted to play on even terms. He was already 'heartily sick' of cricket against odds. An easy win for Hawke was enlivened by an entertaining 81 from Frank Mitchell, a dust storm, a plague of locusts and (for the amateurs) gifts of valuable ostrich feathers. Hawke complained that they had travelled 6,000 miles to play three 'Test' matches to find that they were now playing two. Hugh Bromley-Davenport, on his third tour with Hawke, tried to improve the mood with songs from the piano.

4.2 Albert Trott (and a footnote on Neville Cardus)
Albert Trott burst on to the cricketing scene against Stoddart's 1894/95 English tourists. In a sensational debut, he plundered 38 not out and 72 not out and, moustache bristling, annihilated the

---

147 *Sportsman*, 7/1/1899
148 *Sportsman*, 6/2/1899

England second innings with 8-43, driving Australia to a 382-run win. It was to be more than 50 years before Alf Valentine equalled his feat of taking eight wickets in an innings on Test debut. Albert scored 331 runs and took 35 wickets during that tour, yet he was ignored for Australia's next tour of England selected and captained by his brother Harry. The two had a notably frosty relationship.

He went to London, qualified for Middlesex, caught Lord Hawke's eye, and spent the close season coaching at The Wanderers and was already a hero to the locals and a terror to the batsmen. Matting wickets suited him, as they had done Briggs, Ferris and Lohmann. Trott bowled with a round-arm style which gave him a good out-swinger and was an aggressive spinner of the ball. His variations in pace were supplemented by a well-disguised fast yorker and he bowled a vicious bouncer when this was a rarely used weapon. He had, he said, never seen a matting wicket on which he could not turn the ball and on this surface was described by Warner as a 'perfect masterpiece of a bowler'.[149] He was a fine fielder and the first proponent of the slide, gather and pick up in a single motion, in which he was 100 years ahead of his time.

Albert finished the tour with 169 wickets at under ten, from 802.1 overs, and hit 472 runs including an unbeaten hundred against the Transvaal. He drank hotel bars dry, broke the hearts of many South African women, and did not resist the siren songs of the bookies outside his Cape Town hotel. Hawke told of his request for an advance 'to send to his brother' which Hawke provided. When a further request was made, Hawke asked for the address of his brother, so he could send the money directly. No more was heard of it.

For Frank Mitchell, 'Not everyone is gifted with the temperament and stomach of Albert Trott to whom everything came alike, fair weather and foul, good food or no food, sleep or no sleep.' After the tour he dressed up, Rasputin-like, as a Russian Orthodox priest for the fancy dress ball. He demolished English cricket with 1,000 runs and 200 wickets in each of the next two seasons and hit a ball through the twin pillars of the Lord's pavilion. He was unquestionably the world's best all-rounder.

---

149 Warner, *Many Climes*, 192

Then came a slow decline as the booze and pressure took their toll. There was time for the famous benefit when Middlesex played Somerset. In Somerset's second innings, Trott took four wickets in four balls and then a hat-trick. He bowled, in Cardus's myth-making phrase, 'himself into the bankruptcy court'. In fact, he achieved this unsurpassed feat on the last day of the fixture, with the gate money already secured.

This hero briefly became a first-class umpire, but eventually his demons caught up with him and he ended his life in his lodging house room.

The Eastern Cape meander continued with a match in Grahamstown, against an Eastern Province XV won by the tourists by ten wickets. The town was in a mood to party, with the circus visiting, the last night of the great exhibition, a balloon ascent, a concert and a military tattoo.

4.3 The no-balling of Peter Madden

Peter Madden had played against all four touring teams. In his five games he had taken 29 wickets at 13.55 and conceded a mere 1.6 runs an over. He had demolished Read's XI with figures of 33-10-39-8. He was a fast and skilful bowler, but, ironically for a policeman, he was under constant suspicion of breaking the law on throwing. Locals considered his action at least as fair as Fry, and Hawke, who fulminated against 'chuckers', had no scruples about using Fry.

Madden completed 16 overs on the first day, taking 1-34 without a word, but in the first over of the second day Hawke's umpire A. White called the second and third balls presumably after overnight discussions. 'A more palpable chucker I have never seen,' was Warner's take on it.[150]

Then came the traditional two-day trip by Cape cart jolting over rough tracks to King William's Town. They stopped overnight and

---

150 *Ibid*, 207-208

by the light of a brilliant moon, some of the amateurs walked to the nearest kraal and poked their noses into the huts, talking to the inhabitants and passing round tobacco. Warner, replete with multiple imperial stereotypes, described how an elderly man 'with a face like a Chinese idol became most obstreperous in his demands for brandy'.[151]

With aching limbs from days of being tenderised in the carts, they beat a Border XV by an innings, with Trott taking half the wickets to fall and a reversed batting order. Giddy reprised feats from earlier tours, hitting a Jessopian 66 in 45 minutes during which he hit 16 off an over from Haigh and 17 off four balls from Milligan. It was the end of four weeks in South Africa's Arcadia. Sterner tests were to come.

Forty-five hours on the train brought them to Johannesburg via the border post on the Vaal. There was no hostility from the Boer officials, according to Warner 'the most offensive men in the world'. Warner's hostility to all things Afrikaner was unescapable. At the end of the platform, he reported, 'The extremely ugly and inartistic Transvaal flag was flying in all its glory. Somehow it annoyed us.'[152]

Amid the clamour of Johannesburg, the amateurs relaxed at the Rand Club despite the ruinous whisky prices. The game against a Johannesburg XV provided a first glimpse of Jimmy Sinclair. On a lightning-fast wicket, Sinclair made 56 in the second innings, with powerful driving off the back foot. With the ball, thanks to Lohmann's coaching, he used his height well and varied his pace cleverly, and 'Barberton' Halliwell showed why he was the best wicketkeeper in the world. The game was drawn.

The match against a Transvaal XI was the second 11-a-side contest on the tour. Halliwell injured a finger and Vincent Tancred, his replacement, complained, 'Only a damned fool would keep wicket of his own free will.' Vincent was the brother of Augustus Bernard Tancred, South Africa's best pre-Anglo-Boer war batsman. A.B. had been made an honorary member of MCC when he visited the UK in 1897 as a lawyer acting on behalf of the Jameson Raiders. Despite

---

151 *Ibid*, 211
152 *Ibid*, 215

a failure from A.B., the Transvaal accumulated a respectable 211, but the English with hundreds from Mitchell, Johnny Tyldesley and Trott (101 not out to go with his match figures of 11-140 in almost 70 overs) smashed 537/6. For Transvaal, Sinclair had the exhausting analysis of 2-186 in 58 five-ball overs in a defeat by an innings and 203 runs. It was a lesson, if any were needed, about the challenges posed by 'evens' matches. The tourists headed north to Pretoria.

4.4 Paul Kruger and his secret police

After the famous silent treatment from Kruger on the last tour, even Lord Hawke preferred not to beard 'Oom Paul' in his den again. Frank Mitchell and Clem Wilson, anxious to experience the frisson of engaging with the enemy, were the exceptions. They found the president smoking on his step, wearing a frockcoat of a 'cut and colour that would have excited attention in Piccadilly', and a top hat 'that might have belonged to an unpopular referee'. Sadly, Kruger's view of his visitors and their attire is unrecorded.[153]

The president was in a much better temper without Lord Hawke in attendance, launching a charm offensive as the empire tightened its grip around his state. Hawke's mistakes were avoided and Kruger was glad to hear they liked his country (unlike most of their compatriots). He had no time for cricket but explained his grandson, Tjaart Kruger, was a keen cricketer as well as chief of his secret police. It was Kruger's way of indicating he was fully informed but would be conciliatory for as long as he could.

On their return to Johannesburg for the first Test, the team were in demand. Percy Fitzpatrick, chief of Werner Beit, the largest mine-owner on the Rand, and veteran of the reform committee, invited both teams to a garden party. Fitzpatrick and Abe Bailey had initially been sentenced to death before Rhodes bought them out in 1896 and they were banned from politics for three years. The period was up, and Fitzpatrick was a key player in Milner's plan to force Britain into war against Kruger. Abe Bailey also hosted a banquet, which included

---

153 *Ibid*, 224

speeches from ex-reform committee detainees. President Kruger's health was drunk and the 'Volkslied' – the national anthem of the Transvaal Republic – was sung as propriety (and the secret police) required. The police hardly needed to report that their rendition of 'God Save the Queen' could have been heard several miles away.[154]

For the first Test, South Africa included Charlie 'Buck' Llewellyn who, on the recommendation of Major Poore, had signed with Hampshire and had also toured North America with Ranji. Bailey employed him at The Wanderers. While from a similar ethnic background to 'Krom' Hendricks, Buck played cricket in Natal where the white population were less concerned at drawing a line against 'coloureds' than they were about turning Zulus from warriors into workers. Hendricks' misfortune was to live in the Cape where he became the primary victim of their particular social and political racial exclusions.

Hawke won the toss and batted on the super-fast Wanderers surface. The English team struggled to 145 all out at less than two runs an over strangled by South Africa's quartet of Middleton, Rowe, Graham and Llewellyn. Sinclair's sublime 86 took South Africa to 251, the first time they had led on the first innings in Tests.

The second innings appeared no better. Middleton took 5-51 and only Warner offered any resistance. But on the verge of a famous first victory, nerves overcame the South Africans. Five catches were spilled off Llewellyn's bowling alone. Warner was 97 not out overnight in his debut Test, and had Solomon taken a difficult catch at point early the next day, the game would have been over. When Warner was on 82, Llewellyn had him smartly stumped by Bisset with the first ball of a new spell, but he was given not out by the umpire, Alfred Soames. 'That's a bit of luck for England,' said Plum Warner when Soames replaced the bails. Soames later admitted that he had made an 'incredible blunder' and cost South Africa their first Test win.

Warner carried his bat for an undefeated 132 out of 237. It was a remarkable debut which gave his team a sniff of a chance. *The Owl*

---

154 *Ibid*, 227-229

considered that the press reports of Warner's 'fine' innings were a misprint for 'five' innings. South Africa's poor catching had left them with exactly 132 to win.[155]

They were cruising at 58/2, having lost Sinclair caught off a skier by Cuttell for four and Francis bowled by Cuttell for 29, when Trott tore through the rest of the order. Cuttell, in support, bowled nine consecutive maidens, and despite Bisset battling for two hours for his unbeaten 21, South Africa were dismissed for 99. It was the closest they had been to that elusive first win. Hawke thought that South Africa had been a one-horse show, overreliant on Sinclair.[156] This was not true, but they lacked the confidence to get over the line against a determined opposition. The psychology of empire meant no one yet knew how to close out against the mother country.

There was still no direct line to Kimberley and Hawke's men had to take a circuitous route through the Cape ready for their next fixture. The Griqualand West XV started well with 236 on the usual glass-like outfield. Bill Shalders stroked an elegant 76, forcing himself into the South African side for the second Test. Hawke's men piled up 367 with fifties from Mitchell, Warner, Cuttell and Wilson and Griqualand West collapsed the second time round to Trott, everyone's favourite nemesis. They were so demoralised that even Hawke took a wicket with his lobs.

Their innings defeat did not quite warrant Cape Town's premier paper gleefully putting the boot into their rivals, 'Of the many collapses – which like wrecks bestrew the path journeyed over by Lord Hawke's team – there is none so crushing and complete as the Griqualand West XV.' 'The capitalists of Kimberley,' the newspaper crowed, 'instead of giving Maxim guns to their citizen soldiers to play with, would be doing a greater service to the Kimberley community by importing a few good English professionals.'[157] The gun not the cricket bat was rapidly becoming the capitalists' weapon of choice.

---

155 *The Owl*, 17/2/1899
156 *Cape Times*, 24/2/1899
157 *Cape Times*, 1/3/1899

4.5 Jameson and Zimbabwe's 'first war of liberation'

The ubiquitous Dr Leander Starr Jameson, once company doctor at Rhodes' De Beers compound for African labour in Kimberley, was Rhodes' representative on the Pioneer Column which invaded Matabeleland and Mashonaland in 1890. He declared war on Lobengula's Ndebele in 1893 and led the botched and foolhardy Raid on the Transvaal Republic in 1896.

The Jameson Raid emptied Matabeleland and Mashonaland of police and guns and provided the perfect opportunity for the African population to fight back in the 'first war of liberation'. The 'rebels', lacking political structures, were led by 'spirit mediums' such as Nehanda, who gave women a formidable voice.[158] Olive Schreiner recounted the brutal suppression of the uprising in her novel, *Trooper Peter Halket of Mashonaland*. While the war continued into late 1897, the iron rooster advanced into the heart of Matabeleland, with the first train puffing into Bulawayo on 4 November 1897.

Hawke's men flew the Union Jack on the front of their train from Kimberley. After a three-day journey they arrived at Bulawayo, the old capital of Lobengula, ex-paramount chief of the Matabele. Rhodesia had been won by trickery and the maxim, and 'owned' by Rhodes' British South Africa Company provided with a charter by The Queen.

4.6 Getting there

The three-day rail trip was a picnic in comparison to the journey faced by the five Salisbury-based members of the Rhodesian cricket team led by Harry Taberer. Taberer had played against Aubrey Smith's tourists in 1889 as a schoolboy at St Andrew's. He was a double blue at Oxford for rugby and athletics and played cricket

---

158 Arthur Keppel-Jones, *Rhodes and Rhodesia*, (Kingston: Queen's University Press, 1983); T.O. Ranger, *Revolt in Southern Rhodesia*, (London: Heinemann, 1978)

for Essex for three years. Rhodes had appointed him chief native commissioner of Mashonaland in 1895.

The 239-mile wagon trip between Salisbury and Bulawayo normally took four days, but this was rainy season and Harry Taberer and his four Salisbury team-mates had allowed a fortnight. At the impassable Hunyani river, Taberer, who could allegedly throw a cricket ball 100 yards standing in a barrel, hurled a ball attached to a rope across the swollen waters and they hauled themselves and their cricket gear across while the mules swam across towing the coach. Then came the mud, forcing the coach to be pushed wheel turn by wheel turn. Eventually, it stuck so deep that 36 oxen were needed to dislodge it. They finally arrived the day before the match.

Lobengula's council and parade ground had been commandeered only three weeks before. Hawke's men easily disposed of a Bulawayo XVIII – 'Too much like a joke,' commented *The Owl*.[159] In the big match against a Rhodesian XV, Harry Taberer, unaffected by the rigours of the journey, fielded brilliantly, and took 5-62 in 38 overs, but failed to prevent a comfortable win. Taberer was to play his only Test as captain of South Africa against the famous 1902 Australians. He enforced the follow-on against Trumper and co., but the match was drawn.

The locals had shipped in a ten-course dinner, including oysters, turtle soup, salmon, chicken, lamb, turkey, pheasant, grouse, wild duck, and an assortment of desserts which even W.G. Grace would have found satisfactory.[160] The amateurs climbed the World's View in the Matopos to indulge in imperial dreams, while the professionals held a sports day and went souvenir hunting. Trott, Cuttell and the others boarded the train armed to the teeth with battle axes and assegais.

Another 60 hours on the train saw Hawke's men back in Kimberley facing a Griqualand West XV. After scoring over 350 last time, the tourists were reduced to 54/9 before Milligan and Archer put on 72

159 *The Owl*, 10/3/1899
160 Gerald Howat, *Plum Warner* (London: Unwin Hyman, 1987) 28

for the final wicket. Haigh took a hat-trick, but Bertie Powell, who had taken 6-48, trumped this with 72 out of 85 while he was at the wicket. His array of shots through the leg side as well as his cutting and driving made this, for Warner, the best innings played against the tourists. Griquas took a 74-run lead before a fascinating contest was ended by a thunderstorm.

The team visited the De Beers compound where the African labour force was incarcerated for the length of their contracts. It was a Sunday and the workers, bribed by additional beer and meat rations, put on a 'dance' which terrorised the tourists. It was, Warner admitted, 'rather a creepy performance'.[161]

The tourists' view of the Cape railways descended even further when the brakes failed and the train rolled backwards down a steep hill, colliding with another train. The collision gave Mitchell two black eyes and dislocated Trott's thumb. They stopped at Matjiesfontein to sample the usual James Logan hospitality and played a friendly. Lohmann bowled beautifully off a short run and batted elegantly despite the advancing symptoms of tuberculosis.

4.7 Class, gender and justice in Cape Town – Logan in court again

Soon after the team's arrival in Cape Town, James Logan, now a Member of the Cape Legislative Assembly, sponsor of and supremo of the tour, was prosecuted for attempted rape on Maud Stevens. She was a young, coloured cleaner employed at Poole's Hotel which he owned. Logan had called her into his room and closed the door. Despite a statement of events from an inevitably frightened Stevens, and support from the hotel manager, Charles Munday, the courts cleared Logan. The hearing was held behind closed doors, and much of the evidence supplied against Logan was dismissed. He blamed the incident on a conspiracy orchestrated by Munday.

After the case, Logan accused Maud of perjury. The alleged crime rested on her own defence of her character. Despite her lawyer arguing that this could not constitute a crime, the magistrate found

---

161 Warner, *Many Climes*, 253

her guilty of intending to make the court believe she was a virtuous woman and imposed a six-month sentence. 'If people of her class were allowed to make such statements,' he said, 'no man would be safe.' Despite ill health she was required to stand in the dock. As a coloured servant facing a member of parliament, Stevens was humiliated and had her reputation formally destroyed. As she told the court, 'I have felt very bitterly through the whole of the matter, the misfortune of being poor.'[162]

Back in Cape Town for the final time, the visitors lost a match to a combined Colleges XXII amid wild excitement. Hawke characteristically demanded that the fixture be expunged from the tour statistics, arguing that it was not on the programme, though it was a substitute for a cancelled match. M.W. Luckin's official history obediently omitted the scores.[163] Hawke was determined to keep his unbeaten record.

The tourists routinely dismissed a Cape Colony XI by an innings and 29 runs, with Haigh getting a hat-trick. Then came the selection issues for the second Test. First was the third fruitless campaign for the selection of 'Krom' Hendricks, ignored despite still being the outstanding performer in Cape cricket. Second, 'Buck' Llewellyn who had been a key performer in the first Test withdrew 'for business reasons'. These were not explained, but it is likely that the sensitive Llewellyn, aware of the racist treatment of Hendricks who shared his antecedence (Dutch father and St Helenian mother) and dependent on professional cricket for his living, may not have wanted his future exposed to the reactionary glare of the Newlands establishment. Western Province continued their antagonism towards 'Barberton' Halliwell, following his support for Hendricks. Port Elizabeth had dropped Halliwell for the abandoned first Test in favour of Prince, so Western Province came up with a crazy compromise, playing both wicketkeepers, Prince and Halliwell, and effectively handing

---

162 *Cape Times*, 24/3/1899, 3/3/99, 6/3/1899, and 7/4/1899
163 Luckin, *History*, 535-546

Murray Bisset, himself an excellent wicketkeeper, a ten-man team.

Wisden described the second Test as a 'truly sensational game'. In front of a record crowd and in glorious sunshine, England batted first and were in charge at 61/1. Then Sinclair, who had not bowled in the first Test, tore the innings apart, ripping out Warner for 31, Tyldesley for 13, and Cuttell, Trott, Milligan and Board for single figures. He made great use of his height and bounce and varied his pace with subtlety and control in claiming 6-26. He was ably supported by Middleton who took 4-18. Nine wickets had fallen for 31 runs, Hawke's men were all out for 92 and the South Africans were ecstatic.

Trott and Haigh were equally threatening on the Cape Town mat, running through the home team apart from Sinclair, whose commanding batting was thrown into sharp relief by the clatter of wickets at the other end. At the close he was undefeated with 59 out of 126/7. The next day, he stepped up his assault by crashing Trott over the ropes and into the pond until Johnny Tyldesley took a brilliant catch on the boundary to dismiss him for 106 out of a total of 177. He had hit 48 out of 51 in less than 30 minutes in front of 7,000 delirious spectators. As Warner put it 25 years later, 'A cricketer … sees innumerable fine innings many of whom are forgotten after a while, but a few will always remain in his memory. In my case Sinclair's 106 will be one of these … the bat looked like a walking stick in Sinclair's hand.'[164]

South Africa led by 85, but Hawke's team were no strangers to fightbacks. Tyldesley's century shepherded the score to an impregnable-looking 330, a lead of 245 as Lord Hawke strolled contently around the ground carrying a Box Brownie camera and taking snaps for a lady friend. Sinclair again had the best South African figures with 3-63 off 31.2 overs. He had taken 9-89 off 43.2 overs and hit 106 out of 177, an achievement of almost unprecedented dominance. But could he sustain this level of performance to bring South Africa their first victory?

---

164 P.F. Warner, *My Cricketing Life*, (London: Hodder and Stoughton, 1924) 106

Faced with a score of 246, he tried the only way he knew. At 27/5 he drove Trott deep to long on, but Milligan reached far back over the ropes and into the crowd and just hung on to the ball with the fingertips of one hand. It was the catch of a lifetime and eight runs later South Africa had collapsed in a shocking tumble of wickets, suffering 'as sensational and decisive a defeat as ever befell a representative team'.[165]

They were routed for 35 in 65 minutes. Schofield Haigh was unplayable, jagging the ball back fiercely from the off to take 6-11. Trott was no less a threat, ending with 4-19. The crowd were stunned into silence. Not for the first time in the series, a tight contest was followed by a humiliating capitulation. As *The Owl* put it, the outcome was 'too bad of Lord Hawke to give our representatives such a liberal supply of rope and pull us up with such a jerk'.[166] The familiarity of this disaster made it even harder to bear.

At the farewell dinner Hawke continued to protest allegations of money-making. They were, he said, 'Here as the guests of Mr Logan who did not care a rap whether he would have to pay up or not.' Given Logan's courtroom battle over his investment with Read and Ash in 1891/92, this may have been questionable. Never one to avoid airing a grudge, Hawke harked back to the professionals' strike and encouraged their employment at the Cape but only to coach youngsters, not to play. The amateurs then headed off to a private dance in their honour.[167]

Hawke was determined to remain unbeaten, ignoring those pesky college students. Trott and Haigh were among the best bowlers in the world and ideally suited to matting wickets. There had been a significant improvement in South African cricket. Sinclair, who topped the test averages with 200 runs at 50, Halliwell, Llewellyn, Kotze, Graham, Bisset and Shalders promised a competitive future.

---

165 *Cape Times*, 5/4/1899
166 *The Owl*, 6/4/1899
167 *Cape Times*, 5/4/1899

For Plum Warner the tour was a triumph, topping the batting averages with a series of well-crafted innings stabilising a team which often struggled on mat, and developed his reputation as leadership material. He wrote up the tour for *The Sportsman* and dedicated his book to his mentor Lord Hawke, who was his best man when he married in 1904.

Albert Trott, treated as a god by the crowds, revelled in the fun and fellowship of the tour. The autocratic Hawke regime was mitigated for the professionals by the snobbishness of the amateurs who travelled and lodged separately, the two camps meeting mainly on the field. Class had its advantages for the lower orders. Perhaps, as Warner put it, with less certainty than a decade earlier, these touring teams did something from a political point of view 'in bringing our cricketing kinsmen across the seas in touch with those of the mother country'. [168] But no longer was cricket binding together the empire. With cordite already crackling in the air, the war clouds closed in.

---

168 Warner, *Many Climes*, 269

PART 2:

EMPIRE AND UNION

5

Googlies: Plum Warner 1905/06

THE WAR which followed Lord Hawke's autocratic sashay across the sub-continent in 1899 was a ruinous and long drawn-out struggle costing the lives of hundreds of thousands of soldiers, and of civilians dying of starvation and disease in the infamous concentration camps.

This bitterest of wars was followed by an uneasy peace. The Treaty of Vereeniging in 1902 ushered in a decade of reconstruction as Lord Milner and the British Colonial Office sought to restore the mining industry as the economic engine of a single new political union. The suffering of the Afrikaner population was to determine South African politics for the rest of the century.

Though this was described as a 'white man's war', hundreds of thousands of black South Africans were involved as combatants and support workers and as civilians suffered most from the conflict. Prime minister Lord Salisbury had promised that after victory, 'Due precaution will be taken for the philanthropic and kindly treatment of these countless indigenous races of whose destiny I fear we have been too forgetful.' His words were empty. Those who had hoped that their sacrifices in the imperial cause would win political and land rights were sadly disillusioned. The peace terms, as Winston Churchill effectively admitted, hung Africans out to dry.[169]

---

169 *South African News*, 17/3/1906

This disappointment gave rise to the South African Native National Congress (SANNC) and a host of new organisations. They became a national presence, and a mushrooming of political and self-help organisations heightened black public and political awareness. Sol Plaatje, the first general secretary of the SANNC, recalled reading the news as a boy to groups of men sewing blankets around the kraals.[170] Africans would need to free themselves.

For whites, the perennial issue remained how to create and maintain a cheap and readily available pool of labour.

As a short-term solution, Britain, having failed to force or entice black workers down the mines, imported thousands of indentured Chinese from 1904. The furore over this policy formed the backdrop to Warner's tour.

5.1 Harry Taberer, cricketer and labour recruiter

Harry Taberer had been appointed chief native commissioner by Rhodes in Rhodesia during the Ndebele and the Shona uprisings against the British South Africa Company regime in 1896/97.[171] Taberer captained Rhodesia against Lord Hawke's tourists and, in 1902, in his only Test, captained South Africa against the Australians. He took one wicket: Victor Trumper.

In 1903, he was appointed secretary of the Lagden Commission set up to establish a subcontinental approach to 'native policy' focused on the mobilisation and control of labour. The commission's report not surprisingly favoured Rhodes' segregationist approach to land tenure. Simply put, reducing African access to land would force labour into the mines and farms, the basic principle behind the 1913 Native Land Act.

Following the repatriation of Chinese labour from 1907, Taberer became head of the Native Recruiting Corporation, delivering millions of African migrant workers across the subcontinent. For the next 30 years, he was a god-like figure at the head of the huge labour recruitment machine for the gold mines. He managed the

---

170 André Odendaal, *Founders,* (Cape Town: Jacana Media, 2012); André Odendaal, *Vukani Bantu!,* 63

171 Ranger, *Revolt*

beating heart of the South African economy and the immiseration of millions of migrant workers.

He personified, perhaps more than anyone in South African history, the heady combination of conquest, imperial and company rule, political and industrial strategy, and administrative organisation on a gigantic scale.[172]

As cricket writer and poet Alan Ross was to discover 50 years later, every Transkei trading station had an adjacent Native Mine Recruiting Organisation shed bearing the legend 'Kwa Teba' ('Here is Taberer').[173]

James Logan promoted a South African cricket tour to England in the middle of the war in 1901 to the disapproval of those such as Arthur Conan Doyle who thought that able-bodied cricketers should be fighting not playing. No representative matches were played. The star attraction was Jimmy Sinclair, who by the age of 25 had played top-level cricket for ten years, served in the British forces, been captured, escaped and had run a refugee camp in the Orange Free State.[174]

After the war, Lord Milner, Abe Bailey and the mining industry drafted in available talent from the subcontinent and abroad. Bailey recruited Frank Mitchell and Reggie Schwarz, who would determine the direction of South African cricket over the next decade. Both had toured North America in 1901 along with Bernard Bosanquet. Jimmy Sinclair and 'Buck' Llewellyn had already displayed a maturity and confidence that would serve as a platform for the successes of the next decade and this was taken to the next level by promising performances against the powerful 1902 Australian tourists.

---

172 *Cape Times*, 'Sports and Sportsmen in South Africa', (Cape Town: Cape Times, 1929) 497

173 Alan Ross, *Cape Summer*, (London: Constable, 1957) 185

174 Captain J.H. Sinclair was commended for the general state of the Springfontein camp as well as innovations such as a regime of daily inspections by a committee comprising inmates. Thanks to Dale Slater for this information.

5.2 *Australia's first visit to South Africa*

The 1902 Australians called in at the Cape on their way home from England where they won the Ashes but lost the fifth Test at The Oval by one wicket. Jessop's whirlwind century turned the game and Rhodes and Hirst, one of history's strongest tenth-wicket pairs, completed the job but not, as legend had it, in singles.

In South Africa, Victor Trumper preserved his status as cricket's Zeus, but his team proved surprisingly human. Conditions were unfamiliar and the opposition competitive. 'Buck' Llewellyn took 25 wickets in the three-match series, a South African record which still stands – his nearest challenger being Duanne Olivier with 24 wickets against Pakistan in 2018/19.

South Africa piled up 454 in the first Test at Johannesburg with 97 from debutant Louis Tancred and 90 from Llewellyn. In reply, Clem Hill hit a hundred before lunch and in the end the game was tantalisingly poised with South Africa on 101/4 chasing 215. In the second Test at the same venue, Jimmy Sinclair scored a breathtaking hundred and Llewellyn took 5-43 to give South Africa a 65-run lead. But despite their individual brilliance, South Africa could not close. An undefeated 159 from Warwick Armstrong dragged the tourists to 309 and the locals collapsed in the second innings for 85.

In the final test, at Newlands, South Africa played under their third captain of the series in 'Barberton' Halliwell. Trumper made a brilliant 70, and South Africa followed on. This did not faze Sinclair, who gave an exhibition of controlled hitting that would have left Jessop open-mouthed. His 104 is a strong candidate for the greatest inning ever played at Newlands, but even he could not save South Africa from a ten-wicket defeat.

Abe Bailey had guaranteed £2,000 and the tourists earned £200 a man for just over a month's work. Bailey and the public were aware of the political significance of two major cricketing powers playing each other for the first time, without England. It pointed towards an equality which Bailey would persuade the ICC to formalise seven years later.

In 1904, the South Africans again toured England under Frank Mitchell. South Africa lost only three of 26 fixtures, and the match against Middlesex ended with Albert Trott sending Kotze's middle stump cartwheeling for a tie. The turning point of the tour was Reggie Schwarz unveiling his googly against Oxford University. He went on to capture 96 victims at an average of under 15. Schwarz was the first to recognise that a method which in England had got wickets partly through novelty value could be lethal on the turning and steep-bouncing matting wickets in South Africa.

Frank Mitchell criticised the weak opposition but for the domestic clubs the County Championship was more important than a touring team. Only the Australians were worthy of Test matches and without internationals the tour was a financial failure. Intriguingly a match against India, to be captained by Ranji, had been arranged but the Indian tour was unfortunately cancelled.[175] Another opportunity missed.

A possible visit by the 1905 Australians was vetoed. The Australians were too expensive and the South Africans too vulnerable. The Cape aristocracy in leafy Newlands felt that the class advantages of a visit from the English establishment far outweighed the Australian professionals. SACA invited MCC who had taken control over tours, but MCC were nervous about the financial risk and worried that South Africa might demand Tests in England.

Bailey and Schwarz negotiated a deal at Lord's under which MCC received a large guarantee and the SACA was responsible for all professional fees and expenses for a 1905/06 tour. As usual South Africa wanted as many good amateurs as possible to oppose their amateurs. But few top English amateurs had the time and resources for a long tour.

Warner believed that while his side was a strong one it would probably lose the Tests. The team included three professionals in David Denton, Schofield Haigh (who had toured with Hawke) and Colin Blythe, who had played in the last Ashes series. The *Cape*

---

175 *Cape Times*, 18/02/1904

Times ran a positive rule over the players: Denton 'has so supple a wrist and so grand an eye'; Haigh 'bowls a snorter ... and cleans bowls a higher proportion than any other man in England'; Crawford 'impresses through his supreme confidence even more than his skill'; Lees 'gets the life from the pitch away swing and back break'; Relf, who had learned his cricket 'on matting in Norfolk, did the double last year'; Lilley's record as stumper 'is second only to Kelly'; and Warner proved 'one of the best batsmen of the year and as captain of a touring team has no superior ... except F. S. Jackson'.[176]

The *Kinfauns Castle* ran into a storm in the Bay of Biscay savage enough to make the ancient mariner blanche. Waves swept over the ship, bulwarks were stove in and windows shattered. Storm over, William Milton, a fellow passenger, was no doubt happy to offer reminiscences and insider advice to the amateurs. Warner was certainly well briefed. He mentioned a triangular tournament in England, already a pet project of Abe Bailey, and paid tribute to Milton who had created 'one of the finest grounds in the world' at Newlands. He acknowledged that the balance of South African cricketing power had shifted to Johannesburg, but the Cape were the pioneers. A new cricketing power had arisen in the southern hemisphere.[177]

Warner was pleased that five Tests were scheduled for the first time. In front of a South African audience, he argued his team was infinitely stronger than Hawke's. All six bowlers had played for England or were on the verge of doing so. Warner said, 'When one has become accustomed to the South African light, the matting and the pace of the ball has no terrors.' And of course, there was a little flattery as he added, 'Taking everything into consideration cricket in South Africa is more pleasant than in Australia.'

Western Province cricket was under a cloud, monopolised by cliques, and the spectators had voted with their feet.[178] Warner was

---

176 *Cape Times*, 18/10/1905

177 *Cape Times*, 29/11/1905

178 *South African News*, 28/11/1905

realistic at the first practice, 'After 17 days on board ship some of us looked as if we had never made a run in our lives ... One young Malay, a fast left-hander, hit my middle stump nearly every ball.' C.J. Nicholls was a 'coloured' professional restricted, like 'Krom' Hendricks, by the WPCU racist constitution from playing senior cricket. He was one among many who were denied a chance to take on the tourists, a cruel fate and desperate waste of talent for an underpowered Western Province.[179] The supposedly lightning-fast J.J. Kotze proved to be out of practice and condition and had his pace compared unfavourably with Hendricks.[180]

Rain had slowed the outfield but sharpened the edges of the mountain. The crowd and the promenade at lunch reminded Warner of Eton versus Harrow. The English team settled in against a pedestrian attack despite the peculiarities of playing on matting: of maintaining footing without getting entangled when stepping out to drive, the different feel of ball on bat, and the bounce, cut and turn that varied with the tightness of the mat. Denton made 78 and Warner, Fane and Relf all made fifties in a total of 365. Only a superb spell of left-arm fast bowling from local professional George Whitehead (6-100) kept the score just the right side of humiliation.[181]

Despite ideal conditions, a nervous and ill-prepared looking Province capitulated to Haigh's reputation in the first innings and Crawford's sharp break and confidence, 'reminiscent of a young Sammy Woods' in the follow-on, losing by an innings and 127 runs. Warner reminded Western Province that they had always done well against English teams – beating Warton in 1888 and Hawke in 1895, drawing (and losing) with Read, while Hawke in 1898 only got home by a short head.

The local verdict was despairing. Cape cricket was 'under a cloud with no silver lining. No new talent, no coaching ... increasingly slow

---

179 For more on Nicholls, see Chapter 8
180 *Cape Times*, 11/12/1905
181 George Whitehead was believed to be a player of colour. For his story, see Winch and Parry, *Too Black to Wear Whites*, 165-172

methods of batsmen would … soon cause it to become as extinct as the dodo.' [182]

5.3 Jim Phillips' last tour

This was Australian umpire Jim Phillips' last tour. The *Cape Times* noted, 'For last few winters he has gone in hot and strong for studying mining engineering at Camborne and for dieting. With regard to the former, he has done remarkably well and as to the latter he has rather overdone it.' As a professional himself, Phillips was called upon to give negative verdicts to professional players with whom he socialised, cricketers likely to have a good growl when losing prizes or having their careers jeopardised but he maintained his popularity through scrupulous fairness.[183]

He was central to the great Victorian throwing controversy. 'None of us will readily forget that afternoon at Old Trafford when [Phillips] proceeded to no-ball Arthur Mold 16 times in ten overs and practically ended his first-class career,' reported the *Manchester Guardian*. 'How the crowd raged and fumed … but he was a splendid official; up at Lord's his integrity was especially appreciated.'[184]

On 14 December, the tourists piled into the railway coach which had been assigned for the duration of the trip, a far cry from the chaotic travel arrangements on previous tours. But as Warner claimed, it 'would be absurd to expect rail travelling in SA to be as comfortable as in England but engineering difficulties and a narrow gauge need not necessarily imply a narrow and extraordinarily hard sleeping berth while it would be easy to provide better bedding'.

They passed through the Hex River Valley, the train climbing into the northern Cape until halted by a swarm of locusts so deep that the track was impassable for several hours. They played twice against Griqualand West, but the Kimberley's star had fallen from the

---

182 *Cape Times*, 19/1/1906
183 *Cape Times*, 6/12/1905; 29/12/1905
184 *Manchester Guardian* quoted in *Cape Times*, 29/12/1905

heady days of the early 1890s. Griqualand West insisted on fielding 15 players. Warner, who was strongly opposed to playing against odds in the main centres, reprised the Hawke playbook, and played 12 but fielded 11. It gave at least one bowler's soles some respite from the burning hot gravel 'field'.

5.4 Warner in the Kimberley labour compound

Warner noted, '[The] compound of the De Beers mine was one of the main attractions of the town, but it did not appeal to some of us who thought it unedifying and not the sort of spectacle one wants to see twice. Hundreds of creatures were yelling and shouting around us as if they were mad and … gave us a war dance which was not very amusing and only raised the dust.

'In the galleries … all was dirt and grime, and half-naked men bathed in perspiration were hammering, shovelling, picking and keeping up a chant which here, echoing about the bowels of the earth, sounded weird and awe-inspiring.'

Warner and his team were clearly intimidated by the African workers, whose frustration as to their own exploitation would have been evident from their performance. It was a time of crisis where insufficient black migrants were available at minimal wages and Warner had been briefed to support the Chinese labour lobby on the gold mines.

Johannesburg was not the same place that Warner, Haigh and Board had visited seven years previously. The war, fought over the mining industry, had almost destroyed it. By 1902, the workings were flooded, machinery ruined and the African workforce had vanished. Africans were not attracted by below subsistence wages, nor was it politically possible to employ whites at less-than-inflated wages. Reconstruction was reliant on importing Chinese labour from 1904.

It wasn't just wages. The *Mining Journal* reported that Rand fatality rates among black miners were the highest in the world with many due to incompetent blasting. Total fatalities in this period amounted to 26 per cent of the work force as opposed to an already high rate of three per cent in the UK.

The *Mining Journal* pointed out, 'Through indifference or parsimony numerous lives are lost which could otherwise have been saved.' It was 'more economical' to pay an occasional fine than invest in life-saving gear such as chain ladders in shafts.

'The slaughter continues while the native is charged with being slothful because he does not want to work in death traps,' wrote *South African News.*[185]

In these circumstances, reconstruction was reliant on importing indentured Chinese labour who had no knowledge of local conditions.

After five easy wins in the Cape the tourists faced their major challenge of the tour at The Wanderers.

Transvaal started poorly in front of a packed crowd and Denton's not out 132 secured a lead of 130. The fightback started with 66 from Shalders and a 46-run ninth-wicket partnership between Aubrey Faulkner (63 not out) and Smith (27). The MCC needed 176 to win against Reggie Schwarz (4-80 and 5-34), who turned his googlies prodigiously off a good length, pitching well outside off to hit or even miss leg stump at pace. Faulkner (3-62), who turned it both ways, had an easy and natural action and disguised his break which came off the mat at medium pace. Warner's MCC crumbled to 115 all out.

Transvaal had achieved the first victory against an English touring team on level terms in South Africa. It was a huge moment in the balance of power.[186]

Eight of the Transvaal team wore South African colours in the first Test. For Warner, the threat from Schwarz was clearly significant but the googly phenomenon was not yet confirmed. Faulkner had taken only two first-class wickets before the Transvaal game. Gordon White took 56 wickets on the 1904 tour but had hardly bowled since and Ernie Vogler had only nine wickets in two seasons. But the Transvaal result had convinced local cricket fans that they were on the verge of something special.

---

185 *South African News*, 11/4/1906
186 *Cape Times*, 30/12/1905

> ## 5.5 Gandhi, cricket, and segregation
>
> Thousands of white spectators crowded into The Wanderers for the first Test. But Johannesburg had a large population of coloured and Malay builders, artisans, and drivers; of African clerks and interpreters; as well as Indian launderers and traders. They were associated with cricketing communities rooted in the Cape, mission schools and Indian traditions and had dozens of clubs. Their treatment by the establishment as potential spectators (playing against them was now beyond the colonial imagination) reflected their place in the reconstructed postwar South Africa.
>
> In 1903, M.K. Gandhi who had recently arrived in the Transvaal, requested admission for coloured spectators. George Allsop said there was insufficient space. A petition raised the issue again in 1905. The chairman, seconded by founder Jacob Swart, moved that the request be referred to the annual meeting in March, when MCC would be long gone. The motion was carried. In September 1906, Gandhi unsuccessfully tried to hire the hall on behalf of the British India Association and in 1912 he requested the room for a reception for visiting members of the Calcutta Legislature, but a response to his request was delayed and he was then told that the hall was already booked.[187]

Perhaps the most sensational Test of the 20th century, rivalled only by Jessop's match in 1902 and the Australia-West Indies tied Test in 1960, took place at the Wanderers from 2–4 January 1906. South Africa's six debutants Faulkner, Schwarz, Sherwell, Snooke, Vogler and White, all of whom would dominate South African cricket in the next decade, joined Sinclair, Nourse, Louis Tancred, Hathorn and Shalders.

It started with a bang. Warner won the toss and took the first ball from Schwarz, which he cut deftly for four, but was tucked up by extreme spin and caught at short leg in Schwarz's second over. Denton slashed at the next ball and was brilliantly held by Faulkner running backwards from slip. Fane gave a chance to Tancred at

---

187 Thelma Gutsche, *Old Gold*, 118

mid-on in Schwarz's third over, escaped, but then steered Faulkner into Schwarz's hands at slip and MCC were in deep trouble at 15/3. Schwarz and Faulkner reprised their performances for Transvaal. The former bowled huge-spinning googlies and top-spinners and the latter mixed googlies with leg breaks.

Wynyard and Hayes consolidated. Wynyard changed his hands on the bat on occasion to counter the sharp break from the off and, according to reports in the *Johannesburg Star*, this 'curious left-handed stroke' helped the ball along with the spin to the boundary. There is seldom anything new in cricket – not even the reverse sweep.

Vogler replaced Faulkner and got Hayes caught and bowled off a skier with his first ball in international cricket. Wynyard perished charging at Schwarz and Relf padded up to White's leg breaks but only kicked the ball into his stumps. Crawford and Haigh used the long handle to put on 48 and England were all out for 184 in 190 minutes, the 19-year-old Jack Crawford top-scoring with 44.

South Africa's much-vaunted batting line-up ran into immediate trouble against Colin Blythe and Walter Lees. Nervous aggression undid the top-order and when Jimmy Sinclair was caught and bowled off the first ball he received from Walter Lees, South Africa were reeling at 39/5. Arthur William 'Dave' Nourse came in at 43/6 and playing with 'nerve and confidence' shepherded the home team to 91, still 93 behind. But it looked like the Transvaal win had been a false dawn.

Schwarz opened the bowling with the fast-medium of 'Tip' Snooke, rather than Faulkner. Fane went quickly, but Denton stroked six fours in his 34 before Faulkner bowled him with a vicious googly. When Vogler bowled Warner for 51, MCC were 113/5 and over 200 ahead. Crawford made a destructive 43 before being bowled by Nourse, who then trapped Haigh in front at 174/7. His figures at this stage were 3-3-0-2. MCC's innings closed shortly after tea on day two for 190, 283 runs ahead.

Given that neither side had made 200 in the match so far, this seemed an unassailable target. After Tancred and Hathorn departed at 22/2, it looked all over. But White and Shalders dug in and South Africa ended the day on 68/2. They needed 216 to win, with eight wickets to fall. South Africa had hope but not much else. Warner, on the other hand, was confident despite the loss of Schofield Haigh with a stomach problem. Lees and Blythe started the day with four maidens. Trying to break the pressure, Shalders went for a quick single off a misfield by Warner at point, White didn't move and Shalders couldn't regain his ground and was out for 38 (68/3). Snooke was soon trapped in front by Lees for nine (81/4). South Africa's Jessop, Jimmy Sinclair was set on emulating the great man's 1902 effort. He drove a four off Lees and lifted the next ball high over the bowler's head. Fane sprinted around the boundary at long-on skipping over the legs of the spectators and brought off a superbly judged catch to dismiss Sinclair for five (89/5). With every run precious, White tickled the ball into the off side, called for a run and wicketkeeper Board chased and threw down a single stump on the turn. The dangerous Faulkner was well short of his ground and out for six (105/6). The locals had shot themselves with their own gun.

South Africa were 178 runs behind with four wickets in hand in a game which had so far averaged around 15 runs per wicket. Even Hope now had its hat and coat on. Nourse and White concentrated on crease occupancy just batting the overs. At 117, Nourse skied the ball over the slips but Crawford running back dropped a difficult chance. After lunch, White reached 50 with a cut to the boundary off a Relf full-toss. Crawford was having a bad day, bowling a succession of rank long hops, and Warner, trying everything, resorted to captain Wynyard's lobs. At 190, Nourse reached his half-century after an hour and a half's batting and Hope sat down on the edge of its seat. Relf finally beat White with a bail trimmer. White's classical and chanceless 81 had added 121 in 136 minutes with Nourse (226/7). It was back to miracle territory when Vogler was clean bowled by Hayes for two (230/8).

Immediately after tea Relf caught and bowled Schwarz for two, throwing the ball high into the air in triumph (239/9). South Africa's captain and wicketkeeper Percy Sherwell, in his first Test – a singles tennis champion away from cricket – strode to the wicket. An unprecedented 45 runs were needed for the win, a thunderstorm hovered overhead, and the air was thick with dust. Sherwell had replaced the ageing Halliwell, still universally acknowledged as a world-class keeper, and probably a better batsman. Sherwell was chosen for his captaincy, but he had not had a good Test so far. The batting order had not worked, the top order being overcrowded with stroke players, his bowling changes were ineffective and his keeping untidy against the googly's sharp turn. He had conceded 23 byes in the English second innings of 190.

'Dave' Nourse said that Sherwell appeared full of confidence. When the odds are so stacked against you, you have nothing to lose. Sherwell placed the last ball of Relf's over calmly to the leg boundary. Runs came quickly and bowling changes veered from the tactical to the panicked. At 259, with 25 needed, Lees came back on and traded maidens with Relf at the other end. Nourse cut Hayes and straight drove Lees for four, Sherwell on-drove him for four more. The tension could have been cut with an axe. One spectator, as cricket tradition dictates on such occasions, gnawed through the handle of his umbrella. The windows of local shops displaying updates were besieged with stressed and wildly excited onlookers.

Sherwell brought up 280 with a snick for four through the slips off Lees. Neither Relf nor Hayes went for it. Relf started a new over. Nourse hit an on-drive, which Sherwell sprinted to turn into three and tie the scores on 283. The spectators flung their hats into the air, the uproar forcing a break in play. Warner's field closed in, vultures round the bat. Ball two was wide of off, Sherwell cut ball three to slip who fumbled it. A 'yes … no … get back' routine in mid-pitch narrowly avoided a disastrous third run out. Ball four was pushed back along the ground, then ball five was a full-toss. Sherwell stepped out and sent it in the direction of the midwicket boundary.

The ball never found the rope. The crowd had already hoisted 'Old Dave' on their shoulders. He finished on 93, an innings of calculated aggression built on sound defence, spiced with pugnacious back-foot drives and a booming square cut. The game was to all intents over when he went in at 105/6 and he kept his head when wickets fell and when apprehension gave way to excitement. He batted for 180 minutes, with 11 fours. It was the innings of a cricketer with ice in his veins.

5.6 Old Dave

'Dave' Nourse remembered the final moments. The MCC team were 'so close that it looked as though they were all on the mat. While watching the ball I was conscious of a sea of faces looking at me, and when at last Relf bowled a full-toss on the leg side to Sherwell, from which the winning hit was made I heard Warner say, "Good God, Bert," and I started to run.' Before Dave could reach the other end, the crowd made a bee line for Sherwell to shoulder him in. He said, 'No, go after Dave.' Dave had made a dash towards the tennis courts but was caught by the crowd and shouldered into the pavilion. It was 'one of the happiest moments of my life' when they at last let him down on firm earth.

Then he had to climb the steps which were packed with celebrating supporters. 'One of the first men I met was George Kempis, who held out his hand to congratulate me' with a gold coin in his palm. 'At least seven congratulated me in a similar fashion before I was halfway up … It was the only time I wished those stairs were another 50 steps higher. In fact, I felt half inclined to go down and come back up again.'[188]

Dave received £100 from a grateful Bailey, a collection worth £87 and sold his bat to The Wanderers. He had taken an excellent catch to get rid of Crawford, had two cheap wickets, and scored 18 not out and 93 not out. He was at the beginning of 45 consecutive Test matches between 1902 and 1924. He was still playing at the age of 57 when he made 55 for Western Province against the 1935/36 Australians that included Bill O'Reilly. The 'Grand Old Man of South African cricket' filled in his time between representative appearances as a soldier, railway guard, billiard marker, saloon keeper, commercial traveller, manager of an athletic outfitters, coach to Cape Town University, and father to Dudley, one of South Africa's greatest batsmen.

---

188 A.W. Nourse, 'A Peep into the Past' in M.W. Luckin, *South African Cricket*, 1919–1927, (Johannesburg: published by the author, 1929) 49-57

A shell-shocked but still articulate Warner summed up, 'In all my years of experience of cricket, I have never seen a side fight a better game than yours, and though beaten and naturally the first person to be sorry, yet I am also the first person to appreciate the magnificent and splendid pluck which has brought victory to you.'

He made his excuses, the absence of Haigh on the crucial last day and Crawford's lack of form with the ball, but the batting was the real disappointment. Warner said, '[The] leg break bowlers were extraordinarily difficult to play on matting wickets as the ball turns twice as quickly and bounces. It was extremely difficult to jump out and drive while there was the danger that one might find one's right leg caught in the end of the mat, and the intended drive end up in an uncomfortable straddle.' South Africa's all-round strength meant England never had the game won, despite experience suggesting any other result was a virtual impossibility.

SOUTH AFRICA v ENGLAND First Test, The Wanderers, 2–4 January 1906

ENGLAND

P.F. Warner*	c Snooke b Schwarz	6	b Vogler	51
F.L. Fane	c Schwarz b Faulkner	1	b Snooke	3
D. Denton	c Faulkner b Schwarz	0	b Faulkner	34
E.G. Wynyard	st Sherwell b Schwarz	29	b Vogler	0
E.G. Hayes	c and b Vogler	20	c Schwarz b Snooke	3
J.N. Crawford	c Nourse b Sinclair	44	b Nourse	43
A.E. Relf	b White	8	c Sherwell b Faulkner	17
S. Haigh	b Faulkner	23	lbw b Nourse	0
J.H. Board	not out	9	lbw b Faulkner	7
W.S. Lees	st Sherwell b White	11	not out	1
C. Blythe	b Sinclair	17	b Faulkner	0
Extras		16	Extras	31
Total		**184**		**190**

Schwarz	21-5-72-3	8-1-24-0
Faulkner	22-7-35-2	12.5-5-26-4
Sinclair	11-1-36-2	5-1-25-0
Vogler	3-0-10-1	11-3-24-2
White	5-1-13-2	4-0-15-0
Nourse	1-0-2-0	6-4-7-2
Snooke		12-4-38-2
Fall of Wickets	6, 6, 15, 53, 76, 97, 145, 147, 159, 184	3, 55, 56, 73, 113, 166, 174, 185, 190, 190

SOUTH AFRICA

L.J. Tancred	c Board b Lees	3	c Warner b Blythe	10
W.A. Shalders	c Haigh b Blythe	4	run out	38
C.M.H. Hathorn	b Lees	5	c Crawford b Lees	4
G.C. White	c Blythe b Lees	8	b Relf	81
S.J. Snooke	c Board b Blythe	19	lbw b Lees	9
J.H. Sinclair	c and b Lees	0	c Fane b Lees	5
G.A. Faulkner	b Blythe	4	run out	6
A.W. Nourse	not out	18	not out	93
A.E.E. Vogler	b Crawford	14	b Hayes	2
R.O. Schwarz	c Relf b Crawford	5	c and b Relf	2
P.W. Sherwell*	lbw b Lees	1	not out	22
Extras		10	Extras	15
Total		**91**	**9 wickets**	**287**

Lees	23.1-10-34-5	33-10-74-3
Blythe	16-5-33-3	28-12-50-1
Crawford	7-1-14-2	17-4-49-0
Haigh		1-0-9-0
Relf		21.5-7-47-2
Wynyard		3-0-15-0
Hayes		9-1-28-1
Fall of Wickets	5. 11, 13, 35, 39, 43, 44, 62, 82, 91	11, 22, 68, 81, 89, 105, 226, 230, 239

South Africa won by 1 wicket

Both teams partied long into the night at Abe Bailey's and amid the hangovers next day was the satisfied sense that South Africa, through tenacity and perseverance, had come of age. Even the news of the election of the Liberals under Campbell-Bannerman on a platform of ending Chinese labour could not dampen spirits on the Witwatersrand. Bailey said they knew Warner was going to Australia to collect the Ashes and hoped that in a year or two Warner would come back to South Africa for the same purpose. The Ashes would, he implied, be contested for among these three teams and not just between England and Australia.

For Bailey, this victory was a historical opportunity to change the face of international cricket. South Africa would be an equal part of the sporting triumvirate with Australia and England, effectively a full and independent partner in empire. He was to spend the rest of the decade working towards the foundation of the Imperial Cricket Conference and its flagship triangular tournament, which would finally take place in 1912.

But not everyone was happy. In Cape Town on the same day, secretary general Dr Abdurahman's speech to the ('coloured') African Political Organisation pointed out that when a coloured man thought of South Africa today, he could not feel anything but depressed at his miserable wretched home. Abdurahman quoted Abe Bailey as saying, 'If the coloured man thought himself equal to the whites there would be a bloody racial war in the country.'[189]

The South Africans had learnt from their blunders in the field and nerve-jangling performance with the bat in the previous Test in 1899. A new generation of South Africans had arrived. Only Jimmy Sinclair was still representing South Africa, while three MCC players – Warner, Haigh and Board – had appeared in that game. Amid the general euphoria, the resolutely anti-Transvaal *Cape Times* criticised the Bailey-engineered inclusion of his 'private secretary' Reggie Schwarz who was not South African-born, had represented Middlesex in the summer and arrived a few weeks earlier to find a place 'had

---

189 *South Africa News*, 10/1/1906

been snugly kept for him'.[190] Plum Warner needed to snatch back the momentum. Instead, with a two-month break between Tests, he met SACA to discuss playing against odds. He argued that anything other than 11-a-side reduced the cricket to a farce, was inappropriate in major centres like Port Elizabeth and if the objective was to ensure games went the distance, hours of play should be cut. He went on to suggest that The Wanderers act as the MCC of South Africa. He claimed his sole object was the future welfare of SA cricket while waving a red flag at PE and the Western Cape cricket establishment.

PE's *Cape Daily Telegraph* was unhappy, 'Mr Warner is taking upon himself the role of dictator ... By offering to curtail the hours ... Mr Warner has no feelings for the paying public. As for odds, the team broadly represents the population of England and it is ridiculous to expect a population of 15,000 Europeans to pit itself against it on equal terms.'[191]

On the train through Natal, J.C. Hartley regaled his team-mates with his memories of his storming Pieter's Hill with the Royal Fusiliers. The veteran Pieter de Villiers, who had taken 5-56 against MCC, had been captured in this exchange and sent to a prisoner of war camp in Ceylon. He had no intention of fighting another war. Next time he would stay at home and sell horses.

Once in Durban, despite a superb hundred from Dave Nourse, an even better innings according to Jim Phillips than he had played in the Test, and two lively spells of fast left-arm bowling, Natal lost by four wickets before a 7,000-strong crowd. Nourse, who played the 'big drum' in the Durban Light Infantry Band, received yet another collection, this time of £46. He did not forget the band bugler boys, who were the delighted recipients of £10.

Warner compared Nourse with the great left-handers such as Clem Hill and Joe Darling. On the bowlers, he said, 'Faulkner was one of the very best bowlers we have met. He bowled the leg break too fast to jump out to the pitch of the ball. That Reggie Schwarz

---

190 *Cape Times*, 6/1/1906
191 *Cape Times*, 24/1/1906

puzzled us was obvious to any observer, but I think we should not find him so difficult next time.'[192]

Plum should not have been too puzzled. He was the godfather of the googly. He had captained both Bernard Bosanquet and Reggie Schwarz at Middlesex while Bosanquet was developing his googly. Bosanquet was Warner's secret weapon in 1903/04, winning the Ashes under his captaincy with a spell of 5-12 in the fourth Test. Bosanquet took 9-107 for a strong MCC and Ground team and had Schwarz stumped for a duck. Schwarz himself learnt the delivery from his close friend, who named his newsreader son after Reggie, and unveiled the googly himself for the first time against Oxford University, taking five wickets. Three games later, Bosanquet made a hundred for Middlesex, and Schwarz took 5-48 for the South Africans, trapping Warner lbw. The match ended in a thrilling tie.

Warner 'hoped and believed' that with four Tests to go they would win the rubber. Privately, Warner must have doubted that his team's batting was equal to the task. He feared that he was unable to deal with Schwarz's vicious turn from off to leg at pace off the matting wicket and became fixated on the googly, while ignoring the serious threat from the quicker bowlers, 'Tip' Snooke and Jimmy Sinclair.

The tourists headed for East London and the scenic part of the tour playing against odds in King William's Town (the depleted army garrison), Queenstown (the centre for African labour recruitment for the mines), Cradock (the wool industry base), Grahamstown (the educational capital of the Eastern Cape) and two games in Port Elizabeth.

Cricket had made significant strides in Johannesburg and Natal, but Warner saw no progress in the smaller towns. In King William's Town, he wondered why they had to play such 'an appallingly weak team, the exhibition we made of them cannot serve any useful purpose' and their 'sorry display would have disgraced any ordinary village second XI'. His frustrations came from many days on the road, playing against non-cricketers clogging up the field and lengthening the interminable batting order. In Port Elizabeth, they had to adjust

---

192 *Cape Times*, 5/2/1906

to a slow, matting wicket on grass, the precise opposite of what they were to face shortly in the next Test in Johannesburg.

Johannesburg was in a frenzy of excitement for the second Test. There was a row over umpiring and an overnight thunderstorm produced a slower wicket favouring the visitors, but neither this nor excellent fielding and good bowling could disguise the abysmal English batting. Warner, Denton, Board and Haigh scored a dozen runs in the whole match. For South Africa, nine batmen reached double figures in the first innings total of 277, lit up by a whirlwind 66 from Sinclair. The googly bowlers were outbowled by the fast-medium Snooke (who dismissed Warner for two and nought) and Sinclair. The South African victory by nine wickets showed that they were a multifaceted team strong enough to be successful in any conditions against any opponents. Warner's men were outplayed in all departments.

5.7 Plum Warner and Chinese labour

The Tests were punctuated by a visit to the Simmer and Jack mine where 4,000 Chinese miners were employed (100,000 indentured Chinese were transported to the Rand between 1904 and 1907). Warner arrived to a crescendo of criticism from both sides – racists howling 'yellow peril' and UK liberals alleging 'slavery'. But MCC's weight was solidly behind the Rand mining industry.

When Warner's tour spent two hours in the Chinese labour compound, he praised the Bath House with *hot and cold water* [Warner's emphasis], delicious looking boiled beef with gravy, carrots, Chinese rice and vermicelli, and large airy rooms though the wooden bunks would not appeal to 'you and me'. New arrivals were paid a shilling a day for the first six months. Warner saw no evidence of 'slavery' in his two hours in the compound

A shilling a day was equivalent to half a cup of tea (costing two shillings) at the Carlton Hotel where Warner was staying. Thanks to its shilling a day indentured Chinese labour force, the mining industry led by Lord Harris' Consolidated Goldfields paid out dividends of around 100% on investments for 1905. With the Liberals in power, Chinese indentured labour was on borrowed time. Harry Taberer and the Chamber of Mines and the colonial government had to develop new plans were developing new plans for forcing black labour on to the mines.

The tourists had to win the third Test to have a chance of saving the series. South Africa won the toss. All 11 batsmen got into double figures and the last five wickets put on 176 runs in a total of 385. Major contributions came from Gordon White (46) and Dave Nourse (61) who built a platform for Maitland Hathorn's stylish 102. Walter Lees bowled beautifully to take 6-78 but without support. England's reply of 295 was dominated by Fred Fane's 143. South Africa used eight bowlers, flaunting their embarrassment of all-rounders, with Snooke and Schwarz taking four wickets each.

With a 90-run lead, South Africa's batsmen expressed themselves. Louis Tancred stroked a polished 73, Dave Nourse contributed a pugnacious 55, and Sinclair hit 48. But Gordon White batted on a different level. He drove with awesome power, timing the ball with uncanny precision. It was the innings played by a cricketing god at the peak of his powers. His chanceless 147 out of 349/5 declared was the highest and unanimously agreed to be the best innings played by a South African in a Test match.

The tourists disintegrated. They missed four straightforward catches, and according to the *South African Cricket Annual*, 'Their defence was not worthy of men of such reputations.'[193] Behind by more than 400, only David Denton with 61 had the resilience to resist and South Africa had won their third Test in a row by 243 runs.

White's sublime innings has overshadowed Snooke's performance. In a team stuffed with high-quality spin bowling, on the batsman-friendly matting wicket, 'Tip' Snooke's figures of 31.4-8-70-8 in the second innings and 53-9-127-12 in the match were nothing short of sensational. Snooke hurried the batsman with his pace and bounce and captured six of his wickets with balls that moved away with the arm. South Africa had not won a Test before this tour. Now they had won three in a row and secured a five-Test series with two matches still to play. Abe Bailey wasted no time in cabling London regarding the planned 1907 tour and demanded three Tests against a full-

---

193 J.T. Henderson (ed), *South African Cricketers' Annual*, 1906/07
(Pietermaritzburg: Times Publishing, 1907) 165

strength England side. South Africa would soon be an equal imperial partner with Australia and England. Bailey's ship had come in.

MCC made a brief visit to Bloemfontein. Reconciliation was not advanced when the cricketing veteran and ardent Afrikaner nationalist Charles Fichardt took a bouncer from Haigh in the face. Then it was back to Cape Town on a more comfortable train paid for by gate profits. The South Africans had a week getting used to conditions at Newlands; England returned with a day to spare.

Nothing pulls in politicians like sporting success and the first day of the fourth Test saw the governor, the chief justice, the prime minister, several ministers and the leader of the opposition crammed in with 7,000 enthusiasts. A cinematographer took up a position at third man and the crowd whistled an accompaniment as he filmed the partnership of Aubrey Faulkner and Gordon White for an audience 6,000 miles away. Hartley's tobacco distributed free samples, but the loud gentleman on stilts served no purpose whatsoever.

Sherwell won a toss he would have been better to lose and Colin Blythe, on a rain-softened wicket, sent back five South Africans for seven runs with only 44 on the board. Blythe kept a precise length, extracted significant turn from leg, and sent down a deadly straight ball with no discernible change of action. The god-like Sinclair tried to drive one that bounced, was beautifully caught by Board and left very slowly dragging his bat. This was followed by a trademark lower-order recovery, which Lees tried to stem by bowling wide outside off to an eight-man off side field. White was caught at the wicket for 41, Faulkner went for 34 and Snooke and Schwarz then added 63 in a merry 45 minutes. Schwarz hit Blythe over the trees on to the railway line and Snooke was last out for 44 in a respectable total of 218.

On the following day, the tourists fought to within 20 runs of the South African total. When South Africa batted again, White launched a one-man show putting immense power into his off drives, cutting delicately and pulling fiercely. 'He would,' said Warner, 'have been welcomed by any eleven in the world.' Finally, he was bowled by a shooter from Lees for 73 sublime runs out of a total of 97/5 at stumps.

Colin Blythe wrapped up the South African innings for 138 the next day, setting England 159 to win. The pitch had little in it for the googly bowlers. Schwarz was used for two overs, and Vogler not until the match virtually over. From a winning position with the tourists floundering on 34/3 and Hayes ill, overconfidence overcame the locals and Fane was able to lead his team home with a fighting unbeaten 66. The local press castigated the fielding. Hard drives and cuts passed unhindered, and pick-ups and returns were unreliable and inaccurate.

A relieved Warner noted that his MCC had now won all three games at Newlands. He admitted they had struggled badly at The Wanderers where South Africa were the better team, with no tail and bowlers able to make the ball talk. England believed they had a better than even chance in the fifth Test, again at Newlands, due to start three days later.

Warner won the last toss of the series, but within five minutes had lost the advantage. His first ball from Schwarz was a slow off break which curved round his half-raised bat into his wicket. It was the shot of an exhausted man mesmerised by a bowler who had destroyed his self-belief. Then Snooke bowled Denton to reduce England to 5/2. The teenage Jack Crawford less trammelled by doubt came to the rescue with a faultless display of free hitting, but when he played on to Sinclair for 74, the innings tailed away to a below-par 187.

South Africa, the team without a tail, again showed their strength as a batting unit. Honours were even at 87/4 with Nourse and Sinclair together at close of play. The next day, a Saturday, saw 10,000 noisy enthusiasts shoehorned into the ground. They were rewarded by a day of varying fortunes, falling hopes and brilliant batting. Sinclair swiped mightily at the first ball of the day – a yorker from Blythe – but was a split second too late and South Africa were 100 runs behind with five wickets in hand. Rumour had it that Nourse had a fiver at 25/1 on a fifty and he batted patiently against Crawford until caught for 36 at slip by Relf off the keeper's gloves. Snooke (60) and Faulkner (45) produced some stylish hitting but, when the ninth wicket fell, South Africa were only 52 ahead, and in deep trouble.

But this was a special team and Vogler partnering Sherwell proved yet again the depth of South African talent. Vogler's magnificent driving relied on timing rather than force. One hit disturbed the wood pigeons in the trees near the entrance, a second landed near the pond and a third was deposited into the hat of a delighted spectator. An hour's hitting turned the game and the last-wicket stand of 94 was only ended by a leaping one-handed catch by Blythe at mid-on. Fittingly, the series had concluded with another game-changing, tenth-wicket partnership. Vogler's 62 not out from number 11 earned a £47 collection.

The demoralised tourists, 146 behind on the first innings, were disposed of for 130. Apart from a pretty 33 from Moon, the team had nothing left to give. Five hundred spectators arriving at 10.35am on a train from Cape Town and hoping for some last-ditch English resistance on the last day saw two balls and the players walking off the field.

Warner's men had played 24 games, won 16 and lost five. They had lost four out of the five matches that mattered, one by the narrowest of margins. Previously, South Africa had played a total of 11 Tests (status retrospectively awarded) against five touring teams. This was South Africa's first five-Test series, which gave the home players who lacked domestic competition a chance to find a rhythm and build their strengths. It put unprecedented strain on the resources of the touring team. South Africa achieved the rare feat of using the same 11 players for the whole series. No previous South African team had been able to get its best side on to the field, let alone retain them for five Tests. The stability of selection relied on a semi-professional system under Bailey's patronage where players were given cricket-related jobs or sinecures such as Dave Nourse's regimental band.

South Africa also escaped significant injury. As befits a touring team, England were beset by illness, injury and exhaustion were constant companions. In four months they played 66 days of cricket and travelled 5,348 miles by rail. Too many games and too many miles, said Warner, who designed a schedule for succeeding tours to minimise travelling at night and the matches against odds. They had spent 22 nights braking, jolting, and shunting in miniature sleeping accommodation on the narrow-gauge rail network. Four out of the five Tests were shoehorned into the last five games of the tour. The tourists put in a Herculean effort to secure the fourth Test but collapsed, completely out of puff, in the fifth. The South Africans were simply the better team.

5.8 The Manx Cat

Once the fifth wicket falls, a fielding side can hope to wrap things up. But in the seven innings when all 11 South Africans batted in the series, the first five wickets contributed 588 runs at an average of 17 per wicket, while the last five wickets scored 1,031 at the astonishing average of more than 30, far greater than the top five in either team. The last five wickets outscored the front five in five out of seven innings. This was a source of excruciating frustration for the fielders and a winning platform for the batsmen.

The remarkable difference between the performances of the top and bottom five reflected the nine all-rounders plus a batsman-wicketkeeper in the South African team. The batting order was stable over the series. After Nourse's heroics in the first Test, he replaced Snooke in the top four, and the only other changes were in the bottom three where Sherwell shuffled himself, Schwarz and Vogler. This worked no matter what the combination. The top five apart from White and Nourse, who averaged 54 and 48, respectively, underperformed as a unit. They were propped up by the batting of Snooke, Sinclair, Sherwell and Vogler.

Cricket is a team game played by individuals. But it is also played in pairs and the partnerships down the order tell the real story. While the top-order was vulnerable to the tireless Lees and Blythe who took 65 per cent of the wickets, the rest of the batsmen fought, not necessarily through huge partnerships, but by a refusal to collapse. The partnerships for the sixth to the tenth wickets in the last innings of the fifth Test epitomised this fight – 53, 42, 44, 13 and 94. As Warner said, 'Like a Manx cat, they had no tail.'[194]

---

194 *South Africa News*, 11/4/1906

Interestingly, the tourists were also surprisingly adhesive down the order. In their nine completed innings, 982 runs were scored for the first five wickets at an average of 22 and 706 for the last five at an average of 16. But this said more about the failure of the top five batsmen. Only Fane and Crawford averaged over 30 and only Relf and Moon over 20. Warner made an embarrassing 89 in ten innings, with a top score of 51, averaging less than nine; Denton averaged 17.2 and Hayes 13.8. These were the top three tourists in the previous English summer with first-class batting averages of 43, 42 and 35, respectively.

Conventional wisdom was that the googly bowlers won it. They certainly got inside Warner's head. Schwarz destroyed him five times in the eight innings he faced him, four times for single figures, and Vogler and Faulkner got him once each in his ten innings. But overall, despite the huge difficulty of playing googlies on matting, the medium-pacers – Snooke (24), Sinclair (21) and Nourse (six) – took 51 wickets between them against 44 from the spinners – Schwarz (18), Faulkner (14), Vogler (nine), White (two) and Shalders (one). The tourists thought Vogler the least predictable and best of the bowlers though – his strike rate (62 balls per wicket) and average (22) did not bear this out, but his day was still to come.

It was a matter of horses for courses. The first three Tests were at The Wanderers. In the critical first Test, the four googly bowlers took 14 wickets (Schwarz 3-96, Faulkner 6-61) from 71 per cent of the overs bowled. Then the tourists had two months to let their paranoia about googlies take root. In the second Test on the same Wanderers pitch, the spinners defeated 11 English batsmen (Schwarz 6-46) and in the third Test only five (Schwarz 5-98). Schwarz didn't take a wicket in the fourth-Test loss in Cape Town, where Warner dropped himself down the order to avoid him, but got four in the fifth Test, including Warner twice. What went around came around for the godfather of the googly who, in battling his personal demons, might have lost sight of the real dynamics of the Test matches.

Despite the heroics of White, Nourse, Sherwell, Vogler and Schwarz, the man of the series was the unobtrusive 'Tip' Snooke, whose fast-medium away swing snared 24 wickets at an average of 15 and economy rate of 2.54, and who in addition scored 190 runs in seven innings at an average of 27. Snooke played initially as a batsman and didn't bowl in the first innings of the series. But ultimately all 11 players contributed in a variety of roles, stepping up when it really mattered. It was a rare moment in Test cricket and MCC back home did not see it coming, or as Warner perhaps suspected, simply did not care.

South Africa did. The legacy of bitterness created by the war required reconciliation and South African cricket as the cultural arm of the mining industry needed to express itself as a unifying force. Politically, the road to South African union was under way, only Nourse and Schwarz were born outside South Africa, and the team was an important piece in the unification jigsaw. Warner noted, 'The cricket matches had done a great deal more to bring together the two great races [Dutch and English] of South Africa than all the efforts of the politicians.' It was to be highly significant for South African cricket and for the nation itself over the next 65 years. It provided the platform for Abe Bailey's efforts in conjunction with Lord Harris to ensure that South Africa was accepted as an equal member of the Test triumvirate and as a cornerstone of the empire.

The 1905/06 tour showcased a team performance by an almost uniquely talented group of 11 players. The series was threaded through with Warner's nightmares about the googly bowlers, and his old colleague Reggie Schwarz. But appropriately the googly, itself a master of disguise, was a red herring drawing Warner's fevered attention away from the weaknesses (notably the top-order) and strengths of the opposition. On his return, he insisted that the next team to tour should have a genuinely fast bowler and as many leg break bowlers as could be found.

By the next Test series, the foundations of the new Union, resting on African labour control and exploitation, had been laid. The conundrum of a large indigenous population, yet insufficient unskilled labour willing to work for starvation wages, was a perennial frustration to the colonists. But the Chinese labour experiment was over, and Natal's colonial regime ruthlessly enforced a poll tax along with a hut tax aimed at driving Zulus into the labour market.

Colonial divide and rule policy used the traditional authorities to enforce the tax system. Chief Mgaqkwa said his people were unable to pay. The Natal secretary for native affairs, H.W. Winter, told a convocation of chiefs that the 'cows the government was milking had run dry, but it was necessary that the pots should be filled, and it was for the natives to help the government just as the white man had'. Ten days' work on the railway in the districts by their subjects would provide the means.

Zulu communities reluctant or unable to send all their able-bodied males as migrant labour in the white economy fought back. The Natal military were hard pressed and Abe Bailey himself organised and sent 100 sharpshooters and 200 infantrymen 'Rosebuds' recruited from Yorkshire and Lancashire. The Bambatha rebellion, which started in the Greytown District between the first and second Tests, became the focus of resistance. Chief Bambatha and his followers hid in the Nkandla Forest on the border of Zululand and had to be starved out. Meanwhile the Natal police under Col. Leuchars destroyed his untended huts and crops. 'The hills tonight are marked by the glowing embers of the ruins. Bambatha's country has been desolated,' Leuchars reported.[195]

Bambatha was murdered in June at Mome Gorge, and his death was the catalyst for a further wave of resistance, again brutally suppressed. By the end of the rebellion at least 3,500 Africans had been killed, 4,000 jailed and a similar number lashed. Bambatha's rebellion was the last significant act of traditionally based armed resistance against the colonial regime in South Africa. By 1909, the number of Africans from Natal and Zululand working on the Rand increased by 59 per cent, and 80 per cent of adult males in Zululand were migrant workers.[196]

---

195 *Ibid*
196 Omer Cooper J.D., *History of South Africa*, (London: James Currey, 2nd edn., 1994) 154

6

Union and Lobster:
Henry Leveson Gower 1909/10

IN SOUTH Africa, the grand reconciliation of Union was under way. Britain sought to placate the Afrikaners and build a united and imperial white South Africa. This meant white advantages and an economy built on cheap migrant labour, which would inevitably require the removal of African rights to land ownership, political engagement and freedom of movement.

After the war, General Smuts asked the British High Commissioner, Sir Alfred Milner, to defer the question of African enfranchisement until after the granting of responsible government to the colonies. Milner agreed. He saw political equality for blacks as undesirable and in 1905 set up the Lagden Commission which offered the guiding principles for what would become apartheid. As Milner offensively but accurately put it, 'You only have to sacrifice the "nigger" absolutely, and the game is easy.'[197]

6.1 Africans and the road to Union

Even though no South Africans officially attended, the 1900 London Pan-African Conference sent a petition to The Queen listing South African grievances, including the compound system, indentured labour, forced labour on public works, passes and the

---

197 Mostert, *Frontiers*, 1263, 1273

restriction of African land and voting rights.[198] By 1907, separatist 'Ethiopian' church movements as well as traditionalist revolts such as Bambatha continued to counter the message that white domination and control were necessary and inevitable.

The white movement leading to Union called for a uniform 'native policy' throughout the subcontinent. *Izwi Labantu* editor A.K. Soga described the movement as part of a grand design for a capitalist-dominated South Africa, controlled by Rand magnates and based on cheap labour. He warned, 'Unless some miracle happens to fend off federation under their auspices … this will be a glorious country for corporate pythons and political puff-adders, forced labour and commercial despotism, but no fit place for free men to live in.'

But some still hoped that Britain would ensure that African rights would be respected. Britain's betrayal of Africans lay in their decision to leave African interests to the tender mercies of a self-governing South Africa.

Plum Warner's humiliation resonated across the empire and the alliance between mining capital and state-building in South Africa underpinned the decision in 1907 to play Tests against anyone other than Australia for the first time in the UK. Bailey and Lord Harris seized the moment and MCC granted equal status to South Africa on and off the pitch, a development which was to structure relations between MCC and the South African cricket and political establishment until 1968.

In 1907, Bailey achieved his political objective. On the pitch, England captain R.E. Foster noted that the tour would be remembered for the miserable weather, the soft wickets and the South Africans' googly quartet. They proved that googly bowling was not only possible on soft turf wickets, but the ball still turned quickly, and the variable pace and bounce were more difficult than on hard wickets.

---

198 Odendaal, *Vukani Bantu!*, 86-87

6.2 Deconstructing the googly bowlers

On the 1907 tour, Reggie Schwarz claimed 143 wickets at 11.51 (9 at 21.3 in the Tests). Disdaining deception, his weapon was in plain sight. He only bowled googlies spinning from off to leg, there was little variation in the flight and the challenge was to counter the sharp pace off the pitch and the degree of turn. Vogler (15 wickets at 19.7) was, according to Foster, the finest bowler of the quartet, and relied on variations in pace, and deception in flight and turn. He was a bowler of 'infinite variation and unbounded resource', bowling fast-medium off-cutters, swerve, and slow-medium top-spinners as well as breaking both ways with an almost identical action.

Faulkner (12 at 18.2) and White (4 at 31.7) were 'to all intents the same bowler', but Faulkner was more dangerous, quicker through the air and off the pitch, and with greater degree of turn. Foster was concerned with the threat posed to batting. As googly bowling improved, 'the wonderful drives of some of our great batsmen will become a thing of the past' (Sherwell stumped Hayward three times as he advanced to drive) and the result will be a combination of rigid defence and risky hitting.[199]

The googly threatened to turn the period into a golden age of innovative bowling rather than classical batsmanship. Following the long, drawn-out and brutal South African conflict, the country now needed to present itself as forward-looking and innovative, contributing like Australia and Canada in the senior common room of the empire. Schwarz not only recognised the significance of the googly; he became its key proponent on the mat and anthill wickets of the Transvaal as well as the wet wickets of a miserable English summer. Schwarz was a key figure even without ball in hand. His role as private secretary to Abe Bailey linked cricket and the South African political economy just as had the collaboration of Rhodes and Milton, which 25 years previously refined the concept of segregation through cricket. The Bailey-Schwarz alliance built South African cricket into a dynamic force, an advertisement for investment and a promise of the coming Union as a stalwart of empire.

199 R.E. Foster. South African Bowling (1908) in Benny Green, *The Wisden Papers*, 84-92

Losing the three-Test series 1-0 in England was disappointing, but only Snooke and Faulkner averaged over 30 on damp turf wickets. The tourists were understandably apprehensive at Lord's in their first Test outside South Africa and left reeling by a partnership of 145 for the sixth wicket in 75 minutes between Len Braund and Gilbert Jessop. Vogler excelled with figures of 7-128 in a total of 428. Percy Sherwell, having promoted himself to open, batted superbly to make only the second hundred by a keeper in Test history and South Africa hung on for a draw.

Colin Blythe's 15-99 dismantled South Africa in the dismally damp second Test at Leeds where every run was worth its weight in gold. Faulkner's 6-17 reduced England's first innings to 76 all out, but the tourists were unable to build on a small first-innings lead and ultimately fell 53 runs short of the 129 needed for victory. The final Test at The Oval featured a masterly 129 from C.B. Fry who had worked out how to play the googly bowlers. South Africa had to chase an unlikely 256 at 96 runs an hour to save the series and ended on 159/5.

South Africa's googly bowlers had proven themselves. But it was the overall variety of their attack, including J.J. Kotze, Snooke, Nourse and Sinclair, which, as in 1905/06, constituted its real strength. Plum Warner had been fixated on the googly and even Sherwell tended to see the googly as his strike weapon, under-bowling Sinclair, Snooke and Nourse. The weather gave the speedy Kotze little opportunity and while the tailless batting order was still intact, it was nullified by the wet wickets.

The 1909/10 MCC tour came at a critical moment in South African political history and MCC needed to be led by a safe pair of hands. Surrey's Henry 'Shrimp' Leveson Gower fitted the bill. After Warner's near meltdown, MCC employed a player-diplomat who was worth more than his runs. He was considered an experienced batsman and an excellent captain. (The row in 1909 when Jack Crawford was expelled from Surrey was overlooked.)

Before leaving, Leveson Gower asked W.G. Grace how he would have played the googly bowlers. The Old Man stroked his beard thoughtfully. 'I would have played them on their merits,' he said.

Leveson Gower's country house credentials were impeccable, he even stayed with the archbishop of Cape Town in Bishop's Court when the tour ended.

The team as selected included the six amateurs requested by the South African Cricket Union, including captain E.G. Wynyard, who had done much of the organising, Fred Fane who had been successful on the previous tour, and eight professionals. The MCC sought to match South Africa's batting line-up. In the absence of a googly bowler, they moved the novelty index way past the Schwarz setting in selecting the lob bowler George Simpson-Hayward.

Jack Hobbs and Bert Strudwick started their journey to South Africa by stopping a donkey barrow in the street and marching solemnly behind it to their local station.[200] On board the *Saxon*, Leveson Gower hobnobbed with two of the conspirators in the Jameson Raid 13 years previously. Mining supremo Lionel Phillips had been bought out of a death sentence following the Raid, then spent a decade holed up in his English country estate. Rhodes' ubiquitous old crony, 'Dr Jim' Jameson, recently prime minister of the Cape colony and minister of lands in the Transvaal, was the inspiration for Kipling's *If*. 'Shrimp' got an extended first-hand briefing on the state of the mining industry and the dynamics of the road to Union, now only a few short months away. The skipper's brief was to reinforce the British requirement for a strong and loyal Union.

For Hobbs, who was allergic to the sea, the voyage was a cake walk in comparison to the trip to Australia. At the fancy dress ball, Bert Strudwick (Struddy) dressed in a monkey skin (with Simpson-Hayward as an Italian organ-grinder) and leapt agilely from table to table gibbering wildly at the ladies. Colin Blythe had a more cerebral cruise playing violin in the ship's orchestra.

The ship docked under the mountain which 'dominated Cape Town with a dwarf's village beneath it', as Hobbs described the scene. Struddy was struck by the 'parched' land. It looked almost too hot to land. The team faced a battery of cameras. Wynyard

---

200 Jack Hobbs, *Playing for England*, (London: Victor Gollancz, 1931) 45-46

explained that Fry was unavailable and 'Crawford's little difference' had removed him from consideration. The fast bowlers, Buckenham and Thompson, had had successful seasons as had the left-handers Blythe, Rhodes and Woolley. Simpson-Hayward was a one-off. He had already shown off his lobs at Newlands when touring South Africa with an English football team.

The amateurs stayed in the Vineyard Hotel, the professionals in less salubrious accommodation. Struddy found hundreds of ants in his meat pie. 'When I mentioned it, I was told not to be so particular,' he said. He and Hobbs tried to distract the ants by leaving apple cores in the fireplace. The *Cape Times* hoped the snobbish Western Province Cricket Union would avoid 'flagrant favouritism … with good men omitted because they don't happen to move in the exalted ranks of suburban society'.[201] Readers were provided with an instant assessment of the first practice. Thompson 'comes up to the wicket like an animated windmill and gathers pace and bounce off the mat'. Rhodes' forcing strokes to the off and his wonderful timing on the leg side marked him as one for whom matting had no terrors. Buckenham was not one of those tearaway dispensers of charmed lightning, and used his inches to rare advantage and made the ball turn very sharply. Simpson-Hayward stooped to conquer and like Bosanquet's googly had developed his technique on a billiard table. An audible snap of his powerful fingers produced vicious off breaks. Hobbs was disappointing. One critic suggested it might be better if he simply got back on the boat. [202]

The *Minstrel* tradition, with its white supremacist 'black face', so popular on Smith's tour, resurfaced as the tourists watched Mick Commaille, who was to play for South Africa in the series, in the *Minstrel Musicales*. A warm-up game against a Colts XVI reminded them of the wealth of cricketing talent unwillingly unearthed by Lord Hawke's team. But Hobbs made a quick hundred and the Colts were unable to repeat their earlier triumph. This was the first outing of the Hobbs and Rhodes opening partnership.

---

201 *Cape Times*. 23/11/1909
202 Hobbs, *Playing for England*, 47

The serious business started with the match against Western Province, the Currie Cup champions. The speedy J.J. Kotze was not available, and incompetence and the weather made it a less-than-auspicious occasion. A large crowd huddled in the bitter north-west gale which howled among the firs and regular showers sent them scurrying for the tea shed which was besieged all day. At close of play, the spectators fought to get out of two tiny gates and join a stampede for the train back to town.

In between, Hobbs made 114 using his full palette of shots. One moment he was driving the fielders back to the boundary then tap-tap-tapping with Rhodes; the singles superbly judged and smartly run, he drew the field in and pushed them out in a constant battle of wits, like the great Barcelona football team's midfield a century later. The locals were convinced they had a system of secret signals.

The selectors, as the *Cape Times* had feared, relied on reputation rather than youth and form. Western Province were rolled over twice on the second day in perfect batting conditions for a total of 218 runs and the innings-and-133-run defeat was almost identical to that inflicted by the previous tourists. Blythe's slow left-arm bowling concealed break, pace and flight, and his opponents failed to deal with his metronomic accuracy and 8-1 off side field. Only Murray Bisset retained some of his reputation in a black two hours of cricket for Western Province.

The MCC boarded the train to Kimberley. They played 12 against 15 in the baking heat and Buckenham torpedoed local resistance with 7-17 in the second innings. They moved on to Bloemfontein, winning by 200 runs, and finally Johannesburg, where the tour began in earnest. The amateurs stayed with Abe Bailey who with his secretary, Reggie Schwarz, had arrived back from London in mid-December to supervise the tour. The Wanderers ground celebrated its 20th anniversary in 1908 with a 'war dance' which celebrated the return of African mine labour. Culturally and ideologically these occasions reinforced the 'otherness' of African cultures and the triumph of white over traditional African institutions, while providing safe thrills for the white audience. It was an extension of the safari park with humans as exhibits.

The representation of Africans as fauna rather than people had a long tradition. It was the mirror image of the Minstrels in black face which sought to portray black culture as docile and compliant. But they also provided Africans with an opportunity to subvert their roles. As Hobbs described it, 'On Christmas Day we drove out to see a native war dance … the blacks came from their compound in all sorts of attire, from full war paint to reach me downs. They started off slowly then worked themselves off to a perfect frenzy. They seemed to go quite mad, banging tom toms, shouting, brandishing spears and knobkerries, until we were wondering if we were quite safe and expected to get a clout on the head at any moment.'[203]

6.3 The black vote

The draft South Africa Act of Union prohibited black South Africans from voting in Natal, OFS, and the Transvaal but, provided they could meet a high education and property qualification, they could continue to do so in the Cape. Most whites accepted this as the price for Union and anticipated that the Cape franchise would soon disappear. For Africans, it was a total betrayal. As A.K. Soga put it, 'This is treachery … at one stroke they sweep away the dearest possession of 20,000 voters'.

The first South African National Native Convention met in March 1909 in Bloemfontein with delegates from the four colonies. The convention called for all persons to have 'full and equal rights and privileges … applicable alike to all citizens without distinction of class, colour or creed'. In the Cape, as in the rest of South Africa, the franchise status quo was a necessary compromise. Former prime minister William Schreiner disagreed with the colour bar which he saw as a blot on the constitution.[204] During the Cape's ratification process, he spoke 64 times against the racial franchise but all four colonies ratified the act, with Schreiner one of only two dissenting voices.

Attention then turned to the Westminster government.

---

203 Jack Hobbs, *My Cricket Memories,* (London: Heinemann, 1924)
204 Odendaal, *Vukani Bantu!,* 191

A warm-up game against The Reef XI was rained off after Vogler laid down a marker with 6-58. The Transvaal match, effectively a full Test trial, began after Christmas. Fifties from Snooke and Schwarz gave the Transvaal a 64-run lead on the first innings despite five wickets from Thompson, and MCC wilted. In the second innings, Faulkner made 148 not out and Simpson-Hayward took four wickets with his donkey drops to the scorn of the crowd. Faulkner took the ball and grabbed 5-34 to go with his 4-49 in the first innings. The MCC lost by a record 308 runs.

'Tip' Snooke was selected as captain and nine of the Transvaal side were joined by Mick Commaille and Dave Nourse. Bailey secured Gordon White's release from Robinson Mine. Transvaal's Tom Campbell, who regularly kept to the googly bowlers, replaced Murray Bisset. England dropped Blythe, who they considered less effective on hard wickets.

Zulch was bowled by Simpson-Hayward's fourth ball to the bemusement of the 6,000 strong crowd. Then Faulkner danced down the track to the 'lobster', missed, but Strudwick was unsighted. The giant Sinclair tried to kick away a big-spinning off break and was bowled. Commaille amused spectators by his forward and back 'concertina method', but lost patience as the crowd barracked him, charged, and this time Struddy did the rest. Simpson-Hayward finished with 6-43. He had brought the art of lob bowling back from the dead. Aubrey Faulkner held the innings together with 78 out of 208.

In reply, Hobbs steered Vogler's first ball to the leg side boundary. He and Rhodes dominated the googly bowlers and by close of play the English had put on 147 without losing a wicket (Hobbs 77, Rhodes 57). Another day and a different game. At 159, Vogler bowled Rhodes with a leg-stump yorker and the rest followed for less than the opening partnership. Nonetheless, England had a 102-run lead, with Vogler and Faulkner sharing the wickets.

Aubrey Faulkner was a one-man team. He came in with South Africa staring defeat in the face on an effective score of 27/4 and put on 99 in partnership with Snooke (47) for the sixth wicket and 74 with Commaille (19) for the eighth, before completing his first Test century and ultimately reaching 123.

This was a superlative innings, from a cricketer at the height of his powers. South Africa had scored almost 60 per cent of their runs for the last five wickets. It was déjà vu for 'Shrimp', who had watched Sherwell and Nourse in 1905.

The game was delicately poised. The key was how close Hobbs could get them to their target of 244. At 47, he turned a Vogler full-toss into a yorker. But instead of subsiding to the comeback kings, England began to stage their own fightback. Thompson swung the bat and White went for 18 in an over. Thompson and his captain added 70 for the eighth wicket and when White caught Simpson-Hayward off Vogler, England needed 34 for the last wicket. Struddy defended desperately, until Thompson (63) misread a Faulkner googly and was bowled with the tourists short by 19 runs. Vogler finished with 12-181 in the match and Faulkner scored 201 runs and took 8-160 in 50.2 overs.

It was 'the game of a decade, every ball of consequence, every run of value,' according to the *Cape Times*.[205] Faulkner's was an extraordinary all-round performance in a match which rivalled the first Test on Warner's tour. Once again South Africa after a disastrous start had climbed the mountain and were 1-0 up.

All 20 wickets had fallen to Vogler and Faulkner, who together bowled more than 70 per cent of the overs. Snooke's strategy was vindicated.

But the psychological war worked both ways. Simpson-Hayward bet Sinclair a sovereign that he would not score a fifty against him in the series.[206] He bowled him twice, for three and nought, respectively. 'It was the height of the ridiculous to see Sinclair baffled,' wrote the *Cape Times*.[207] Instead of a relic of the past, the lob was beginning to look like the wave of the future.

---

205 *Cape Times*, 5/1/1910

206 Herbert Strudwick, *25 Years Behind the Stumps*, (London: Hutchinson, 1926) 146

207 *Cape Times*, 4/1/1910

6.4 The imperial government:
union trumps African rights

An official delegation sailed to London in 1909 to support the passage of the bill for South African Union through the British parliament. William Schreiner led a counter delegation of black South Africans representing an emerging national movement, including Walter Rubusana, Matt Fredericks, Thomas Mapikela, John Tengo Jabavu and Dr Abdurahman. M.K. Gandhi said that Indians looked with despair on a whites-only Union.

The government delegates set out to discredit Schreiner and British public opinion and parliamentarians showed little interest in the opposition case. The British government had no intention of interfering in the delicate balance of English-Afrikaner interests in the Union construction, which they described as the domestic affair of South Africa. Black South Africans were on their own.

During the debate in the House of Lords, the archbishop of Canterbury said it was justifiable to place restrictions on the black population equivalent to those on children because most of the population would be unfit to share equal citizenship for generations to come.

In the Commons, Liberal prime minster H.H. Asquith said they regretted the colour bar, but any relaxation should be introduced by South Africa itself. Speakers including Charles Dilke, Keir Hardie and Ramsay MacDonald argued against the colour bar, but the front benches agreed that Union trumped African rights. The bill was passed without a division on 19 August.[208]

The unification of South Africa would take place on 31 May 1910.

The tourists headed south to play two games in Natal's intense heat. Herby Taylor, in his first major match, made 55 and Dave Nourse scored 129 and 54 not out. In reply, Hobbs stroked a classical 163. Many years later, Frank Woolley called the match the 'most astonishing case of "attempted umpiring", one cannot call it umpiring

---

208 Odendaal, *Vukani Bantu!*, 225

– in the whole of my experience'. Five MCC batsmen were given out lbw. The admittedly diminutive Leveson Gower was given out hit under the armpit and Woolley was triggered by a ball he had hit cleanly to the square-leg boundary. Leveson Gower told his bowlers not to appeal when Natal batted a second time. It did not bode well for the second Test.

Durban's first ever Test began with friendly byplay as the 'Shrimp', who had lost four previous tosses in a row, pretended to win the toss and Snooke looked dejectedly towards his dressing room. The grumbles of Snooke's team-mates were silenced when the English skipper went into the South African dressing room and said plaintively, 'I suppose you'll bat, Snooke?' 'I should think so,' was the cheerful response.[209]

The weather allowed for only two hours of play on the first day. Simpson-Hayward had seven men on the off, including four in the slips, when Sinclair came face to face with his nemesis, the lobster. His futile efforts to play the innocuous-looking deliveries had the crowd in hysterics. After 45 frustrating minutes he skipped out to drive, hit over the ball and was bowled for 12. Simpson-Hayward had 4-42 and South Africa 199, a score which was exactly matched by England for the first time in a Test.

The third day saw spectators crowding ten deep around the rails, in trees and up telegraph poles. South Africa were faltering at 23/3, with the openers and Faulkner in the hutch. Nourse arrived in silence, another slip was added, Thompson got a ball to swing away late, the left-hander felt for it, but the chance went begging.

It was a key moment. Nourse and White began to rebuild, umpire Frank Smith dozed off and allowed Rhodes to deliver nine deliveries in a six-ball over. A rising ball struck Nourse on the wrist and was caught by Rhodes. Umpire Frank Grey declined the appeal, to English consternation. White added 143 with Nourse and a further 79 with Mick Commaille, making a brilliant 118 before being defeated by a prodigious off break. Sinclair's arrival saw Simpson-

---

209 *Cape Times*, 22/1/1910

Hayward grinning at the other end. Desperate to fight his way to form, Sinclair hooked Thompson three times to the boundary in an over, then hit over the top of a Woolley yorker and went for 22. The innings ended on 347, and the next day's headline read, 'Sinclair not bowled by [Simpson] Hayward'.[210]

With 348 to win, Hobbs demonstrated the slide-rule exactitude of his strokes, pull-sweeping good-length googlies with the spin, sending them humming between the tightly set field. Faulkner made the ball turn 'quite a yard' and time and again beat both wickets and batsman. Ernie Vogler took four catches at slip off Faulkner in his 6-87, including Hobbs for 70. Vogler also bowled 29 overs to seal another victory by 95 runs.

The Durban Test attendance of 20,500 realised a gross of £1,575, and enough profit to pay for a professional for the following season. MCC batsmen Fane, Denton and Woolley were still struggling to deal with the pace of the ball off the pitch. Meanwhile, the South Africans were still vulnerable outside the off stump. The lobster had 15 wickets at 14 in the two Tests so far. On mat stretched over a hard surface, underarm deliveries spun as effectively as googlies. Leveson Gower helped the ground staff stretch it to the maximum himself. Simpson-Hayward's style gave Gordon White 'lockjaw'. Like the googly, the lob depended on getting the batsman to eschew his normal game, and it soon began to prey on the mind.

The *Sporting Life* bemoaned the parlous state of English cricket. South Africa had won four out of five in 1905/06, and Australia the same in 1907/08 before retaining the Ashes in England. Leveson Gower lashed out in print against the criticism. The *Pretoria News* hoped that for the sake of journalism, members of the next MCC touring party would be forbidden to write for the press.

After Thompson had failed to teach his opening partner Buckenham to swim in the tidal pool, the team departed Durban for the Eastern Cape.[211] The Border team drew on the strong but

210 *Cape Times*, 26/1/1910
211 Strudwick, *Stumps*, 144

unacknowledged tradition of local African cricket and arranged African net bowlers to provide batting practice. Leveson Gower told the *Cape Times*, '[You] can't expect [white] amateurs to work themselves to a standstill. Two or three of them were very useful bowlers.'[212] But the local council vetoed allowing Africans on to the ground as net bowlers. The visitors won by four wickets, but all was not well with Border cricket. Only three of Border XI turned up to the farewell banquet. The speeches were described as 'not interesting'.

In Queenstown, the start was delayed when the wicket was found to be 32 yards long. Then a young batsman nicked a ball from Buckenham to Struddy. Everyone appealed, but the umpire gave it not out. Struddy shied at the stumps, missed, and it went to the boundary for four. The scorer asked whether it was a hit or byes. 'Hit,' roared the umpire. He was the batsman's father. Really.

The MCC steamrollered Eastern Province by an innings and 139 runs before catching the train back to Johannesburg where they again took on the Transvaal. White hustled three wickets in nine balls without conceding a run. He finished with 5-42. But Dave Denton, the Yorkshireman, reinvented his technique against the googly and scored 139 out of 291 in the first innings and 138 out of 271 in the second, winning the game on his own.[213]

In the third Test, South Africa got off to a bad start against a confident England. From 30/3, White (72) fought a rearguard action with the irresistible Faulkner (76), and South Africa recovered to 305. Denton replied with his third hundred in successive innings against the same attack. It was scored in even time and his collection made another century, earning him £104.[214] Taking a leaf out of their opponents' book, Woolley and Strudwick added 69 for the last wicket, turning a deficit of 52 into a 17-run lead.

Billy Zulch came out to bat with a feather which he placed on a good length just outside the off stump. Struddy asked him what

212 *Cape Times*, 25/12/1909
213 *Cape Times*, 23/1/1910
214 Hobbs, *Playing for England*, 51

it was for. Zulch replied that if Simpson-Hayward pitched the ball 'outside that feather', he would play it with his legs. 'Very good idea,' Struddy retorted, picking it up and putting it in his pocket.[215] Simpson-Hayward spun his web, reducing the hosts to 123/7. At the other end, Frank Woolley conceded only 16 scoring strokes off 108 deliveries, but a 55-run partnership for the eighth wicket and a further 69 runs for the last two wickets gave South Africa hope of a series victory. With MCC needing 221 to win, the fifth day was set for a momentous struggle. Hobbs had sunstroke and had made a groggy 11 batting down the order in the first innings. This time he came in at 42/3. Initially nervous and fidgety, his eye recovered its keenness, his mind its will and back came that lightning turn of the wrist, that half-careless, indolent glide, illustrating the difference between Test cricket and genius.

Vogler and Faulkner had the series in in their sights at 93/6 when Morice Bird joined Hobbs. But Bird possessed an iron nerve and put on 95 with Hobbs. Finally, Leveson Gower helped Hobbs (93 not out) carry the English over the line by three wickets. Hobbs was chaired off and the crowd demanded a speech. But Hobbs was not a talker, and the 'Shrimp' was left to tell the crowd that this was one of the proudest moments of his life. The series was still alive and Cape Town, the venue for the fourth Test, was delighted.

The tourists had momentum and a wicket which suited them more than the Transvaal batsmen. Psychologically, the defeat of the googly was a significant blow for South Africa. The Cape Town press criticised the googly fetish which put all their eggs in the same basket and meant that Murray Bisset, South Africa's premier wicketkeeper, was 'shamefully' overlooked. Leveson Gower stood down with a damaged hand, Blythe came in and Fred Fane reluctantly took over the captaincy. For South Africa Schwarz and Sinclair replaced Floquet and Pegler.

A large marquee with a staff of skilled telegraph operators was set up to meet the demand for real-time updates. England won the toss

---

215 Hobbs, *Playing for England*, 50

and the tent was soon in pandemonium with the shock dismissals of Hobbs (caught by Faulkner off Vogler for one), Rhodes (caught by Faulkner off Snooke without scoring) and Denton (caught by Commaille off Snooke, also without scoring) leaving England on 2/3. Vogler swung the ball like a baseball pitcher and Snooke bowled at lightning pace, getting sharp bounce off the wicket. It was left to Woolley (69) and Bird (57) to bail them out. Woolley's self-belief was back, and he sent the ball repeatedly whistling past point. Snooke manipulated the bowling skilfully, blending googlies with Sinclair's length and his own expresses but the English clawed their way to a respectable 203.

The hosts, with Commaille promoted to open on his home ground, put on 47 for the first wicket, and the English looked in trouble until Bird sent White's middle stump cartwheeling with the last ball of the day to leave the score at 93/2. W.E. Howell, the Australian medium-pacer who took 4-18 and 5-81 opening the bowling in Cape Town in 1902 had said, 'Newlands is the finest wicket in the world, for a bowler … No other ground produced the same sequence of surprises as matting stretched on turf.'[216] The next day Thompson's off-breaks seemed to whip off the wicket and break back with redoubled pace. It took Schwarz and Vogler's 35 for the ninth wicket to give the locals a four-run lead.

It was déjà vu all over again. Hobbs was caught for a duck by Campbell off Snooke miles down the leg side and the same bowler knocked out Rhodes' off stump. Denton skied a pull off Vogler which was dazzlingly held by Faulkner one-handed and diving at full stretch: three in the hutch with 17 on the board. Woolley and Fane rescued the innings with an aggressive 100-run partnership until Vogler bowled Woolley for 64, Fane went to Faulkner for 37 and the last five wickets fell for 49 runs in 59 minutes.

South Africa needed 175 to win. Claude Buckenham targeted the dangerous Commaille and dispatched his off bail in a 50-yard parabola to the fence. But bowling at high speed, he caught his foot

---

216 *Cape Times*, 9/3/1910

in the worn part of the matting and badly strained a thigh muscle. His departure was the cue for another Nourse-White partnership. Gordon White's innings was typical of the player – bright, breezy, and invigorating. At the other end was Nourse, 'big, bluff and burly, blocking every ball and drawing the fielders in by making a sharp sprint down the wicket then nonchalantly trotting back'.[217]

White, Nourse and Snooke fell to Blythe and Thompson and South Africa were suddenly 91/5 with 84 needed and the series in the balance. Faulkner gave an early chance which was refused. His square cutting was perfect, his defence impregnable and lob bowling held no terrors for him. Lobs held plenty of terror for Sinclair, but he batted with huge discipline and restraint, scoring 19 in a partnership of 71, until he was bowled by Thompson with 13 to get. Schwarz knocked off the runs, Faulkner finished undefeated on 49 and South Africa had won the Test and their second consecutive series at home against MCC. No one on the winning side made 50 and 13 wickets fell to the googly, though for the first time in the series Sinclair and Snooke found a wicket where they could contribute with the ball. Jack Hobbs saw Buckenham's injury as the turning point, but Sinclair's quiet innings was a revelation.

The Western Province ground failed to live up to the intensity of the struggle. The start was delayed as no regulation ball was available, the tiny sight screen needed constant shifting (Hobbs had said visibility was a serious problem), the worn matting put Buckenham out of action and, finally, the catering charges, well 'sixpence is ridiculous for a cup of tea no matter how badly one may need it'.[218]

The final Test began 24 hours later. With the series won, South Africa brought in Samuelson, 'Pompey' Norton from East London and home favourite Murray Bisset. England had run out of options and replaced injured fast bowler Buckenham with the wicketkeeper Tufnell as Strudwick had a touch of malaria. Fane continued as captain. Two teams of exhausted players who had played three

217 *Cape Times*, 10/3/1910
218 *Ibid*

consecutive Tests were performing in front of a sated public with the series already decided.

Fane won his second toss. Jack Hobbs strode to the crease as the hungriest cricketer around after one and nought in the previous Test. The dog-tired South African bowlers paid as he put on a world record 221 for the first wicket with Wilfred Rhodes. Hobbs gave no chances until he trod on his wicket while pulling a ball from debutant Norton, having made 187, his first Test century. Rhodes made a chanceless 77 before Nourse bowled him off his pads. The indefatigable Faulkner made the ball turn a great deal, but the Newlands wicket was too slow. The fresh Norton took his chance with 4-47 in 15 overs, the first time in five Tests that anyone other than Faulkner and Vogler had taken more than two wickets in an innings. And in other firsts for the series, South Africa were kept in the field all day and MCC passed 400.

6.5 Hobbs and Rhodes

Fire, and the abandon of youth, were exemplified by Hobbs who, quick and precise as a cat, had built his game under the watchful eye of Tom Hayward. Rhodes started as the deadliest left-arm spinner in the world and became an outstanding batsman. Hobbs 'just loved opening with Rhodes'.[219] They drove the field to distraction, dragging the field in to counter almost telepathic singles, and then flashing the ball through the gaps and parting spectators pursued by harassed fielders. The Test record partnership of 221 runs was scored in two hours and 24 minutes on what was considered a bowler's wicket.

Following this hammering, South Africa collapsed in a heap to the cunning Blythe. From 48/7, a last-ditch rearguard involving Schwarz and Zulch dragged them to 103. Billy Zulch demonstrated endurance, grit, and determination despite taking some nasty knocks from Thompson in his undefeated 43. He became only the second

---

219 *Cape Times*, 12/3/1910

South African (after A.B. Tancred's 26 not out in South Africa's second Test) to carry his bat through a completed Test innings.

Following on more than 300 runs behind, Faulkner put on 120 for the fourth wicket with Snooke (47), until Woolley controversially caught him for 99. The unlucky Faulkner found out too late that one of his singles had been incorrectly credited to Sinclair. Sinclair, meanwhile, played like a millionaire, rattling up 37 and leaving the 'Lobster' wicketless, but lost his bet that he would make 50 in the series. A final partnership between Schwarz (44) and Bisset (27), with nine fielders stationed on the off side to cancel out Schwarz's driving and cutting ensured that England had to knock off 16 runs before they finally won by nine wickets, and the series ended 3-2.

6.6 *William Schreiner, Union and MCC*

MCC's farewell banquet was held at the Mount Nelson Hotel. William Schreiner remembered the Aubrey Smith tour in 1888. He understood that Simpson-Hayward had nine separate species of lobs. For him, lobs not only introduced an element of humour into the game, but they marked a new epoch demanding attention. He was closer to his comfort zone when he spoke about how 'South Africans were as united in sport as they were politically' and in achieving this 'owed a debt to MCC'.[220]

Schreiner more than anyone was aware that while unity among the white population may have been reinforced by MCC, Union had been built on the backs of the black population whose interests had been betrayed not only in South Africa but by the imperial government.

Leveson Gower responded that South Africa was now a cricketing great power. He had received 100 letters most of which related to Hobbs, whom he proposed as the new prime minister of a united South Africa. Leveson Gower thought five Test matches and three continuous weeks of Test cricket at the end of the tour were too exhausting. He recommended neutral qualified umpires, whose

---

220 *Cape Times*, 14/3/1910

decisions could not possibly be misinterpreted. It would be 70 years before these would be introduced.

Dave Denton in the *Yorkshire Post* criticised Abe Bailey's concentration of talent in Johannesburg, which diluted the standard elsewhere. The South African team to Australia contained nine members of the Wanderers club. The best players played with rather than against each other, increasing their skills but widening the gap between Test players and the rest.

The series had been a titanic and unpredictable battle between evenly matched teams. In three of the four Tests, the differences between the teams' first innings scores were 17, zero and four respectively. The margins of victory in four Tests were 19 runs, 95 runs, three wickets and four wickets. Winning positions were repeatedly reversed. In the first Test, England were fewer than 50 runs behind with ten wickets in hand on the first innings but lost by 19 runs; in the second they were 105 behind with ten wickets in hand, this time losing by 95 runs; the third Test saw England recover from 42/4 to win by three wickets; the fourth saw South Africa win from 91/5 in the last innings chasing 175. Only the last Test, with the series gone, was a cakewalk.

The outstanding Hobbs-Rhodes partnership put on 559 runs for the first wicket at an average of 79.85, and the remarkable Simpson-Hayward took 23 wickets at 18. Thompson received little publicity, but stole the all-rounder honours with 23 wickets at almost 27 and 267 runs at 33.

Ranged against them were South Africa's two all-rounders, Ernie Vogler and Aubrey Faulkner. South Africa used 12 bowlers, but Vogler and Faulkner took 65 out of 85 wickets (76 per cent), bowling two-thirds of South Africa's overs. Vogler collected 36 victims, a record until Hugh Tayfield broke it against MCC in 1956/57. Faulkner took 29 wickets and both bowlers averaged below 22. On the previous tour, Snooke, Sinclair and Schwarz had all grabbed more wickets than the pair. Much can change in three years, but it was remarkable that this time Snooke, Sinclair and Nourse took only four wickets each and Schwarz bowled a mere eight wicketless overs. Snooke's strategy of getting Vogler and Faulkner on and keeping them on won him the series.

Faulkner's performance was doubly amazing. He also scored 545 runs at an average of over 60, almost twice the aggregate and average achieved by the next best South African batsman, Gordon White. He was indisputably the greatest all-rounder in the world.

Political union was two months away when the tourists headed for home and the eternal mine labour crisis reached a new stage as the last Chinese miners sailed home on the day the series was decided. Bailey and Lord Harris backed up on the pitch by Schwarz, Vogler, Faulkner and White had forced South Africa into the triumvirate of cricketing and imperial great powers. But could they stay there?

6.7 Herbert Strudwick goes home

Struddy was nominally a wicketkeeper, but his energy carried him all round the field. He would defeat slip in a race to the leg boundary and leap over the stumps to reach a ball cocked up in front of the bat. He was the tour's Jonah, involved in two car smashes and attacked by a dog to the detriment of a borrowed coat.

With typical commitment, he had played in the final Test despite a 'touch of malaria' that confined him to the outfield. With the inexperienced Tufnell behind the stumps, 25 byes were conceded in the South African second innings. This might have been significant had Murray Bisset, with little experience of keeping to the googly bowlers, not conceded 30 byes. But the 'touch of malaria' serious. Struddy was prohibited by medical advice from the post-tour trip to Rhodesia and found himself back in bed in the 'ant-hotel' in Cape Town.

If he couldn't go to Rhodesia, he had to go home with the others. His pals packed his trunk and when the doctor came, Charlie Blythe distracted the medic, Struddy removed the thermometer and he was given the all-clear. He staggered to the docks in a malarial haze, found his bunk and did not get up until Southampton. He spent another two weeks in bed with a high temperature, 'but anything was better than staying at that place with those ants'. Two lion cubs were born in Cape Town Zoo and named Hobbs and Struddy.[221]

---

221 Strudwick, *Stumps*, 150

7

Barnes and Taylor: Johnny Douglas 1913/14

THE FIVE years between the 1909 Act of Union and the outbreak of the First World War was a period of intense change. The immediate goal of urban capitalist English speakers was to revive the mining industry on which the profits of the empire depended, but this conflicted with the interests of poorer, rural, Afrikaners. Meanwhile, black South Africans were concluding that they, not the Afrikaners, had been the real losers, betrayed at the peace and again over Union.

After Union, the state emphasis moved from the franchise to reducing access to land to force out labour. The Native Land Bill, passed into law into 1913, was intended to deprive black South Africans of land ownership rights and restrict their opportunities as tenant farmers. It was opposed by the South African Native National Congress (SANNC), renamed as the African National Congress (ANC) a decade later. South African Indians too, led by Mohandas Gandhi, developed the concept of Satyagraha, or passive resistance, against the application to Indians of increasing state restrictions on space and movement.

On the mines, Africans replaced Chinese labour from 1907. But wages and appalling conditions brought African mineworkers out on strike. The police drove the workers back down the shafts with clubs and rifle butts. African workers' grievances went unheard and unmet.[222]

---

222 Jack and Ray Simons, *Class and Colour in South Africa*, (London: IDAF, 1983 160

7.1 The Native Land Act, 1913

'Awakening on Friday morning, 20 June 1913, the South African native found himself, not actually a slave, but a pariah in the land of his birth,' as Sol Plaatje, the first general secretary of the SANNC, explained. 'South Africa has ceased to be the home of any of her native children.'[223]

Minister of native affairs, J.W. Sauer rushed the Native Land Act through parliament. As a Cape 'liberal' pre-Union, and a major recipient of African votes, he had traded his principles for cabinet rank. Overcrowded and uneconomic 'reserves' were created, and it was illegal for Africans to purchase or lease land from Europeans outside the reserves. This protected white landowners from competition and forced male Africans onto the mines. It divided South Africa into a country based on segregated landownership, where the white population (around 13 per cent of the total) would own 87 per cent of the land.

In 1912, SANNC was created to fight for 'equal rights for all civilised men'. It was not a mass movement but relied on progressive constitutionalism. SANNC sent a deputation to demand the withdrawal of the Native Land Act (as it had become after being enacted into law, having initially been the Native Land Bill), a petition to the prime minister and finally a deputation to the UK in 1914, only to be told, as they had been in 1909, that the act was an internal South African matter.[224]

The previous MCC tour had featured see-saw contests, knife-edge finishes and victories for the home side. Leveson Gower had been prepared to take risks and accepted defeat with some equanimity. To call Johnny Douglas pugnacious is not to trade in metaphors. When he deputised for Plum Warner in Australia he announced, 'I can't make a speech, but I will box three rounds with any man in the room'. There were no takers,

---

223 Sol. T. Plaatje, *Native Life in South Africa*, (London: King and Sons, 1916) 21
224 Edward Roux, *Time Longer than Rope*, (Madison: University of Wisconsin Press, 2nd ed., 1964). 74

Johnny Douglas had won gold in the middleweight division of the 1908 Olympics.

Even after his Australian success, Johnny Douglas was not first choice to captain MCC in South Africa. But Warner was too old, Fred Fane too reticent and neither Fry nor Foster available. Douglas was the last amateur standing and was determined to avenge the defeats inflicted on Warner and Leveson Gower. He selected the strongest touring side yet to visit the subcontinent. Schwarz in 1905/06 and Faulkner and Vogler in 1909/10 had turned the googly into a psychological X-factor on matting wickets. But in 1906 the googly was itself a sleight of hand disguising their real strengths – a consistent and penetrative seam attack and a reversible batting order.

Building on South African success and cricketing innovation, Abe Bailey from Consolidated Goldfields, a key representative of the Rand mining industry and effectively CEO of South African cricket, persuaded England and Australia to join South Africa in a tripartite Imperial Cricket Conference. It made South Africa equals on the cricketing world stage and enhanced its investment profile.

But the seeds of disintegration were already apparent. The domestic game was poorly administered, played by 'shamateurs' supported by sympathetic employers, primarily Abe Bailey himself and the mining industry. Class snobbery, limited crowds in the domestic game and a racist system which blocked potential black professionals ensured that South Africans resisted the professionalism which might have created a stronger cricketing foundation.

There was too much international cricket. In eight years, South Africa had toured England three times (including the triangular tournament), played ten Tests against MCC in South Africa and another five in Australia. Given travelling and the duration of tours, this created unsustainable pressure on a small pool of talented players. By 1913, the golden goose was distinctly off-colour.

The Test squad in Australia in 1910/11, skippered by Percy Sherwell, faced a new reality when Australia took apart the googly bowlers and piled up 494/6 on the first day of the first Test in Sydney. South Africa fought back in the second Test, but threw away a winning position where they collapsed to 80 all out against the left-arm swing of J G Whitty with only 170 needed. They won the third Test by 38 runs in a high-scoring but gripping match in Adelaide, but, apart from Schwarz, their bowling failed, and the series was lost 4-1.

The 1912 Triangular Tournament was billed as the cricketing event of the decade with the three countries meeting on equal terms. It came three years too late for South Africa and was drowned by a sunless summer. South Africa's damp and dreary performances showed they were incapable of challenging the top two on grass wickets. Faulkner was crushed by his workload, Schwarz's elbow injury rendered him ineffectual, and only wrist spinner Sydney Pegler was a success with the ball. Herby Taylor showed promise, but played too many shots too early and failed to make a century in 57 first-class innings. After a start against Australia which included an astonishing double hat-trick for the tiny leg-spinner Jimmy Matthews, they then ran into Sydney Barnes who took an extraordinary ten wickets in each of his three tests against South Africa – ultimately totalling 34 wickets at 8.29. It was the end of an era as Faulkner, Schwarz, Llewellyn and Pegler stayed on and the rest headed back by instalments, glad to be out of the rain.

By the time that Douglas crossed the Bay of Biscay, the stalwarts of the previous decade (Sinclair, White, Shalders, Snooke, Faulkner, Sherwell, Vogler, Hathorn, Schwarz and Pegler) had dropped out of the game or were unavailable. South African cricket had pressed the restart button.

7.2 Jimmy

The changing of the guard was marked by the death of the great Jimmy Sinclair from cirrhosis of the liver and cardiac failure in February 1913.[225] He had been South Africa's first sporting superstar and, on his day, the world's leading all-rounder. He could take any game by the scruff of its neck and was electrifying with the bat and irresistible with the ball.

---

225 As stated on his 'Form of Information of Death'.

Averages of 23.23 with the bat and 31.68 with the ball in 25 Tests provided little clue to the man and his impact. Numbers meant little to him. He lived in the moment, but in trying to please his supporters sometimes failed to meet expectations. He died tragically at only 36 when an 'incurable affliction turned his great frame into a gaunt and skeletal structure that could not support his great spirit'.[226]

Hobbs, Rhodes, Woolley, Bird, Relf and Strudwick were all on their second tour to the sub-continent. Add in Phil Mead, Jack Hearne, the ebullient Lionel Tennyson and South Africa's worst nightmare, Sydney Barnes, and this was a formidable side. Johnny Douglas had got his way.

The perennial spat between the provinces and the propensity of the Western Province Cricket Union to shoot itself in the foot meant there would be no Tests at Newlands. Two each were allocated to Durban and Johannesburg and one to Port Elizabeth.

7.3 The white miners' strike

In 1913, a manager at New Klipfontein Mine cut the pay of five white miners and unleashed a worker strike demanding trade union recognition and an eight-hour day. Some 18,000 workers from 63 mines came out and Africans were forced down the pits as scabs. On the night of 3 July Johannesburg was on fire. Mobs set fire to the railway station, the *Star* newspaper and the Rand Club, hated symbols of the industry. Botha and Smuts called for support from British imperial troops. A volley was fired in Market Square; 22 people were killed and 47 wounded. The panicked government conceded all the strikers' demands. But the city remained a powder keg.[227]

The team arrived in Table Bay in November after some rough weather, stoically endured by Hobbs and Woolley, best of batsmen and worst of sailors. Cape Town welcomed them on a glorious early

---

226 Gutsche, *Old Gold*, 151-152
227 Simons and Simons, *Class and Colour*, 158-160

summer morning with the old mountain showing up against the clear blue of the sky, and the Bay a sheet of turquoise glass.

Jack Hobbs regretted that he had not yet been able to fulfil his promise of spending a season in Cape Town. Bert Strudwick was looking forward to a happier time than on the last tour. Sydney Barnes, always a special case, was arriving later with his wife and son and would have no opportunity to measure his progress at Newlands since his time as Claremont's professional in 1899.

Douglas would have taken a stroll down Adderley Street. He and his father John Douglas, a well-known boxing referee, had supported Andrew Jephtha, a black welterweight boxer from Cape Town who won his first British title in 1907. By 1910, Jephtha had lost his sight after repeated blows to his eyes. His tobacconist business failed because of his blindness, and he returned to Cape Town where he scratched out a living sitting on the Adderley Street pavement among the flower sellers, offering his booklet *A Black Boxer in Britain* for a shilling.[228]

7.4 Johnny Douglas

Johnny Douglas praised the all-round ability of the team and pointed out that Mead, Hobbs and Hearne had each scored over 2,000 runs in the previous season. 'We also have Tennyson – provided he can get going I think you will see him hit the ball out of the ground. If he has the same good season here as he had on board the *Saxon*, I think he will come out on top of the averages,' he said to loud laughter.

He told the story about batting in Melbourne with a railway running alongside the ground. 'Two members were talking in the pavilion when I went out to bat,' he said.

First member, 'Here comes Douglas, now you'll see something like cricket.'

Second member, 'I'll make a bet with you that more trains will pass in the next hour than Douglas will make runs.'

First member, 'Done.'

---

228 Thanks to Dale Slater for making the connection between Douglas and Jephtha

> R.P. Fitzgerald, chairman of Western Province Cricket Union,
> 'Who won?'
>
> Johnny fixed his questioner with a mournful stare. 'Trains,' he
> replied briefly, 'By 23.'[229]

Strudwick had been deeply scarred by the 'war of the ants' on the
last tour and rather than risk a repeat he booked into Cape Town's
premier hotel, the Mount Nelson, at his own expense. Once bitten,
twice shy.

As Hobbs said when he and Rhodes broke the Test record for the
first wicket, Newlands was the most perfect run-getting wicket in
the world *if* you knew how to play on it. Western Province won the
toss and, without Barnes, Douglas was unable to stem the flow of
runs. Plum Lewis made a brilliant 151 out of 376 and the Western
Province attack dismissed the tourists for 199. Following on, MCC
battled in high winds, a dust storm and a last hour of drizzle, to
secure the draw.[230]

A chastened MCC played against odds at Robertson and
Oudtshoorn. Having missed the first two games, Barnes took 7-11
at Oudtshoorn in the second innings and proved irresistible in the
next match against the Cape Province in Port Elizabeth, which was
won by an innings and 67 runs thanks to 170 from Hobbs. Douglas
told his opponents not to feel too bad – all but two of the MCC team
had played Test cricket for England.

A memorial match for Jimmy Sinclair raised £105 while the
swallows, like the cricketers, arrived in their summer homes. Ringed
swallows from Ayrshire were found in Orange Free State and a group
from Staffordshire moved into their seasonal quarters in Utrecht in
Northern Natal.

The team played themselves into form and by the first Test had
five innings victories in the bank. 'The name of Barnes seems to
stand out in bold letters everywhere and on everything. It is Barnes

---

229 Lionel Lord Tennyson, *From Verse to Worse*, (London: Christopher Johnson,
    1936) 118

230 *Cape Times*, 10/11/1913

who established the funk at the Bay, it is Barnes who is relied upon to do the needful so a train can be caught … No wonder that locals should be trembling and hearts palpitating on facing up to the one and only Barnes,' wrote *The Star*.[231]

The tour headed south to take on the Currie Cup holders, Natal, captained by Herby Taylor. Douglas left out Barnes, to avoid giving Taylor a sighting until the real business began. Rain demolished most of the first two days and Taylor carried his bat for a chanceless 83 not out in a total of 124, and 42 not out of Natal's 69/0 in the second innings. Douglas made 70 not out but 'was no more attractive than expected from a player whose reputation for slowness and lack of initiative has preceded him'.[232]

First Test previews were full of foreboding. Only Taylor, Nourse, Hartigan, Ward and Cox were retained from the 1912 tour and the 'attack' featured neither googlies nor pace. The selectors even appeared to have selected the wrong Tapscott from the Kimberley cricketing family. South Africa picked their youngest team, with an average age of 25 compared to their opponents' 30.

Herby Taylor won the toss and batted. Barnes swept gracefully in towards the wickets, snapping the ball at speed from the top of his high action. After Taylor hit him through the leg side for four, Barnes turned to leg theory with six fielders on the leg side and three within a few yards of the bat. On 20, Taylor glanced one low and fine to Woolley at leg slip but he couldn't hold on. Wickets fell at regular intervals until Taylor hit Douglas out of the ground before being caught behind for a remarkable 109 out of 182. Barnes's five-wicket haul took him past Hugh Trimble's record of 141 Test wickets.

7.5 Motoring in Amanzimtoti

On the Sunday of the Test, Hobbs, Strudwick and Booth were on the way to Amanzimtoti when their driver tried to overtake a horse-drawn cart near a bridge, hit a bank and turned over. Strudwick was thrown clear, while Booth and Hobbs were hauled out from

---

231 *The Star*, 4/12/1913
232 *The Star*, 11/12/1913

under the vehicle by passers-by. Booth had rib fractures and Hobbs's hand was badly cut. Strudwick watched the driver vanishing into the distance covered in blood.

South Africa posted an attacking field but spilled 11 chances, several by wicketkeeper Tommy Ward who had dislocated his little finger but did not seek medical attention until the tea interval. Hobbs stroked 82 and Douglas completed a stubborn first Test century in the face of a wearying attack. Lionel Tennyson was badly missed three times before he finally got in the way of a straight one from Nourse on 52, his only significant score of the series. The innings ended with three wickets in four balls, but England had an unassailable lead of 268.

South Africa's second innings was over in less than three hours. For Barnes the mat was a magic carpet, generating a huge amount of spin and bounce, perplexing, alarming and defeating a succession of batsmen, while the game also had to be stopped to treat Strudwick for an injury to his cheek bone after one particularly severe kick. Barnes trapped Taylor in front for eight; Percy Lewis, the hero of Newlands, went for a pair, twice caught Woolley in the slips off Barnes; and only Dave Nourse dug in. Even Nourse was nonplussed by Barnes' top-spinner and retreated so far into his crease that he eventually trod on his own wicket on 46. The last three wickets couldn't get out of there fast enough and fell in three balls. South Africa had lost by an innings and 157 runs with Barnes collecting 10-105.

The Star reflected that South Africa 'were beaten by a margin more decisive than the most pessimistic thought likely'.[233] The young players lacked experience and confidence, it was reported. The selectors had failed to rejuvenate the ageing team over the previous five years. Their start 'has been so long delayed that many have to get off the mark together and the failure of one is apt to end in disaster to all'.

Douglas demonstrated a determination to wear the opposition down. 'There is far more at stake than the rubber – the status

---

233 *The Star*, 18/12/1913

of South Africa's future involvement in international cricket,' trumpeted *The Star*. It was to be an ongoing theme. Could South Africa maintain her seat at the top table? It was 'very discouraging' for those trying to revive cricket in SA. For the failure of the South Africans in the triangular tournament, 'Certain reasonable excuses could be made, but the Durban rout comes into another category. With the brilliant exception of Taylor, the losers played poor cricket.'[234]

The party headed north to the Rand. Barnes travelled with the South African rather than the English players. Sir Lionel Phillips from the Corner House mining group, Bailey's fellow mining grandee, had invited MCC to stay but before they arrived Phillips was shot in the street by a gunman. The would-be assassin blamed him for being jailed for 'causing disturbances' by over-vigorous debt collection among African miners whom he had supplied with fruit and vegetables.

The MCC arrived in Johannesburg and an inexperienced Transvaal XI led by Louis Tancred subsided to another innings defeat. But the elements of a strategy to play Barnes began to emerge. At 26 for no wicket, Barnes switched to leg theory. Billy Zulch played out three maidens before hooking the first ball not on a perfect length for four. Zulch made a careful 47 and Roly Beaumont crafted a couple of equally watchful fifties. They adopted the MCC tactic of risk-free batting, aiming to wear Barnes down and wait for the loose ball instead of trying to hit him out of the attack. Even Barnes, they hoped, was human. But hundreds from Woolley and Hobbs showed that it was not just Barnes but the MCC batting which would be a threat in the second Test. The Transvaal approach was imported wholesale into the Test team to the annoyance of Western Province, who saw their selections vetoed. Mick Commaille and Mars were on the Cape Town platform saying goodbye to their supporters when they were told not to bother boarding the train. Lewis, Cooper, Baumgartner and Tapscott were dumped and Zulch, Beaumont and

---

234 *Ibid*

Louis Tancred brought in along with the promising googly bowling all-rounder, Claude Newberry.

Christmas Day had seen heavy thunderstorms. Despite the ongoing labour crisis, the professionals had been taken to see African dancing at the Vogelfontein mine compound, while Tennyson and Douglas relaxed as the guests of Sir George Farrar, yet another member of the Corner House group. The following day, Taylor won a toss he might have preferred to lose. He batted first in front of a 7,000-strong crowd. At 22, Zulch was caught at slip off a kicking ball; Hands was taken by Rhodes at short square leg and Beaumont caught behind. Barnes had taken three wickets in seven balls. Nourse was bowled by Barnes and then at 63, with his own score on 29, Taylor had his leg stump uprooted by a ball that had pitched outside off.

Gerald Hartigan energetically kicked away anything pitched outside leg and Barnes was finally rested after another heavy shower, having taken all six wickets to fall so far. The other bowling held few terrors and Hartigan put on 77 for the seventh wicket with Ward. Douglas, never a man to use diplomacy when force would do, fell over spectators seated on the ground when chasing down a boundary. The umpires had to intervene before the slanging match came to blows. Peace restored, Barnes polished off the two final wickets for figures of 8-56. Conditions had been in his favour and the defensive strategy had not succeeded. After a 20-minute delay, MCC went out to bat but appealed against the light before a ball was bowled. The large crowd left incensed by Douglas' interruptions and his go-slow tactics.[235]

The second day dawned bright with a faster wicket and outfield. The new googly bowler, Newberry, was manoeuvred around the ground by Hobbs and Rhodes and the South African total of 160 was passed in two hours with only one wicket down. Cox tried leg theory and in his third over Rhodes refused to even look at his leg side deliveries as the crowd shouted for him to bowl them on the wicket. Rhodes batted for 309 minutes for a patient 152, shutting out the boisterous crowd and Phil Mead made a hundred in 228 minutes.

---

235 *The Star*, 27/12/1913

England lost their third wicket at 333, but Newberry, giving the ball plenty of air, and Jimmy Blanckenberg (5-83) took the last seven wickets for 70 runs.

Despite this shift in momentum, another innings defeat loomed. Zulch and Taylor dug in, putting on 70 for the first wicket, before Barnes had Taylor caught at short square leg by Rhodes. From 106/4, Hands and Nourse shared a fifth-wicket partnership of 71. Barnes blazed through the remaining defences, taking 6-21 in this last spell and 9-103 in the innings. South Africa lost by an innings and 12 runs. Half an hour later thunderstorms swept the ground. Barnes had routed the South Africans with 17-159, an analysis that would not be challenged until Jim Laker visited Manchester in 1956, 287 Tests later.

7.6 Barnes the Terrible

What made Barnes so lethal? He was tall and strong, a commanding and intimidating presence. He had started as a fast bowler, learnt to bowl a fast off break and then began to extract appreciable turn from leg at fast-medium pace. He bounced in with short steps accelerating into leaps with the ball held out waist high before the last stride and a long loose circular swing of the arm in a high arc. He delivered the leg break from the same height and with the same trajectory as the off break, digging it in instead of tossing it up. For both balls, he gripped the ball the same way, imparting off spin with the first finger and leg spin with the third. The huge amount of spin he put on the ball swung the ball in the opposite direction to the spin. His speed through the air and off the pitch gave batsmen no time to assess the break.

Spin, bounce and nip off the pitch, allied to a late and disconcerting swerve, projected at every variety of pace from slow-medium to fast, made him the complete bowler. Taylor played him as he had the googly bowlers, focusing on the ball in the hand and finger movement as the ball left the hand.[236] He then used exaggerated foot movement – forward if he could smother

---

236 Chris Greyvenstein, *Giants of South African Cricket*, (Cape Town: Don Nelson, 1971) 17

the spin, right back into the stumps if he could not. Strudwick complained of Taylor getting so far back that he would put one foot behind the stumps and slice his bat through the air around the wicketkeeper's head.[237]

The South Africans 'played the game in the highest spirit of amateurism' according to *The Times*. It was taken as a compliment, but apart from Taylor and Nourse, who were effectively professionals, South Africa's cricketers were part-timers without regular competition. *The Star* in Johannesburg quoted an unnamed MCC player to the effect that Newberry 'had strokes all round the wicket but does not seem to be able to keep his head for more than three overs ... he has not taken the game sufficiently seriously.'

They faced a team of hardened and experienced professionals, exemplified by Barnes himself, who in pursuit of social and economic independence, had turned down a trip on Lord Hawke's second South African tour to retain his winter job at the ironworks in Stoke.

The third Test at The Wanderers was started after a single day's break. The *Cape Times* was reduced to appealing to the goddess of luck, 'Cricket is a game of such possibilities that a surprise might easily occur through the effect of weather or an unaccepted chance or two.'[238] Rows of empty benches at the start showed little faith in luck or the recuperative power of the South African team.

England won the toss. Hobbs and Rhodes put on a century partnership for the first wicket, but from 158/1, MCC collapsed to 238 all out. Taylor was the unlikely hero. He took 3-4 by relying on length and variations of pace rather than spin. Jack Hearne, playing in his first Test of the series, dominated when South Africa batted. His variety of deliveries, including the googly, captured 5-49. Barnes bowled 13 overs without taking a wicket, but then bagged three in his last three overs and South Africa's opportunity had vanished. England had an 87-run lead and drove home their advantage.

---

237 Strudwick, *Stumps*, 151-152
238 *Cape Times* 1/1/14

Douglas, dropped twice in three balls, finished on a dogged 77, Mead made 86 with beautifully timed cuts and drives through the leg side, and South Africa were left to chase an unlikely 396. At close of play on day three they were 124 for no wicket, and the optimists were blowing on the embers of hope.

The next day, Relf got rid of Taylor for 70 and Zulch for 82 as 153/1 became 173/6. Then South Africa found something at the bottom of an apparently empty barrel. Ward put on 44 with Newberry for the seventh wicket and a further 78 for the eighth with Blanckenberg batting tenaciously for 59.

But just when hope again peeped around the corner, Johnny Douglas dismissed both Ward and Blanckenberg. South Africa, with only an hour to survive, had lost by 91 runs. They had fought back gallantly with both bat and ball. Barnes finished with the merely human figures of 5-102 in 38 overs. It was the fourth time that 300 had been scored in the last innings of a Test, but two salvageable games had not been saved and the series was lost.

7.7 The general strike, Lionel Tennyson and the third Test

A strike that had begun in the coal mines in Natal spread to the railways and culminated in a national event. Shortly after the third Test, Jan Smuts declared martial law and 70,000 members of the newly constituted South African Defence Force took over the streets of Johannesburg. The Wanderers grounds were commandeered by the military and a civil guard created. The state trained a field gun on Trades Hall, the strikers eventually surrendered and Smuts deported the labour leaders.[239]

The MCC party were signed up as special constables allowing them to be out during the curfew. On the first evening of the third Test, Lionel Tennyson found himself dining at the home of a woman whose husband had been called away on defence duties. The husband returned unexpectedly. 'You must fly, you don't know how jealous he is, you are a dead man if he finds you here,' whispered

---

239 Simons and Simons, *Class and Colour*, 168

the wife, as Tennyson dived down a rose-covered trellis without his jacket. He got back to the hotel pouring blood and had to get his wounds dressed. His fielding the following day was, he claimed, excellent despite the circumstances.[240]

When Tennyson visited E.G. Wynyard, the maids were allegedly instructed to lock themselves in their rooms before 'The Honourable' went upstairs.

With the Wanderers commandeered by the military, the Transvaal game had to be moved to Pretoria and the team headed north by train. Barnes as usual had made his own arrangements and did not play in this game or the next against a Transvaal XI at Vogelfontein. Without Barnes's edge, both matches were drawn amid almost no interest at all.

7.8 The African mine workers' strike and the racist state

While white mine workers received 'courteous' treatment in Pretoria jail, African miners suffered serious casualties in another so-called riot that resulted from the brutal suppression of an African strike. On 9 January 1914, 8,000 black workers at the Jagersfontein mine struck work after a white overseer had kicked a black worker to death. When the manager refused to have the perpetrator arrested, the workers tried to break out and join miners in other compounds. White miners cornered the black strikers and fired on them, killing 11 and wounding 37. Most went back to work, but the remaining 250 who refused were marched to jail. A judicial enquiry was held, and while the white witnesses disagreed over the necessity for the shooting none of those responsible was prosecuted.[241]

Barnes resurfaced again against Griqualand West in Kimberley, knocking over ten more wickets inside 19 overs to bring MCC another innings victory. MCC then travelled to Bloemfontein, capital of the Afrikaner heartland of the Orange Free State, where

---

240 Tennyson, *Verse or Worse*, 118
241 Simons and Simons, *Class and Colour*, 168; *The Star*, 10/1/1914

relations had been less than cordial on previous visits. Johnny Douglas had arranged to meet family and 'forgotten the mayor's reception'. The team under Morice Bird departed from the far end of the train avoiding the large welcoming contingent, Afrikaner notables and all, at the other end.

7.9 Struddy and the gramophone

The team partied hard in the staid Afrikaner capital of Bloemfontein and their gramophone was a source of considerable annoyance to the other hotel guests. The manager tried to get them to leave and Strudwick barked at him on the stairs, not improving his mood. Finally, he located the gramophone along with several of the party who insisted on him joining them for a drink. 'I don't know what time they let him go but he was our only pal in Bloemfontein the next day,' said Struddy.

When they returned to the hotel for lunch, they ran over an African pedestrian who was forced by local bylaws off the pavements and into the street. Strudwick thought he was dead, but he got up and calmly walked away.[242] No further action was taken.

The game rubbed salt into Bloemfontein's wounds. Bird made 200, Jack Hearne stroked a century and Barnes bowled right through both innings to claim 13-79. Johnny Douglas always believed in fighting fire with fire and MCC won by a shockingly punitive innings and 374 runs.

In early February, after drawn games against Transvaal and Northern Natal, the travellers returned to Durban to play Natal. They won the toss but, without Hobbs, struggled to 132, their lowest total of the tour. Natal were as much a one-man team with the bat as the tourists were with the ball and this was the start of the duel between Taylor and Barnes. In Natal's first innings, Taylor, playing a different game, made 91 out of 153, a lead of 21.

A moderate second innings, with Johnny Douglas top-scoring with 33, set Natal 215 to win. Dave Nourse came out to join Taylor

---

242 Strudwick, *Stumps*, 155

at 26/2. Struddy, fielding as a sub, dropped Taylor's top-edged pull off Barnes when he was on nine with what was claimed to be 'the biggest sitter you've ever seen', the ball bouncing off his chin. Taylor celebrated with three consecutive fours off Barnes. By now Nourse had had plenty of experience of the Staffordshire devil, but allegedly told Taylor he couldn't pick the top-spinner and Taylor set out to take on Barnes. For over after over he farmed the strike.

At the beginning of each over, Barnes found Taylor at the business end and his intended victim Nourse out of reach until finally his patience was exhausted. 'It's Taylor, Taylor, Taylor, all the time.' he roared, threw down the ball and strode off to the pavilion for a rub down and a large whisky and soda. Nourse hit Woolley for a big six and was finally caught on the boundary trying to repeat the treatment. 'Why did you do that?' asked a frustrated Taylor. 'That bastard is coming back, I saw him on the veranda getting ready,' hissed Nourse.[243] When Barnes did come back it was too late. Taylor was caught Woolley off Hearne for 100, but the last few runs were knocked off for a four-wicket win.

MCC had lost for the only time on the tour. Taylor not only monopolised Barnes but scored 191 (for once out) out of Natal's total of 369 in the game. In the second innings he put on 146 with Nourse (59) for the third wicket which took them to within 43 of the total. Barnes ended up with second-innings figures of 2-70.

Taylor moved batting into the modern age by the speed of his assessment of length and the strength of his play off the back foot. His footwork was no less revolutionary than Schwarz's googly.[244] The main annoyance for the tourists was the usual – the umpiring. Barnes struck Taylor repeatedly on the pads and complained that they were playing 13 men. Douglas then had a batsman given out before the umpire changed his mind and reversed his decision. As a contemporary report put it, 'Mr Douglas expressed himself strongly on the matter.' The umpire, Josh Steele, refused to resume after tea

---

243 Greyvenstein, *Giants*, 20

244 Louis Duffus, *Cricketers of the Veld*, (London: Sampson Low, Marsden and Co, 1947) 18

until Douglas apologised. And when Woolley finally caught Taylor, Barnes shouted, 'Not out.'[245]

Three Natalians – Claude Carter, who took ten wickets in the match, Dan Taylor (brother of Herby) and Joe Cox – were selected for the fourth Test in Durban. Spectator interest had declined with the loss of the rubber. Barnes claimed 7-56, but England were all at sea against the left-handed Carter bowling round the wicket into a strong wind. His 6-50 inspired a collapse from 92/0 to 163 all out and gave the South Africans a seven-run lead on the first innings.

Taylor played another masterly innings of 93 in the second innings and was able to declare on 305/9, with seven more victims for Barnes. His exhibition of patience and technique contained only three fours and 60 singles. Hobbs (97) and Rhodes (35) put on 133 for the first wicket, but then Blanckenberg took three quick wickets. A violent thunderstorm finished matters off with MCC teetering on 154/5, still 158 behind. This was the first Test against England in South Africa not played to a finish.

The team sailed to Port Elizabeth for the final Test. Struddy, the insect magnet, was delighted to escape the dozens of Durban cockroaches that scampered up his bathroom walls and swam in his cups of coffee. To the disappointment of the small crowd, Barnes allegedly had a throat infection and was unable to play. South Africa won the toss and batted with justified optimism following the previous Test. The top five all got into double figures, but only Taylor (42) and Hands, with an excellent 83, kicked on. Douglas wrapped up the tail with a bristling spell of 4-14 as South Africa slid to a disappointing 193.

England revelled in the conditions. Almost everyone made runs, with the consistent Phillip Mead hitting his second century of the series. Bill Lundie, South Africa's new fast bowler, bowled 46.3 overs into a gale, ending with 4-101 including Hobbs, Douglas and Tennyson. Newberry and Blanckenberg were leg weary and tired of

---

245 Luckin, *History*, 618

Test cricket. One could have forgiven Taylor for feeling the same way, but he (87) and Zulch (60) fought back to reduce the 218-run deficit, putting on 129 for the first wicket. England missed the great man and used eight bowlers in the blazing heat of the fourth day, but Taylor's departure effectively raised the white flag except for a defiant 49 from P.A.M. Hands. South Africa went down to a ten-wicket defeat and a 4-0 series loss.

It was a tame ending to what would be the last day of Test cricket for almost seven years. All members of both teams, except Barnes, were entertained by the local branch of the Society of St George. Johnny Douglas was characteristically defensive. He was unhappy that they had been the recipients of 'scathing and nasty remarks which were quite unwarranted … we tried to do our best and when a man does his best he should be excused of his faults'.

The tourists arrived back in Cape Town in the first half of March. Barnes had disappeared from the tour after not playing in Port Elizabeth. The final match at Newlands ended in an exciting draw with the last Western Province pair battling it out to survive. And apart from winning a game of soccer played by the team in their street clothes against a local league team, the tour was over.

Or almost. The South African business manager, Ivor Difford, had not made himself universally popular. Rumours circulated during the team's stay in Johannesburg that they were drinking heavily. Tiger Smith denied this, saying Difford had simply failed to return the beer, wine and spirits which had been supplied free of charge for the team's use. He also claimed that Johnny Douglas hardly touched a drop. The latter proposition seemed unlikely.

Whether or not Difford lined his pockets on the proceeds of leftover alcohol, he reduced the bonus payouts for the team based on their behaviour and absences. He looked to deduct £50 from Tiger Smith because he hadn't played the full tour, Relf was £10 short, Phillip Mead lost a fiver for missing two matches through illness, and Jack Hearne was docked his bonus because he had been in hospital in Durban. With SACA picking up the tab, Difford was presumably instructed to minimise outgoings. But Johnny

Douglas told Difford some home truths and the lads all got their full £200 bonus.[246]

Barnes's 'indisposition' in the final Test was often explained by the incendiary relationship between two of the most difficult personalities to play for England. But Barnes blamed the tour management, not the captain. He was promised a collection when he did anything outstanding. He considered 49 wickets in four Tests and 125 scalps at less than ten in all matches an outstanding achievement, not to mention his 17 and 14 wickets in the second and fourth Tests. Difford had not arranged a single crowd collection, so Barnes refused to play in the last Test.

This may have only been part of the story. Barnes's record and behaviour suggested a deeper rift. Barnes travelled out on a different ship to the team, and missed eight games out of 22, including the final Test. He often travelled between Tests with the South Africans rather than with his own team and returned on a later vessel. And there were several on-field incidents. Douglas's obsession with winning meant he had to put up with his behaviour which must have strained relations to the limit. No doubt Ivor Difford fell out with Barnes, but he may have been a convenient scapegoat.

Bill Ferguson, legendary baggage master, and scorer for several decades, gave an inkling of what it was like touring with Douglas. In addition to his other duties, Bill was ordered by Douglas to whiten his boots and pads on a daily basis, dry his belt between sessions, and be at Douglas's hotel at 8am every day just in case he needed anything. Fortunately, said Fergie, 'There were not many skippers like him.'[247]

Despite the volatile mix of Difford, Douglas and Barnes, there was enough cricketing respect to save the tour from imploding. It was a two-man series in a way that few others have been. Herby Taylor averaged 57 in 10 innings against the greatest bowler of his generation, and 50.80 in the five Tests. He was only dismissed once

246 David Lemmon, *Johnny Won't Hit Today*, (London: Allen and Unwin, 1982) 71-74
247 W.H. Ferguson, *Mr Cricket*, (London: Nicholas Kaye, 1957) 52-53

in single figures, lbw to Barnes. The only time MCC lost was when Taylor made 91 and 100 in Natal's four-wicket win.

He was not simply a batsman, he was a captain at 24, both of his province and his country. Twenty-three players were used by South Africa, five played all of the games and only three did themselves any justice with the bat – Taylor, Zulch and Hands. They were utterly inexperienced, except for the out-of-form Nourse, and wholly dependent on Taylor's ability as an opening batsman to blunt the Barnes threat.

It was a case of Barnes against boys. In Barnes's four Tests his strike rate was 27.67 balls per wicket, at an average of 10.93. The other bowlers in the MCC team in the same four Tests had a strike rate of 74.36 balls per wicket, at an average of 31.76. Barnes was physically remarkable, mentally unshakeable, tireless, relentless in line and length, and voracious in his appetite for wickets on matting, which accentuated his pace, spin and bounce. He was so skilled as to be almost unplayable to anyone lacking the lightning-fast reflexes and ice-cold brain of a Taylor. He was backed behind the stumps by the spring-heeled Strudwick, whose agility, superabundant energy and fierce concentration earned him 15 catches and six stumpings in the series. It was a team mismatch, but it did elevate Herby Taylor into cricketing immortality.

After gathering gloom, blackness closed in and international cricket vanished. The bright young talents, Bill Lundie (who faced the last ball to be bowled in a Test before the outbreak of hostilities) and Claude Newberry (who planned a professional career with Tennyson's Hampshire), walked off the Port Elizabeth pitch forever. They went off to war a year later but never came home. Nor did Reggie Schwarz, Gordon White and Arthur Ochse who had played in South Africa's first ever Test.

PART 3:

PITCH AND TURN

8

Strike! Frank Mann 1922/23

NINE YEARS after Sydney Barnes had steamrollered his way across South Africa, the world was struggling to look beyond the horrors of the Somme, the freezing wastes of the North Atlantic, the mass starvation in Bengal and the cruelties of South West Africa, among the hundreds of tableaux of death. The war to end all wars, with 17 million dead and 23 million wounded, more than in all the wars preceding it, was immediately followed by a more relentless enemy, the influenza pandemic which fed on the mass migrations of the dispossessed across the globe. It is estimated that between 50 and 100 million died.[248]

The upheaval of war translated into the struggle over labour. Immediately after the war, white municipal workers in Johannesburg won a successful strike, but the state reacted ferociously when voteless black workers used the same tactic. In 1919, an African National Congress campaign against passes gained thousands of adherents. At one meeting alone, 2,000 passes were handed in before the meeting was broken up by white thugs with guns and clubs and 200 Africans were put on trial. The black crowd outside the courtroom sang 'Nkosi Sikelel' iAfrika' as mounted police charged the demonstrators.

---

248 Laura Spinney. *Pale Rider: The Spanish Flu and How it Changed the World*, (London: Vintage, 2017), 4

Black mine workers earned one 20th of the wages of white miners and since the start of the war these had stayed static, while white wages had gone up by 40 per cent. In February 1920, 71,000 African miners came out on strike with ANC support. The Chamber of Mines sang a familiar song – that any increase in black wages would make the mines uneconomic and put white miners out of work. On Smuts's orders, troops invaded the labour compounds, shot and beat black workers and drove them back to work. The involvement of the ANC in mass action was short-lived and the newly formed African Industrial and Commercial Workers Union (ICU) under Clements Kadalie began to play an activist role.

8.1 Bulhoek and Bondelswarts resistance

State-directed violence was not confined to strikers. Opposition movements in South Africa have often taken on a religious Ethiopianism as a remedy to land hunger and ethnic beliefs. In 1920, a millenarian sect of about 500 'Israelites' camped at Bulhoek Common near Queenstown to celebrate Passover and stayed awaiting the end of the world. The believers could not be persuaded to disperse and 800 police and soldiers opened fire with machine guns and rifles, killing 120 and severely injuring many more.[249]

A year later, when the Bondelswarts, a Khoi community in South West Africa, refused to pay the heavy tax increase on the dogs they needed for hunting, they were attacked by a force of 400 men with air bomber support and again more than 100 died.

South Africa returned to world cricket with a visit from Herbie Collins' Australian Imperial Forces in 1919. The two representative games did not rank as Tests and the tourists, spearheaded by Jack Gregory's hostile fast bowling, were too strong for the locals without Herby Taylor. Two years later, Warwick Armstrong arrived with his triumphant 1921 Australians fresh from a 3-0 Ashes victory, although the 'Big Ship' himself was injured. Australia had won eight Tests in a row against a still reeling old enemy. To its surprise, South Africa

---

249 *Time Longer Than Rope*, 135-143

managed to draw the first two Tests. In the second, Jack Gregory hit the fastest Test century (119) in 70 minutes. South Africa survived thanks to Charlie Frank's obdurate 152, before losing the third Test by ten wickets. The Australians presented a 'Champion Barracker' bat to the spectator at The Wanderers who had punctuated Frank's innings with stentorian shouts of 'You'll never get him out'. He was proved wrong, but only after 512 minutes.[250] The South Africans had displayed fight, but there was room for technical improvement. The first MCC tour for nine years would provide a gauge of the state of South African cricket.

On 11 March 1922, Jack Board, the Gloucester wicketkeeper who had toured with Hawke and Warner, was umpiring a grudge match between King Edward School and Jeppe High School, the two leading school sides on the Rand. A few hundred yards away, strikers fought a pitched battle with the police and army. Planes bombed the insurgents and fleets of ambulances ferried the wounded to the hospital. It capped the lot as far as his cricketing experiences went, said Board.[251] This was the culmination of a week-long occupation described by the pro-mining *Star* as the 'phantasmagoria of a frightful dream'.[252]

The strike began in January as a labour dispute, but turned into a civil war. The mine owners sought to employ more cheap black labour and the white labour force fought to retain their access to privileged employment at enhanced rates. Or in the parlance of the day, it was over the location of the 'job colour bar'.

Many Afrikaners without skills or experience had gravitated to the mines during the war. The death of Louis Botha in 1919 had decreased Afrikaner support for the Smuts-controlled South Africa Party, the party of the mining industry. The 1922 rebellion marked the re-emergence of Afrikaner nationalism in alliance with white labour. From the mining industry's perspective, a 32 per cent increase in production costs made mines uneconomic unless the job colour bar

---

250 Luckin, *History*, vol 2, 185
251 *Ibid*, 65
252 *The Star*, 15/3/1922

was 'balanced' by employing more cheap African labour to recognise economic realities. For the white workers, the mine owners were destroying South Africa as a 'white man's country'.

The job colour bar was as old as the mines. White supervisors who set the blasting charges were paid £500 a year. Africans who did the digging, drilling and hammer work earned £30 per year. In total £10m was paid annually to 20,000 Europeans mineworkers and £6m to 200,000 Africans. The gap was widening. African wages had risen by nine per cent since the start of the war, white wages by 57 per cent. The – white – Mine Workers Union, according to the mining houses, earned wages at a level far more than the value of their services. This the capitalists considered to be 'economic suicide to the strains of the Red Flag'.

It was a struggle for the country. White and black workers had fought in the European war and followed the Bolsheviks with huge interest. Massive immigration of displaced persons after the war had focused white radicals on a South African revolution, overthrowing a mining system dictated by stock markets in London, Paris and New York. This international cabal, they believed, used African workers to systematically undercut the interests of whites. It was an incendiary mixture of international revolutionary socialism, anarchism, xenophobia, white racism, nationalism and violence. For some, the goal was the establishment of a republic separate from the British Commonwealth based on a state-owned mining industry, for others the destruction of capitalism itself.

The strike had been spontaneous in 1913/14. From January 1922, it was led by military-type commandos and the East Rand mines were at the centre of the struggle. The Fordsburg Commando with its banner of 'Workers of the World Unite and Fight for a White South Africa' and other commandos of men and women roamed the Rand in search of 'scabs'.

Thousands of Africans became the victims of white brutality and intimidation. The strikers attacked Africans to stampede them off the Rand or provoke them into a race war. In early March, at Ferreiratown, strikers armed with rifles and revolvers attacked a group of Africans armed with sticks and pangas. While the police looked on, 16 Africans were killed and dozens injured. Charles Ward, a miner who had arrived only eight months previously from Scotland, was arrested with a pocket full of dum-dum bullets designed to inflict maximum carnage.

After ten weeks of armed skirmishes, a white worker council called a general strike and so began a week of civil war, pitched battles with police, dynamited pylons and a city plunged into darkness. A railway official who witnessed one such battle said the police cut through the strike commando 'like a train going through a flock of sheep'. A few days later, while the Boksburg commando sang the 'Red Flag' outside the jail where their colleagues were imprisoned, the police dropped to their knees and fired at the strikers.

By 10 March, the worker committee controlled Johannesburg. The Smuts government proclaimed martial law. A day later, the artillery fired into commando positions and planes flew raggedly over the city dropping 32 bombs on commandos and civilians alike. The middle classes overlooked the deadly battle for the town. While the schoolboys of King Edward School and Jeppe High School fought their battle on the cricket field, the Wanderers tennis club focused on a vital league match.[253]

8.2 The Wanderers and the civil war

By 19 March it was officially all over; 687 people had been killed or wounded and hundreds of arrests made. The Wanderers was transformed into a hospital with segregated wards for police and army, and strikers and commandos. Casualties overflowed into the dance hall and gym and prisoners huddled on the slope of the banked cycle track. Others filled the makeshift morgue. Victor Kent, dictatorial president of the Wanderers, denounced 'foreign socialistic influences' and the trade unions that had incited the revolution. He demanded that uneducated immigrants be prohibited because 'it was impossible to make sportsmen of them'.[254]

---

253 Thelma Gutske, *Old Gold*, 158-161
254 *Ibid*

It was the closest South Africa would come to a revolution, driven by privileged white workers fighting to increase the deprivation of the black labour force.

The mining industry backed by the firepower of the state had gained a vital victory but black workers were the perennial losers as they plodded back to the mines.

Eight months later, MCC arrived. Frank Mann was Plum Warner's choice to lead the tourists.

At 16st he was a cruiserweight by comparison with the 22st Warwick 'Big Ship' Armstrong, but he was still the biggest man to have represented MCC in South Africa. He was an aggressive bat with a drive like 'Gulliver's sneeze among the Lilliputians'.[255]

He had been hardened by years of active service in France where he was wounded for the third time in 1917. After a long convalescence he succeeded Warner as Middlesex captain after Warner finally won the County Championship in 1920.

After their thrashing from Johnny Douglas, SACA insisted on six amateurs to balance the sides. The MCC delivered. Phil Mead and Frank Woolley returned, Hobbs stayed at home with appendicitis, Patsy Hendren was overlooked and the colourful Cecil Parkin deemed a behavioural risk.

The voyage claimed the usual casualties in the Bay of Biscay and light entertainment was choreographed by amateur impresario Percy Fender. The highlight was the Blue Riband race with lady 'jockeys' cutting down the middle of ten-yard-long tapes with nail scissors on a pitching deck and Fender on commentary. Away from the track, he was always willing to sing his signature song 'Why do these tortoise shell rims hide those wonderful eyes?'. He had a 'violent row' with the short-fused Arthur Carr on the ship. Meanwhile, A.C. McLaren's unofficial tour was sailing to Australia and New Zealand and Archie could be heard performing on the flute in the Sports Committee Jazz Band.

---

255 Brian Rendell, *Frank and George Mann*, (Cardiff: ACS Publications, 2015) 19

Frank Mann had no previous Test experience, but he was a war hero, heir to the Mann brewing empire, a successful county captain and a man of considerable personal charm. He faced 63 days of cricket, even more social engagements and an itinerary which covered more miles than ever before. Plum Warner gave him a full endorsement, 'Mr Mann is the right man in the right place, compels affection and respect and in Mrs [Enid] Mann has a charming and tactful chief of staff.'

Wives, that is Cecilia Gilligan, Ivy Carr and Dora Woolley (and her two young children), were part of the tour party for the first time. This gave Mann plenty of additional headaches. Although SACA paid single first-class accommodation for the players, the latter had to bear the additional costs for their wives. The professional Woolley and his family could only afford second-class fares and Dora was excluded from some official functions.[256]

The press wondered how Mann would handle the awkward and disruptive George Macaulay and Vallance Jupp. Mann told them that he had booked return passages for each of them. Any problems and they would be on the first boat back. Arthur Carr was also, in his own words, 'a bit of a handful' and would have his own run-ins with the skipper.

The welcome in Cape Town was warm. Mann praised South Africa for its contribution to the war and the popular Frank Bond was appointed as travelling manager. Only four players had previously played on mat and the rest soon discovered that sharp spin and steep bounce put a premium on the back foot and gave little opportunity for the silky off-drive.

Soon after his arrival, Mann was approached by a coloured cricketer, who asked him if he wanted a fast bowler. Mann allegedly thought it was a joke. But subsequent racism has almost certainly obscured how C.J. Nicholls was employed as a baggage master and net bowler.

---

256 *Ibid*, 50

8.3 C.J. Nicholls, Tancred and the First World War

C.J. Nicholls came from the 'Malay' tradition of 'Krom' and Armien Hendricks who had given Walter Read's English tourists a rare working over in 1892 and had challenged Warner, Hayward, and the other tourists in the nets in the 1890s. In 1897, A.B. Tancred admitted in *Cricket*, 'Hendricks is a good fast bowler, but in the opinion of the great majority of South African cricketers it would not be advisable to send him [on tour to England], on account of the colour question which in England you no doubt find difficult to understand ... there are two or three native bowlers coming on well; one of them, a "Cape boy" is as fast as any bowler we have ever seen.'[257]

It is likely that he had Nicholls, a left-handed fast bowler in mind. The 'Hendricks law' prohibited persons of colour from playing professionally or in representative games. The Western Province Cricket Club (WPCC) employed him as a net bowler and general staffer at Newlands. Plum Warner described how Nicholls had hit his middle stump nearly every other ball in 1905 and Colin Blythe had invited him to qualify for Kent, but he had turned down the chance.

Nicholls had been baggage handler for Douglas' team in 1913/14. After the outbreak of war, WPCC's Vollie van der Byl took command of the coloured Cape Labour Battalion and Nicholls became an unofficial batman to Van der Byl and Battalion cricket coach and organiser in France. During the 1919 Australian tour, he was appointed as baggage master by the Australians. The latter played three matches in Cape Town, but their request for a game against coloured servicemen and fundraisers was turned down.[258] You could die for the empire alongside white comrades, but you couldn't play cricket against them.

He was baggage master and unofficial manager to the 1921 Australians, and Mann's and Stanyforth's MCC tours, and was involved with Roslins in Cape Town as player, coach and administrator for half a century.[259]

257 *Cricket*, 22/7/1897, 294
258 *Cape Argus*, 6/11/1922
259 Odendaal, Reddy and Merrett, *Divided Country*, 26, 64-65

The MCC could certainly have used another quick bowler. Arthur Gilligan's first ball of the tour disappeared for five wides and the second for four byes.[260] Izak Buys, a left-handed fast bowler from Stellenbosch, reduced the tourists to 93/6, but Fender struck a typically belligerent 96 and Mead a resolute 97. This ensured victory in the tricky first fixture and the team began a month's perambulation through the Cape heartlands through, as Fender put it, 'rain, rain, rain'.[261]

Smooth progress on the field was not always matched off it. Frank Mann considered breakfast to be the most difficult part of the tour. He prided himself on being always accessible at mealtimes, but found himself in the firing line as the players channelled complaints from their wives about seating at functions the previous evening. The gradations of class within the touring party and by reference to local dignitaries were a subject of perennial dispute. Mann also discovered that the wives complained more about selection decisions than their husbands.

Cecilia Gilligan was very unhappy. Over the course of the tour, Mann and Carr appeared in every game, Frank Woolley only missed two, while Gilligan, statistically the most successful fast bowler, played in only 14 out of 22 matches. He played in the first (as an emergency call up for Jack Russell) and last Tests, averaging 22 with both bat and ball.

R.M. Ballantine, the one-man press pack, said the wickets were dangerous and some of Gilligan's deliveries might have damaged his opponents.

This was not the real reason for his omission. His stamina and attitude towards Mann were suspect, Gilligan believing he should have been captain. In any event, Mann underplayed a potential trump card.

---

260 *Cape Argus*, 10/11/1922
261 *Sportsman*, 27/12/1922

8.4 Arthur Gilligan and the fascists

Politics may have been a factor in the rift. In 1924/25, Gilligan led MCC in Australia and with Frederick Toone (secretary of Yorkshire under the presidency of Lord Hawke) as manager. Both Gilligan and Toone were proselytising members of the British Fascist Party. As Robert Brooke later put it, Gilligan spent his spare time extolling the virtues of Benito Mussolini's fascists. After the tour, the Commonwealth Investigation Branch discovered that British Fascists branches had been established in the major Australian cities through which the tour passed, using enrolment forms and propaganda printed in Britain. On his return, Gilligan wrote an article for the *British Fascist* entitled 'The Spirit of Fascism and Cricket'.[262]

In 1927, he apologised for not attending a Fascist meeting at Hove. He had been ordered to take a month's complete rest on his return from captaining the 1926/27 MCC tour to India. It was a marathon of 34 fixtures, against opposition often selected on community lines – Europeans, Hindus, Mahommedans and Parsis. They even played, and lost to, Delhi Ladies. Gilligan played 22 of the games, scoring under 500 runs and taking ten wickets in 88 overs. His recommendation was instrumental in the inclusion of India into the ICC in 1926.

Gilligan told the British Fascist organisers, 'My heart and soul is with the movement, and I think that the object of the meeting is magnificent ... we shall never have red gold monopolising our wonderful country and empire.'[263] The *British Lion* published his 'clarion call to all who know what it is to play the game and can help to carry this same spirit into our entire national life ... Be a sport and save your own countrymen from the red tyrant. He has had enough rope. It is time he was hanged by the rope of fascism, the one rope he dreads. Help to draw it tight. If you don't, they'll draw their noose around you.'[264]

---

262 www.cricketmash.com

263 'Playing Cricket: A.E.R. Gilligan's straight bat to the Reds', *The British Lion*, June 1927, no.19, 10

264 *Ibid*

The team had two wicketkeepers, George Brown and Walter Livsey, who a few months earlier had both made hundreds in a record ninth-wicket partnership for Hampshire. In perhaps the most remarkable match ever, Hampshire won by 155 runs after being bowled out for 15 in the first innings. Livsey did not have a good tour. He was horribly sea sick, fell ill soon after arrival and played only two games before he broke a finger keeping to Gilligan at Queenstown. He went on to become the 'manservant' of the hon. Lionel Tennyson.

Brown was unfit against Griquas at Kimberley and Carr was forced to take the gloves. 'Stevens and Fender did most of the bowling and neither had any control of length or the foggiest idea of where the ball was going. Still, I only conceded 27 byes,' he said.[265]

The next fixture against East Rand was memorable for the return of the 41-year-old 'Tip' Snooke, who made 76, and a sandstorm which levelled the tents, and dyed everything a rich brick red. The match against Transvaal catapulted 22-year Bob Catterall to national attention. Catterall's father trained him like a racehorse. Monday to Wednesday was devoted to practice and running. Thursday night was 'cascara' night to clear his vision and on Friday, 'I just had an ordinary gallop.'[266] It worked. Bob hit 128 in 195 minutes with two sixes and 13 fours. He was the only player to cope with Valance Jupp's leg theory – sharp off-cutters bowled on leg stump to a seven-man leg side field.

Catterall and 20-year-old Buster Nupen, who had taken five wickets for Transvaal, became instant certainties for the Johannesburg Test. Billy Zulch and Charlie Frank who had carried the fight to Australia in the postwar series were overlooked. Frank, who had been badly gassed and dug out of a shell hole on the Western Front, had played one of the greatest ever defensive Test innings against the 1921 Australians. But SACA decided that fielding was the priority and that Frank was not up to standard. The side also lacked a googly bowler which in South Africa was like Hamlet without the prince.

265 Actually it was 37 byes. A.W. Carr, *Cricket with the Lid Off*, (London: Hutchinson, 1935) 184; Luckin, *History vol 2*, 259

266 Brian Bassano, *Mann's Men*, (London: J.M. McKenzie, 2004) 128

The 46-year-old Ernie Vogler had written to offer his services – having apparently retained his bowling skills and improved his batting. But he failed to arrive on the promised steamer.

There was optimism in the Transvaal air. The distressing series of court cases dealing with the savagery of the Rand Rebellion and its aftermath were over and the death sentences were all commuted. At the other end of the continent, Howard Carter had broken into Tutankhamun's tomb and the world had its first shared global moment marvelling at the wonders of ancient Egypt.

Both sides fielded five debutants. Bob Catterall, passed fit after dislocating his thumb, faced the first over from Gilligan, the smallest player on the field but the fastest bowler in England. He covered an 18-pace run in ten strides and a ferocious delivery leap. Catterall was dropped in his first over, but by Gilligan's third over his pace had noticeably slowed. Jupp replaced him and switched to leg theory. Catterall opened his shoulders and drove his first ball straight back past him for four. Taylor played very uncertainly against Jupp, Hearne played across a straight one, and suddenly leg theory became an attacking weapon. At the other end, Alex Kennedy turned it both ways and 92/2 at lunch turned into 148 all out. Advantage MCC.

South Africa's bowlers proved equally adept. Jimmy Blanckenberg moved the ball both ways off the mat at medium pace and finished with 6-76. Andy Sandham, who scored 26, explained his dismissal, 'I didn't know anything about the first ball and the second. The third ball woke me up with the noise. I turned around and saw two stumps flat and had a headache as I saw the groggy third stump. I should like someone to preserve that last ball to see what Jack Hobbs would have done with it.'[267] Alex Kennedy's 41 not out and a last wicket partnership of 30 with Gilligan gave England a lead of 34.

In the second innings, Herby Taylor performed like a cricketing god. He rewrote the record books with the highest score for South Africa against England at home until readmission. His majestic 176 steered South Africa to 420 in front of a delirious Boxing Day

---

267 *The Star*, 26/12/1922

crowd. Gilligan took 3-69 and Kennedy 4-132 and England needed an unlikely 387 in the final innings. The game was effectively over at 124/4. Frank Mann was beaten so often by Nupen that he laughed at his predicament. He finished on 28 not out and South Africa won by 168 runs. When asked for a speech, Sir Abe Bailey just pointed to the scoreboard.[268]

There was no time to celebrate South Africa's first win in 17 Tests since Adelaide in 1911. The players clambered wearily aboard the train to Cape Town for the second Test.

For South Africa, Buys was replaced by the left-hander Alf Hall, a Newlands specialist. For MCC, Russell had recovered, and Macaulay was welcomed back. Vice-captain Gilligan cooled his heels in the pavilion to Cecilia's chagrin.

The South Africans, drawn almost entirely from outside the Cape, showed their inexperience on the Newlands mat laid on grass. George Hearne was caught for a golden duck off Macaulay's first ball in Test cricket. Kennedy skilfully exploited the cross wind and Percy Fender swung it dangerously late and the locals were all out 113 before tea. England crawled to a 70-run lead, featuring a 50 from Jack Russell and a wild 42 from Carr. The fielding led by Catterall was exceptional.

Newlands was feeling its age, the facilities antiquated and even the sight screens inadequate. The unhappy Hearne dragged a ball on to his stumps for a pair, but Catterall (76) and Taylor (68) ground out a second-wicket partnership of 155. Taylor defied Kennedy's guile, the speed and turn of Macaulay, Fender's swing and Jupp's leg theory. This was a new Taylor, a man of iron will rather than the brilliant and dashing batsman of his youth. Macaulay took five wickets and MCC faced a target of 173.

After Blanckenberg trapped Russell lbw at 20/1, it became the Alf Hall show. He bowled an impeccable length and varied his pace and spin. He shouted for a succession of lbws and stumpings with the crowd chorus behind him. Hall took his fifth wicket at 86/6 when Jupp joined Frank Mann. After a sleepless night, Mann had

---

268 *The Star*, 29/12/1922

added only a single before hitting a sitter straight into Taylor's hands at cover. It went in, then out again, falling at his feet. The crowd fell silent. In the following over Nupen could not take a return catch and a few runs later Brann dropped Jupp at extra cover.

Riding his luck, Mann pulled two huge sixes. The score rose to 154, the finishing line in sight. Taylor brought Hall back and Jupp was stumped for 38. With six to win and three wickets in hand, Mann decided to win the game with a single hit. His top edge spiralled upwards and nestled safely in Blanckenberg's huge hands.

Brown came out to join Kennedy who played the ball past gully for an apparently safe single. But Taylor was loitering with intent at wide third man. He pounced and with only one stump to aim at smashed the wicket on the full an instant before George Brown slid in his bat. Five runs to win, last man in. Bob Catterall was on the fence at deep square leg and called in 20 yards by Jimmy Blanckenberg. He moved in but sidled out again as Blanckenberg went back to his mark. Jimmy spotted him and called him in again and this time Catterall stayed in. Alex Kennedy 'took a wahoo and hit it over my head to the exact place I had been standing'. Four runs and the scores were tied.

Hall bowled the next over to Macaulay, both men in their debut Tests. 'Mac was white as a ghost,' it was reported, knees knocking, and the first ball missed his off stump by a whisker. The next delivery pitched on leg stump, straightened and a howl arose from thousands of throats. George Thompson, who had played for MCC on Leveson Gower's 1909/10 tour, was umpiring his first Test. He pulled his hand out of his pocket, but shook his head instead of raising his finger. The *Star*'s 'Olympic' in the press box was outraged, 'Statisticians may produce chapter and verse …but spectators and players alike say that Macaulay was well and truly out.' The whole fielding side were within a yard or two of the striker and Macaulay coolly pushed the following delivery about ten yards for the single and sprinted for the safety of the pavilion only to end up, along with Kennedy and Alf Hall, chaired in by the crowd. [269]

---

269 The *Star*, 5/1/23.

SOUTH AFRICA v ENGLAND Second Test, Newlands, 1–4 January 1923

SOUTH AFRICA

R.H. Catterall	c Brown b Fender	10	b Macaulay	76
G.A.L. Hearne	c Fender b Macaulay	0	b Kennedy	0
H.W. Taylor*	c Fender	9	c Jupp b Kennedy	68
A.W. Nourse	lbw b Fender	16	b Fender	19
W.V.S. Ling	c Mann b Fender	13	c Fender b Macaulay	2
W.H. Brann	b Kennedy	0	lbw b Macaulay	4
J.M. Blanckenberg	c Carr b Jupp	9	b Kennedy	5
C.M. Francois	run out	28	c and b Macaulay	19
T.A. Ward	b Jupp	4	not out	15
E.P. Nupen	c and b Macaulay	2	b Kennedy	6
A.E. Hall	not out	0	b Kennedy	5
Extras		22		23
Total		**113**	**9 wickets**	**242**

Kennedy	18-10-24-1	35.2-13-58-4
Macaulay	13-5-19-2	37-11-64-5
Fender	14-4-29-4	20-3-52-1
Woolley	2-1-1-0	11-3-22-0
Jupp	9-3-18-2	11-3-23-0
Fall of wickets	0, 22. 31, 60, 67, 67, 96, 108, 111, 113	2, 157, 158, 162, 170, 200, 212, 212, 224

ENGLAND

C.A.G. Russell	c Catterall b Hall	39	lbw b Blanckenberg	8
A. Sandham	c Francois b Blanckenberg	19	lbw b Hall	17
F.E. Woolley	c Francois b Hall	0	b Hall	5
C.P. Mead	c Francois b Blanckenberg	21	lbw b Hall	31
A.W. Carr	c Ward b Hall	42	c Brann b Hall	6
F.T. Mann*	lbw b Blanckenberg	4	c Blanckenberg b Hall	45
P.G.H. Fender	c Hearne b Hall	3	c Nourse b Hall	2
V.W.C. Jupp	c Hearne b Nupen	12	st Ward b Hall	38

A.S. Kennedy	c Hearne b Blanckenberg	2	not out	11
G. Brown	not out	10	run out	0
G.G. Macaulay	b Blanckenberg	19	not out	1
Extras		12		9
Total		**183**	**9 wickets**	**173**
Nupen	15-2-48-1		24-8-41-0	
Hall	25-8-49-4		37.3-12-63-7	
Blanckenberg	24.1-5-61-5		24-7-56-1	
Francois	4-1-13-0		3-0-4-0	
Fall of wickets	59, 59, 60, 128. 134, 137, 147, 149, 155, 183		20, 29, 49, 56, 59, 86, 154, 167, 168	

England won by 1 wicket

England's one-wicket win was a classic of cricketing fluctuations. They were in an almost unassailable position at the end of day one with a lead of 15 and six wickets in hand. By the end of day two, Taylor and Catterall had turned a deficit of 70 into a lead of 64 with nine wickets in hand. The home team's chances appeared to vanish when Taylor's dismissal sparked a collapse and England had 173 to get on the equivalent of an English turf wicket. Nervous tension enveloped the players and the shock of Taylor's missed catch spread panic through his inexperienced side. South Africa's inspirational captain froze when his opposing captain offered up his wicket and the match, and the youngsters Nupen, Brann and Hall immediately passed up straightforward chances. Taylor's miss was 'the greatest tragedy to befall South African cricket'.

Bob Catterall, no less feisty a quarter of a century later, blamed Taylor for the defeat. Taylor was the greatest batsman South African had produced, but he was 'a bad captain, a bad tactician and a bad coach'. During their second-innings partnership Catterall was seeing the ball as big as a football. But Herby told him to 'button up and not take a chance'.[270] He did what he was told and fed Taylor the strike. Seven runs were scored in the last half an hour as Herby

---

270 Brian Bassano, *Mann's Men*, 129

tapped back tempting half-volleys. The momentum shifted and the game, for Catterall, was lost. Taylor's caution critically undermined the team's self-belief.

A thousand elements can decide a Test, and this turned on the tightest of margins, including a rejected lbw appeal with the last man at the crease. The game was remarkable for the number of unsuccessful lbw appeals. 'The English batsmen use their legs very much indeed and as the matting wickets lend themselves to exceptionally fast zipping off the pitch often appeared to be asking for trouble,' wrote *The Star*.[271] Mead, Russell, Sandham, Brann, Mann and Dave Nourse were out lbw. For Nourse, the Newlands pitch was not fit for Test cricket. It was slow and uneven; the same ball would bounce three or four feet, or three or four inches. The only thing the ball did not do was creep under the mat.

The real hero was on the losing side. Alf Hall, on debut, took 11/112 in the match with his accurate and incisive left-arm fast-medium.

8.5 Cricket and the start of the communications revolution
The Newlands Test produced the greatest race with the clock in the history of South African journalism.

Twelve minutes after stumps at Newlands, a telephone rang in *The Star*'s offices 1,000 miles across the wires in Johannesburg. Reports of SA's final scores went by pneumatic tube to the printing office, were typeset and hurried to the press. Twenty minutes after the game ended at Newlands and outside the Johannesburg town hall, newsboys were selling *The Star* outside the town hall.

The manuscript was translated into Morse code and sent over the wire at up to 300 words a minute. This was a dozen times faster than the sound key. For the first time, news was available as it happened and 'wherever one turned in Johannesburg, in the club, the restaurant, the workshop and the tramcar, the prospects of the teams were the only topics' according to the newspaper. Technology and the Test turned South Africa into a practical, political (and cricketing) union.[272]

---

271 *The Star* 5/1/1923
272 *The Star*, 2/1/1923

The next Test, to be played at Kingsmead, was drowned out by the Durban rain, but not before Mead made a marathon 181 in 454 minutes. He had the honour of planting the first tree for making a hundred at the new Kingsmead ground, a tradition that continues. The series was level at one match each, with two to play, after three Tests. The tour returned to Johannesburg for the eagerly awaited fourth Test.

In Johannesburg, the workers' revolt had been quelled by Smuts's armed forces, and the mining industry returned to normal. Black workers from the Transvaal had to pay a poll tax for which they were obliged to work in the mines, then they had to provide free labour for three months for the privilege of living in a hut on a farmer's land.[273] Outside the mine compounds, domestic workers were expected to wash, iron, cook and do the garden in addition to the normal kitchen duties for the sum of £2.10 a month, a reduction to pre-war levels. Many walked away, desperation created a crime surge and the state responded with new repressive instruments.

Umpiring had been a running sore throughout the series. Taylor was given not out in the first Test when the whole ground, including Carr on the boundary, heard a nick and Taylor went on to make a hundred. The umpire, Frank Grey, was a South African selector. And the second Test hinged on umpiring decisions, notably when George Thompson turned down the lbw against Macaulay with the scores tied. Neither Thompson nor Grey stood in the fourth Test.

The Wanderers had house full signs up, while thousands outside hoped to get a glimpse of the action. After lunch on the Saturday, play was delayed as spectators spilled over the boundaries and hundreds scrambled on to the superheated and flimsy tin roofs over the stands. A catastrophe was averted, but in this hothouse the cricket was tense from the start. Frank Mann won his second toss and MCC crawled to 244 in more than 100 overs. Alf Hall on an unhelpful surface took 6-82 in 36.4 overs and Carr stonewalled his way to his only Test 50 of the tour.

---

273 *The Star*, 6/1/1923

Tommy Ward held the South African innings together with Dave Nourse, and 'Doodles' Tapscott on debut hit a carefree 50, which gave SA a 51-run lead. But these were initial skirmishes and Russell and Sandham put on 153 for the first wicket in reply. Frank Woolley was on his third South African tour and it was not until his 14th Test in the subcontinent that he finally demonstrated his real class. His first ball clipped but did not dislodge his off bail and he stroked an elegant and chanceless hundred. South Africa were set 326 in four hours and Nourse and Taylor took them within 79 runs of victory with six wickets in hand.

8.6 The 'almost teetotal' amateur: Arthur Carr

'I believe in beer for fast bowlers,' said Carr. 'I can drink with anyone, but I am decidedly against excess where cricketers are concerned. Too much to drink is bad for the eyesight, the nerves, and the wind … You can be quite a moderate drinker most times, but if you do happen to take a few extra ones, you can be quite sure that there will be plenty of people saying, "Oh he drinks too much."'

Carr almost lost his place after a bender forced Frank Mann to hurry to Eastbourne, but Carr reassured him that he would not set South Africa alight or drink it dry. In Johannesburg, Carr was prevailed upon to 'get up on his hind legs' after more than sufficient port and brandy. In his speech, Carr slammed the South African abilities, claimed that half the team would not get into his Notts team and bet £50 that they would not beat Notts, who duly defeated the 1924 tourists. Next, he found himself in full evening dress refereeing a boxing match. He did not enjoy Mann's revenge. Mann forced him to field at long leg at both ends in the heat of the fourth Test. Jupp tried to change positions, but Mann ordered him back.

Carr thought Mann 'one of the best and most popular of county captains … and if he had been a shade better batsman and not put on so much weight early in life, he might have been a great England captain'. He could not move quickly in the field or get down to the ball unless it came straight to him. But, said Carr, 'I still stick up for Frank Mann – blast him.'[274]

---

274 Carr, *Cricket with the Lid Off*, 164-184

Both sides had reason to be confident on their return to Durban. With the series locked at 1-1, the game would be played to a finish. MCC recalled Gilligan, and for South Africa the selectors replaced Buster Nupen with a local medium-pacer, 'Conky' Conyngham. 'Tip' Snooke returned for a farewell appearance. Mann batted first on a damp and slow wicket. Jack Russell and Phil Mead added 139, almost half the total of 281. Russell, in a monumental feat of endurance in the sapping tropical heat, was ninth out for 140 and headed straight to bed with a high fever.

Taylor and Catterall opened against the pace of a fired-up Gilligan desperate to show Mann what he had been missing. Taylor nicked the last ball of Gilligan's third over to slip, and Ward was caught at short leg. Macaulay bowled Catterall to leave South Africa on 41/3. Nourse and Francois put on 39 for the fifth wicket, but South Africa could only manage 179, giving England a lead of 102.

Brown and Kennedy were dismissed quickly and at 26/4 Russell rose shakily from his sickbed. He had advanced steadily to 60 cocooned in his own semi-delirious bubble when last man Gilligan came to the crease at 149/9. By the time that Russell was caught by Francois, the last wicket had put on 92 and he had emulated Warren Bardsley in scoring two hundreds in a Test. Jack planted two trees.

Gilligan with 39 not out had helped Russell boost the lead to a comfortable 343. The series came down to the last innings. Catterall and Meintjes put on 42 before Catterall skied a drive off Gilligan. Taylor and Nourse, the old warhorse, came together at 64/3 and batted tenaciously as Mann rang the changes, but bad light stopped play with South Africa on 111/3. South Africa needed 233 runs, MCC seven wickets. Eleven had been added on the morning of the fifth day when Nourse nibbled once too often at Kennedy and Brown took the catch. Gilligan sent Francois's off stump cartwheeling at 149/5 and Snooke's Test career ended lbw to Kennedy for one. Taylor soldiered on with Tapscott and then Blanckenberg and after overnight rain 141 runs was needed for the series with three wickets in hand. Gilligan eluded Blanckenberg's forward push to flick the off bail. Taylor threw caution to the winds and on-drove Kennedy high into the stands to reach his third century of the series, and his fourth overall. But it was his last scoring shot before he nicked one to slip and Hall was caught to leave South Africa 109 runs short, and England series winners, by two Tests to one.

The game was marked, as *The Star* put it, 'by most strange fortunes'. Sandham was agreed to have been caught off his pad, and Fender was bowled by Hall off a delivery that slipped and bounced twice. Hall apologised as the ball was delivered, but when Fender missed it and it demolished the stumps Alf roared with laughter.

South Africa's fielding had been brilliant early in the series but struggled under pressure. 'Doodles' Tapscott, an excellent fielder, dropped a sitter off Sandham at fine leg when he had two and dashed off in the wrong direction trying to catch a pull from Russell on 38. Then Russell played the ball to square leg, Tapscott slipped and Mead ran, with both batsmen ending up at the same end. Tapscott threw wildly towards the end occupied by both batsmen. The throw was wide and somehow Mead scampered back to his ground.

There was plenty of individual heroism: the match-winning twin hundreds by the ill Russell, the rearguard action by Nourse in both innings, Taylor's determination and unwavering concentration in the last innings, and Kennedy's 5-76 in the second innings in 49.1 overs. On several occasions Arthur Gilligan swung the momentum back England's way. Bowling with 'a determination, power and vitality worthy of a Gregory', he took 3-35 off 23 overs, made 39 not out in the crucial last-wicket partnership of 92, and took a further 3-78 in 36 overs in the second innings and contributed a brilliant run out.[275] It was Russell's Test, but Cecilia Gilligan would have been feeling smug among the frosty group of travelling wives.

The series had more than lived up to expectations. England averaged 27.17 per wicket to South Africa's 27.06. Frank Mann spoke warmly about the opposition. Matting 'was always preferable to a bad turf wicket', and taught batsmen to watch the ball much more carefully.

---

275 *The Star*, 19/2/1923

The official amateur expense allowance was £110. Arthur Carr estimated that the tour cost him about £500 and that Mann spent about £1,000. Carr was a beacon of British upper middle-class snobbery and prejudices. He and his wife thought South Africa 'was trying to be a poor imitation of London'. He admitted to an obliging bookie who fixed him some winners through the jockey club and greyhound associations. There was plenty to enjoy even though 'some of the team were not on speaking terms'.[276]

Mann recommended that wives be banned from future tours. He went back to Middlesex and Arthur Gilligan was chosen as England captain in the five-Test series against South Africa in 1924. In the first Test at Edgbaston, South Africa batted for 75 balls and 48 minutes, making 30. No one apart from extras made double figures. Gilligan's figures were 6.2-4-7-6 and Maurice Tate in his debut Test 4-12. Gilligan went on to lead the 1924/25 Ashes tour in Australia and push his British Fascist agenda. Forty years later, he was president of MCC and present at the selection meeting when Basil D'Oliveira was omitted for the MCC tour in 1968.

---

276 Carr, *Cricket with the Lid Off*, 177

9

Dominium: Rony Stanyforth 1927/28

FOLLOWING THE abortive Rand Rebellion, the 1920s saw a restructuring of the relationships between English and Afrikaners; mine owners and mine workers; farmers and farm labour. White workers may have lost the battle of Johannesburg, but they won the political war.

The 1913 Native Land Act prohibited African land ownership, exiled them to inadequate and unproductive land in the reserves, and consequently drove them into the cash economy. Mines, industry and farming did not need to pay sufficient wages for family subsistence as migrants were 'supported' by the reserves. Tenant farmers became serfs on white-owned land.

Soon after Frank Mann had sailed for home, the 1923 Urban Areas Act was passed, which removed African rights to own property or even to live in the towns unless they could prove they were employed. The legal framework was in place but implementation would take longer.

In 1924, a pact between white Labour and the Afrikaner nationalists ousted Jan Smuts's pro-capitalist South Africa Party. As Ronald Stanyforth's tourists prepared to take on Transvaal in the run-up to the first Test in early December 1927, Colonel Cresswell, the minister of labour, proclaimed, 'To save the country and the crushing of the [white] working classes, the nationalists and the Labour Party have joined hands ... In every country eight per cent of the population is unsuited for anything but unskilled manual labour. In South Africa, the [white] eight per cent cannot get [unskilled jobs] because the native can get [them] at a lower wage.'[277] They were turning the country from one of employers and mining capital to a 'white man's country'.

The eight per cent of whites had votes of course, African workers did not.

The Industrial and Commercial Workers Union (slogan, 'I See You, White Man') led by Clements Kadalie responded to the slew of racist labour practices threatening African economic survival. It had begun among Durban dock workers in 1919 and by 1927/28, as Stanyforth's team criss-crossed the country, the ICU's impact was at its height.

Rural Africans formed the bulk of its estimated 250,000 membership and defiance in the countryside underlay the heightened race fear driving white social and political preoccupations.[278]

Stanyforth was an emergency captain. Guy Jackson, the Derbyshire amateur, had withdrawn through illness and Percy Chapman, England's captain against Australia in 1926, had declined.[279]

Stanyforth had toured South America under Warner in 1926/27, had played for the army but not a county, and was optimistically described as the best wicketkeeper in England. As emergency stand-in skipper, he demanded the final word on whether he played in the Tests.

Stanyforth's tourists, with the usual six amateurs, were described as 'strong but not fully representative'. The batting lacked Hobbs and Hendren and relied on the big four – Sutcliffe, Holmes, Tyldesley and Hammond. George Geary and 'Tich' Freeman, with his leg spin and googlies, were the impact bowlers.

---

277 *The Star*, 8/12/1927
278 Helen Bradford, *A Taste of Freedom*, (London: Yale, U.P., 1987) 2
279 MCC Minute Book, 1927–1933, MCC/SEC/1/6

9.1 Wally Hammond

Cape Town welcomed back Wally Hammond. Hammond had contracted a life-threatening illness in the West Indies in 1925/26 and he did not play in England in 1926. David Foot, in a provocative yet sympathetic biography of Wally, suggested that this was syphilis which, when treated with mercury, profoundly affected his subsequent personality and behaviour.[280] Late in the 1926/27 season, Wally Hammond built up his strength and confidence playing for Green Point CC in the Cape sunshine.

His ghostwriter was later effusive in his praise for 'this magnificent African port where one finds splendid modern buildings cheek by jowl with cupolas and minarets while gloriously clad Malays jostle negroes and Chinamen, white men and Indians, in the long straight streets'.[281] But despite Hammond's skill and power, matting wickets and slow recuperation meant that he was only moderately successful.

Back in Gloucestershire, he was a man reborn. He scored 1,000 runs in May for the first time since W.G. Grace and ended up with 2,969 runs, with twelve centuries at an average of 69. He was the first name on the touring team sheet. 'With so many happy memories … I thought myself the luckiest man in the world to have a chance of going there in the company of masters such as Sutcliffe, Geary, Holmes and Tyldesley, and under so universally popular a skipper,' Hammond said. His long association with South Africa was just beginning.

Labour's Colonel F.H.P. Creswell, joint leader of the Labour and nationalist coalition government, and Jan Smuts, now leader of the opposition, welcomed the players to Cape Town underlining the continued relationship between 'British' South Africa and the empire. General J.B.M. Hertzog, leader of the Afrikaner nationalists, did not attend. In 1926 the Balfour Declaration had proclaimed equality between the Dominions and Britain and in Hertzog's view was the basis

---

280 David Foot, *Wally Hammond, the Reasons Why*, (London: Robson Books, 1996)
281 Wally Hammond, *Cricket My Destiny*, (London: Stanley Paul, 1948) 31

for full independence for South Africa. He was anxious to limit the connection with the empire and rejected the idea of a federal imperial parliament. His membership saw a continuing direct relationship with the empire as a sell-out to mining capital and British interests.

On the cricketing front, with the West Indies about to become the next Test-playing nation, South Africa was under pressure to justify its founding position in the ICC, particularly when it was obvious that no South African tours to the West Indies were likely to take place. Unsurprisingly, this issue does not appear to have been raised either by the ICC or MCC itself, but by sanctioning a two-tier cricket world they missed a huge opportunity to put global cricket on a non-racial basis. Instead, in 1929, MCC dropped K.S. Duleepsinhji to assuage South African sensibilities.

Cricket in South Africa was considered an English minority sport among the minority white population in a divided country. But it was also played at a comparably high standard by black South Africans, who played in a common competition on a regional basis. From the late 1920s, the sport began to reflect the increasing ethnicisation of the country and the black cricketing population sub-divided into Africans, Indians and 'Coloureds' – Muslim and Christian – all playing in their separate provincial tournaments. Whites were entirely ignorant of the achievements of black cricketers and this racist myopia was shared by their MCC visitors.

Smuts thought MCC would carry all before them and Creswell wished South Africa all the luck – they would need it. This was not just hyperbole. South African cricket was at its lowest ebb since the 1890s. The 1924 tour to England was officially described as 'South Africa's most tragic overseas experience'.[282] A dismal summer and soft wickets flummoxed the batsmen. The debacle in the first innings of the series, dismissed for 30, left deep scars. Bob Catterall averaged twice as many as the next best batsmen, Susskind, and Herby Taylor did not pass 65 in eight innings. The team suffered three hammerings followed by two miserable draws watching the rain fall.

---

282 Luckin, *History vol.2*, 309

9.2 Ian Peebles and J.J. Kotze

Ian Peebles, a self-confessed feckless 19-year-old, had stayed up all night to see the lights of Cape Town as they docked. As he enjoyed the scent of the pines drifting across Newlands, the 'most beautiful ground of all', J.J. Kotze was lovingly tending an experimental grass pitch on the boundary edge, prodding here and sprinkling a little water there. When he replenished his watering can, a couple of women wandered near it in high heels and he came charging out of the trees, bellowing with rage and anxiety, and drove them away with menacing gestures of the can.

Kotze was just as terrifying without the ball as he had been as South Africa's fastest bowler. He chauffeured the petrified MCC team at speed around blind bends on Chapman's Peak Road with steep drops to the sea. A long cut in a front tyre was just waiting for a convenient moment to blow.[283] Somehow, they got back alive.

The Western Province game – played on matting over grass – was ruined by rain, but 'Tich' Freeman with 5-15 showed early form. The team headed for Kimberley's heat and dust endurance test. Sutcliffe and Tyldesley made hundreds and Hammond complained of 'eating thick red dust for days afterwards, mouth, nose, ears, eyes and clothes were stuffed with it and no amount of washing seemed to make it go away'. Bloemfontein offered better cricketing conditions but no resistance. Peebles took 10-80 in the match and Percy Holmes hammered a hundred in 73 minutes on the grassless outfield. Stanyforth declared on 592/7 with Holmes on 279 not out.

Transvaal and a South African XI provided the first real opposition. In the two drawn games, 'Nummy' Deane's tactical exploitation of the chinks in the visitors' batting armour made him an automatic pick as captain, and J.P. Duminy, who scored 224 for once out, and left-arm spinner Cyril Vincent with 16 wickets forced their way into the Test team. For MCC, Holmes hit another big hundred at Pretoria, Wally Hammond stroked 132 and Geary took

---

6-75 at The Wanderers. After taking a mere three wickets in the first seven games of the tour, Hammond destroyed a South African XI with 6-32.

This was the final series played entirely on matting unless it was tied after four Tests, in which case the final game would be on turf. While some like Victor Kent at The Wanderers would resist turf to their last breath, Kotze at Newlands, H.L. Crockett in Durban, and Taylor and Commaille were strong advocates of the change. The current state of turf wickets internationally was not encouraging for the balance between bat and ball. As Geary took his six wickets at the Wanderers, Bill Ponsford was breaking his own world first-class record with 437 for Victoria versus Queensland and a young colt called Don Bradman scored 118 on debut for New South Wales.

The night before the Test, the cricketers spent an evening at the Johannesburg Empire. It was a gift for the comics. 'Tich' Freeman roared so loudly that the comedians offered him a free pass, Percy Holmes turned tomato red at his adventures on the voyage being recounted, and Peebles's youthful indiscretions came in for much chaff.

The selectors omitted the 48-year-old Dave Nourse, veteran of 45 consecutive Tests, and six new caps were awarded to cricketers from five provinces. Ten players were born in South Africa with the eleventh, Buster Nupen, born in Norway. Deane won the toss at The Wanderers and Duminy, invulnerable in the provincial games, lost his leg stump to Geary first ball on Test debut. Bob Catterall held the innings together with 86. The players were buzzed, David Gower-like, by three aeroplanes 20 feet off the ground, and sat on the mat until the last plane lumbered off into the distance. George Geary bowled at medium pace, combining a sharp leg-cutter with a big off break to capture 7-70 in 27.3 hostile overs. South Africa were 196 all out.

Denijs Morkel trapped the in-form Percy Holmes in front for a duck. But Sutcliffe, the Valentino of Test cricket and a firm favourite with the crowd, and Ernie Tyldesley put on a record 230 for the second wicket. Promnitz, right-arm medium with a quick break, reversed the flow and MCC lost their remaining nine wickets for 83.

South Africa, 117 behind, still had a sniff, but not for long. Hammond sent down seven consecutive maidens at lightning speed and bowled Taylor, Duminy and Catterall. With Geary's tight-fistedness at the other end, South Africa found themselves without a paddle on 38/7. Hammond's match-winning spell was a surprise to the Green Point faithful, who had only seen him go through the motions with the ball. 'Shunter' Coen and Vincent put on 80 for the ninth wicket, doubling the home score. But a ten-wicket loss soon followed. Hammond took 5-36 in the innings and George Geary 12-130 in the match.

As both teams rattled through the Northern Cape dust bowl, locals demanded Dave Nourse's return. The *Cape Argus* wanted a team for the present not the future.[284] Was Hammond the real deal, a deadly accurate, match-winning, fast-medium bowler? Or was it just nervous batting? England appeared reliant on their four professional batsmen and George Geary. Sutcliffe, Tyldesley and Hammond had scored 275 out of 288 in the first innings.

George Bissett, the local fast bowler who had only played second league cricket, was a shock inclusion for his raw pace in the second Test at Newlands. Deane won the toss and put England in on a wet wicket. With a south-easter at his back, two balls in Bissett's first over reared unpleasantly and Sutcliffe was fortunate to get away with an edge to third slip. Holmes had his leg stump removed, Tyldesley played on two balls later, Sutcliffe skied an attempted pull to slip, Stevens flicked a bouncer to Cameron behind the stumps and Bissett trapped Wyatt in front with a ball that kept low. Bissett had taken the first five wickets to fall with 66 on the board. Vincent took three for six, while Nupen tied up Hammond with leg theory. England were all out for 133, Bissett taking 5-37 and Vincent 4-22.

In reply, South Africa were 128/3 when 'Tich' Freeman forced Taylor so far back that he trod on his stumps on 68. The next day, South Africa took a 117-run lead thanks to 39 from Buster Nupen. England crawled to 140/1 in reply, with the bowlers hampered by

---

a persistent drizzle. South Africa saved three runs through a smart piece of fielding by a fox terrier at cover, but it was England's day. The spectators were less impressed. A loud appeal from Nupen brought a 'Don't shout so loud, you'll wake us all up' from the crowd.[285] Sutcliffe broke his bat on 99 and his new bat did no more than edge a full delivery into his stumps. Holmes (88) and Tyldesley (87) provided a platform for Wyatt's painstaking 91. He admitted it was 'a far from chanceless knock' and received dogged support from Hammond and Geary with a single in half an hour.

South Africa needed 312 to win in 275 minutes. Geary, the standout bowler, went off with an elbow injury that was to ruin his tour. Commaille and Taylor put on a century partnership in 85 minutes. Hammond dismissed Commaille at 115, and disaster struck on 126 when Taylor, on 71, played the ball to short leg, called Cameron for an impossible single and changed his mind halfway down the pitch. Hammond, running away from the stumps, slid, gathered, turned and whipped the ball back to the keeper in a single movement.

The familiar doubts crept back in. Hammond bowled the aggressive Jock Cameron and completed his day with three slip catches off 'Tich' Freeman. Astill took three wickets and South Africa collapsed to defeat by 87 runs with half an hour to spare. The press was scathing. South Africa had had control until Morkel grassed the simplest of chances off Wyatt. 'Cypher' in the *Natal Advertiser* again called for the in-form Nourse to add resilience and experience. South Africa trailed 2-0 with three Tests to go.

9.3 Keable Mote and the ICU

The ICU's African leadership faced an ongoing harassment campaign. Keable Mote, Transvaal provincial secretary of the ICU, and three others were charged with holding a political meeting. The mayor of Springfontein accused them of agitating against the banning of African trade unions, calling for the abolition of passes and for wages of 8s a day. Mote argued that the council had assumed

---

285 *Cape Argus*, 5/1/1928

an unreasonable and autocratic position in prohibiting a peaceful meeting. The defendants cross-examined the mayor to the delight of the black spectators crowded into the court. The police described the meeting as moderate in tone and the magistrate sentenced them to a 10s fine.

Mote was then arrested at Kroonstad for sedition at a meeting at Vrede ('Freedom'). The public prosecutor failed to establish the charge but sent him to Vrede for a preliminary examination anyway. The Vrede magistrate said that without the full charge, he could not fix bail and Mote was kept in custody until a charge was decided upon.[286] No African could expect justice.

The MCC collapsed to 49 all out against Eastern Province with Ocshe taking five wickets, then, after beating Border by an innings and 109 runs, they headed for Durban. They had previously played Natal on turf, but it was back to matting for the third Test. Deane won the toss and batted. In Geary's absence, occasional bowler Bob Wyatt opened the bowling in the teeth of a gale. His length and swerve proved unplayable, and he conceded a single in 66 balls and bowled Taylor for seven. Despite resistance from local debutant, Fairless Nicolson, South Africa staggered to 146/7 before Nupen and Deane put on 95 for the eighth wicket. Deane scratched around like a 'hen in a pen' for 77, but Nupen's scintillating 51 lifted the total to 246. Wyatt finished off the innings ending with the remarkable figures of 13-10-4-3.

Hammond (90), Tyldesley (78), Holmes (70) and Greville Stevens (69) gave England a 184-run lead and South African cricket was staring down the abyss. Taylor nicked Hammond's first ball of the innings to Stanyforth, who dived but grassed it, and then missed Jack Siedle down the leg side. Taylor, Nicolson, Catterall, Deane and Nupen all made half-centuries, with the latter pair putting on a South African sixth-wicket record of 123. South Africa declared on 464/8, their highest total in Tests against England, and the match was drawn. South Africa proved that they could bat against a Geary-less attack. But could they overturn MCC's 2-0 advantage?

---

286 *The Star*, 26/1/1928

If the South African state were focused on crushing the ICU, white labour was treated with kid gloves. Two hundred white miners came out on strike in Randfontein because a white miner refused to share the lift cage with a few black miners and had been dismissed. He was quickly reinstated.[287]

The team were back at The Wanderers for the fourth Test and the South Africans felt the faster wicket and a third Test in three weeks would maintain their momentum. Alf Hall returned for South Africa, but Geary was still injured. Deane won the toss, and despite the depleted England attack sent them in to prevent them batting out a draw in the fourth innings.[288] Hall captured 6-100 in 42.2 overs and South Africa were chasing 265. Taylor stroked the first ball of the innings for four and hit South Africa's first century of the series, out of 170. There was plenty of support. Jock Cameron drove, pulled and square cut 50 in 37 minutes and the lower order kept hitting. South Africa scored their runs at 82 per hour, England at 47.

Three of the big four were out, with MCC only 20 ahead in their second innings after Holmes made 63. Wyatt and Stevens resisted stubbornly to set South Africa a tricky target of 153. Hammond had Taylor caught behind with the total on 14, but there was no panic. Morkel, Nicolson and Catterall got them close, Cameron failed to finish things off with a massive six before Nupen drove the winning runs. This was South Africa's first Test win for five years. They had improved with every game and in Bissett (4-43 and 4-70) had found an aggressive and consistent strike bowler.

Neville Cardus in the *Manchester Guardian* praised Deane for his imaginative captaincy and psychology, particularly bowling first. Just as the matting wicket was about to make its final bow, Cardus mischievously suggested that matting replace the industrially rolled and cultivated wickets on which batsmen with a third of Trumper's ability put up records beyond him.[289]

---

287 *The Star*, 27/1/1928
288 *The Star*, 28/1/1928
289 *The Star*, 3/2/1928

As the South Africans celebrated at The Wanderers, the Rhodesian prime minister Howard Moffat banned the ICU, shut their offices and deported their agent. Moffat said he would 'not tolerate propaganda which stirred up strife among natives or ill feeling between natives and Europeans'. ICU Leader Clements Kadalie was defiant, 'Despite your ban we shall find means to get our message to our fellow workers to enable them to uphold the banner of freedom.'

Both teams arrived at Durban for the final Test showing significant wear and tear. For England, captain Stanyforth was injured and stood down. Geary's arm was still very stiff. Harry Elliott won his first Test cap along with Eddie Dawson who was celebrating his engagement to a girl he met during the Natal match. Greville Stevens took over the captaincy. With the series in the balance, England rejected SACA's umpires and both captains requested Arthur Laver to stand in the last Test.

'Test match fever has all SA in its grasp ... Few events of recent years even those of national political importance has been watched with as much anxiety as the struggle now in progress,' wrote *The Star*.[290] But cricket has as strong a capacity for anti-climax as Durban does for rain. The first day was a washout. Deane won his fifth consecutive toss and now with only three days to force a result, he sent MCC in for the third time in the series on the quickest pitch Durban could produce.

Bissett had Holmes caught behind in the first over, but a graceful and correct hundred from Ernest Tyldesley and fifties from Sutcliffe and Hammond put England firmly in control of the series on 240/4. But Buster Nupen ran through the soft underbelly of the English batting, snatching four of the last five wickets for seven runs in 31 balls and England were all out for 282. Catterall, fielding on the fence, took three crucial catches, running in to claim Wyatt with the ball swinging away from him and sprinting 30 yards to bring off a brilliant shin-high grab from Hammond. With two days to go, Stevens countered Taylor's aggression with extreme leg theory.

---

290 *The Star*, 4/2/1928

Staples bowled ten overs for five runs and even Taylor was limited to a single in 42 minutes. Having fought back to parity, South Africa's chances were sliding down the leg side.

Bob Catterall was joined by Jock Cameron at 95/4. Cameron gave a chance to square leg and jumped for joy when it was put down. The pair put on 135 in 90 minutes. Cameron hit four successive balls from Freeman for three fours in a row and then a six, and when he finally crashed Freeman down long leg's throat the pair had taken South Africa to 230/5. Catterall's 119 was his best innings for South Africa in South Africa. Deane, Nupen and Vincent swung the long handle, 215 runs came in 100 minutes and Deane declared with South Africa 50 runs ahead.

Not many batsmen demonstrate their personality without playing the ball, but Percy Holmes was an exception. He would leave the ball by leaping high in the air the bat flailing above his head, touching down with both feet outside off stump, ending in a crouch with a broad grin. Bissett had him for a duck in the first innings and there were various suggestions that the young Bissett might be a bit too quick for a man of his mature years. 'I could play Bissett with a bloody broom handle,' Holmes said. Bissett bowled, there was a resounding thud into pad, a loud appeal and Holmes was back in the pavilion cheerfully explaining that this was the first time he had 'bagged 'em'.[291]

On the final day, England were 20 runs behind with nine wickets in hand. Bissett bowled with a gale behind him and five slips. At 43/3, and three of big four gone, he hit Wyatt twice and the batsman retired for treatment. The window was open. Bissett, bowling like a man possessed, was two yards quicker than Deane had ever seen him while maintaining his perfect length.

After lunch, a short rain break raised tensions even further. But Bissett continued to storm through the English middle order and acting captain Stevens saw his worst-case scenario unfolding in front of his horrified eyes. Eddie Dawson, playing in front of his new

---

291 Bob Wyatt, *Three Straight Sticks*, (London: Stanley Paul, 1951) 51

fiancée, put up grim resistance until Deane took a superb catch diving backwards at silly mid-off from Stevens. With England on 103/8, an exhausted Bissett had taken 7-29 in 19 overs backed by sensational catching. Wyatt returned and tried to hit England out of reach, but Vincent cleaned up and when the last man, Freeman, was caught by Hall at mid-on, South Africa needed 69 to win. Fittingly, Catterall smashed the winning runs amid a cacophony of excitement as dark clouds banked up over the ground.

'Nummy' Deane credited the victory to the 'extraordinary spirit of the team'. When the first day's play was lost to rain, he had to take every risk to try and win it. The ultra-aggressive cricket lasted throughout the three days. The match turned on 'the partnership between Cameron and Catterall, which got us in a position to go for a win and the outstanding bowling of Bissett' according to whom Deane's decision-making framed the win – putting England in, declaring their first innings when 50 ahead, and motivating Bissett, his batsmen and fielders into an ultimate last-ditch effort.

For the *Natal Advertiser* this was a side finding itself after years of cricketing transition. Ernest Tyldesley wrote to Deane on behalf of the English professionals, thanking the South Africans for playing the series in such a sporting spirit and congratulating him on his captaincy. 'Olympic' in *The Star* argued that the English professional is the backbone of English cricket but is not accustomed to change his game. An audacious and discerning opponent had the psychological edge. 'Deane with characteristic Dominium freedom from the thraldom of precedent and tradition disturbed the conventional and complacent English concept. He gained the initiative halfway through the third Test and kept it,' wrote 'Olympic'.

Changing fates on the pitch were mirrored in the political forums of the empire. The 1926 Balfour Declaration had given South Africa and the other Dominions equality with Britain, and Hertzog celebrated with the introduction of a new flag and a national anthem. Deane's efforts represented and reinforced South Africa's own political independence and identity. The rise of Afrikaner nationalism and the subjugation of black workers underpinned the emergence of South

Africa from the imperial identity into its own peculiar future. As Olympic put it, the South African performance 'expressed the free spirit of the Dominions. Some of the things the Springbok skipper did so daringly and so effectively an English captain would hesitate to do. He would lack precedents for them.'[292]

---

292 *Ibid*

10

Confusion: Percy Chapman 1930/31

THE 1929 Wall Street crash widened the fault lines of global inequality. It was the beginning of permanent impermanence, where economic uncertainty drove political processes, whether black or white, and the priorities and impact of labour and capital. Widening inequality created differential pressures across the range of South African communities, which all reacted in their own ways. This was not a binary juxtaposition of black and white but a multifaceted struggle between communities to exploit changing economic conditions resulted in mass migrations into urban environments.

The prevailing mindset underlay a cricket series which suffered from hastily taken decisions and exuded a sense of flailing in the dark, of transience and fragmentation.

In South Africa, Afrikaner nationalism dominated politics. Before the crash, Hertzog won what was described as the 'swart gevaar' (black danger) election, although this label could have been applied to any since 1910. Hertzog ran on the preservation of white privilege and removal of the few remaining political and economic rights available to Africans. He won a majority but not the two-thirds needed to disenfranchise the small number of remaining black voters in the Cape. Instead, he diluted any possible black impact, doubling the white vote by including white women on the roll, and focused on formalising restrictions on African ability to live, work and trade in urban areas.

By 1930, the depression was beginning to bite deep but as the world's major gold producer, Hertzog insisted on retaining the gold standard. This reduced export profits, exacerbated destitution among white farmers, turning the drive towards far-right Afrikaner nationalism into a stampede. The impact on black tenant farmers was even more severe in a shrinking rural economy as, under the 1913 Native Land Act, they were expelled from white-owned land.

The African Industrial and Commercial Workers Union (ICU) faced a tsunami of white hostility and lacked the resources to counter the myriad oppressions suffered by rural and urban Africans. All aspects of African economic life were under attack. A new state monopoly on beer brewing, for example, destroyed the primary source of income available to African women. Beer profits, which had previously remained in African hands, were commandeered by municipal monopolies over beer halls, and used to pay for infrastructure for whites – roads, civic buildings, and swimming pools – as well as intensified police control. Beer monopolies (known as the 'Durban system') were used across Southern Africa, and made Africans pay for their own repression.

The ICU was attacked head on. A.W.G. Champion, leader of the Natal branch, was banished to the Cape. ICU secretary-general Clements Kadalie was banned from speaking on the Rand and moved to East London where a general strike over wages had created almost total paralysis. As a national force, the ICU was effectively dead by 1930. The African National Congress might have filled the political void, but the radical James Gumede lost his bid to be secretary-general to the more conservative Pixley ka Isaka Seme, and for the remainder of the decade the ANC focused on the fruitless task of protecting black access to the Cape's property-based franchise.

The cricketers were only dimly aware of the political state of the country, but they were familiar with the economic misery and instability caused by the depression. In South Africa, following the Balfour Declaration, Britain was one among equals and Percy Chapman understood that their role was to win friends for the empire.

South African cricket was in a positive phase. An exceptional young squad had toured England in 1929, ably led by 'Nummy' Deane. They lost the series 2-0, but the performances of 'Tuppy' Owen-Smith, Bruce Mitchell, Denijs Morkel and Jock Cameron suggested a brighter future.

England was less sanguine. Don Bradman had panicked the MCC. After captaining the first four Tests, Percy Chapman was replaced for The Oval by the reliable Bob Wyatt, and Chapman was a victim of the new ideology of cricket as accumulation not style. As *Wisden* put it, 'A defensive policy was foreign to [Chapman's] nature.'[293] The change made little difference. Bradman posted his third-highest score of the series in The Oval Test – a mere 232 – and Australia duly won by an innings. But before being replaced for The Oval, Chapman was named as captain for South Africa and on arrival in November 1930, although he could not be persuaded to smile he insisted that there was no hostility between him and Wyatt, who was in the party. Apparently Wyatt wasn't the problem; Percy had broken a front tooth on a ship's biscuit.

The touring party included four Maurices (Tate, Leyland, Allom and Turnbull), three England captains (Chapman, Wyatt and White) and the captain's wife, Beet, described as a 'whisper from heaven'.[294] Patsy Hendren was officially appointed 'Head Professional'. The team arrived on a blazing Cape summer day and George Duckworth, who decided he had misjudged the weather, sold his coat to a local professional. Percy Chapman was pleased that they had already named a peak after him.

Chapman's light touch went down well. He was enthusiastic about the attack spearheaded by Maurice Tate, Bill Voce, 'Farmer' White and Ian Peebles, but more doubtful about the batting. Hobbs had recently retired from Tests but not yet first-class cricket. MCC authorised the inclusion of Herbert Sutcliffe and asked the SA Board of Control (SACBOC) to cover his salary, but they refused, Sutcliffe

---

293 Alan Gibson, *The Cricket Captains of England*, 144-145
294 Maurice Turnbull and Maurice Allom, *The Two Maurices Again*, (London: E. Allom and Co, 1931) 21

diplomatically pleaded an Indian engagement and Andy Sandham was the only recognised opener.

The tour's itinerary resembled the gyrations of a drunken and directionally challenged spider. The MCC's sketch map criss-crossed the continent with little regard to geography or distance. The team made three separate trips each to Cape Town, Durban and Johannesburg and travelled to the Victoria Falls on the Zambezi. They spent 34 nights at sea, 25 on trains and 105 in hotels. As Maurice Allom described it, 'Heat, sweat and dust filled our days.' He added, 'The train crawled and twisted like some caterpillar as it ate its way into the withered heart of the country.' Lightning took flashlight photographs, or 'an unbelievable sunset would bring a majesty and a mystery to the wilderness'.[295]

'Bowser' Dalton was baggage man, 'nimble in neither mind nor body', and the party included two press 'hangers on' – Louis Duffus ('Vagrant' in *The Star*) and R.M. Ballantine.

The latter's broadcast talks 'were greatly to be feared'. For the only time, MCC would play five Tests on two completely different surfaces randomly distributed between the centres: matting (Johannesburg), turf (Cape Town), turf (Durban), matting (Johannesburg) and turf (Durban).

This unprecedented confusion of geography and playing surfaces would strain the resources of Chapman's team and test the fitness and adaptability of both sets of players. The tour was notable for illness and injury, but both sides recognised that winning the series meant winning at The Wanderers on matting. Tests on the flat turf wickets were likely to be drawn.

The MCC lacked Sutcliffe, Duleepsinhji, Larwood, Woolley and Geary.

South Africa had lost the spine of the 1929 England tour. 'Tuppy' Owen-Smith, Denijs Morkel and J.A.J. Christy were in England and 'Nummy' Deane had announced his retirement.

---

295 Turnbull/Allom, *Two Maurices*, 33, 46

10.1 Dropping Duleepsinhji

K.S. Duleepsinhji was a nephew of Ranji (who had made 53 and 146 not out for C.W. Wright's XI against the 1894 South African tourists).[296] In 1929, as the most promising cricketer of his generation, he made his debut in the first Test against South Africa. Amid mutterings from the SA camp, and scores of 12 and one, Duleepsinhji was unceremoniously dropped and never faced South Africa again.

He returned to the side immediately after the South Africans went home, touring New Zealand and proving himself according to his captain, A.H.H Gilligan, the best player of spin on a wet wicket he ever saw. He played 12 Tests between 1929 and 1931, averaging a remarkable 58.5 with three centuries, including 173 on debut versus Australia. He might have been an all-time great but for the pulmonary disease which forced his retirement at the age of 27. He was apparently not considered for selection for the South Africa tour as MCC did not challenge South Africa's racist requirements. A few decades later, a similar issue would not be so easily swept under the carpet.

The Duleep issue mirrored South Africa's exceptionalism as Test cricket began to go global. The West Indies played their first Test at Lord's in 1928, New Zealand in January 1930 and India in 1932. England's cricket world had doubled in size, but although the white South African Cricket Association (SACA) were delighted to take on – and beat – New Zealand in 1931/32, no formal consideration was apparently given to playing India or the West Indies. While not legally impossible, as it became under apartheid, segregation made it effectively unthinkable.

The MCC and the ICC made no attempt to grasp the nettle and require all its members to play each other. They were comfortable with a two-tier system of 'white' Test-playing countries, and then others and maintained this until South Africa's eventual exclusion

---

296 Luckin, *History*, 653

from 1970. Apart from Duleep's single appearance, SACA's 172 Tests were played against 'white' opposition.

The tour kicked off at Newlands on J.J. Kotze's prized turf wicket with the 'backdrop of the towering mountain changing its expression with the angle of the sun amid the floating streams of cloud'. Kotze thought the wicket was good for 1,000 runs. Chapman's bowlers, however, instantly repaid his confidence in them as Tate took 5-18 in 12.3 overs. The Western Province batting was 'so lamentable as to beggar description'[297] and hundreds from Wyatt and Hammond meant a massacre by an innings and 177 runs.

Matting wickets had been in their thoughts since England and Kimberley gave the tourists their first taste of how the bowlers could get the ball to spit at speed off a length and jag sideways. Kimberley was a 'dead city', effectively a vast prison camp with barbed wire, armed guards and forced searches of every worker after every shift. The mines used convict as well as contract labour and only the red shirts of the lifers relieved the dusty drabness. De Beers excavated 5,000 tons of earth a day and kept the diamonds they found out of circulation for three years to preserve their market scarcity.[298] On the field, Ken Viljoen and Xenophon Balaskas showed enough fight to play themselves into the South African team before a dust storm spectacular even by Kimberley standards ended proceedings.

An African waiter in the Kimberley Club, fearful, of his ultra class-conscious masters, created another storm by refusing to serve the professionals, who, unlike the amateurs, had not been given honorary member status. For the Glamorgan amateur, Maurice Turnbull, class was more important than team, 'In England the relationship between amateur and professional is a very wonderful thing provided neither oversteps the mark … in South Africa the professionals lose sight of the fact that the club must be allowed to confer membership on whom it likes. It is amazing how often we are welcomed en bloc to

---

297 Turnbull/Allom, *Two Maurices*, 39
298 Turnbull/Allom, *Two Maurices*, 49

clubs but if they wished to make only two or three of us members, I do not see why the rest should have reason to feel hurt.'[299]

The match in Durban was overshadowed by yet another motor accident. This time, Andy Sandham was involved in a collision on Durban North Road with a vehicle driven dangerously by an inebriated champion jockey. When Hendren and Hammond visited Sandham in hospital, he was very groggy. Chapman, already beset by illness and injury, put a brave face on it but Sandham did not play again on the tour.

On arrival in Johannesburg, Chapman waded into the matting/turf debate by arguing for a turf wicket at The Wanderers. It would have to be laid almost over the dead body of the autocratic chairman, Victor Kent. A blanket of depression had settled over the Rand. On the day after MCC's arrival, the Robinson mine, dating back to 1888, was put up for auction. It had yielded gold worth £25m and paid out dividends of £12m. It was sold by the liquidators for £4,700.[300]

10.2 Satire, pith helmets and a chief called Brandy

Every touring team had been 'introduced' to the African population through 'native' dances and compound inspections. Harry Taberer, South African cricket captain in 1902, SACA vice-president and South Africa's head of labour recruitment, portrayed business as usual at the City Deep compound. For Maurice Turnbull, the xylophones, tin drums, singing, rhythmic and ferocious stamping of feet, clashing of assegais and beating of shields created an eerie and threatening effect.

But the dances were not just urban repetitions of indigenous culture. African workers satirised their circumstances and sent up the watching whites. The MCC watched a performance involving a man with a pith helmet and a dilapidated gun, a chief called Brandy wearing peacock feathers and a witch doctor and his bones. Brandy presented an assegai and a shield to Percy and gave Beet Chapman a knobkerrie that she could use to bash in Percy's head if he chased other women.

---

299 Turnbull/Allom, *Two Maurices*, 55-56
300 *The Star*, 27/11/1930

For the only time, the MCC leadership had access to another side of African life. Taberer invited the Chapmans to a reception for C.J. Piliso who had won a scholarship to study medicine for two years in New Zealand. The two speakers were Dr Xuma, the only African medical doctor practising in Johannesburg, and the legendary sportsman, polymath and politician, Isiah Bud-Mbelle. The Chapmans were accompanied by Dorothy Hodgson, lecturer in history at the newly founded University of the Witwatersrand and future wife of W.G. Ballinger, who was an advisor to the ICU.

There were clear associations with cricket. Taberer's Native Recruitment Corporation had presented a cup for African cricketers to encourage the engagement of Africans educated at mission schools who had learnt cricket to fill key roles as translators and clerks in the industry. By limiting it to Africans, the cup intensified ethnic stratification between Africans, Coloureds and Indians who had set up their own sports bodies from the late 1920s, mirroring the country's increasing focus on race and ethnicity.

A touring team from India played a local Indian side at the same time as the MCC match. The home team scored 102 against the tourists' 71. The Rev Bernard Sigamoney, trade unionist, boxing promoter and Anglican priest, took most of the wickets for Johannesburg. Sigamoney would play a key role in encouraging 'non-racial' cricket first through Africans, Indians and Coloureds competing in the same competition in communal or 'Inter-Race' tournaments as in India, then in the development of non-racial teams under SACBOC. The Indian ambassador, Sir Kurma V. Reddy, entertained the teams to lunch and the municipality provided a bus tour before the Indian team left for Kimberley.

This was the beginning of a golden age for African cricket with the players drawn from the mine 'malabanas', the elite class of mission school-educated clerks and interpreters. Frank Roro, Piet Gwele, Sol Senaoane and many others provided cultural leadership in the atomised environment of the Rand. It was a small world. Isiah Bud-Mbelle, apart from his many political achievements including the founding of the ANC, had been the president of the non-racial

Griqualand West Cricket Board set up in the 1890s, and C.J. Piliso, who had received the scholarship, was the son of the president of the SA Bantu Cricket Board (SABCB), H.B. Piliso. In the 1930s, the SACB asked for matches against touring teams but received no response and the tourists showed minimal curiosity about South Africa's black cricketers.[301] The goal of the authorities was not to showcase African sporting skills, but to counter the beginnings of anti-South African criticism by suggesting that opportunities were available to a tiny African minority. The tourists focused on their exotic colonial experience.

10.3 Ian Peebles in Rhodesia

The team headed for Bulawayo, Victoria Falls, and colonial adventures. Ian Peebles refused to pay a shilling to hire an oilskin for the Falls jungle walk, setting off in his swimming trunks and was eaten alive by an insect guard of honour. He played in a friendly match the next day, but while he tried to soothe the stings in the river, he was ruled out 'absent bathing'. He then ignored protocol, bowling the formidable Captain Wardroper, chief of police, under whose auspices the match was played, for a golden duck. That night he was driven home from the post-match party by a wildly inebriated and erratic Wardroper who refused to give up the wheel until physically restrained by his terrified passengers.

Two matches were planned against Transvaal on matting. The first saw the home side only 52 runs behind with six wickets in hand when stumps were drawn. In the second match, a curtain-raiser to the first Test, Chapman crashed 87 in 66 minutes with five sixes, one of which sailed over deep point and out of the ground. Maurice Tate showed his ability to perform on any surface with five wickets. But rain brought proceedings to a halt and MCC spent their cash at the Turffontein races.

---

301 R. Parry, 'African Cricket on the Rand: Piet Gwele, Frank Roro and the Shaping of a Community', in Murray, Parry and Winch, *Cricket and Society in South Africa*, (London: Palgrave Macmillan, 2018) 101-136

10.4 Zulus, pass burnings and Johannes Nkosi

In Durban, a red standard proclaimed, 'Down with Pirow's [Minister of Mines] slave laws: Burn your passes on Dingaan's Day', and during a mass demonstration on 16 December more than 2,000 passes were burnt in the pouring rain. The demonstrators led by the ICU's Johannes Nkosi marched to the city hall. The police attacked. Twelve Africans with bandaged heads appeared in court on public order offences. Nkosi died from a severely fractured skull. A few weeks later, his mother spoke heartrendingly of the death of 'her support and her star' and how proud she was of him.

After their victory in Cape Town, MCC had drawn their next five games. The pre-series debate was over 'Nummy' Deane's possible return as captain. He had retired from first-class cricket after the 1929 tour but retained his role as selector alongside Tup Holmes and J.T. Tandy. The press clamoured for his return. Deane resisted. He was out of practice and his business commitments made it impossible.[302]

Buster Nupen's persistent knee injury meant he had played little cricket, but he suddenly found himself not only in the team but South Africa's captain. Nupen was a shrewd, engaging personality with a keen tactical brain and capable of changing a game in minutes with bat or ball. Herby Taylor had not recovered from a blow in the kidneys playing for Transvaal. Ken Viljoen and Xenophon Balaskas who had impressed for Griquas, and Sydney Curnow were selected in South Africa's youngest-ever team. The XI was not named until the morning of the match and Bob Newson, the opening bowler, assumed he had not been selected for his first cap and turned up at work. His colleagues showed him the newspaper and rushed him to the ground.

The two Tests on matting (first and fourth) at The Wanderers were most likely to produce a result. The changing surfaces confused everyone. Even Louis Duffus, who wrote the official history, got the surfaces wrong. Preparations were leisurely. On the day before the

---

302 *The Star*, 15/11/1930

match, Balaskas and Viljoen went to The Wanderers nets to face two men bowling in lounge suits and black shoes. On the main ground, the professionals Tate, Leyland, Hendren and Goddard spent an easy hour in a net. Percy Chapman, with 80, 37, 48, 48 and 87 in his previous innings, preferred a round of golf with Deane.

The following day, Chapman won the toss and put South Africa in. England wore black armbands in memory of Johnny Douglas, who had drowned diving into the freezing waters of the Kattegat, the strait between Denmark and Sweden, trying to rescue his father. Maurice Tate later said of Douglas, 'He was a great cricketer and for all his funny ways, was both a splendid man and a lovable captain.'[303]

South Africa were unable to cope with Tate, Bill Voce and Peebles. At 81/9, Quintin McMillan lobbed the ball gently into Chapman's hands at mid-off. Peebles was already taking his sweater from the umpire when Chapman dropped it, and McMillan and Bob Newson went on to put on 45 for the tenth wicket, dragging the total from the disastrous to a merely inadequate 126. Voce, who started fast then turned to cutters, bowled unchanged through the innings for figures of 26-11-45-4. McMillan top-scored with 45 not out and then, still floating on a cloud of adrenaline, announced his engagement.

Nupen took 5-63 and England closed on 193, a lead of 67. The tourists complained about 'unsportsmanlike' behaviour. Voce nicked a ball to Bruce Mitchell, who threw it up as if he had made a clean catch. While Voce was allegedly trying to establish if he was out, he wandered out of his ground and Mitchell threw his wicket down. England blamed Mitchell for sharp practice but the umpires chose to believe that Voce was attempting a run.

South Africa cut the lead to 33 when Curnow perished on a suicide single and Siedle got in front of a straight one from Voce. But Mitchell and Catterall put on 122. England's wicketkeeper, George Duckworth, appealed 28 times in the innings. In the last over before tea, Catterall played a ball from Hammond which ricocheted off his foot or off the ground. Duckworth shouted 'catch it', Hendren

303 Maurice Tate, *My Cricketing Reminiscences*, (London: Stanley Paul, 1934) 165

held on, and umpire Treadwell signalled out. Catterall pointed to the ground but was forced to trudge back. The Voce and Catterall incidents would have uncanny resonances on Peter May's tour 25 years later. South Africa were five wickets down and 115 runs ahead. An attacking 51 from Cameron got their noses further in front, but Nupen was hit in the mouth and left the field streaming blood.

Needing 240 to win, MCC were surprised by the fast-medium swing of Bob Catterall who reduced them to 30/3. But Hammond, supported by Maurice Turnbull, was unmovable in a stand of 101 for the fourth wicket. Turnbull played a ball from Nupen and the bails fell off. The umpire signalled out, but Turnbull appealed to him, convinced that Cameron had knocked off the bails. They were lying in front of the wicket and the stumps were facing forward.[304] *The Star*'s sporting editor was not impressed, 'The wickets were inclining forwards because the ball hit the base of the stumps.'[305]

10.5 Nupen

Nupen bowled round the wicket off a short run with his body leaning forward and long fingers clamped around the ball. A yard before the crease, he bent his body back like an archer drawing his bow. Then forward it came in a sweep that dragged the toes off countless cricket boots. The arm came over in a high arc, the ball gathered pace off the pitch, bounced and turned prodigiously from the off which he varied with a leg cutter.

Hammond had fought his way to 63 but had no confidence in the tail. He charged Vincent and Jock Cameron had the bails off in a flash, reminding Hammond of how he had done the same at The Oval in 1929. Tate tried to hit his way to victory. At 195, he nibbled at Nupen and Mitchell did the rest. Nupen switched to leg theory with England needing 45 to win and the last men at the crease. Duckworth and Peebles put on 16 amid the barracking of the largest

---

304 Turnbull/Allom, *Two Maurices*, 100-103
305 *The Star*, 28/12/1930

crowd seen on a South African cricket ground. Finally, Nupen nailed Duckworth dead in front, the finger went up and South Africa had won by 28 runs.

The local press hailed this as the 'second-best Test victory' (after the first win in 1906) with its constantly shifting advantage and brilliant individual performances: Cameron behind the stumps and his forceful half-century, the excellence of Mitchell's innings and his slip catching, Catterall's daring batting and his five triumphant overs, and the contributions of Viljoen and Vincent. But Nupen's bowling heroics (5-63 and 6-87) in his first Test as a captain were the dominant performances of the entire series. South Africa fought back from an appalling start, found the confidence to fuel their second innings batting performance and applied enough pressure to force Hammond, the best batsman in the world not called Bradman, into making a crucial mistake when he could have steered England home.

Nupen stood in front of the crowd with three stitches in his wounded chin, his knee heavily bandaged, an aching strain in his side and the knowledge that he had captained his first and possibly only Test team to victory. It was one of the greatest days of his life, 'I am terribly proud to have skippered the winning team and I am glad to have been of some use to the side … Our opponents have not yet settled down and may be harder to beat in the other Tests. You can tell the people of England that I'm tickled to death.'[306]

Tate and Peebles had played through injuries. Peebles had jumped into a flower bed on Christmas Day, straining his groin to escape the attentions of Cocky, a parrot. MCC accepted their defeat less than stoically, throwing hard-boiled eggs at the cheering throng. For them, the game had been trench warfare – Mitchell's running out of Voce, for example – amid the ferocious barracking of the crowd. South African officials who poked their noses into the England dressing room quickly regretted it. The MCC left, muttering 'Wait until we get them on grass'.[307]

---

306 *Ibid*

307 Turnbull and Allom, *Two Maurices*, 104

It was the best news to happen in South Africa for years. The cinema showed a highlights reel featuring both sides tucking into a Christmas pudding; Maurice Allom had recorded the game on his cine camera and showed his footage to mining magnate Solly Joel and his guests with a commentary. When he turned the lights up, only one person was still awake. But he did receive a touchingly honest marriage proposal from an admirer, 'I was considered most beautiful in my teens, but truly, like the flower I have faded, if not attractive I am still useful.'

10.6 Christmas on the mines

Over the Christmas period, shifts and supervision were reduced and qedeveke, a home brew famous for its kick, was readily available. It was a time for score settling in a violent and brutal workplace.

'Faction fights' were treated by whites as primordial and deaths as inevitable, but the roots of the conflicts were structural rather than behavioural. While work gangs were always mixed, workers were housed in ethnic groups and generated strong 'home-boy' networks. The mine labour hierarchy favoured the earliest arrivals by ethnicity. Basutos and Mozambiquans ('Shangaans') held more lucrative and less dangerous posts as African police and compound officials. The later-arriving Mpondo ended up as underground diggers. Tightening margins in the depression were transmitted to the underground workforce. Conditions, brutal at the best of times, became intolerable for the Mpondos. They fought back against their immediate oppressors.[308]

On Christmas Day 1930, on Randfontein Mine, a Basuto was allegedly murdered by an Mpondo. This started the worst violence for 25 years both on the surface and underground. Basutos and their Shangaan allies protested they had been attacked. 'If you see a snake wants to bite you, what do you do?' asked their spokesman.[309]

Four Mpondos were killed in revenge and ten more workers were killed, and hundreds injured before the violence finally ceased at the turn of the year. As if the loss of life had not been enough,

---

308 T. Dunbar Moodie, *Going for Gold*, (Berkeley: UCLA, 1994) 180-210
309 *The Star*, 26/12/1930 and 30/12/1930

> grim reality returned on New Year's Day when hanging rock in the East Rand Premier Mine collapsed and 12 African miners died under the rubble.[310]

Even before Buster drove his troops to victory, the selectors announced that Deane would captain South Africa for the remainder of the series. Deane's employers had capitulated to popular demand and he agreed to fulfil the will of the selectors (of which he was one), his employers and the country.

The victorious team had four days to travel to Cape Town, recover, regroup and to adjust to turf under their new captain. Herby Taylor had recovered and fast bowling 'turf expert' Sandy Bell was brought in. MCC were unchanged. Between them the two teams fielded six past and present Test captains.

The wicket was a featherbed and Deane laughed when he picked up the coin. Bruce Mitchell and Jack Siedle put on a record 260 for the first wicket, destroying any chance of MCC quickly achieving parity. South Africa declared on 513/8, with hundreds from Mitchell, Siedle and Taylor, while Maurice Tate returned the exhausting figures of 43-13-79-3.[311]

Hammond kept wicket despite a poisoned toe when Duckworth injured his hand and then opened the batting with a runner. England faced an uphill battle against Bell's hostility and McMillan's guile. Despite Hendren making 93, Hammond 57 and Leyland 52, England failed by 14 runs to avoid the follow-on. Deane enforced it despite having spent 120.4 overs in the field. Patsy Hendren (86), again supported by Hammond (65), patiently blunted the exhausted attack. England were finally all out for 252 when time was called, and the draw achieved.

The following day, *The Star* published an 'astonishingly frank' interview with Deane. He was, the paper admitted, mentally and physically exhausted. 'Oh, for a Denijs Morkel or an Owen-Smith,'

---

310 *The Star*, 31/12/1930
311 *The Star*, 3/1/1931

said Deane. 'With them in the side, I think we would have won the match.' He criticised the team's misfields, including his own, dropped catches and general slackness. He thought Buster Nupen's efforts were nullified by the surface and said that Nupen would be dropped for the next Test.

Tactically, he had banked on the pitch crumbling by the third day but it was too well prepared and when the bowlers did create openings, the chances were not taken. Asked if he enjoyed the captaincy, he said, 'I do and I don't. It is all right if you have a lot of earnest young fellows under you all determined to fight to the last ditch and snatch the most insignificant advantage. But half-heartedness and blackness spreads through a side and you must keep spurring them on all the time.'

It was a strange interview. This was a man who had been forced to return against his will.[312]

Deane's commiseration with the treatment Chapman received from the English press was heartfelt. He said, 'No one had more experience of the "scare writers" than I … Many newspapers tried to put me in an embarrassing position. Had they saved their caustic meanderings they might have made my job a little less difficult as I acted with the best interests of SA cricket at heart.'

When the article appeared, he complained that it was a gross distortion. He had been disappointed with the fielding – but largely his own. The batting had never been excelled by a South African side and the bowlers did remarkably well on an unresponsive wicket. But the damage had been done.

And on to Durban, which gets summer rain, for the third Test again on turf. Despite loss of time, Chapman's desperate attempts to create a sniff of victory on a fast turf wicket turned the third Test into a nailbiter.

Nupen was dropped as promised, Deane won his ninth toss in 12 games and South Africa batted in heavy humidity. Tate and Voce reduced them to 59/4 before the rain washed out a day and a half.

---

312 *The Star*, 6/1/1931

On the third day of four, Voce's leg cutters claimed 5-58 as South Africa crawled to 177 at less than two runs an over. England, thanks to aggressive batting from Hammond, playing on his favourite South African ground, finished the day only 47 behind with all ten wickets in hand.

On the final morning, Allom and Turnbull inspected the wicket clad in swimming trunks and yellow striped dressing gowns, to the surprise of the mynah birds. Wally Hammond duly completed his first Test century in South Africa (136 not out) and in a bold bid to force victory Chapman declared 46 ahead at 223/1. It almost worked. Jack Siedle was lbw to Tate with the first ball of the innings and Mitchell and Curnow followed quickly. In a tense final session, Taylor's 64 not out earned the draw. It was his 50th Test innings against England and one of his best.

The three-week gap before the crucial fourth Test back on The Wanderers matting gave the teams a chance to draw breath. A few days after the Durban Test, Deane resigned without explanation, simply stating, 'I have resigned and that is all I want to say.' Deane would continue as a selector, retaining de facto control of the team and its evolution.[313]

Given Nupen's match-winning first Test as captain, he seemed the obvious replacement on his home ground. But Jock Cameron, who was more familiar with the Newlands turf, was appointed South Africa's third captain in four Tests. There was clearly a rift between Nupen and Deane, but if Nupen could be overlooked as captain he could not excluded as a bowler on matting. Nupen aside, the selectors asked nine bowlers to stand by. Nineteen players were invited to attend trial nets and, even then, the team was selected at the last minute. Hall and Nupen came in for Quinn and Bell; Viljoen replaced Deane.

Andy Sandham's ankle had gone under the knife and MCC called up Harry Lee, who had been coaching in Grahamstown, to open the batting. Duckworth had pleurisy and was replaced by Farrimond.

---

313 *Rand Daily Mail*, 28/1/1931

> ### 10.7 The Wanderers and crowd psychology
>
> On the eve of the match, *The Star* played the psychology card. The reputation of The Wanderers as the 'Bull Ring' goes back a long way. The newspaper wrote, 'Physical conditions are difficult, light, altitude, matting, ground and heat – but these can be adjusted for – there is something else, the overpowering impulse which comes from the crowded stands. Imagine you are an MCC batsman coming out of the pavilion. Some 20,000 pairs of eyes are glued on you. A few are friendly, some are highly critical, the majority are decidedly unsympathetic.
>
> 'There are two ways of fighting it. A sense of humour will do it. When Duckworth came out to bat in the nerve-jangling second innings of the first Test, he met the leg pulling section of the crowd by ironically raising his cap. He had mastered The Wanderers. The second is by sheer will power. The mastermind is Hammond. His indifference is almost pachydermatous. He masters The Wanderers every time and refuses to be hypnotised. When he proceeds to dig himself in, those big silences – like psychic air pockets – have no effect. To most men they would prove fatal. There are some who seem victims to these unsympathetic waves. Chief among them is Chapman. Patsy Hendren is a further victim.'[314]

For South Africa, Cameron's captaincy brought a new focus. Herby Taylor scurried about in the covers and Nupen was as aggressive as ever. But England were no longer the rudderless outfit of the first Test. Lee protected Hammond from the new ball risk, and Hammond nursed Leyland until he had played the punishing innings that he had threatened all summer. Wally and Jock continued their duel. Hammond missed an off-drive and dragged his foot until in Cameron's view it was on the whitewash. Cameron whipped the bails off and appealed for the stumping. Not out, said the umpire at square leg. Convinced that Hammond's toe was still on and not over the crease, Cameron pulled a stump out and bellowed a louder appeal.

---

314 *The Star*, 14/2/1931

Still not out. No one moved. 'I am appealing for a stumping,' shouted Jock as he removed the remaining stumps. 'OWZAT!' 'NOT OUT,' roared the umpire in return.[315]

England took their 'matting' bruises on hip and thigh and Hendren was hit three times on the finger. But Leyland (91), Hammond (75) and Hendren (64) laid the foundations of a potentially match-winning total which increased in tempo when Bill Voce, batting at 11, treated the crowd to three sixes off Nupen. His 41 not out in a tenth-wicket partnership of 57 made for a comfortable total of 442. But there were twists and turns to come.

South Africa started confidently with half-centuries from Mitchell (68) and Siedle (62) taking them to 166/2 and parity at the close of the second day. So often did fortunes vacillate on the third day that it was hard to unpick the confusion of collapses and recoveries, interruptions, drizzle and an early close amid smoke and gloom. Hammond found his old matting devil with the new ball. He made it swing, nip, bounce and shoot. Taylor batted grimly through the best bowling he had faced in years. Hammond's spell of 12 overs conceded 16 runs, but the wickets went to Peebles, who, like a hyena feasting on Hammond's kill, took 6-63, including Taylor who trod on his stumps. As the duel with Barnes two decades previously had shown, Taylor's technique relied on his exceptional footwork, getting either right back into his stumps or right forward. Occasionally, he went too deep in his crease, but he had averted the follow-on with South Africa 149 behind and time was running out for England.

Catterall induced edges from Lee and Hammond to Mitchell, amid a great roar from the crowd. England had lost three wickets for 23, but Hendren, Leyland and some free hitting from Tate allowed Chapman to declare on 169/9. Nupen (6-46) had showed his ultimate mastery in the last Test to be played on matting.

South Africa had four hours to survive or score the 317 to win. Curnow's 12 in 80 minutes at the top of the innings made their priority clear. But a free-scoring 74 from Mitchell and a partnership

---

315 Wally Hammond, *Cricket My World*, (London: Stanley Paul, 1949) 67

between Catterall and Cameron whispered an audacious reversal. Catterall pulled his first ball after tea for six before he was lbw to Peebles. Viljoen rattled the score along until Hammond grabbed a low slip catch and hugged the ball with delight. McMillan and Cameron hit out, but when McMillan went, 56 were needed in half an hour. Cameron and Nupen might have done it, but they instead settled for the draw. South Africa ended 37 runs short with England needing three wickets.

It was equally dramatic off the field. While Catterall and Nupen waited to bat, they were shocked to be told that they were dropped for the final Test in Durban and for the Australian tour. The papers lambasted Deane and the other selectors' 'amazing display of irresolution and ineptitude' culminating in this 'preposterous omission'. The Transvaal Cricket Board described the selection committee as 'grossly incompetent' and demanded that the selectors be replaced before the team for Australia was chosen.[316]

Harry Lee was delighted to have played for England after a long county career. He had received permission to play from the sports master at St Andrew's, but wires had been crossed, the school complained and MCC refused to give Lee his blazer and cap until he apologised for not getting formal permission. He refused and presumably his blazer and cap are still waiting for him in a Lord's cupboard.[317] It was his first and last Test.[318]

The larger-than-life Percy Chapman, who held the tour record for consuming over 200 oysters at a sitting, was 'glad to have played at the Wanderers but extraordinarily glad not to have to play there again'. The matting wicket and the bare outfield were unsuitable for Test cricket. Chapman had seen a patch of turf grown under a stand at The Wanderers that was infinitely good enough to have played on. The experimental grass pitch under the stand was studiously ignored by the authorities.

---

316 Turnbull/Allom, *Two Maurices*, 185-186

317 Bill Edrich, *Cricketing Days*, 98

318 H.W. Lee, *Forty Years of English Cricket*, (London: Clerke and Cockeran, 1948) 95

Chapman had to win to tie the series, but his chances were reduced by the turf wicket and Bill Voce's damaged finger. The home selectors, not content with the storm of controversy over the absence of Catterall and Nupen, unveiled J.B. Cochrane as their new bowling surprise, replacing Alf Hall. After practice on the day before the game, England were singing in the showers while the locals debated what the selectors thought they were doing.

Being Durban, it was either raining or about to rain. Chapman won the toss and put the opposition in to exploit the wet conditions. To Percy's fury, the umpires discovered that the bails did not fit the new large-size stumps and there was a 20-minute delay while his advantage slipped away and the wicket dried. He made a formal protest. The South African Cricket Board apologised; the wrong bails had been included with the new stumps, but nothing could be done. Rain was the winner as South Africa finished on 32/0 at close of play on the first day.

Siedle and Mitchell put on a century opening partnership and England could not match South Africa's total of 252. Cyril Vincent bowled with metronomic accuracy to take 6-51. Bad light on the third day ended the game as a contest and the match petered out into a draw with neither side close to forcing a win.

South Africa had somehow held on to their advantage from the first Test by their fingertips despite the challenges of different surfaces almost every Test, capricious weather, chaotic selection, incompetent officialdom and incomprehensible internal politics.

For Percy Chapman, the best side lost, 'The first Test we should have won but lost. The second Test South Africa should have won but didn't. The third in Durban's rain, I leave to you. The fourth Test was one of the finest matches ever played with magnificent performances on both sides. In the fifth, well South Africa and the rain gods did what was needed to hold on to the series. Congratulations to them.'

South Africa's third series win, the first since 1910, was achieved despite the selectors, Tandy, Deane and Holmes, whose performance verged on sabotage. Deane played the central role as selector and captain (for two Tests) effectively undermining the whole series. The capriciousness of selections, catastrophic communications and last-minute decision-making seldom got the best team on the park or let them perform at their best.

Deane's return from retirement in the second Test was not made public until after Nupen's triumph in the first, and he resigned again after the third 'in a manner singularly incompatible with his distinguished service'.[319] No explanation was ever publicly provided.

The selectors' horses for courses principle caused resentment and confusion. Neville Quinn had been South Africa's best bowler on the 1929 England tour and chosen for the rain-ruined third Test, bowled in one innings and was promptly dropped. Sandy Bell played in the three Tests on turf but was not picked on matting wickets. Buster Nupen played three Tests out of five, was dropped twice but still managed to take 21 wickets, more than anyone else in the series, at an average of under 20.

The series was a farce in five acts. In act one, Nupen's knee injury prevented him from playing before the first Test, yet he was also given the captaincy for one game after which Deane would return. But the public didn't know that. The heroic Nupen single-handedly won the game and could not be omitted for the second Test. In act two, Deane returned as captain. Unhappy with his own substandard performance, Deane publicly blamed the team and dropped Nupen for the third Test on turf. The next act saw Deane quit the captaincy but retain his role as selector. In act four, he selected Nupen, who was again the outstanding performer coming close to bowling South Africa to another Test win. It was the last Test to be played on matting and even though there might have been concerns over Nupen's bowling on turf, he and Catterall were dispensed with for non-cricketing reasons while the team fought to save the game and the series.

In act five, the selectors chose the team for Australia without Nupen and Catterall, whose careers were ended 'on grounds other than cricketing ability', and selected Denijs Morkel, on whom

---

319 Louis Duffus (ed.), *South African Cricket, Volume 3, 1927–1947*, (Johannesburg, SACA, 1949) 108-109

Deane had lavished praise in Cape Town, as vice-captain for a tour eight months away. Morkel had spent the African summer playing rugby in the UK, fractured his wrist and was wearing a plaster cast when selected. 'Was there,' asked *The Star*, 'ever a worse cricketing injustice?'[320]

---

320 *The Star*, 27/2/1931

11

Waiting for Godot: Wally Hammond 1938/39

WALLY HAMMOND'S MCC team criss-crossed the country to the echoing creak of ox wagons inching towards Pretoria. The tour shared a canvas with the centenary of the Great Trek, a self-conscious reinforcement of the mythology of Afrikaner nationalism, and the ideological foundation for a new South Africa after 1948. MCC's peripheral involvement reflected some unease over the direction of travel as the English press repackaged these developments as 'white unity' rather than Afrikaner exclusionism. Meanwhile, in central Europe the tanks were massing on the borders while the cricket tour culminated in the Beckettian absurdity of the 'timeless' Test (which wasn't).

The tourists viewed the sunshine and gaiety of this most hospitable of tours through a darker lens. They set sail in a haze of late-summer cricket colours, streamers and cheers, knowing that they could soon be crowding the decks of troopships. Yorkshire's Hedley Verity carried military manuals to prepare for future battles. For Bill Edrich, the possibility of bombing raids 5,000 miles away 'affected our cricket for cricket is a game that needs to be played with an undivided mind'.[321]

It was the first MCC tour to South Africa for eight years. Don Bradman had started the decade as a phenomenon within the game.

---

321 Bill Edrich, *Cricket Heritage*, (London: Stanley Paul, n.d.) 78

By the end, he had changed the nature of cricket itself. Deane's selections for Australia, picked six months in advance, ran into Bradman, and crashed to a 5-0 defeat. Only once, in the third Test, when Bradman was dismissed cheaply and the heroic Sandy Bell took 5-69 (one of his three five-wicket hauls in the series), did South Africa take a first-innings lead. Then the Don and Bill Woodfull crushed their hopes with a record second-wicket partnership of 274.

The switch from matting to turf, so long in coming, apparently reaped immediate rewards with a first-ever series win on turf in England in 1935. But ironically Mitchell's masterful 164 not out, the tragic Jock Cameron's 90 in 111 minutes and match figures of 9-103 by leg-spinner Xenophon Balaskas, all happened on a Lord's pitch which, ravaged by insect 'leather jackets', played like South African matting. Australia, minus Bradman, toured South Africa a few months later. Grimmett and O'Reilly's leg spin and the Richardson/Fingleton leg trap burst the hosts' bubble. Aside from a monumental 231 by Dudley Nourse – son of Dave – in Johannesburg, batting inadequacies doomed South Africa to a 4-0 home defeat.

The 1938/39 itinerary reflected the now standard double circuit of the sub-continent. Colonel Rait-Kerr at Lord's agreed to SACA's request that the team play a fixture in Pretoria during the 1938 celebrations. In return, SACA agreed to exclude covered wickets, an issue for MCC because of the precedent it might set for Australia. If he played on covered wickets, Warner feared, Bradman would be batting until judgement day.

In the event of a tied series the last game would be played to a finish. Uncovered wickets and timelessness were to combine in the bizarre spectacle of the final Test, when Ken Viljoen got his hair cut twice. SACA, who paid the expenses, limited tourist numbers to 15. Professionals were paid £300 and amateurs £100 in addition to expenses. Of the £300 allocated to the MCC manager, £50 was described as 'expenses' to placate the Inland Revenue and £150 provided to cover tips.

The team paid more than usual attention to boat drill. Together with manager 'Sherlock' Holmes, senior pro Les Ames, and unofficial vice-captain Norman Yardley, who made up the selection committee, Hammond ensured the boat voyage contained enough traditional nonsense, bow-tie days and wrong-handed drinking to entertain and bond the players.

11.1 The personal Hammond

Warner persuaded Wally Hammond to turn amateur in 1938 and he was quickly appointed England captain. Lord Hawke, despite his 'once a pro always a pro' attitude, wished him all the best. Hammond's personal and leadership style had little in common with Hawke. The latter was not shy to impose his morality on his players, including universal church attendance on Sundays. Hammond argued that there should be as few as possible regulations on tour; his view was that cricketers were men not children and could be trusted to behave themselves.[322]

Wally was as enigmatic a captain as he was a man. As author Derek Birley has noted, behind his dashing batsmanship, good looks and the faultless Savile Row tailoring was a strange, rootless, chronically insecure individual.[323] He was a popular choice as skipper but could be 'moody', as Tom Goddard reckoned, and his personal agenda made him a remote and occasionally ruthless figure. According to E.W. Swanton, Hugh Bartlett was the only player on the tour not to play in a Test because he had shown interest in a girl Hammond had his eye on. Wally's philandering was hardly a secret. Eddie Paynter, when asked what he thought about Hammond's captaincy, was succinct, 'Wally, well yes, he liked a shag.'[324]

As in the previous series, MCC and SACA agreed to forbid wives. By mid-tour Hammond was juggling relationships with female friends as well as his wife who had headed for South Africa after seeing press pictures of Hammond with Sybil Ness-Harvey, the Durban beauty queen. Sybil would soon become his second wife.

---

322 Wally Hammond, *Cricket My Destiny*, (London: Stanley Paul, 1948) 142-143

323 Derek Birley, *A Social History of English Cricket*, (London: Aurum Press, 1999) 255

324 David Foot, *Wally Hammond*, 172

In 1932, Hertzog's nationalists and Smuts's South Africa Party agreed to abandon the gold standard. The price of gold and the profitability of the mines skyrocketed, and they were jointly elected as a 'fusion' government which would become the United Party. It was a signal for a further tightening of restrictions on Africans in urban areas, the 'white man's country' as Hertzog put it. Much depended on enforcement. A magistrate in Johannesburg tried Africans in batches of 140 per hour for pass law and liquor offences. Sir James Rose Innes, the liberal former chief justice, described the 'full-blooded fascist flavour of proceedings'.[325] In 1936, Smuts repaid Hertzog's bargain over the gold standard by agreeing to abolish the vestigial black access to the franchise in the Cape. Smuts was in practice no less a ruthless oppressor of Africans than the nationalists, but black votes had proved useful to his party in Cape marginals.

11.2 The end of the ICU

The ICU had for most of the previous decade been a successful mechanism for giving a voice to the voiceless rural poor. It provided a mechanism for mitigating oppressive treatment by white landlords and a rallying point. As ICU organiser Jason Jingoes put it, 'When you ill-treat the African people, I See You; if you kick them off the pavements, then I See You; when an African women and baby is knocked down by cars in the street, I See You.'[326]

By the early 1930s, it had been crushed. The ruthlessness of the state reaction was a testament to the movement's successes among black rural workers and its disruption of white landowner tyranny, once again African challenges to Hertzog's restrictions focused on the retention of the franchise.

Afrikaner nationalists saw the newly formed United Party as a sell-out to English capital. D.F. Malan broke away from Hertzog to form the 'Purified' National Party building on the platform of the Broederbond, the shadowy organisation for Afrikaner domination.

---

325 Roux, *Time Longer Than Rope*, 59-72
326 Helen Bradfield, *A Taste of Freedom*, 137

Broederbond ideology mirrored German national socialist principles with an emphasis on the people (or 'volk') as the basic unit of cultural and moral life. Nationalists emphasised the oppression of the volk by British imperialism, the end of slavery which encouraged the Great Trek, the destruction of the Boer republics, the concentration camps and the betrayal of Union. In a stroke of marketing genius, the Broederbond designed the perfect strategy for uniting the volk behind them. In August 1938, several families dressed as 19th-century trekkers set off from Cape Town in eight ox wagons for a four-month journey to Pretoria at slow walking pace. The trek would mark the 100th anniversary of the Covenant with God before the Battle of Blood River, the formative event in Afrikaner mythology.

The oxen were inching through the northern Karoo when the cricketers landed below the skirts of Table Mountain in early November. Both sides were batting heavy and bowling light. The wickets belonged to the batsman, and as Hammond put it, 'Bowlers could break their hearts and exercise every guile in the calendar but not stand a chance of getting a normally careful batsman out in a week.' This was not unique to South Africa. In their previous Test, England had piled up 903/7 with the young Len Hutton contributing 364. A demoralised Australia, with Bradman and Fingleton unable to bat, lost by a ridiculous innings and 579 runs. If this was acceptable at The Oval, it was not surprising that groundsmen, who were preparing uncovered turf wickets for the first time, erred on the conservative side.

The MCC batting took care of itself. Farnes's pace and Hedley Verity's spin would carry the attack, supported by leg-spinner Len Wilkinson and leg spin and googly bowler, Doug Wright. The nucleus of the victorious 1935 South African squad – Mitchell, Nourse, Dalton, Langton, Balaskas, Viljoen and Eric Rowan – were available and in form. Alan Melville was an experienced first-class captain with Sussex even though he had yet to play a Test. Among the bowlers, the fast-medium Norman 'Mobil' Gordon had been the outstanding performer with 39 wickets in the 1937/38 Currie Cup, but they lacked an experienced fast bowler and a wicket-taking spinner.

No surprise then that the top five batsmen would all average more than 59, with Hammond and Eddie Paynter on 87 and 81 respectively. Len Hutton was a relative failure without a century and an average of 44. The bowling figures reflected this carnage – Gordon in a heroic 245.6 eight-ball overs captured 20 wickets at 40 runs each, while 'Chud' Langton's 13 wickets were taken at an average of over 50.

For South Africa, six batsmen, led by Dudley Nourse, would average over 47. Verity's 19 wickets cost an abstemious 29 each, and Farnes took 16 at 32. Captaincy was tough, missed chances always significant and keeping up spirits was hard in the face of such relentless accumulation. Both captains used rapid bowling changes to try and make things happen as well as keeping their fielders interested, but it was the tactics of hope. The lack of bat-ball balance risked cricket disappearing into a land of perpetual present, a series of groundhog days that finally came to pass at Kingsmead. But the series was no less fascinating for that, with each team being forced to engineer small advantages and make them pay.

Cricket soon became a bit player in the costume drama that enveloped the country. The MCC had stumbled (and been pushed) into a climactic moment in the history of white South Africa as the Afrikaner volk re-enacted as a national performance, the recognition of the Afrikaner as the 'chosen race'.

11.3 The Great Trek, the Battle of Blood River and the Covenant

The mass exodus of Dutch pastoralists (the Voortrekkers) north and east from the Cape from 1835 to escape tyrannical British rule became known as the Great Trek and the formative experience of the Afrikaner nation. A wagon train led by Piet Retief and Gert Maritz headed east in 1838 to Natal with the idea of settling in the Port Natal region controlled by Dingane.

This was the start of the origin myth which became known as the Day of the Covenant and rested on two 'covenants': the first was a treaty under which Dingane allegedly ceded land to Retief, which was subsequently found to be a forgery. Dingane invited Retief to his kraal, and once he recognised the nature of the threat they posed they were later massacred. Two more trekkers, Andries Potgieter and Sarel Cilliers, arrived to avenge the fate of Retief's party. They drew up their wagons into a defensive laager – a wagon fort – on the bank of the Nqutu river, and Afrikaner legend records that on 16 December 1838, Cilliers swore a solemn covenant with God that if victorious they would serve him for eternity. The Zulus attacked, the trekkers launched a hail of bullets, and what became known as Blood River to the victors and the Battle of Ngcome to the Zulus was overflowing with the corpses of the Usuthu (warriors).

This combination of the civil and the divine in the Afrikaner foundation myth lay at the centrepiece of the centenary celebrations in 1938. Ox wagons congregated from across the country in Pretoria in the days before 16 December.

A few days before the celebrations, MCC were welcomed to Pretoria by mayor Swart attired in full Voortrekker costume of slouch hat, cord trousers and veldskoen – He professed admiration for the patience of the players and spectators faced with this interminable game.

They met governor general Patrick Duncan and Jan Smuts, the deputy prime minister. Meanwhile, Oswald Pirow, the minister of mines, was in Europe. Pirow reminded the British that they were a minority in South Africa, pointing out that '60 per cent of the [white] population had no British blood in their veins and sentimental appeals cut no ice', before heading to Berlin for talks with Hitler and Goering. It was a delicate political moment and Smuts was far more interested in talking about the prospects for the Test series than developments in Europe. When Len Hutton finally managed to raise the topic of war, Smuts suggested optimistically that the German economy was not strong enough to take on Europe.

There was tension in the air. Hedley Verity and Doug Wright had been walking through the city when they came across a victim stabbed in a brawl and took him to hospital. Hammond panicked when Verity arrived back at the hotel with his hands covered in blood. He thought he'd lost his key bowler.

11.4 MCC and the trekkers

General Hertzog, leader of the governing United Party, and D.F. Malan, leader of the opposition, pledged that the spiritual and moral uplift of the Afrikaner people was above party politics. The celebrations represented a huge boost for Afrikaner nationalism. The British economic elite, including Smuts, the press and the British churches, had no option but to interpret the events as a joint celebration of Boer and Briton coming together in their common white interests.

The MCC and North-Eastern Transvaal met the trek when it arrived in Pretoria as arranged by SACA. Ken Farnes reported that Hammond, Ames, and Verity rode out in the early morning to meet the ox wagons.[327] Next, the wagons trundled at walking pace past Berea Park where the match was under way. The two teams lined up to salute the trekkers as they passed and bouquets were handed over to the trek leader by MCC manager Flight-Lieutenant 'Sherlock' Holmes, and Johnny Lindsay, captain of North-Eastern Transvaal.[328]

Old commandos on horseback, many carrying the weapons they had used in the Anglo-Boer War, descended on Pretoria carrying only a blanket, rusks and biltong. The trek culminated in a mile-long torchlight river of fire and a mock skirmish between hundreds of mounted commandos. On the big day itself, the foundation stone of a huge new monument was laid by three female descendants of the original *Great Trek* leaders. President Paul Kruger's grandson played the role of his grandfather, in unmistakeable beard and tall hat. He read Paul's last speech before his exile. When a speaker had the temerity to speak in English, he was drowned out by several thousand voices singing the new national anthem, 'Die Stem van Suid Afrika' ('The Voice of South Africa'). The minister of defence, J.A. Kemp, symbolically overturned the result of the Anglo-Boer War by

---

327 Ken Farnes, *Tours and Tests*, (London: Lutterworth Press, 1940) 178-179
328 *Rand Daily Mail*, 14/12/1938

renaming the site of the monument Voortrekkerhoogte (Voortrekker Heights), wiping Roberts Heights, which had celebrated the British victory, off the map. The English *Rand Daily Mail* hoped in vain that the government would reconsider.[329]

In Johannesburg, the MCC-Transvaal game was delayed while both teams attended a commemorative service in St Mary's Cathedral. The Anglican bishop called for the Voortrekker spirit not to refight the battles of the past but to go forward in unity (between English and Afrikaner) together.

D.F. Malan, leader of the Purified National Party, spoke at the Blood River site on the banks of the Ncome river. He called on Afrikaners to cherish their religion and racial purity. Differences in race and colour were God's handiwork and not to be interfered with. His address was full of foreboding. Africans were strangers in their midst and a menace to the wellbeing of the Afrikaner, particularly in the towns. There were shades of Enoch Powell's Rivers of Blood speech, 30 years later in Birmingham.

A Nazi-style paramilitary organisation called the *Ossewabrandwag* (the Ox Wagon Sentinel) was dedicated to the spirit of the Great Trek. But it was not just about ideology. The nationalist strategy used emotive appeals to the Afrikaner language and culture to channel the savings of Afrikaners into Afrikaner banks and finance companies. The aim was to break the British monopoly over capital, support the rural population of poor Afrikaners and capture the machinery of state for the Afrikaners to create their ideal republic.

For Bill Edrich, delightful as the tour was, there was a sense of impending political disaster. The strength of feeling against Britain was plainly evident. Neo-Nazi groups chanted anti-Semitic slogans denouncing foreign influences. The trek was an imposing sight but for Edrich, 'Little happiness was to be gained by aggressive nationalism. We have had enough of that.'[330]

---

329 *Rand Daily Mail*, 19/12/1938
330 Bill Edrich, *Cricket Heritage*, 84

Back in Johannesburg, MCC took on Transvaal, traditionally close to Test strength. A hundred from Bruce Mitchell and 97 from Ken Viljoen steered the locals to a comfortable 428/8 declared. In reply, Len Hutton faced the fiery Eric Davies, the quickest bowler in the country. His third ball was a chest-high bouncer, Hutton ducked too late and it hit him on the back of his head, knocking him out and dislodging a bail. Hutton dropped out of the first Test. Davies, a national hurdles champion, bowled his way into the Test side with 6-82 but could not prevent a draw.

The first Test began on Christmas Eve on the flattest of flat Wanderers wickets. Paul Gibb replaced Hutton and seized his chance with both hands. Eddie Paynter became the fifth Englishman to score hundreds in both innings of a Test and Gibb fell seven runs short of joining him. Jim Swanton broadcasting back to England found little to say during a century partnership between Nourse and Mitchell. Then he struck radio gold. Off-spinner Tom Goddard knelt and examined the surface closely as if he knew it was about to give him considerable help and posted two slips and a gully. Nourse chipped back and was caught and bowled. Next ball, Gordon, nightwatchman in his debut Test, lunged out of his ground and Ames whipped the bails off. Billy Wade watched his first delivery turn sharply past his groping bat and take out his middle stump.

Tom Goddard had the first hat-trick in England versus South Africa Tests since Lohmann. But there were few other incidents. South Africa's five new caps had contributed four runs, and a century by Eric Dalton coming in at number eight gave the scorecard a lopsided look. There was no possibility of engineering a result. As William Pollock wisely suggested in the *Daily Express*, four days for the Test was either not long enough, or too long.

The circus travelled in air-conditioned railway carriages to Cape Town for the new year Test. Wally Hammond won the toss on another batman's paradise, but much of the first day was lost to rain. An unhurried Hammond declared on 559/9 with hundreds from himself, Ames and Bryan Valentine despite the late swing which gave Gordon his second five-wicket haul in two Tests. There was little chance of bowling South Africa out twice. Mitchell rammed home the lesson with a comatose 42 in 255 minutes. Perhaps the most apposite contribution came from a well-oiled sailor up a tree who kept up loud encouragement for Ken Viljoen. Viljoen was behind his desk in Johannesburg.

The coin again came down heads in the third Test in Durban and England piled up the runs with Eddie Paynter's record 243 the basis for a declaration on 469/4. Newlands had taught Hammond the need for urgency. Paynter was finally caught by Melville diving full length at second slip off the only ball that lifted in the match. His partnership of 242 with Hammond came in 178 minutes.

South Africa stonewalled in reply until Van der Bijl ran himself out and Ken Farnes, scenting blood, bowled with accuracy and disconcerting pace. Gone was the breathless Farnes who had dragged himself through 30 uncomfortable eight-ball overs at altitude in Johannesburg. The shocked South Africans crumbled from 60/0 to 103 all out. They paid the penalty for not exploiting a batsman's pitch. Following on, 366 runs behind and with more than two days to play, Mitchell, Viljoen and Rowan batted positively but South Africa were convincingly defeated by an innings and 13 runs.

11.5 Eddie Paynter

In the third Test, Paynter scored 243 out of 431 while he was at the wicket. The rate of scoring over the innings was 5.3 per eight-ball over, a significant psychological hammering. It contributed to the South African collapse in their innings – losing all ten wickets for 43. This was the key moment of the series. After his innings, Eddie received plenty of liquid hospitality from someone calling himself Trufucious Paynter, allegedly his father's cousin. Eddie's father had never heard of him.

Eddie is almost a forgotten hero outside Lancashire. His average was 81.62 for the series; he scored a century in each innings of the first Test, before his 243 in the third. He made his first-class debut at the late age of 24, after having lost the tips of two fingers in an accident and played the first of only 20 Tests at the age of 29 in 1931. His overall Test average of 59.23 is second only to Sutcliffe among English batsmen and he averaged over 80 against Australia despite a duck in England's 903/7 in 1938.

Eddie was tough and independent-minded, refusing Bill Woodfull's offer of a runner when he came out of hospital to bat in the Bodyline series. He later deplored the fact that South African black cricketers like Basil D'Oliveira were forced to play in the UK.[331]

During the Test, Lord Nuffield was given access to the players' balcony. He was so excited that he promised £10,000 for a national annual schools cricket tournament. While it built a strong relationship between white schools, clubs, first-class cricket and representative honours, the Nuffield programme massively widened the gap in opportunities and resources between white and black cricketers. No one suggested including representatives of black schools.

Durban wouldn't be Durban without a motoring incident. Paul Gibb had been given an old banger of a car without functioning brakes. A downhill run and a fruit stall had an inevitable result and as usual the locals bore the brunt. The accident cost Gibb his pride and the value of the stall.

Back at The Wanderers for the fourth Test with a 1-0 series advantage to protect, Wally Hammond won his eighth consecutive toss. England batted and thanks to Hutton's 92 scrambled to 215. 'Chud' Langton, using a mixture of pace, swing and spin, was the destroyer with 5-58. Rain washed out much of the second day and South Africa led by 34 runs with seven wickets in hand by the start of play on the third. But a persistent downpour turned South Africa's advantage into another draw as England batted out the final 60 overs with few alarms, keeping their 1-0 series advantage with one Test to go.

On the Day of the Covenant (generally known as 'Dingaan's Day'), the tourists were confronted by 'hundreds of chanting, shrieking, jumping, dancing and leaping' descendants of the

---

331 Eddie Paynter, *Cricket All the Way*, (Leeds: A. Richardson, 1962) 65-66

warriors who had attacked the colonists 100 years previously. The men in head dresses carried spears, the women in beads and bangles waved umbrellas. On command they charged with spears raised at the touring party. It certainly had impact. 'I was frozen in my seat as they came to a halt with the spears reaching over the rope less than three feet away. I was more than slightly alarmed,' said Eddie Paynter.

Wally was pleased to be back in Durban and see Sybil, though his wife Dorothy's arrival must have made life complicated. Getting out on the pitch would have been a relief. The series had come down to the last Test in Durban. This would be played to a finish – standard practice in Australia. England rotated their attack, bringing in Reg Perks and Doug Wright.

The pitch was typically overprepared. Norman Gordon had won a threepenny bit from Hutton at cards and passed it on to Alan Melville, who spun it in the air. Perhaps distracted by the different coin, Hammond changed his call to tails and lost the toss for the first time in the series.

South Africa clearly intended to pile up as many as possible until the wicket broke up. Farnes bowled off 11 paces and was the only bowler to extract lift from the wicket. He peppered Pieter van der Bijl and forced the former boxing blue to bat swathed in towels. It was turgid stuff until, as if stung by a cartoon wasp, van der Bijl smashed four boundaries in successive balls from Wright and put a ball on to the grandstand roof. Perks bowled him for 125, which despite this flurry of activity had taken 438 minutes.

Day three was the first rest day. Heavy rain fell and groundsman Vic Robins used the heavy roller to produce a new wicket. South Africa ground remorselessly on. The normally aggressive Dudley Nourse made the slowest Test hundred by a South African and when the innings eventually closed for 530, Reg Perks had taken 5-100 in 41 sharp overs.

England lost their way when they finally got to the wicket. Leslie Ames with 84 and Paynter with 62 provided major contributions. Hammond was tied down by Gordon's exacting length and late out-swing until he lost patience and charged Eric Dalton's leg spin. Jock Cameron had tragically died of enteric fever in 1935 but would have smiled as Ronnie Grieveson removed the bails. On the fifth day, England finished on 316. In a timeless Test, there was no benefit to enforcing the follow-on.

Ames took the English opening bowlers while standing up to the stumps. Shortly before the close, the remaining scattering of dozing spectators was rudely jerked awake. Mitchell trod on his stumps, Rowan was beaten by a slower ball, both off Verity, and van der Bijl, on 97, was deceived by Wright. He had been surprised by a full-toss and patted it back to the bowler. In his annoyance at the missed opportunity to become the first South African to score two hundreds in a Test, he hit the next ball straight into square leg's hands.

With South Africa 506 ahead on day six, Reg Perks crawled back on to the field after lunch on his hands and knees. No one was sure if he was joking. By day seven, the second Thursday of the match, the officials had thrown open the gates. England were chasing the small matter of 696. Hammond apparently believed the target to be achievable provided the pitch continued to sap the energy of the bowlers and didn't become a raging powder keg.

11.6 Edrich's redemption

Bill Edrich had made 21 runs in the whole series. He was crippled by self-doubt, the bat squirming in his hands as he walked out to the middle. He had tried everything, including rationing his consumption of alcohol and smokes, but a sedate lifestyle had done nothing to improve his nerves. 'Tuppy' Owen-Smith threw a party on Thursday night and Bill slipped the leash. He was helped to bed sometime in the small hours and awoke smiling.

Hutton made a cultured 50 before being bowled by Bruce Mitchell, the slowest bowler in world cricket. Hammond, who seldom offered personal encouragement, told him, 'If you can see it, hit it.' As he left the pavilion, Reg Perks slipped a tiny ivory elephant into his hand. 'It'll break the spell, Bill,' he said. The South

---

Africans were cheered up by the appearance of England's walking wicket and Mitchell had a broad grin on his face at the end of his one-pace run-up. Mitchell bowled on leg stump. Edrich hit it for four through the on side and repeated the shot in the following over. He was smiling when he passed his previous highest Test score of 28. And he was smiling even more broadly when he reached his hundred in three hours after one of the most fraught baptisms in Test history. Gibb polished the drizzle off his spectacles at the other end, while Edrich had waited until day seven of the fifth Test of the series to save his Test career.[332]

Rain cancelled day eight and the following day was a rest day. They came back on Monday to a newly rolled pitch looking as good as when they had started. Edrich and Gibb pushed their partnership on to 280 before Gibb was dismissed for 120 in 451 minutes.

South Africa had gone into the game with a lightweight attack. Bob Newson was playing his first Test for eight years, 'Chud' Langton had gone lame, Bruce Mitchell and Eric Dalton were part-time leg-spinners and Norman Gordon, who had bowled 37 overs in the first innings without getting a wicket, carried the attack. There had been a remarkable shift in momentum. Far from being impossible, E.W. Swanton thought it was just a matter of time for the target to be achieved.

The normally imperturbable Bill Ferguson started worrying about whether he would have enough space in his scorebook. Eventually an exhausted Edrich was caught by a diving Gordon at short leg for 219 (447/3) in 436 minutes, almost too tired to smile. England were 496/3 at stumps with exactly 200 to make, seven wickets in hand, Hammond and Paynter together.

Overnight, the South Africans announced that the game would have to end on the following day, Tuesday, to allow the team to catch a train to Cape Town and connect with the *Athlone Castle*. They should have boarded it a week earlier. The shortage of shipping as

---

332 Edrich, *Cricket Heritage*, 83

the war clouds gathered meant this reunion couldn't be missed if they were to be home for the 1939 season.

The tenth day was frustrating and gripping. Rain was predicted, but Hammond and Paynter seemed oblivious and scored only 82 in the pre-lunch session. Hammond completed the sixth century of the match, his third of the series and the 21st of his career, equalling Bradman. Swanton discovered that, 30 minutes to the south, it was raining hard. The message went out with a pair of gloves and the batsmen set about the bowling on a pitch which had started breaking up. There were two short rain stoppages, then Hammond darted down the wicket to be stumped off Dalton for the second time in the match. Just an over later – two balls into Gordon's 56th over of the innings – the rain swept in and cricket was over. England were on 654/5, 41 runs behind.

It was an absurdist anti-climax after a game which demonstrated the folly of turning pitches into roads and bowlers into cannon fodder. There were many ironies. The MCC, anxious for balanced cricket, had resisted covered pitches. A covered wicket would probably have crumbled by day five. It is debatable whether an England win would have done more than provide some sort of closure for the participants and the handful of spectators who had remained to the bitter end. But the real irony was that the so-called 'timeless Test' wasn't. There was a suggestion that the remaining batsmen should stay on and fly to Cape Town the next day but enough was enough. Wally Hammond, the singular man, ignored the MCC prohibition on air travel and flew to Cape Town, while his team took the 1,000-mile train ride to meet the *Athlone Castle*.

For much of its duration the Test was an exercise in Zen thinking where inner meaning elbowed out action. It developed according to its own internal rules and calendar in conditions which almost made the actual participants bit players. Conducted at a snail's pace and with fewer than half a dozen bursts of significant activity over ten days, it became a curiosity, a dreamscape and museum piece while it was still under way. It was only on the last day, with a finite conclusion in sight, that it became a cricket match. But the inflexibility of the administrators, Hammond's lack of urgency and the Natal weather gave it perhaps the only fitting Beckett-like result – a timeless Test that ended in a draw.

It was an especially poignant counterpoint to the marching of jackboots across Europe. Cricket became the ephemeral repository of a vanished dream in a world of fundamental change. By the next time the teams met, millions would be dead and a new world order begun. In South Africa, the rumbling wheels of the second mythologised Great Trek were constructing their own reality in the guise of apartheid. Godot had arrived.

PART 4:

EYES OPENING, EYES CLOSED

12

Nazis and Nationalists:
George Mann 1948/49

BETWEEN THE sepia-toned stasis of the timeless Test and the glare of postwar industrialisation, one world had become another. A British population weary of war and hungry for a better future shocked the conservative establishment by voting in a Labour government a few months after VE Day. The jewel and foundation of empire vanished on 15 August 1947 when India gained independence in the chaos of partition. In South Africa, Malan's far-right National Party exploited a rural constituency bias and won the watershed election in 1948 with 443,719 votes (79 seats) against the opposition's 662,252 votes (74 seats), building a racially based neo-fascist system on neo-colonial segregation. They would remain in power until a new democratic South Africa emerged in the early 1990s.

As a bastion of elitist conservatism, fed by gentlemen's clubs and public schools, how would the old imperial club of international cricket deal with the new postwar power arrangement?

After a gentle opener against India in 1946, Hammond's Ashes tourists in 1946/47 were battered by tropical storms and Australian batsmen, seven of whom made hundreds in the first four Tests. The 1947 season was as welcome as it was unexpected. In endless blazing sunshine, the Middlesex twins, Compton and Edrich, built haystacks of runs. Between them they scored 2,057 runs against the South African tourists alone.

South Africa had started well. Bruce Mitchell hit the first ball of the series for four and left-armer "Tufty" Mann began his Test career with eight consecutive maidens. Alan Melville and Dudley Nourse had recovered from illness and injury and made big hundreds. England followed on and batted for 226.2 overs to set a target of 227 in 160 minutes. South Africa timidly turned down the challenge and had no more chances until the last Test at The Oval when Bruce Mitchell's 189 not out, his second century of the match, took them to within 28 runs of victory. But they were already 3-0 down in the series.

Postwar, neither South Africa nor England had yet found a way of channelling young talent. South Africa's runs came from Nourse, Mitchell, Melville and Viljoen, all in their late 30s. Bradman's 1948 Invincibles had both youth and Bradman himself. England were steamrollered 4-0.

Following the Nazi invasion of Poland on 1 September 1939 and the Allies' declarations of war, the South African parliament voted on whether to join the war on their side. A narrow margin of 80 to 67 votes declared for war on the side of the empire. General Hertzog, who had backed neutrality, resigned and the Smuts wing of the United Party formed a war coalition with the pro-British Labour and Dominion parties.

Black South Africans were prohibited from bearing arms, but thousands were recruited to dig, fetch and carry for the white troops. Daily pay for a white private with a wife and child was 12s; Coloureds and Indian soldiers 7s; and Africans were paid 2/6.[333] The African National Congress called for the inclusion of all sections of the population in the military on equal terms but were ignored just as this issue had been in previous wars. Some 'Coloured' troops enlisted in the British army at private rates, enraging Smuts who feared they would return with 'impudent ideas'.

The white craft unions fought relentlessly to restrict Africans and Coloureds to unskilled roles in industrial war work. The

333 Simons and Simons, *Class and Colour*, 536

wartime skills gap was instead met by training white women to manufacture armoured cars, guns and shells. Abroad, Smuts was an advocate of a world safe from racist totalitarianism. At home, he was an architect of a minority racist regime and consistently opposed improving the condition of black South Africans who gave their lives for his cause.

The war marked an economic turning point, a second revolution from a mining to a manufacturing economy. Smuts temporarily relaxed influx controls on Africans in 1942. Shanty towns sprang up; overcrowding and poverty bred crime and violent confrontations between Africans and police. Whites feared that their monopoly on semi-skilled labour was under threat from industrialists intent on reducing labour costs. Smuts adjusted segregation to the needs of industry, but ensured African labour would remain cheap, powerless and tightly controlled.

12.1 Vorster's storm troopers

White South African politics was fragmented. Hertzog had died in 1942 and three Afrikaner parties now opposed the Smuts coalition – D.F. Malan's reconstituted National Party, the Afrikaner Party led by N.C. Havenga and Oswald Pirow's New Order, which supported a single master race in a racially structured republic on Nazi Herrenvolk principles.[334] All refused to fight in Britain's war, all supported a German victory and had as their goal a white man's republic. And beyond these three 'constitutional' parties, the violent Ossewabrandwag, led by the Nazi J.F.J. van Rensburg, and the future prime minister B.J. Vorster, rejected representative democracy, built an army of Nazi-style storm troopers and embarked on a sabotage campaign.

South Africa's Nazi supporters fed on early Allied defeats, but the reversals in North Africa created a shift in local opinion. Smuts won a landslide election in 1943. The Broederbond, torn between constitutional and Nazi direct action factions, finally threw in its

---

334 Omer Cooper, *History*, 184

lot with Malan's Nationalists who promised a constitutional path to Afrikaner control.

Jan Smuts had a key role in the drafting of the UN charter and the ANC drew up its African Claims document, a bill of rights based on Smuts's UN model calling for universal suffrage. Smuts ignored at home what he advocated abroad. He had rejected African appeals for 50 years and refused to meet ANC leaders to discuss what he saw as their 'wildly impracticable' proposals.

The struggle entered a new radical phase. The ANC Youth League, created in 1944 by, among others, Anton Lembede, A.P. Mda, Oliver Tambo, Nelson Mandela and Walter Sisulu, refocused African resistance on concrete oppression rather than constitutional abstractions. During the Alexandra bus boycotts, the youth wing supported the thousands who walked 18 miles a day for seven weeks to force the bus company to rescind its penny fare increase. The new radicals supported mass anti-pass campaigns and resisted the bulldozing of squatter camps.

The end of the gold standard had massively increased mining profits. Shareholders, state and white workers shared the benefits, but as ever black mine workers were frozen out and their condition continued to deteriorate. Black wages were lower in real terms in 1946 than they had been a decade previously. Following an African miners' strike in the same year, all black trade union activity was banned.[335]

The Lansdown Commission into African worker conditions cynically and erroneously concluded that as migrants had legal access to communal land in the reserves, their wages were effectively 'pocket money'. The evolution of apartheid was about maximising the unequal distribution of resources. Eighty per cent of the total population had access to 13.5 per cent of the country's poorest land without minerals, fertility or infrastructure. Industry failed to pay the reproduction costs of black workers and their families and condemned them to grinding poverty.

---

335 Omer Cooper, *History*, 187

12.2 Black mine workers and the 1946 strike

By August 1946, postwar galloping prices and food shortages resulted in a reduction in compound rations. The illegal African Mineworkers Union (AMU) demanded a minimum wage of 10s a day, adequate food, and the right of free association. The Chamber of Mines refused to negotiate, and 76,000 workers came out on strike.[336]

They brought the goldmining industry to its knees and almost precipitated a general black workers' strike. Smuts blamed 'agitators' and met the 'war' the only way he knew, with the full savagery of the police apparatus. Police drove workers out of their compounds, beat them with clubs and rifles, and fired on them when they gathered or marched to reclaim and destroy their passes. No policeman or civilian was attacked. Nine deaths and 1,248 injuries were reported, though the full number of African casualties was never published. Eventually they were forced back to work at the point of a bayonet. The *Rand Daily Mail*, the mouthpiece of the mining industry, complimented the police for 'their courageous and skilful behaviour' in challenging 'agitators [who] led an ignorant and barbarous people to ask for the impossible'.[337]

In the 1948 election, Malan's National Party targeted Smuts as an internationalist in the pocket of the mining industry and sacrificing the country for his greater aggrandisement. The 78-year-old Smuts had run out of steam. He had not abolished unpopular wartime measures, his domestic platform was incoherent and even his international star was waning.

His role on the world stage had a hollow centre. His internationalist principles ran contrary to his segregationist treatment of the black population at home, and his own country's tragedy owed much to his evasion and manipulation.[338]

336 Simons and Simons, *Class and Colour*, 523
337 *Rand Daily Mail*, 14/8/1946
338 Mostert, *Frontiers*, 1278

The fight against fascism was coming home. India attacked the restricted access to land for South African Indians in the UN General Assembly and the UN refused Smuts's request to incorporate South West Africa into South Africa. Smuts failed, 'more beloved in Lambeth than in Lydenburg', and the Nationalists ushered in a philosophy of baasskap (white supremacy). The nationalists proclaimed their narrow victory as the volk's manifest destiny, where divine providence made them the chosen people on the African continent.

In South Africa, one of the least useful generalisations contrasts supposedly racist Afrikaners with allegedly liberal and urbane English.[339] Political control by the empire and its acolytes such as Smuts had put in place a racist framework, which would be reinforced in a more coherent if abhorrent architecture by National Party ideologues. More than 300 laws came to regulate where and how black South Africans could move, work and live. These included pencil tests to determine racial identity, bans on interracial sex and the prohibition of political and economic rights. Africans were forced to carry passes confirming they had approved employment and were summarily arrested if they did not have them on their person. As South Africa industrialised, ideas of racial superiority became institutionalised, codified and entrenched.

When the English cricket tourists arrived in October 1948, it was clear that the high-level political welcome, including cosy chats with the prime minister, would not be repeated with the National Party's D.F. Malan. Afrikaner nationalism saw no need for fraternisation or cricket.

The MCC began, as always, with a hunt for an amateur captain. Norman Yardley was not available, nor was Bill Edrich who had become an amateur in 1947. Tom Dollery had gone to public school but was a professional. Finally, George Mann had captained Middlesex for a year, and his father, Frank, had been popular in South Africa in 1922/23. George was enthusiastic, a natural leader

---

339 Paul Maylam, *South Africa's Racial Past*, (Aldershot: Ashgate, 2001) 171

and a fine fielder but an unproven batsman. Billy Griffith went as vice-captain and back-up wicketkeeper to fill in as Test skipper if the Mann gamble failed. It didn't, Mann won over his team-mates by reaching his hundred with a straight six in his first game at Newlands.

Postwar SACA changed its tune on amateurs. Amateurs had been encouraged as their natural class (and competitive) counterparts, but SACA's Algy Frames now asked MCC to send England's best team. Colonel Rait-Kerr agreed not to send 'second-rate amateurs' but 'shamateurs' were given little encouragement. Trevor Bailey, assistant secretary with Essex, was sounded out in late July. Bailey explained that as a married man he would have to carefully consider the financial side. Rait-Kerr told him that SACA would provide an allowance of £150 to cover equipment and out-of-pocket expenses but would not pay for loss of time.[340] Bailey declined the invitation, and so did Wilf Wooller and John Dewes. Charles Palmer and Reg Simpson were selected instead, but only the latter played a Test, scoring five and nought in Durban.

The professionals were told to bring a dinner jacket and black tie, a warm suit and an overcoat. Derbyshire miner Cliff Gladwin accepted his invitation, calling it, 'The crowning achievement of any cricketer's life.' But there were practicalities. He had to go back to the colliery at the end of the season to qualify for a coal allowance through the winter for his wife and family, so needed leave of absence from the Ministry of Labour. Then there was the problem of kit and rationing. He requested 148 clothing coupons. 'This is my first trip abroad and I haven't a quarter of the kit required in my personal wardrobe,' he explained. Rait-Kerr replied that this request was 'rather a bombshell' which far exceeded requests from any other player (in fact the amateur Charles Palmer had asked for 150 vouchers).

The MCC required the professionals to sign their contracts before even telling them their wages. Local prices had doubled but SACA paid £450 and a £50 end of tour bonus via the MCC. This was a meagre return for players who had to meet maintenance costs in

---

340 MCC/CRI/5/1/51, Bailey to Rait-Kerr, 9/8/1948

England, were deprived of any other earnings in the close-season and were forced to contribute to extensive hospitality to promote the goodwill of the tour. The manager, Brigadier Green, told Rait-Kerr, 'Hutton, Washbrook and others talked a good deal too much about the pay they got as compared with South African and Australian players … I warned the players about the talking and tried to give them something else to attack.' SACA agreed to pay an additional £75 for incidental expenses.[341] But this created an existential challenge to the amateur-professional cricket framework on which power at Lord's rested.

12.3 Tax Avoidance and MCC

Income tax was deducted by MCC at 9s in the pound (45 per cent) on all earnings received by the professionals but not the expenses paid to the amateurs. The likely tax treatment of the additional £75 set alarm bells ringing in the committee rooms. The 1948 Income Tax Act had tightened up the definition of taxable income. If the additional £75 for expenses was taxable, then this would call into question the £150 expenses received by the amateurs. As Rait-Kerr put it, if they received taxable income amateurs *were being paid for playing cricket* (authors' emphasis) and should therefore lose their amateur status.[342] Brigadier Green suggested the expenses be paid directly by SACA with MCC as agent avoiding the need for PAYE deductions at source.[343] But this did not resolve the question of the ultimate taxability of the payments.

The MCC secretary Ronnie Aird met the Inland Revenue, who refused to create special rules for the cricketers, saying, 'Players will in general get better treatment by exerting their charm on their local chaps.' Leaving aside the class-based implications of the Revenue's response, MCC thrust responsibility on to the players and swept the issue vigorously under the carpet.

---

341 *Ibid*, Green to Rait-Kerr, 16/3/1949
342 MCC/CRI/5/1/53, Rait-Kerr to Green 10/3/1949
343 *Ibid*

The party were prohibited from communications with the press before, during or for 12 months after the tour, without written consent. No wives or families were allowed nor was air travel, aeronautics or racing of any kind without consent. The MCC provided one blazer, two caps and two ties. The players had to find the rest.[344]

SACA received total gate receipts of over £90,000 against expenses of around £26,000. Less than £7,000 was paid to the players. By contrast, South Africa's professional cricketers are now guaranteed a percentage of the gross income of the SACA, which was over one billion rand in the 2019/2020 financial year, with nearly 200 million rand set aside for the men's national team operational expenses as well.

After five straight wins in the Cape and Orange Free State and a draw against Natal, the tourists took on North-Eastern Transvaal in Benoni. A routine game became extraordinary when Cliff Gladwin took the last four wickets of the local innings in five balls, including a hat-trick. Then Compton arrived at the crease, was missed off young leg-spinner John Stokes-Waller and in a kaleidoscope of cricketing genius smashed 300 in 181 minutes with five sixes and 42 fours, the last 100 coming in 37 minutes. This is still the fastest 300 in first-class cricket. After the match, Compton said Stokes-Waller – with figures of 23-0-171-2 – was the best leg-spinner he had faced on tour. It is hard to know if he was joking.

Alec Bedser recalled that Compton's innings 'contained freak, super and brilliant shots all the time'. On one occasion, he moved down the wicket to a full toss and without any backlift jerked his bat not more than a foot and sent the ball over long-on for a carry of around 120 yards. Godfrey Evans saluted 'vintage Denis, the unstoppable irresistible Denis, who seemed to lose himself in a whirlwind of cricket inspiration'. After the details were cabled back to England, scorer Bill Ferguson noticed that a run had been lost and Compton's partnership with Simpson ended on 400 instead of 399. No one cared. And few noticed that the fixture had been won by Roly Jenkins's match haul of 11-137.

---

344 MCC/CRI/5/1/5, Manager's Report

Before the first Test, the tourists played Transvaal at Ellis Park and the nature of the pitch and imbalance between batting and bowling resulted in MCC's first innings of 513/7 declared being surpassed by Transvaal's 560 as the match snored to a draw.

12.4 MCC and the Afrikaner nationalist government

And so to the traditional big moment, the first Test. In Johannesburg, as usual? Not this time. Under SACA's itinerary, the tourists and most of the Transvaal team headed south to Durban to play the first Test at Kingsmead.

Since the 1890s, the English cricket team had been a distraction, a unifying and rallying point for the colonial regime in the face of political difficulties such as the Jameson Raid and the Rand Rebellion. Hammond's tourists had played a walk-on part in the centenary of the Day of the Covenant. This time, MCC was relocated to the heart of 'British' South Africa on the sacred day of 16 December, spiritually and geographically far from Pretoria. D.F. Malan's speech at the Voortrekker Monument repeated what he had said at Blood River a decade before. 'Natives' would always be the enemy and unless white supremacy was now implemented through apartheid, there would be many more Blood Rivers.

In the eyes of the South African state, the tourists were seen as allies of Smuts and the mining industry and potential fifth columnists, but as we have seen this did not deter SACA and MCC from complacently participating in white neo-fascist rituals. At three minutes to 12 on 16 December 1949, the English and South African teams playing at Kingsmead dutifully stood to attention and 'lined up facing the grandstand, waiting for the peal of noon bells signalling the doors of the [huge new] Voortrekker monument were about to be opened' in Pretoria.[345] The government's view of the English cricket team as bent on undermining Afrikaner nationalism, underscored by their reactions later during the D'Oliveira affair, did not stop the English visitors, or English-speaking Natalians in the 'Last outpost of the British Empire', from conforming to apartheid conventions.

---

345 Odendaal, Reddy and Merritt, *Divided Country*, 137

The first Test began during a Durban heatwave. It was a world away from the Kingsmead dreamscape a decade before which had been ended by a thunderstorm and a bolt for the train. War had tragically taken Ken Farnes, on a night flying exercise over Oxfordshire, 'Chud' Langton, who crashed shortly after take-off from Maiduguri airport in Nigeria, and Hedley Verity, who had died of wounds in an Italian military hospital.

Dudley Nourse, Eric Rowan and Bruce Mitchell were still the cornerstone of South Africa's batting, and Len Hutton and Doug Wright were back on a ground they must have hoped never to see again. The Test was to be played on the same strip as the timeless Test. Wally Hammond, watching on, predicted a high-scoring draw.

Umpires Dick Ashman and George Sickler walked out for the start of play just as they had in 1939. Nourse spun a gold sovereign, Mann called heads, it came up tails and South Africa batted. Before the match, Eric Rowan told the MCC players that Roly Jenkins's bowling was asking to be hit. Jenkins came on early with Rowan on strike. Rowan charged down the pitch at his third ball, a leg break which turned, and edged it through to Evans to leave South Africa at 9/1. Bedser and Gladwin swung the ball in the humidity. Cyril Washbrook hit a single stump to run out Billy Wade and two reflex catches from Compton at short leg kept South Africa on the back foot. Wright dismissed Nourse (37), thanks to a full-length diving catch by Allan Watkins at silly mid-off, described by John Arlott as the most important catch in the series and South Africa were all out for 161.

12.5 The local Indian community and empire

The Indian community were segregated in the 'non-European' section of Kingsmead and the gates closed before 9.30am. Indian independence the previous year gave a huge boost to the self-esteem of Indians in South Africa, whose citizens were now politically on equal terms with the English. But within South Africa, the segregationist noose, already irksome, was tightening further. The 'Ghetto Act' restricted Indian access to land and prompted a passive

---

resistance campaign and speeches by India in the UN. Local Indians avidly supporting the tourists demonstrated their opposition to the nationalist regime. Inside the ground, Alec Bedser noted how strange it was to see a block of dark faces amid a sea of white ones. The Indian staff at the Edward Hotel debated the finer tactical points of the game with MCC professionals.

It rained and the wicket began to crumble. Rather than using the heavy roller, Mann decided to keep it spicy. Len Hutton scored 83 out of 146/3, which set the platform for a 92-run lead on the first innings. Denis Compton was dropped off the second ball of the third day and hung on for 72 in a battle of wits with Athol Rowan (4-108 in 44 overs) and 'Tufty' Mann (6-59 in 37.4 overs). He advanced down the wicket in mock charges, often scurrying back and finishing up deep in his crease defending his stumps like a contortionist. With a day to go, South Africa were two runs behind with six wickets in hand.

The surface of the pitch had broken up, but the South African late-order batsmen attacked desperately. Thanks to Wade's 63 and Denis Begbie's 48, England needed 128 in 135 minutes to win. The light was fading, a further 17 minutes was lost to rain and a knee injury to Nourse needed treatment but a season's worth of shifts in fortune were packed into 28 overs.

South Africa's targeted the big three, Hutton, Washbrook and Compton, looking for outfield catches. Washbrook, having started off as if to overtake a train that he had already missed, was dropped by Owen Wynne at deep square leg and the saturated ball then slithered through Cuan McCarthy's anguished grasp and eluded his final despairing grab. England had 79 runs to win and nine wickets in hand. In an inspired move, Nourse brought tall seamer McCarthy back to make amends. The 19-year-old in his first Test was bowling in near darkness with a sodden ball but found extra yards of pace and hostility. He bowled Watkins, had Simpson and Mann caught and shattered Evans's stumps before the wicketkeeper got his bat down. At 70/6, England were going to need a miracle. Compton and Jenkins put on 45 before McCarthy with a superhuman effort sent Compton's off stump cartwheeling. Denis later considered his 28 to be one of the finest innings he ever played. The transfixed spectators peered through the gloom while the tourists huddled in the changing room unable to watch.

12.6 Cometh the Man

Thirteen to get and the unflappable Bedser comes in to face the penultimate over. One run later Roly Jenkins edges behind for a heroic 22. In comes big Cliff Gladwin, boilersmith at Doe Lea pit. He passes a grim-faced Dudley Nourse. 'What are you smiling about?' asks Nourse. 'When the hour comes, so does the man,' says Cliff. He hits his first ball to mid-on. Lindsay Tuckett drops it and Bedser is almost run out going for a panicked second. Off the seventh ball, Alec spars to Dawson at short leg and starts to run. Cliff sends him back. Dawson's throw scrapes the stumps, and they scamper an overthrow.

Last over, eight to win, eight balls to get them in. Just bowl full and straight, Nourse tells Tuckett, make them hit across the line. A big swish from Bedser eludes contact and they run a leg bye. 'Don't worry, my little champion,' Cliff calls over his shoulder. 'We're going to get them.' The next ball is short. Cliff connects. The ball sails into the leg side where Eric Rowan is carefully positioned on the fence at deep midwicket. Cliff has his heart in his mouth, but no, the horrified crowd sees that Eric in his excitement had moved in 15 yards and can't backpedal quickly enough. The ball sails over his head and trickles into the picket fence for the sweetest boundary of Cliff's career.

Cliff hustles another leg bye; Alec manoeuvres a single to long-on and the scores are level. Two balls left. Billy Wade is still standing back; Alec tells Cliff to run the next ball regardless. Cliff forgets his instructions and shouts at Alec to go back. Last ball, one to win. Just bowl on the stumps, says Nourse. Cliff sees it, a bit leg side and a bit short, he swings and is hit on the top of the thigh. Alec roars, 'Run, run' plunging headlong down the pitch like a galleon in a gale. 'Tufty' Mann dives in from silly mid-on and rolls the ball at the stumps. Cliff runs with the hounds of hell at his heels and turns to see Alec under a heap of bodies and the wicket unbroken.

The crowd carried Cliff off on their shoulders. Amid the pandemonium, he wondered what the boys down the pit would think. In the dressing room, Roly Jenkins kissed him on both cheeks. McCarthy was distraught. His 6-43 was the most heroic of debut performances, but the game had slipped away. 'I never hope,' said George Mann, whose debut Test it also was, 'to play in a better Test,' and Dudley Nourse agreed.[346] Many hours later, the England team staggered back to a guard of honour from the Indian staff in the Edward Hotel foyer.

SOUTH AFRICA v ENGLAND First Test, Kingsmead, 16–20 December 1948

SOUTH AFRICA

E.A.B. Rowan	c Evans b Jenkins	7	c Compton b Jenkins	16
O.E. Wynne	c Compton b Bedser	5	c Watkins b Wright	4
B. Mitchell	c Evans b Bedser	27	b Wright	19
A.D. Nourse*	c Watkins b Wright	37	c and b Bedser	32
W.W. Wade	run out	8	b Jenkins	63
D.W. Begbie	c Compton b Bedser	37	c Mann b Bedser	48
O.C. Dawson	b Gladwin	24	c Compton b Wright	3
A.M.B. Rowan	not out	5	b Wright	15
L.T.D. Tuckett	lbw b Gladwin	1	not out	3
N.B.F. Mann	c Evans b Gladwin	4	c Mann b Compton	10
C.N. McCarthy	b Bedser	0	b Jenkins	0
Extras		6	Extras	6
Total		**161**		**219**

Bedser	13.5-2-39-4	18-5-51-2
Gladwin	12-3-21-3	7-3-15-0
Jenkins	14-3-50-1	22.3-6-64-3
Wright	9-3-29-1	26-3-72-4
Compton	2-0-5-0	16-11-11-1
Watkins	3-0-11-0	

346 *Rand Daily Mail*, 21/10/38.

Fall of wickets	9, 18, 69, 80, 99, 148, 150, 152, 160, 161	22, 22, 67, 89, 174, 179, 208, 208, 219, 219

ENGLAND

L. Hutton	c McCarthy b A.M.B. Rowan	83	c Dawson b Tuckett	5
C. Washbrook	c Wade b Mann	35	lbw b Mann	25
R.T. Simpson	c Begbie b Mann	5	c E.A.B. Rowan b McCarthy	0
D.C.S. Compton	c Wade b Mann	72	b McCarthy	28
A.J. Watkins	c Nourse b A.M.B. Rowan	9	b McCarthy	4
F.G. Mann*	c E.A.B. Rowan b A.M.B. Rowan	19	c Mitchell b McCarthy	13
T.G. Evans	c Wynne b A.M.B. Rowan	0	b McCarthy	4
R.O. Jenkins	c Mitchell b Mann	5	c Wade b McCarthy	22
A.V. Bedser	c Tuckett b Mann	11	not out	1
C. Gladwin	not out	0	not out	7
D.V.P. Wright	c Tuckett b Mann	0		
Extras		14		19
Total		**253**	**for 8 wickets**	**128**

McCarthy	9-2-20-0	12-2-43-6
Dawson	3-0-16-0	
Tuckett	6-0-36-0	10-0-38-1
A.M.B. Rowan	44-8-108-4	4-0-15-0
Mann	37.4-14-59-6	2-0-13-1
Fall of Wickets	84, 104, 146, 172, 212, 212, 221, 247, 253, 253	25, 49, 52, 64, 64, 70, 115, 116

England won by two wickets

The tourists returned to the Transvaal for the second Test with the tensions of the Day of the Covenant over and the Christmas celebrations under way. The Wanderers was now part of Johannesburg Station, so the match was played at Ellis Park. George Mann was lucky again, winning the toss when in Durban he had been fortunate to lose it. Hutton and Washbrook put on a world record 359 for the first wicket in front of 35,000 spectators. Compton added a century and England made 608. South Africa fought back, but a draw was all they could ever hope for.

The South African selectors announced the third Test team with a day left to play in the second Test. Alan Melville was called in to replace Eric Rowan, a spiky and ebullient personality, who never wore a box or gloves. Having failed in his three innings so far, Rowan was probably not surprised. But he was determined to prove the selectors wrong. He batted throughout the last day to steer South Africa to safety. As a barracker advised MCC, 'Put the selectors on. They'll get him out.'[347] Out of 270/2 he had made 156 not out. He walked off with a two-fingered gesture to the selectors. 'Victory,' he said. No one believed him.

12.7 Groundsmen

After the Test, Crawford White wrote, '[The] Ellis Park pitch should be blown up and utterly destroyed ... it is killing South African cricket.' The groundsman, Aubrey Saunders, was a 'sunny man with a sunny job'. 'Here I go,' he said, 'making a wicket where they set a world record and the moans begin. Cricket has been waiting 38 years for this partnership so why the grumbles?' The famous 'Bosser' Martin, long-serving groundsman at The Oval, shared this mindset. He had chuckled with glee as England ground towards their 903. When they got to 729 and Hutton passed Don Bradman's record, Martin was heard to mutter, 'One more and I break Harry White's record for Lord's.'[348]

The teams flew to Cape Town for the third Test starting the next day. Everyone enjoyed their first flight except a green and panicked Roly Jenkins. SACA's greed for gates in the holiday season crammed 12 days of Test cricket into 21 heatwave-ridden days. The players were exhausted, and at Newlands the south-easterly wind howled down the pitch with such force that the *Edinburgh Castle* was unable to dock in Table Bay. George Mann won another toss and England's 308

---

347 *Rand Daily Mail*, 31/12/1938
348 *Rand Daily Mail*, 29/12/1938

rested on Washbrook's 74, but Athol Rowan (5-80) with spin, flight and whip off the pitch kept control on another shirtfront. Thanks to hundreds from Bruce Mitchell and Dudley Nourse, South Africa got to 298/2, ten runs behind.

But a huge advantage was overturned by timid batting and Denis Compton's rarely spotted left-arm unorthodox spin. Mitchell made seven in the first hour. Godfrey Evans described Mitchell as being a real headache for the wicketkeeper, 'He always shaped to play and let it go at the last possible moment. He was the most tantalising batsman with his shoulder twitching all the time and his bat moving up and down when taking the ball.'[349] Compton bowled 17 overs in the teeth of the gale, took an acrobatic caught and bowled to get rid of Nourse for 112 and bowled Mitchell for 120 scored from 344 minutes. Begbie and Hanley ran themselves out off consecutive balls and Compton bagged his only five-wicket haul in Tests. South Africa's lead was restricted to 48 and the momentum shifted decisively towards England with half-centuries from Hutton, Crapp, Compton and Watkins. When, against the pleadings of his exhausted bowlers, George Mann declared on 276/3, South Africa had 125 minutes to score 229 for victory, a sniff in a series where such chances were rare. After a brief thrash at the start, Nourse reined in the horses and South Africa ended up on 142/4 in 31 overs.

Despite plenty of press criticism, Nourse later insisted that Mitchell blocking up one end while he attacked at the other had been the right approach. He had taken plenty of chances in his personal duel with Roly Jenkins, driving him through the off side from two steps down the wicket. In the second innings, Roly lured him out of his crease, drifted it past the edge and Evans did the rest.[350] For Nourse, the chance of victory was lost by the middle order batsmen who could not press home the advantage. And Mann's declaration was a sop to the crowd rather than a realistic opportunity for either

349 Godfrey Evans, *Behind the Stumps*, (London: Hodder and Stoughton, 1951) 203

350 W.J. Edrich, *Cricketing Days*, 89

side. A target of 229 in just over two hours could not be achieved with the batsmen at their disposal.

12.8 Two sets of Bedsers

After three exhausting Tests and a helter-skelter travel schedule, the team found themselves in the Eastern Cape. Alec and Eric (who was travelling 'on business' as Alec would not tour without him), discovered that a Mr and Mrs Sid Bedser of Kei Road had given birth to twin boys and named them Alec and Eric. The brothers drove to the village for the christening. A large crowd had gathered to witness the charm of two pairs of identical twins, one huge, the other tiny. As Alec explained, 'We were photographed holding the twins in every conceivable position bar standing on our heads. They were small enough to hold in the palms of our hands. I held Alec junior but in the course of being photographed they changed hands so many times that there was no way of knowing if they were in the right hands at the christening ceremony.'[351]

The team took three days by train to get to Victoria Falls. Godfrey Evans decided to create a human chain above the Falls. Gladwin, Compton, Simpson, Mann and one or two others waded out until an enraged manager, Brigadier Green, took slow but determined steps towards them, and they decided that this was a risk too far. They settled for a canoe through the hair-raising Zambezi and an island picnic.[352]

Back in Johannesburg for the fourth Test, the issue of race was in the headlines. Two hundred Mosleyites had marched through the Jewish quarter in London's East End singing Nazi marching songs. In Johannesburg, Robey Leibbrandt, a South African sporting hero, was charged with a breach of the peace after yelling incendiary antisemitic abuse from a holiday camp stage. Leibbrandt had been a light-heavyweight boxing champion and carried South Africa's flag at the 1936 Olympics. He had bellowed the 'eyes right' command

---

351 Alec and Eric Bedser, *Our Cricketing Story*, (London: Evans Books, 1950)
352 Evans, *Behind the Stumps*, 206

in Afrikaans and on making eye contact with Hitler felt a 'hypnotic force'. He met Hitler and was recruited as a saboteur at the Fuhrer Leadership School. His sabotage instructor assessed him as a fanatic, incapable of working with others.

He was sent back to South Africa to organise the Nazification of the police and finally captured during a plot to assassinate Smuts. Some 349 fellow Nazis in the police were arrested and 52 charged with treason. The police blew up their own storeroom destroying the evidence. In court, he made a stirring speech to implement the ideas of Adolf Hitler whom he thought God had sent to save the peoples of the planet. He told a tearful courtroom. 'To hell with mercy, I demand justice. Long live the Afrikaner volk! Long live National Socialist South Africa!' He was sentenced to death but Smuts, wary of creating a fascist martyr, commuted the sentence to life imprisonment. He was released by the National Party government a few days after it won the 1948 election. He married and had five children – one named Izan (Nazi spelled backwards).[353]

The perennial racist complaint about 'disorderly natives' acquired a new edge under the regime. Operation Clean Up was planned to deal with the 'shebeens' – unlicensed bars – in Johannesburg, but had to be delayed as police reinforcements were needed to deal with clashes between Africans and Indians in Durban. The roots of the violence lay in the exploitation of Africans by Indian traders and landlords. African and Indian community leaders struggled to resolve the conflict and work together against white domination.

When Operation Clean Up got under way, 270 police destroyed more than 1,000 gallons of illegal skokiaan and other alcohol. Several hundred Africans 'suspected of murder and housebreaking' were arrested. Some escaped to the Bantu Sports Club next door, where a football match was in progress. The black spectators stoned the police who drew their guns and shot into the crowd. At least one man was killed and many injured.

---

353 Max Du Preez, *Of Warriors, Lovers and Prophets*, (Cape Town: Zebra Press, 2004) 167-184

In the 18 months after the election, the apartheid state had outlawed Africans from receiving unemployment benefits, enforced racial segregation in public facilities including trains, prohibited mixed marriages, outlawed sex in all its forms 'between pigmented and non-pigmented persons', created a population register by skin colour and descent, and imposed compulsory residential segregation on all population groups. The Suppression of Communism Act, the political cornerstone of this racist edifice, gave ministers dictatorial powers to prohibit or ban organisations, publications, gatherings and persons, under a definition of communism so wide that it caught any opposition from any source.

The nationalist regime's perspective on sport was shaped more by Robey Leibbrandt than on the cricket pitch. A first generation of opposition was beginning to take root where previously tourists had colluded in and ignored the treatment of Africans for the sake of the Imperial alliance. Bill Edrich, writing in *Cricketing Days* in 1949, praised the efforts of the Rev Michael Scott, 'A thin, ascetic-looking clergyman with saintly features, who has spent a good part of his life trying to break down the segregation of coloured peoples and enable them to win some of the advantages of the white race.' Scott was a strong supporter of black cricket in Johannesburg, but met with violent prejudice from the Malan regime. He appeared at the UN on behalf of the Herero in South West Africa and successfully resisted South African control of the territory to Smuts's fury.

Edrich was told in Johannesburg that there were some fine black cricketers in that area, and he noted, 'Everyone now knows that many South African Negroes have won high esteem as scholars, businessmen and artists.' Edrich hoped South Africa 'will forget about silly colour bar prejudice and turn out its best team'.[354]

Wally Hammond's ghostwritten *Cricket, My World*, also published in 1949, made several references to South Africa's racist policies. He pointed out, in a chapter entitled 'Colour Blind', how South Africa lost potential strength by failing to encourage black cricketers who,

---

354 Edrich, *Cricketing Days*, 87-88

as the West Indies and India had shown, were capable of equalling the best white cricketers in every department of the game. Hammond said, 'Although negro cricket is not yet much developed [in South Africa] ... it is impossible not to admire the persistence with which the game is played by the few coloured teams ... perhaps there is some negro express back on the Highveld under clear South African skies breaking his heart for a chance to show his mettle.'[355]

Even more surprising was Hammond's reference to a forgotten black cricketer, 'Typical of South Africa's perverse fortune is the fact that man who seems to have combined Larwood's accuracy with what was possibly the fastest trajectory ever seen on any cricket field – never came to England at all, though several leading cricketers put forward his name for [the 1894] tour. The bowler in question was a negro called Hendricks, a black Hercules about six foot four inches tall, with extremely long arms, who had been employed in some capacity by a Pretoria Cricket Club and displayed as a local wonder who could bowl down anyone's wicket, no matter how good the batsman, within half a dozen balls because of his ferocious pace.'[356]

Cecil Rhodes banned 'Krom' Hendricks from being selected because he felt, 'It was not right for a coloured man to accompany a white team.' Despite getting his alleged ethnic identity ('negro') and place ('Pretoria') wrong, Hammond had the gist of the story correct. He may have heard about Hendricks from Plum Warner or when he played for Green Point less than a decade after Hendricks had finally retired. In 1930, Warner, in a discussion of Eddie Gilbert and Jack Marsh, had suggested, 'Men of colour, save in the West Indies and India, have rarely made their mark in first-class cricket.' Hendricks, of South Africa, Plum considered, would probably have done so had he been given the chance.[357]

---

355 Wally Hammond, *Cricket My World*, (London: Stanley Paul, 1949) 72, 79

356 Hammond, *Cricket My World*, 88

357 Reg Hayter (ed.) *The Best of The Cricketer 1921–1981, The Sixtieth Anniversary Selection* (London: Littlehampton, 1981). Thanks to John Young for this reference

The shock of the post-1948 nationalist regime jarred the more reflective of the tourists into print. John Arlott, on his first overseas tour (and his last to South Africa), spoke graphically of conditions in the African location outside Grahamstown when he accompanied commentator Charles Fortune.

He said, 'Heavy rain come out of a thunderous sky and Charles Fortune brought out his car to take his clean-as-a-pin and kindly native cook back to her house … Shame, hesitation, doubt, guilt struggled in the mind. Such conditions could, perhaps, exist on the edge of a too-rapidly commercialised city, but here, among these quiet houses and schools, beside a town where one could have grown up, it is not to be understood or accepted. In crawling filth, in houses made from petrol tins hammered out flat, the people who live in that healthless quarter of Grahamstown are fortunate if they have a dwelling with one brick wall supporting a chimney. There are appallingly brave attempts to plant little gardens, to place tiny fences about the houses, but the floor space cannot work out to a square yard per person – probably less. What the rents are it is not possible for me to guess: who the landlords are someone, someday, will demand to know. Meanwhile the conscience cannot throw it off.'[358]

But these were relatively isolated references. Experience for most tourists was of a 'Rolls-Royce safari' surfing on the high end of the privileges of white colonial society. MCC was an establishment institution supporting its South African counterparts and, by association, the state itself. The English tourists had no direct engagement with black cricket and curiosity was not encouraged. After the 1890s, it was a matter of faith for whites that black South Africans, when they did play, did so only at a rudimentary level. Recognising historical cricketing realities could threaten the edifice of white supremacy itself.

Cricket had been played by Africans, 'Coloureds', 'Malays' and Indians since the last quarter of the 19th century and had developed hand in hand with political and social leadership. A colour-blind

---

358 John Arlott, *Gone with the Cricketers*, (London: Longmans, 1950) 105

'Barnato Board' organised national cricket tournaments until the late 1920s and early '30s when the communities split into separate racially based boards. The foundation of the golden era of African cricket on the Rand in the 1930s and 1940s was the cricketing talents and organisational skills of Piet Gwele, Sol Senaoane and Frank Roro among many others. Roro was chosen as one of South Africa's ten cricketers of the century in 1999. From the mid-'30s, the Rev Bernard Sigamoney sought to bring the 'races' together through an interrace competition in Johannesburg. In 1947, Sigamoney launched the non-racial South African Cricket Board of Control (SACBOC) and the first tournament was played in 1951. In sport, Sigamoney argued, 'There should be no difference of race, colour and creed. The South African team is not complete until the membership is open to all races in the country.'[359]

South Africa's selections for the fourth Test reflected at best strategic incoherence and at worst blind panic. Wynne, Begbie, Dawson, Hanley and Melville (who Roly Jenkins had defeated in both innings in Cape Town) were replaced by Eric Rowan, Lindsay Tuckett, the veteran Viljoen, the super-athlete Tony Harris and 'Fish' Markham, a leg-spinner with a quick trajectory reminiscent of Doug Wright, but who had hardly played that season.

12.9 Godfrey Evans

The tourists were not averse to a little light discipline. Godfrey Evans was dropped in favour of the amateur Billy Griffith because he had 'lost form'. His pyrotechnics in the series did not bear this out.

Evans explained his absence as punishment for some over-zealous appealing in a game in Rhodesia against old county pals. The real story emerged later. At the end of the third Test, the players agreed that the next round of drinks would be paid for by the player whose performance had been considered most unsatisfactory. Evans,

---

359 Parry, 'African Cricket on the Rand: Piet Gwele, Frank Roro, and the Shaping of a Community' in Murray, Parry and Winch (eds.), *Cricket and Society in South Africa*, 131

normally the joker himself, was selected as victim. He took it badly and emptied a pint over the redoubtable team manager Brigadier Green. This was not, he admitted, his best career move. When Evans arrived for the fourth Test, he found a handwritten note from George Mann on his pillow informing him that he was dropped from the team.[360] But every cloud has a silver lining. During the Test he partnered South Africa's champion golfer Bobby Locke in a foursome at the Wanderers Club and walked away with the stakes.

England also dropped Doug Wright, his Kent team-mate, for Jack Young, the party's wet-wicket specialist. Wright had lost his rhythm in Cape Town and bowled only 11 out of 150.2 overs, conceding 76 runs. Groundsman Aubrey Saunders, who had created a featherbed for the second Test, this time presented the surprised batsmen with a green top. It looked like a result pitch. Last time out, the openers had put on 359; this time Hutton was bowled by Tuckett in the second over. Spurred on by the pitch McCarthy was tireless, bowling 24 eight-ball overs at full pace on the first day. England reached 379, largely due to 97 from Washbrook and a century from Watkins (111), who squeezed 92 runs out of the last three wickets.

The wicket looked full of runs when Mitchell and Rowan faced the England attack. But the selectors' panic had been transmitted to the players. Mitchell was caught behind for two and wandered off looking surprised by the decision (4/1). Rowan pushed Gladwin back down the pitch, the batsmen went for a run, hesitated and went again. Gladwin lobbed the ball to Griffith and Viljoen was well short (4/2). Rowan and Nourse put on 15 before Rowan played a ball to Jenkins at cover and ran. Nourse stayed put and Rowan had no chance of getting back (19/3). Wade and Nourse put on 106 to stave off disaster. Dudley Nourse's fighting 129 not out saved the follow-on, but left South Africa 122 behind.

When England batted, another immaculate spell from Athol Rowan (4-69 in 34 overs) shackled the scoring, but Hutton's 123

---

360 Brian Rendell, *Frank and George Mann*, 94

produced a lead of 375 when Mann felt comfortable enough to declare. South Africa needed the runs in 265 minutes on a perfect wicket. One match down with one to play and the series on the line, Nourse still did not consider the target realistic and South Africa finished on 194/4. Both captains were criticised for timidity. If South Africa were to level the series, it would have to win the fifth Test at St George's Park, the first Test in Port Elizabeth since Johnny Douglas's ten-wicket win in 1914.

The game of musical chairs continued with the return of Dawson and the debut of Jack Cheetham. Wright was not selected despite dismissing Nourse three times in first-class cricket since the previous Test and Evans had not yet completed his sentence for baptising the manager. Nourse won the toss on a flat pitch with a fast outfield, but South Africa again started badly, losing Rowan and Viljoen with the total on 13. Bruce Mitchell, presumably traumatised by another disastrous start, plodded to 73 out of 219/3 by close of play. The seam stranglehold was epitomised by Bedser, who took 4-61 in 38 overs, ably supported by Gladwin's 3-70 in 30.5 overs. However, a magnificent aggressive maiden Test hundred from Billy Wade (125) carried them to a healthy 379, building on the platform laid by Mitchell (99) and Nourse (73).

The wicket was beginning to crumble, but George Mann's unbeaten 136 not out gave England a 16-run lead on the first innings with one day left. Few England captains, thought John Arlott, could have made their first Test century in the face of such difficulties or at such a vital stage of the game.[361] Athol Rowan's great-hearted 5-167 in 60 overs and Mann's 3-95 in 51 overs once again provided heroic resistance, but lapses in the field counted against them.

On the last day, Mitchell and Eric Rowan put together a century opening stand for the first time in the series, and South Africa appeared to be content to play out time. Suddenly at the end of the tea interval, the light roller appeared and Nourse set England a snap target of 172 in 95 minutes. Washbrook hooked a short ball for six

---

361 Arlott, *Gone with the Cricketers*, 115

in the first over, Hutton hit his first ball for four and the chase was on. They had 23 after two overs, 50 in 25 minutes and 100 in 55 minutes but wickets kept falling and at 125/5 South African fans hoped against hope. Jack Crapp and Cliff Gladwin put together a crucial 27 and with five minutes to go and 11 needed, Crapp drove the ball straight back to 'Tufty' Mann who put it down. With the wind behind him, Crapp hit consecutive boundaries and England had improbably won the final Test by three wickets.

The 2-0 series scoreline broadly reflected the difference between the teams even though it was really decided by Gladwin's leg bye at the end of the first Test. For Nourse, South Africa's fielding and catching was far below the standard required and concentration rather than ability lay at the heart of it. The series had slipped through their fingers.

England had fought as hard as possible in the field and seldom let a chance go begging. As Godfrey Evans explained, they realised that their bowling would not be enough on batsmen-friendly pitches, 'From the opening innings [George Mann] set a fine example in the field, and with the other lads emulating him it was our keen fielding that won us most of our matches.'[362] Washbrook, Simpson and the skipper controlled the outfield; Watkins, Jenkins and Crapp were picking cherries close in, Compton was brilliant anywhere and Hutton always reliable.

With the bat, England were also in a different class. The openers Hutton (577 at an average of 64) and Washbrook (542 at 60) put on more than 50 for the first wicket six times in the series. By contrast, South Africa proved almost incapable of a solid start (18/2; 22/2; 17/2; 19/3; and 13/2) and the middle order were routinely faced with an uphill battle against tight bowling. Alec Bedser struck in four out of the five poor starts. South Africa's other major weakness was, Nourse excepted, their inability to use their feet to Roly Jenkins's leg spin. Flight was a key component on good wickets. 'Stay at home' batsmen could never win glory on an international field, felt Nourse.

362 Evans, *Behind the Stumps*, 197

Test cricket was a huge step up from the weekend game and high-level experience was critical. The selectors picked the same 11 for the first two Tests, but then uncertainly took over. Three players were dropped then reinstated and four others were dropped after only one Test. This was not an environment which allowed players to perform at their best. Selection was a parlour game rather than a means to build a united and focused squad. In addition, the impact of the war on the older players, both technically and psychologically, and the reluctance of the provinces, particularly the Transvaal, to provide opportunities for youth suggests that the failure of South African cricket was one of culture as much as performance.

The tour maintained public interest to the end of the final game and was a huge financial success; a total of 530,000 spectators watched the matches. SACA made a huge profit, but the players benefited from little of the wealth their efforts created. Brigadier Green reported that the accommodation was often poor and sometimes disgraceful. 'We were,' Green felt, 'badly treated in comparison to South African tours to England, or England tours elsewhere.' But the large profits did mean air travel in the last matches to the relief of all except Roly Jenkins.

The English team had a harmonious tour, with only the failure of the enigmatic Wright in the third Test and his subsequent omission, along with Evans, for the last two Tests, to disturb the surface. Wright began well but he never quite secured the Test place his bowling demanded. His unique recipe of medium-pace leg breaks off a long run depended on a rhythm that could be easily lost particularly if, as he admitted to Bill Edrich, he tended to listen to well-meaning but ill-informed advice.

George Mann maintained his enthusiasm and focus throughout the long, hot tour. He had the ability to convey to every new circle of friends that their hospitality was just a little better than the best they had received so far. But class tension between the amateur establishment – captain and manager – and professionals was on the increase, perhaps reflecting the shock electoral triumph for Labour and the row over the failure to redistribute some of the huge profits generated by their performances.

The Evans affair was rescued by Godfrey's good humour, his acceptance that he had overstepped the line, and perhaps his appreciation for a brief rest from his labours in the heat. Evans and the professionals were reminded of their place. But the relationship was changing and by the time England next toured Southern Africa, a professional – Len Hutton – had captained England. But the real location of power had not changed. A Labour government might have been running the country, but the structure of the English establishment still had firm foundations at Lord's.

Sometimes the magic doesn't work. Percy Chapman's mother hands him a sprig of lucky heather before departure, 1930, and a series defeat for MCC.

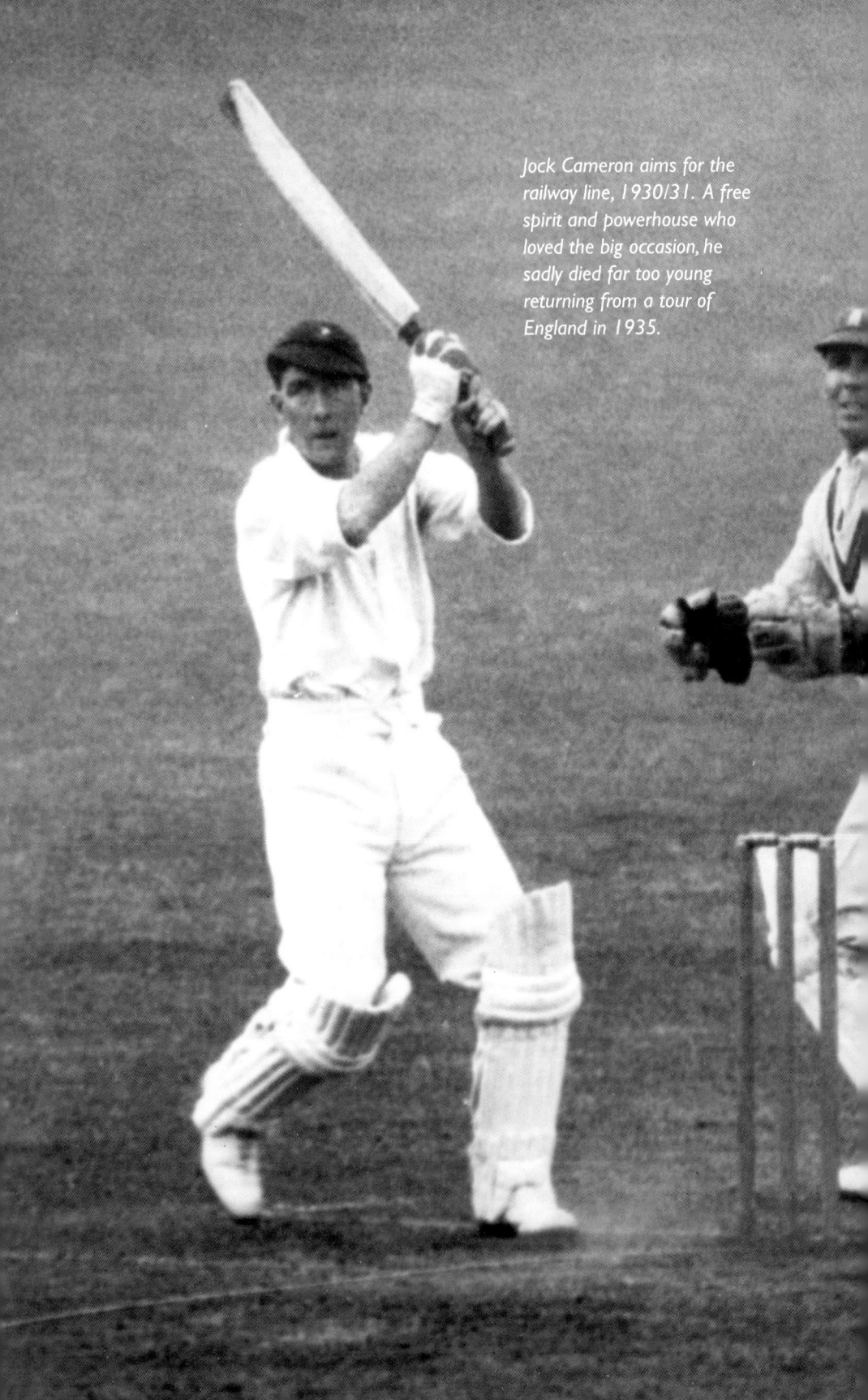

Jock Cameron aims for the railway line, 1930/31. A free spirit and powerhouse who loved the big occasion, he sadly died far too young returning from a tour of England in 1935.

The product of many hours at the wicket in the Timeless Test. Pieter van der Byl's South African cap, 1938/39.

A cricketing picture. George Mann and Dudley Nourse toss at Newlands, 1948

Cricket in the South African shadows. Black South African cricket continued to thrive and the players were capable of performing at the highest level. Frank Roro and the South Africa 'Bantu' Cricket Board XI, 1951. Standing (l-r) B.N. Malamba, M. Sokopo, S. Ntshekisa, Julius Mahanjana, Frank Roro (captain), W. Ximiya, G. Sulupha, G. Langa. Kneeling (l-r) L. Mafongosi, C. Msikinya, C. Scott

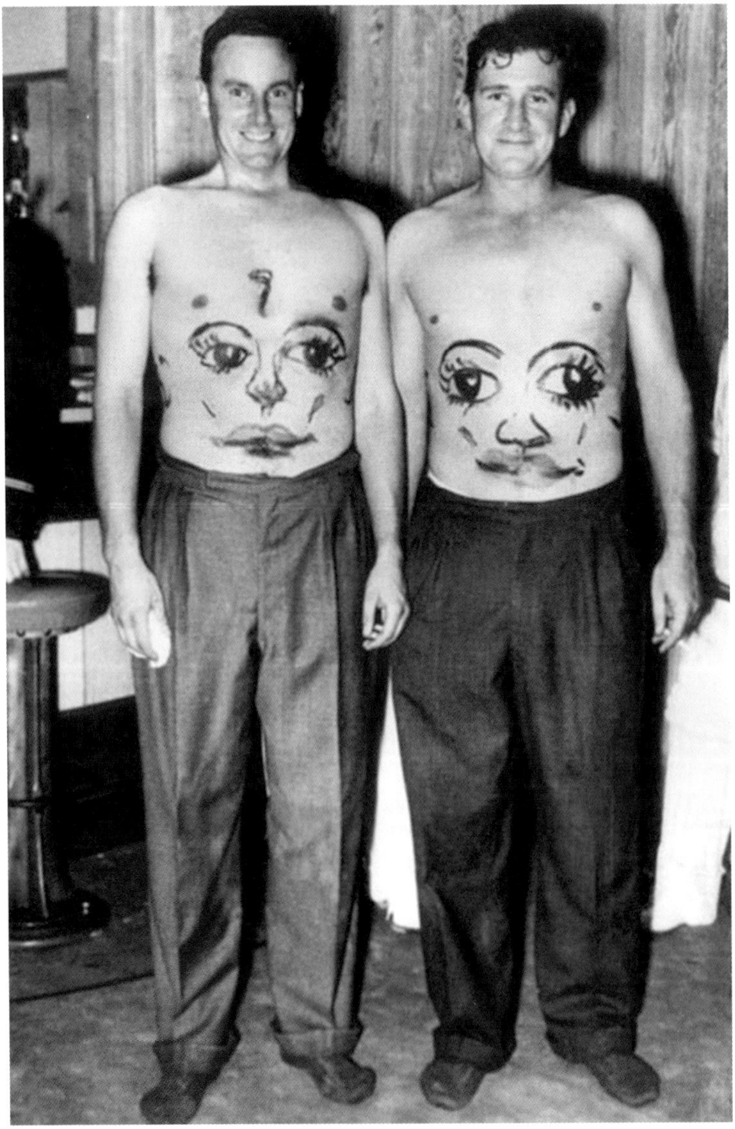

A study in incongruity. Peter May and Jim Laker winning the Edinburgh Castle onboard fancy dress as Tweedledum and Tweedledee, October 1956

Resistance to apartheid's repression. The bus boycotts in Alexandria Township in 1956 won a hard fought victory

On the verge of greatness amidst the acrimony. Tayfield appeals for an lbw against MCC's Brian Taylor for the South African XI, 1956

'When you strike a woman, you have struck a rock'. The Women's March to the Union Buildings in Pretoria in opposition to the Pass Laws led by Sophie Williams, Raheema Moosa, Helen Joseph and Lilian Ngoyi

The South African struggle receives recognition on the world stage with the awarding of the Nobel Peace prize to Albert Luthuli, seen arriving in Oslo in 1964

Hendrik Verwoerd, South African President and the architect of apartheid chats with the captains, Trevor Goddard and Mike Smith, when the Western Province Cricket Club (self-styled 'MCC of the Cape Colony') celebrated 75 years of Test cricket between South Africa and England at Newlands

A characteristic moment of respect between opponents as Mike Smith congratulates Trevor Goddard on reaching his first Test century in the fourth Test, 1965

Basil D'Oliveira during his innings of 158 on the second day of the fifth Test at the Oval 1968. His subliminal batting on a wave of pride and passion, was driven by his determination to make his selection for the MCC tour to South Africa in 1968 incontestable. But the apartheid state abetted by MCC had other ideas.

Basil D'Oliveira: the sky's the limit

13

Defiance: Peter May 1956/57

AS THE *Edinburgh Castle* ploughed through the October swells, the cricketers partied in the state rooms except for a few sensitive souls like Doug Insole, who lay groaning in their bunks. In their wake floated a consignment of books, an anonymous gift distributed to the team. *Naught for your Comfort* was a hard-hitting account by an English clergyman, Father Trevor Huddleston, of living and working among black South Africans. MCC manager Freddie Brown, in a panic at the rumour that it might be banned in South Africa (it wasn't, at least not yet), collected as many copies as he could and hurled them overboard.[363]

At home, Anthony Eden's highhanded effort to 'liberate' the Suez Canal from Nasser's Egypt assumed a UK-French global sway that had long passed to the United States. The US sided with Russia in the United Nations and forced Britain's humiliating departure. Britain's reduced place in the world made it strategically essential to conciliate the nationalist regime in South Africa, effectively one of many decolonisation struggles across the continent.

---

363 Freddie Brown was the third choice as manager after F.G Mann and Maurice Allom. MCC suggested that he and the captain meet South Africa's high commissioner in London to discuss the 'political background' before leaving. Clearly politics was not his strength. E.W Swanton, *With P.B.F. May's MCC Team 1956/57*, (London: Robert Hale, 1957) 234

At the pre-tour dinner, the team were briefed by the MCC president, Viscount Monckton, who had resigned as minister of defence over Suez. Colour was not to be mentioned, and difficult conversations were to be deflected towards the recent Lions rugby tour which had ended 2-2 and contained enough incident to sidetrack a white South African for the remainder of the evening.

Had the cricketers opened Father Huddleston's book (Colin Cowdrey said he did [364]), they would have been exposed to a different reality to that discussed at Lord's: the violence, poverty, misery, and deprivation arising from the impact of 'baasskap' (white supremacy) experienced daily by the black majority.

Instead, fellow passenger Professor Tomlinson, a South African academic, offered to lecture the team on conditions in South Africa. Trevor Bailey, in a chapter of his book bizarrely entitled 'Fanagalo: the magic word from Zululand' (Fanagalo was the lingua franca of command in the mines to enable Africans to obey white orders), spoke approvingly of Tomlinson's 'intelligent, carefully researched, reasoned and considered resume of the situation [which] made a pleasant change from the uninformed, prejudiced and hysterical outbursts to which I have usually been subjected. Although as cricketers we were non-political, we could not shut our eyes to a situation in which there were no satisfactory solutions for the different groups, who not only disliked but were also frightened of each other.'[365]

Tomlinson may have presented himself as a disinterested academic. This was far from the case. He headed the eponymous Tomlinson Commission set up in 1951 to consider the viability of the 'native reserves'. The commission was made up of Broederbond members from the Bureau of Racial Affairs at Stellenbosch University. Tomlinson described all Africans who lived within the Union, but outside the reserves, as 'foreigners' and argued for the principle of total racial segregation, a keystone of future apartheid policy. The report admitted that the reserves were wholly inadequate to support

---

364 Colin Cowdrey, *MCC*, (London: Coronet, 1977) 193
365 Trevor Bailey, *Wickets, Catches and the Odd Run*, (London: Collins, 1986) 179

the population. Additional land and resources would be needed. Hendrik Verwoerd, minister of native affairs, rejected increasing the viability of reserves which would reduce the outflow of labour on to mines, farms or industry in white South Africa.

Tomlinson made the time-honoured white South African plea to his fellow passengers. Wait and see. Keep an open mind. Don't condemn us until you understand local conditions.[366] Bailey, Insole and most of the others were happy to 'wait and ignore' any prickings of conscience while the words of the 'turbulent priest' Father Huddleston sank beneath the waves.

After two weeks of dances, songs, deck sports and shipboard romances, the *Edinburgh Castle* deposited its cricketing cargo on to the pier at Duncan Dock in the shadow of the mountain. Professor Tomlinson had not only laid the foundations for the team's interpretation of South African reality but provided May with a few sentences in Afrikaans to hold out an olive branch to the white supremacist regime at the civic reception. They were there, he said, to play cricket. It was a game not an international crisis. May promised that bright cricket came first and winning was a secondary consideration. Fine words which would come to haunt him. Freddie Brown was more practical. For the first time, MCC would share the financial benefits with SACA. He looked forward to 'pretty high profits'. MCC pocketed a handsome £25,000 in the end.[367]

The team was close to full strength. Fred Trueman was not on board. He was dreaded 'like the Ancient Mariner' off the field with his 'anti-hero' persona, 'rudimentary humour, prodigious memory, and forthright views'.[368] MCC had an uneasy relationship with working-class professionals who had a strong appreciation of their own abilities. Although the 1953/54 MCC team to the West Indies contained 'several players it would not have been wise to take on a Sunday School picnic', Fred was the only player to have his good

---

366 Cowdrey, *MCC*, 193
367 *Rand Daily Mail*, 16/10/1956
368 Birley, *Social History*, 284

conduct bonus withheld. He had also had a poor season in 1956. This was not simply a class issue. As Godfrey Evans, who had his own run-ins with authority, put it, 'Players who may … upset their colleagues either on or off the field should be left at home.'[369]

The Reverend David Sheppard made himself unavailable for political, disguised as clerical, reasons and Tom Graveney's face didn't fit despite finishing top of the averages. Douglas John Insole (named by his Essex supporting father after Johnny Douglas, captain of the 1913/14 tourists), sat on the selection committee and found himself vice-captain. President Monckton 'persuaded' Insole's chairman at Wimpey Construction to let him go.[370]

Described as the 'team of all the talents', England were strongest with the ball. Statham, Loader, Tyson, Laker (fresh from his 19-90 at Old Trafford) Lock and Wardle made up the best attack in the world. The batting was another matter. Cowdrey had been selected as an opener but could not be persuaded to take on this role in Tests, Oakman had a long-term back injury and Compton, with only one kneecap, was a risk at Test level. Doug Insole had played three Tests spread across three series. Jim Parks played one game and was mysteriously diagnosed with sunstroke, back and chest problems, and finally vision issues. He was sent home, but collapsed at the airport when about to return. May did not call publicly for a replacement, but privately and unsuccessfully urged his friend David Sheppard to change his mind.

13.1 Alan Oakman and the Cyclist

Jim Laker described 'a particularly striking example of the general attitude to the coloured folk'. Alan Oakman had borrowed a car to go out for the evening in Cape Town and driving back late hit a coloured cyclist. The man lay in the road in great pain with a broken leg. Oakman was recognised, a crowd gathered and the man on the ground was ignored while the crowd asked for autographs. A policeman came along and the first thing he said was, 'He was

---

369 Evans, *The Gloves are Off*, 180
370 Interview with Doug Insole, 15/6/2017

drunk, Mr Oakman, wasn't he?' The policeman collared one of the onlookers. 'He was drunk, wasn't he?' he demanded, and the person – who hadn't seen the victim – agreed. Another coloured man was picked on. 'You live near this nigger ... he's always drunk, isn't he?' the policeman asked. Slowly fearfully, the black head nodded. This, thought Alan, was what white men called justice. Alan went to see the man in hospital the following day and gave him a few pounds for his family.[371]

England got off to a flyer, winning their first six games by an innings. Insole, with his unconventional, bottom-handed method struggled initially. Journalist E.W. Swanton launched what Insole considered to be a vindictive personal campaign against him and the team closed ranks. May hit four consecutive hundreds, culminating in 206 against Rhodesia in Salisbury. The only way the mayor of Salisbury, Harry Pichanick, could think of to stop him was to present the unflappable Peter May with a live duck.[372] May admitted that 'it did the trick' and added the strangest element to a rivetingly psychological tour.

The real cricket started against Transvaal in Johannesburg. Alan Ross's first impressions were of the 'grey mine dumps with Heath Robinson headgear, the appalling slum shanties of Orlando ... the derelict squatting grounds of the native whose labour is required but not his presence ... no city can so resemble Dante's *Inferno*.'[373]

In a sensational start to the second day, Brian Statham, bowling with the accuracy and control with which he was synonymous, spread-eagled the stumps of Ritchie, Charnas and Heine to record the first hat-trick at the (new) Wanderers Stadium. May came out to a tumultuous reception. Peter Heine landed his delivery on a perfect length and cut it away. May got a deflection and Waite flung the ball skywards, the golden duck beginning an extraordinary lean spell for the England man. Chasing a routine 64 in their second knock, the

---

371 Laker, *Over to Me*, 90-91

372 Peter May, *A Game Enjoyed*, (London: Stanley Paul, 1985)

373 Alan Ross, *Cape Summer*, (London: Constable, 1986) 132-133

blistering pace of Adcock and Heine had England reeling at 36/6 until Frank Tyson steered them to a three-wicket win.

Trevor Bailey later described the series as dull cricket but exciting situations. The battle lines were laid down in the Transvaal match. Ken Funston did not walk and the tourists, who considered the umpires as 'homers', began a lively debate on the merits of waiting for the umpire's decision. Insole was then captain in 'the most miserable game I have ever played in' against a South African XI at Loftus Versveld rugby ground in Pretoria. The wicket had never been used for first-class cricket. It was 'one long drawn-out dogfight, and that is no metaphor', said Charles Fortune.[374] The tourists, including Lock and Wardle, encountered Hugh Tayfield fresh from an unsuccessful season in the Lancashire Leagues with plenty to prove.

MCC's concern over umpiring punctuated the home side's first innings. When England batted, and Peter Richardson was not given out lbw to Tayfield, Jackie McGlew, the Springbok captain, appealed from mid-on for a catch. The umpire raised his finger. It sparked an immediate row with the ubiquitous Insole, who was at the non-striker's end in almost every critical moment on this tour. He said Tayfield was cheating. 'What are you complaining about?' asked Tayfield. 'We had it all the time in England.' He had a point. In The Oval Test in 1955, South Africa were the victim of at least three poor decisions – one of which (an lbw turned down against Peter May before he had scored) probably cost them the match and the series.[375]

When the SA XI batted again, Funston carted a six and two fours off a raging Lock during a match-winning 55. The fixture deteriorated further over McGlew's justified claim for an extra half an hour with England seven wickets down. The batsmen walked off and Freddie Brown had to scurry back to the hotel for a copy of the regulations. MCC played on with bad grace and lost by 38 runs. Tayfield bowled himself into the series with 12-83 in 52.5 eight-ball

374 Charles Fortune, *MCC Tour of South Africa*, (London: George Harrap and Co, 1957) 74

375 Interview with Doug Insole, 15/6/2017

overs. McGlew complained about the MCC's behaviour and May had to read the riot act to his team and issue a formal apology.[376]

13.2 Basil D'Oliveira, SACBOC and the Kenyans

On the same day, Basil D'Oliveira captained the South African Cricket Board of Control (SACBOC) XI against the touring Kenyans in Cape Town. This was the first time a cricket international had been played by a so-called 'non-European' South African team since 1892. Basil missed out on his life's ambition to play at Newlands when SACBOC refused to adhere to apartheid permit regulations and the game was moved to Hartleyvale, a football ground.

SACBOC emphasised no distinctions of race, colour or creed. But its members were the pre-existing racially defined cricket unions (excluding the Malay/Muslim Cricket Union) playing 'interrace' cricket among themselves. Bringing racially defined unions together was a key step in the non-racial unification process and SACBOC's team against the Kenyans was non-racial. Kenya had been the third-choice tourists. India and Pakistan had refused invitations for fear of jeopardising their position in the white dominated Imperial Cricket Council.[377]

D'Oliveira's South Africa won the first Test by six wickets despite a sparkling hundred from Shakoor Ahmed, who had toured England with Pakistan in 1954. Laam Raziet from Stellenbosch made a hundred for South Africa at the Natalspruit ground in Johannesburg to win the second Test, but the third at Kingsmead was ruined by rain. Ben Malamba, who also played lock for the national African rugby team, took 16 wickets with his off-cutters in the series, and D'Oliveira headed the batting averages with 53.[378]

In 1958, D'Oliveira took his SACBOC team on a return tour to Kenya where they won all three Tests by handsome margins and by the end of that year SACBOC declared officially that geography would supersede race.

---

376 Fortune, *MCC Tour*, 78

377 S.J. Reddy and D.N. Bansda (eds.), *The South African Non-European Cricket Almanack*, 1953–54

378 Odendaal et al, *Divided Country*, 246-252

After the South African XI game, MCC needed to repair dents to morale, form and reputation. As in 1948, they were again dispatched to Durban, the most English part of the country, during the 'sacred' Day of the Covenant holiday. May and Insole made hundreds against Natal. Trevor Goddard was characteristically parsimonious with the ball and impressive with the bat, using his feet with a freedom that no Australian had managed against Laker. Natal hung on for a face-saving draw and following a drawn game against North-Easterns at Benoni it was back to Johannesburg for the start of real hostilities.

After Mann's MCC tourists had left in 1949, Malan's National Party had systematically engineered the apartheid edifice. The devaluation of sterling and new discoveries of gold and uranium strengthened economic growth and Afrikaner political control. In 1950, Hendrik Verwoerd, the Dutch-educated architect of baasskap, became native affairs minister and six new seats for South West Africa gave the nationalists a comfortable majority in 1953. Baasskap knitted together the social, economic and political fabric of Afrikaner nationalism including Afrikaans universities, press, churches and the party into a single framework. The nationalists ensured Afrikaners enjoyed preferential rights in defence and the civil service as well as Afrikaner corporations.

Apartheid (translating as separateness) was, as Professor Tomlinson told MCC tourists, 'essential', as the bedrock of the political economy and the mechanism for ensuring ultra-cheap labour. Its power lay in its comprehensive racist legislation which made European fascists and American 'Jim Crow' adherents look like amateurs. Beyond denial of access to land and employment, there were myriad legal mechanisms often labelled with macabre humour to suggest the opposite of what they meant. Detailing the huge body of law, regulation and administrative enactment requires several volumes, but fundamental to apartheid was a belief in racial separation. The Population Registration Act divided South Africa into watertight racial compartments, and inter-racial sex was criminalised. A 'scientific' division by race was impossible, so a white person was defined, *Alice in Wonderland*-like, as one who appeared to be, was accepted by and normally associated with whites. Heartrending anomalies were not slow to appear, as the story of the South African 'non-European' cricketer, Owen Williams, would show.[379]

The next step was control over space – reversing the African influx to urban areas, resettling them in distant locations such as the South Western Townships (SoWeTo), abolishing vestigial property rights and bulldozing squatter settlements. Africans had to carry a single 'dompas' with details of identification, employment, residence, tax payments and police records. The system of controls forcibly regulated industrial labour and served the needs of white voters for farm labour, creating chronic insecurity and anxiety for all Africans. Losing a pass could mean a period of slave labour on prison farms. In 1956, 600,000 Africans, perhaps 15 per cent of the urban population, were arrested for pass offences. Africans were constantly subject to police raids and terrorised by violent criminals (tsotsis) or forced into crime themselves.

But out of this chaos and instability Africans created a rich alternative cultural identity which synthesised aspects of urban and rural life and revolved around the shebeens, music, sport and religion. Alan Ross was one of the few white journalists to notice African cultural identities beyond the mock war dances satirically performed for tourists, feeding the frisson for controlled savagery. Ross described how on Sunday afternoons in Durban groups of Zulus in zoot suits, jeans, beads and Hombergs, dressed cowboy style, or wearing shocking-pink caps and bowlers, formed circles within which pairs of dancers improvised and raved. Nearby, a larger circle formed a ring for boxers who pummelled each other with 'unscientific energy'. After the dances, Ross, peering through colonial spectacles, noted, 'They drifted happily away to put on the sober uniforms of house-boys or cleaners.'[380]

This illustrated another aspect of apartheid, the reduction of capacity through the Bantu 'education' system which would fit

---

379 See Chapter 14 below. Peter Oborne, *Basil D'Oliveira*, (London: Little Brown, 2004) 50

380 Ross, *Cape Summer*, 139

Africans to perform labouring roles ('Make them hewers of wood and drawers of water,' explained Hendrik Verwoerd). This aimed to instil psychological inferiority, withhold knowledge and deaden curiosity, so that racial equality was not only unobtainable but literally unthinkable.

Once in the workplace, Africans were subject to job colour bars excluding them from semi-skilled work, and from the definition of employee, so they could not join trade unions. The law required separate provision of facilities for everything – public transport, emergency ambulances, park benches, beaches and post office counters. It was amended to clarify that these facilities did *not* need to be equal. Nor were they.

Such a draconian system required a comprehensive defensive structure. Physically, this rested on a huge, well-resourced police establishment unaccountable to those they policed. The 1950 Suppression of Communism Act was the all-purpose weapon against resistance to apartheid. The immediate aim was to liquidate the Communist Party, place its members and supporters under police surveillance, hound them out of political life and the trade unions, destroy the liberation movements, and entrench white supremacy behind despotic powers. It applied to anyone 'who professes communism ... or is advocating objects of communism ... or aims at bringing about political, economic or social change ... or encourages feelings of hostility between white and black'.[381] The act provided unfettered powers to ban, prohibit and deport without recourse to appeal.

The state intended to eliminate internal resistance to apartheid. A Defiance of Unjust Laws Campaign had been launched on 26 June 1952 by the ANC and the South African Indian Congress, targeting separate queues in post offices, curfews and railway waiting rooms, by getting arrested, refusing to pay fines, flooding the gaols and making the system unworkable. The campaign was initially successful, but it was hard to sustain without concrete results.

---

381 Roux, *Time Longer Than Rope*, 379-380

Building on these campaigns, a Congress of the People brought together all shades of resistance to frame a Freedom Charter on 26 June 1955. The charter was a radical vision of a free South Africa, which 40 years later shaped the modern South African constitution. 'The people shall govern. All national groups shall have equal rights ... The people shall share in the country's wealth ... All shall enjoy equal human rights.'[382]

The first half of December saw countrywide special branch raids and arrests targeting more than 50 organisations from the Comintern to the National Council of Women and the anti-Bantu education campaign.[383] Professor Z.K. Matthews, Albert Luthuli, Nelson Mandela, Oliver Tambo, Joe Slovo, Lilian Ngoyi, Walter Sisulu, Helen Joseph and 148 others were arrested in dawn raids and brought to Johannesburg for trial on charges of high treason. As Albert Luthuli, in 1960 Africa's first Nobel Peace Prize winner, put it, 'The treason trial must occupy a special place in South African history. That grim pre-dawn raid, deliberately calculated to strike terror into hesitant minds and impress upon the entire nation the determination of the governing clique to stifle all opposition, made 156 of us, belonging to all the races of our land, into a group of accused facing one of the most serious charges in any legal system.'[384]

The Treason Trial preliminary hearings began as MCC returned to Johannesburg. The state's fascist agenda was played out before the international media. The trials started in the ceilingless Drill Hall amid a cacophony of noise from the crowds outside. Inside the court, no one knew the 156 prisoners from the spectators and there were no microphones or interpretation. The police struggled to separate the various prisoners by race group in a cage with whites in the front row. Ironically, the trial, by bringing together the entire defiance leadership in a single place for years on end, did much to unite, build coherence and trust and provided an opportunity to debate strategy.

---

382 Roux, *Time Longer Than Rope*, 398-399
383 *Rand Daily Mail*, 14/12/1956
384 Helen Joseph, *If this be Treason*, (Johannesburg: Contra Press, 1998), 14

It was a lesson that would shape activities on Robben Island and a massive own goal.

The examination was adjourned in chaos after 20 minutes. Outside the court, police launched baton charges and fired at demonstrators; 22 people were taken to hospital. The *Rand Daily Mail*'s headline was 'At Start, Songs; At End, Drawn Guns'.[385] Baton charges and retaliatory stone throwing continued during the next two days while the prosecutor alleged that the prisoners received assistance from overseas to overthrow the government and set up a communist state. The hearings were adjourned to early January.

Trevor Huddleston wrote to the *Manchester Guardian*, '[In] view of the immense importance of the Treason Trials it seems highly incongruous that England should go on playing against white South Africa at this crucial moment of racial tension. Until a new multi-racial constitution is adopted, the MCC should withdraw from any further engagements.'[386]

The MCC were not listening. The first Test began on Christmas Eve at the Wanderers Stadium. Considering Cheetham's spectacular drawn series in Australia and a narrow 3-2 defeat in England which came down to the final Test, South Africans saw a realistic chance of upsetting England for the first time since 1935.

Jackie McGlew was appointed captain for the series. He had refused surgery on an injured knee then dived and landed heavily on his shoulder. It had not recovered, and he withdrew the evening before the Test but did not inform his replacement, Clive van Ryneveld, until the next morning. Ken Funston, the 12th man, who had hit a scintillating 50 in the SA XI game, was ignored and John Watkins was instead flown up from Durban on the morning of the Test. Jim Laker later suggested that McGlew had been pushed down the stairs by one of his team – possibly Funston – who had had 'about six too many' and the rumours continued despite McGlew's denials.[387]

---

385 *Rand Daily Mail*, 20/12/1956
386 *Ibid*
387 Jackie McGlew, *Cricket for South Africa*, (London: Hodder and Stoughton, 1961) 155-158

The MCC had their own problems. May couldn't persuade Colin Cowdrey to open, Alan Oakman's back had not recovered and Trevor Bailey got the nod though he had not opened on the tour so far. Bailey was delighted. May won the toss and before Bailey and Richardson had reached the middle, they had already christened themselves 'Sir Jack' [Hobbs=Bailey] and 'Herbert' [Sutcliffe=Richardson]. Peter Richardson was on five after 75 minutes and had reached 69 not out by the close, with England on 157/3 in 80 overs. Austere as the Karoo his innings may have been, but it was a fighter's knock, and such sparseness had its beauty. That evening a female guest told Richardson and Oakman that she hoped that dreadful boring batsman would get out quickly. Oakman choked on his drink.

She would have to wait a little longer. Richardson reached his hundred in eight hours and eight minutes, the slowest Test century to date. Thanks to him, and 59 from Cowdrey, England crawled to 268. At the end of the second day, South Africa had the edge on 91/1, with Trevor Goddard batting confidently. The next morning Goddard was caught at gully for 49, Keith went for 42, and Bailey trapped the dangerous McLean lbw with a shooter second ball. The remaining passengers dismounted in quick order. Van Ryneveld was brilliantly caught by Bailey at full length at second slip. Neil Adcock, a founder member of the fast bowlers' 'have a go' coalition, smashed his first ball into the 'non-European' enclosure and more than doubled his top Test score with 17. With a 53-run lead, Richardson's achievement was more lifeboat than millstone. By close of play, Heine and Adcock reduced the visitors to 42/3 with the obdurate openers and nightwatchman Wardle back in the hutch.

Compton and Insole stretched England's lead to 137 when the match exploded. Compton, on 32, was dropped at slip by Heine and without adding to his score drove the ball back to Tayfield. Tayfield dived forward, scooped it up and held it aloft. 'Did you?' said Compton. 'I've told you I caught it,' said Tayfield and Compton walked off. Beyond this, no two accounts agree. Insole, the non-striker, admitted he did not see it clearly, but was adamant the ball had bounced two feet short of Tayfield. Compton had walked on

Tayfield's word. Insole argued that the newsreel footage showed Tayfield's cheating so clearly that it was never publicly shown. The South African narrative was that it had been a brilliant catch grabbed an inch from the turf and the umpire gave Compton out on his way back from the wicket. [388]

Peter May arrived in a swirling wind and powerfully drove the ball a foot off the ground into the open gap between square leg and midwicket. Endean, to the right of the umpire, sprinted a few yards, dived horizontally and plucked the ball one-handed out of the air. The remarkable thing was not that Endean had held it, but that he had conceived of the possibility of getting to the ball at all. Perhaps the most remarkable catch on a South African ground, it gave fresh legs to the bowlers and England subsided to 150 all out. South Africa needed 204 to win in more than eight hours. Tyson was in bed with tonsillitis and Bailey had the new ball.[389]

Bailey used the full width of the crease, changing the swing and cut off the pitch. He found lift and fed on the batsmen's weaknesses. Leg cutters did for Taylor and Goddard, caught at slip by Insole, then John Waite chopped on to Statham to make it 11/3. As if conjured up by Bailey's Prospero, the gale increased in ferocity, blew down the sight screens and rain and hail lashed the ground. South Africa ended the day on 40/7 with only Van Ryneveld left and Statham and Bailey sharing the wickets. Never, according to the *Rand Daily Mail*, had the magnificent South African bowling been so recklessly wasted.[390] The following morning May ran out first Heine and then Van Ryneveld as the latter tried to farm the strike against the dangerous Statham. South Africa collapsed to an ignominious 72 all out and lost by 131 runs. Wanderers Stadium had become Heartbreak Hotel. Bailey (5-20) and Statham (2-22) had proved too good for South Africa's batsmen on a blameless wicket. The balance between bat and ball was skewed in favour of the latter for the first time since the introduction of turf wickets.

---

388 Insole, interview, 15/6/2017
389 *Rand Daily Mail*, 29/12/1956
390 *Ibid*

The teams flew to Cape Town for the second Test three days later. McGlew's anger over the collapse in Johannesburg persuaded him to risk his shoulder injury and he put his team through a gruelling fielding session on the day before the game. He lost the toss and was 'a harassed and bewildered man' when he led the team out on New Year's Day into the south-easter.[391] Compton's half century provided moments of nostalgic charm as well as evidence of his current constraints. Cowdrey ground out a snail's-pace hundred over six hours. Godfrey Evans played the most attractive innings of the series. On New Year's Eve, he, Compton and Bailey had missed the midnight curfew by several hours. He appealed for clemency with 62 in 72 balls, giving the Newlands crowd something to enjoy.

Tayfield bowled 424 balls. Only 30 went for singles and England were all out for 369. It was more than enough to unleash Johnny Wardle on a pitch, which he would have wanted to carry around in his cricket bag. He took 5-53 in 23.6 overs as South Africa struggled to 205 with only Roy McLean and John Waite showing any sign of a game plan.

May refused to enforce the follow-on, fearing tiring bowlers and a deteriorating wicket. McGlew also assumed there was no chance of a victory, Adcock had a septic toe and Van Ryneveld a broken finger. McGlew set a purely containing field with no slips or close fielders. May eventually declared, setting a target of 385 in eight hours. South Africa were psychologically beaten, but someone needed to fire the bullets.

Wardle was a supremely versatile bowler, bowling both left-arm 'orthodox' finger spin and wrist spin. He had taken 43 wickets primarily with wrist spin in seven games on the tour so far. Without any discernible change of action, he was able to turn them from off to leg and vice versa. May brought Wardle on in the fourteenth over, but spoilt it by telling him not to bowl wrist spin at Goddard. Wardle said, 'Look, skipper, let me bowl how I want to bowl, and I'll have him out in three overs. I'm not going to bowl the orthodox.

---

391 Fortune, *MCC Tour 1956/57*, 114-115

That would be just like giving him a net.' He bowled a groping McGlew behind his legs then had Goddard caught at slip and the dominoes were falling. 'The wind was blowing. I was bowling almost all "chinamen", drifting the ball out to off and spinning it back into the stumps using Goddard's footmarks'.[392]

Eight wickets went down for 31 in an hour and a half. Russell Endean batted for 40 minutes without scoring. He was completely at sea until an off break from Laker ballooned off his pad above his head and, as a former Springbok hockey player, he instinctively palmed it down. He became the first to be out 'handled the ball' in a Test. Coincidentally he had been the wicketkeeper obstructed when Hutton was given out 'obstructing the field' at The Oval in 1951.

Waite was bewildered by Wardle's googly and caught at slip. Doug Insole was off the field and sitting near the South Africans. John Watkins was picking Wardle ball by ball from the pavilion – googly, chinaman, googly, top-spinner. His time came and he played the first ball from Johnny, a googly, as a chinaman, the second, a chinaman, as a googly and for the third, a googly. After pondering his options, on the first ball of Wardle's next over he took a wild heave and hit a catch straight back to Wardle. He returned to gales of laughter from his team-mates.[393]

Heine was bowled by a straight quicker delivery, but Tayfield was missed off a fierce chance by May at midwicket to deny Wardle a hat-trick. Three runs later, Tayfield was caught behind. Wardle had taken 7-36 in 19 overs and had match figures of 12-89. Wally Hammond considered it 'the finest piece of spin bowling I have ever seen'.[394]

13.3 Mrs Wardle wins the Test

Johnny Wardle had almost not been there at all. He had vowed never to spend Christmas away from his family – he hated the idea of it, and still hated it after the tour but had found his cricketing

---

392 Alan Hill, *Johnny Wardle, Cricket Conjurer*, (London: David and Charles, 1988) 93-95

393 Insole, interview, 15/6/2017

394 Hill, *Johnny Wardle*, 96

El Dorado on the veld.[395] He wrote to his wife Edna that 'she had done more towards winning a Test match for England then any other woman ... we came off at tea and I was buggered but still had the strength to look at the little table where they put the mail; as soon as I saw [your letter] I yelled out, lads we're all right now ... the skipper took me at my word and put me on at the end I wanted. I wouldn't have cared if Bradman or Hutton were batting.'[396]

Roy McLean, who could play Wardle, appreciated his sorcery, 'Wardle tucks his hand away behind his right rump, wheels over his arm and from the back of his palm serves up a mixture of curves and spin that make us look junior school novices.'[397] South Africa had scored 72 in the fourth innings for the second Test in a row. They were 2-0 down and on their knees.

There was a three-week break before the third Test. Jackie McGlew faced a predictable storm. Critics attacked his players, his penchant for late withdrawals, and his psychological fitness for the job. He was out of practice, had played Wardle and Laker very poorly at Newlands and had not touched a bat since. He had contributed to the Cape Town debacle by playing when unfit and his captaincy had been erratic. Perhaps to the relief of the selectors his shoulder injury forced him to rule himself out for the rest of the series. Journalist Alan Ross was generous, 'It is impossible not to feel sorry for McGlew [who was] comparatively inexperienced, led astray by single minded over enthusiasm, lack of tact and prey to a wretched series of injuries.' Doug Insole was contacted by McGlew shortly before his death and the latter spoke frankly about his anguish over the events of the tour and (Insole could not resist repeating) McGlew's negative views about Tayfield.[398]

---

395 Johnny Wardle, *Happy Go Johnny*, (London: Hale, 1957) 180
396 Hill, *Johnny Wardle*, 93
397 Hill, *Johnny Wardle*, 97
398 Insole, interview, 15/6/2017

> ### 13.4 'We shall not ride'
>
> Anthony Eden resigned after the Suez crisis and a chastened Britain under Harold Macmillan wondered what the decline of the empire would bring.
>
> In Johannesburg's black townships of Alexandria and Sophiatown, where child mortality before the age of one was a shocking 23 per cent, the bus company raised fares by a penny. Commuters living on the breadline had first resisted increased fares in 1940. The bus boycott was 100 per cent solid from the first day and around 45,000 people walked nine miles each way chanting 'azikwelwa' ('we shall not ride'). Some were provided with lifts by supporters. The minister reported in parliament that many of these good Samaritans were white women. Nationalist members replied, 'Disgraceful!'[399]

The bus boycott coincided with the reopening of the Treason Trial in a court now guarded by 500 police. Senior defence counsel Victor Berrenge accused the state of a political plot, stoking an atmosphere of violence and treason to intimidate the population and stifle free speech. The prosecution read the Freedom Charter slowly and in full to the court. The defence strenuously denied that it was treasonable. Its ideals were shared by the majority of South Africans and the world. The trial then went to sleep as the state spent the next 33 days meticulously introducing more than 11,000 documents in evidence.

John Waite, a mass of bruises and abrasions from a rolled car in another of the accidents that punctuated English tours, was passed fit and Tony Pithey replaced McGlew. Only 8,000 turned up for the first day of the third Test at Kingsmead, 4,000 down on the attendance against Natal. The public, faced with funereal cricket and a losing side, voted with their feet.

Those who did turn up may have regretted it. May again won the toss and Bailey and Richardson started well, taking 14 runs (all run) off Heine's second over, and reaching 103-0 at lunch. Then 'Barnacle' Bailey shut up like a clam. Tayfield's afternoon spell contained a

---

399 *Rand Daily Mail*, 25/1/1957

world record 137 consecutive dot balls. He bowled 13 consecutive eight-ball maidens without once beating the bat. The tedium was punctuated by Bailey stepping away from the crease when the crowd began slow hand-clapping. Bailey was locked into his own private duel with Tayfield. So much for May's promise that bright cricket was more important than results. Vice-captain Doug Insole at the other end did not shake him out of his bubble and Bailey made 21 in three hours. Despite this, it was the second-fastest first day in the series with a run-rate of 2.4 runs per over.

England subsided from 148/1 to 218 all out (Bailey 80, Richardson 68, Adcock 4-39 and Tayfield 1-21 in 24 overs) with May falling to another incredible catch when a nick from Tayfield ballooned off Waite's gloves and Goddard moving to his left in the slips changed direction and dived high and long towards gully, completing a one-handed catch inches from the ground. It was a remarkable feat of athleticism and co-ordination.

South Africa, thanks to Roy McLean's dominating hundred, took a 65-run first-innings lead. McLean and Funston smashed Wardle and Laker for 27 off two overs and Peter May instantly banished the spinners to the outfield. It was the turning point of the series. May's timidity and lack of confidence in his world-beating spin attack ceded the advantage.

South Africa fancied their chances. Peter Heine, Mr Hyde with ball in hand, snarled down the pitch, 'I want to hit you, Bailey … I want to hit you over the heart,'[400] and broke his little finger instead. But South Africa underestimated the determination and concentration of Insole who was battling his critics as well as Hugh Tayfield. Tayfield hoovered up the rest of the order like a hungry man at the all-you-can-eat buffet. Towards the end of the fourth day, Bailey, who lacked nothing in courage, returned to join Insole with his injured hand heavily strapped.

The last over was due one minute before six on the fourth day. The crowd barracked Bailey and he waited until they settled down

---

400 Laker, *Over to Me*, 95

with the clock now showing one minute past. Tayfield's first ball spun from bat to pad and Van Ryneveld took a sprawling catch at short leg. Tayfield appealed and there was an agonising delay before umpire B.V. Malan lifted his finger. Commentator Charles Fortune said the commentators all thought he had hit the ball but added, 'Bailey would write about it in due course.' Bailey did, 30 years later, 'I pushed forward to Tayfield, very carefully took my bat away, allowed the ball to hit my front pad, told the keeper not to be such a fool when he shouted catch it, and was given out caught at forward short leg. It has been said that I was still standing there in disbelief and anger when the entire South African team had left the field showered and gone home. This is a slight exaggeration.'[401]

England were 127 ahead with four wickets left. Insole's determination not to lose his wicket to Tayfield left him not out on 110, his only Test hundred. Tayfield ended the innings with South African Test best figures of 8-69 in 37.7 overs and, following the last-wicket partnership, South Africa needed 190 in just over four hours.

It was a teasing target and the locals slid to 49/4 when Wardle summoned all his concentration. He recalled, 'I spun it like a top, it had a nice bit of air and McLean's eyes lit up and he rocked back ready to launch it. The spin dragged it down and it came back two feet to bowl him.'[402] May rushed to congratulate him. Wardle told him it was the chinaman. May replied that he shouldn't bowl it again. Wardle's chance of winning the game for England disappeared. For South Africa, Ken Funston and Russell Endean set about the bowling, but when Loader bowled Funston for 44, they shut up shop on 142/6. South Africa were two down with two to play.

Back in Johannesburg, against Transvaal, the home team made 232 and in reply MCC batted on and on to 594/8. Heine was bowling at his fastest and most hostile. 'They are going to drop me, I have to hit someone,' he said, but it was obvious that England's negative approach was a catalyst for his aggression. Insole was disgusted with

401 Bailey, *Runs*, 182
402 Hill, *Wardle*, 103

May's refusal to declare and eventually threw away his wicket on 192. At the time he was embarrassed, though in retrospect he thought 'what an idiot' for not getting to 200 first.[403] May was defiant. Their priority was to win the series not to entertain. He changed his tune from the 'bright cricket' he had promised in Cape Town. That ship had not so much sailed as never made port in the first place.

An interlude in Kimberley produced the non-Test performance of the tour. Griqualand West opener Ray Evans was undefeated on 99 overnight. He sweated through a rest day and the following morning took 50 minutes to scramble the precious single. It was only the second century scored against the tourists. Evans played 24 first-class games in eleven years. Such limited first-class experience made it difficult to identify and nurture talent.

13.6 The Wanderers Cage

The contradictions within white supremacy were illustrated by The Wanderers 'Cage'. The Wanderers Stadium had an enclosure for 'non-European' spectators surrounded by a seven-foot-high chain link fence. The president of the Wanderers claimed that the fence was there to protect black spectators who had allegedly been attacked by white spectators. No such incident was ever reported. Black cricket fans threatened to boycott the Test. The Transvaal Cricket Board (TCB) could not afford the loss of income and while maintaining the sides reduced the front of the cage to 2ft 6in high with an uninterrupted view of the game. The symbolism of segregation was retained.

The bus boycott was still solid. A tip-off and a police raid found workers sleeping illegally in the Wemmer Mine Hostel near the city centre to avoid the exhausting trek back to Alexandria. On the first day of the fourth Test, Johannesburg Magistrate's Court found 1,828 African workers guilty on trespassing charges.[404] The court collected £2,486 in fines. The police were out in force arresting owners of

---

403 Insole, interview, 15/6/2017
404 *Rand Daily Mail*, 16/2/1957

private cars who were providing lifts for 'carriage without a licence'. Trevor Bailey and the majority of white South Africans believed that the strikers were manipulated and intimidated by agitators.[405] He did not mention that police dispersed a bus boycott meeting by firing live rounds with 20 serious injuries.[406]

What was to become one of the greatest Tests was a slow burner. It began with no more than 800 diehards in the stands. Van Ryneveld, clutching a Jewish good luck charm, won the toss and South Africa batted on a shaven pitch. They scored 234/4 in 71 overs, the highest score on the first day of a Test in the series. Roy McLean, given two lives by Insole, led the way with a hard hit 93 before being run out.

Facing South Africa's 340, England, needing only a draw for the series, crawled to 251 by the end of the third day at 28 runs per hour. The game, according to the *Rand Daily Mail* was 'in danger of dying of boredom', a phrase frequently repeated around the ground. Goddard and Pithey started well in response, but South Africa, desperate for quick runs against negative bowling, collapsed from 91/1 to 142 all out. England had a realistic target of 232 and suddenly, from the most unpromising material, the game came alive.

Bailey was caught at short leg off Tayfield, and the following day Richardson and Insole took the attack to the South Africans. At lunch, England had more than 100 on the board and Tayfield's solitary wicket had cost him over 50. Insole flayed Goddard through the covers until a little away movement forced an edge swallowed by Tayfield at slip. Insole could have been forgiven for thinking that with May and Compton to come and 85 to make in three and a half hours, the champagne corks could be loosened.

May tried to cart Tayfield over the infield and was caught by Endean at forward short leg for a duck; Compton was becalmed until he chopped Tayfield to slip for a single; Wardle swept Tayfield for 12 in an over but was caught by Waite slashing outside the off stump; Cowdrey stood firm, passed 50 and England were 186/6.

---

405 Bailey, *Runs*, 179
406 *Rand Daily Mail*, 29/1/1957

After tea, Tayfield bowled Godfrey Evans with a ball which turned 18 inches and kept low. Thirty-six runs were needed in an hour and a half with three wickets in hand. Cowdrey hammered a drive straight back into Tayfield's midriff. Two wickets left, 33 to get. Laker holed out to one of the two long legs on the fence. Last man in. Statham swung and Arthur Tayfield, brother of Hugh, could not hold on. Next over, Loader sent the ball soaring towards the pavilion. Straining every sinew, Arthur again circled underneath it, grasped it with both hands and fell to his knees. South Africa had won by 17 runs.

SOUTH AFRICA v ENGLAND Fourth Test, Wanderers Stadium, 15–20 February 1957

SOUTH AFRICA

A.J. Pithey	c Wardle b Bailey	10	b Laker	18
T.L. Goddard	b Bailey	67	c Evans b Bailey	49
J.H.B. Waite	c Evans b Statham	61	(7) c Cowdrey b Statham	17
K.J. Funston	c Evans b Bailey	20	(3) run out	23
R.A. McLean	run out	93	(4) c Cowdrey b Statham	0
C.A.R. Duckworth	c Wardle b Loader	13	b Wardle	3
W.R. Endean	b Statham	13	(5) c Insole b Bailey	2
C.B. van Ryneveld*	b Cowdrey b Laker	36	c and b Statham	12
H.J. Tayfield	c Bailey b Wardle	10	not out	12
P.S. Heine	not out	1	c Insole b Wardle	0
N.A.T. Adcock	lbw b Wardle	6	run out	1
Extras		10		5
Total		**340**		**142**

Statham	23-5-81-2	13-1-37-3
Loader	23-3-78-1	13-3-33-0
Bailey	21-3-54-3	13-4-12-2
Wardle	19.6-4-68-2	14-2-29-2
Laker	15-3-49-1	7-1-26-1
Fall of Wickets	22, 134, 151, 172, 238. 251, 309, 328, 333, 340	62, 91, 94, 95, 97, 104, 129, 130, 131, 142

ENGLAND

P.E. Richardson	c Tayfield b Heine	11	b Tayfield	39
T.E. Bailey	c Waite b Adcock	13	c Endean b Tayfield	1
D.J. Insole	run out	47	c Tayfield b Goddard	68
P.B.H. May*	b Adcock	61	(5) c Endean b Tayfield	0
D.C.S. Compton	c Pithey b Heine	42	(6) c Goddard b Tayfield	1
M.C. Cowdrey	c Goddard b Tayfield	8	(4) c and b Tayfield	55
T.G. Evans	c Endean b Tayfield	7	(8) b Tayfield	8
J.H. Wardle	c Goddard b Tayfield	16	(7) c Waite b Tayfield	22
J.C. Laker	lbw Tayfield	17	c Duckworth b Tayfield	5
P.J. Loader	c Endean b Goddard	13	c sub (A. Tayfield) b Tayfield	7
J.B. Statham	not out	12	not out	4
Extras		4		4
Total		**251**		**214**

Adcock	21-5-52-2	8-1-22-0
Heine	23-6-54-2	8-1-21-0
Goddard	25.2-15-22-1	25-5-54-1
Tayfield	37-15-79-4	37-11-113-9
Van Ryneveld	8-0-40-0	
Fall of Wickets	25, 40, 131, 135, 152, 160, 176, 213, 227, 251	10, 65, 147, 148, 156, 186, 196, 199, 208, 214

South Africa won by 17 runs

Tayfield had bowled throughout the final day for figures of 37-11-113-9, beating his record figures of 37.7-14-69-8 in the previous Test. The magnitude of his achievement echoed Sydney Barnes in 1913/14. He had bowled three consecutive 37-over spells in the last three innings, taking 21 of the 30 wickets to fall in 895 balls while conceding 261 runs. Each wicket had taken 42.6 balls, cost 12.4 runs and he had conceded 29.2 runs per 100 balls. This was the first time a South African had taken nine in an innings and Tayfield was the only South African to claim 13 in a match, which he had previously done in Australia in 1952/53. Tayfield's triumph had been hard-earned. He had had little success until Insole was out, but never lost faith, and nor did his captain. Unlike May, who was reluctant throughout the series to bowl Johnny Wardle's wrist-spin despite his match-winning performances, Van Ryneveld backed his man whatever the evidence of the scoreboard. Both bowler and captain were vindicated.

13.7 The greatest Test bowling performance

Tayfield's exceptional performance rested on an unshakeable rhythm. He began every over by walking up to the stumps and glaring at the batsman before taking his cap off, planting a kiss on the badge and presenting it neatly folded to the umpire. He tapped his toes on the ground and moved in a couple of paces with his arm coming directly over middle stump and a strong pivot to the off. He gave the ball plenty of air and pitched them all on middle or middle and leg on a perfect length, apart from the occasional one he deliberately drifted outside off.

Tayfield had a precise field: two forward short legs and the area between gully and wide mid-off vacant to encourage the drive. But he was no robot. He had felt sick throughout the last day, but was so focused that he did not realise he had taken nine wickets until later.[407] He acknowledged the superlative catching and Trevor Goddard's miserly supporting role. His spell was rated by *Wisden* as the greatest Test bowling performance of the 20th century. He became an instant national hero.

On the eve of the fifth Test, Alexandria and Sophiatown held bus boycott meetings. The Chamber of Commerce proposed that Africans should pay the additional penny then queue up at the offices and claim it back at the end of the journey. The boycotters, typically described in the press as 'screaming, crazed natives',[408] ridiculed this effort to save the bus company's face and countered that the chamber should pay the penny to the bus company and the fares remain at fourpence.[409] The strike rumbled on.

---

407 Ross, *Cape Summer*, 228
408 *Rand Daily Mail*, 2/3/1957
409 *Rand Daily Mail*, 4/3/1957

Elsewhere in Africa, the breezes of change were stirring the treetops. In Ghana, US vice-president Richard Nixon slapped, clapped and shook his way through the continent's first independence celebrations, joined bizarrely by the South African high commissioner.[410]

South Africa were 2-1 down with one to play and the momentum behind them. Attention was focused on 22 yards of turf at St George's Park in Port Elizabeth. The wicket had been sub-standard earlier in the tour and fearing the loss of South Africa's Test status, it was replaced with a new wicket transplanted from the practice pitches in the outfield. It had not been played on and no one believed it would hold together. Van Ryneveld won his second toss in a row and batted. Statham and Wardle were injured and replaced by Tyson and Lock. Wardle's ritual greeting to both dressing rooms of 'Good morning, workers' was missed.

The wicket had been heavily watered in a desperate effort to hold it together. Bailey and Loader swung and seamed the new ball prodigiously, Bailey took 3-4 in nine overs and the hosts were 21/3. Endean, 'as statuesque as a Follies nude',[411] repelled the tide and reached 50 in four hours. At the close, South Africa had crawled to 138/5. Endean and Van Ryneveld had added an undefeated 60 for the sixth wicket.

Around midday on the second day, the cracks turned from smirks into sardonic grins and the playing surface was an archipelago of saucer-shaped islands in a brown and crumbling sea. South Africa lost their five remaining wickets for 26 runs but finished on 164. What could England do?

It was not a wicket for back-foot players. Jim Laker bet a fiver that he would score more than Peter Richardson in the match. Heine and Adcock got the ball to cut back from a foot outside the off stump or shoot off a length. Richardson was lbw to Adcock for a duck. Bailey stretched way down the wicket, meeting ball after ball with

---

410 *Ibid*

411 Ross, *Cape Summer*, 228

outstretched bat and pad. He added 54 with May and played what he considered to be his best innings in Tests before, on 41, Heine eluded his groping bat. England finished 54 behind on the first innings and it felt like 250. This life-and-death struggle contrasted with the carnival-like atmosphere among the capacity Port Elizabeth crowd, always ready for a party and relishing this gladiatorial contest.

Day three saw South Africa inch to 122/7, an unwanted Test record for a full day's play. The dressing rooms were casualty stations: Compton had bruised his ribs falling downstairs; Loader had taken a crack on the instep from a Heine shooter; Waite had dislocated his shoulder down the leg side; Trevor Goddard, who top scored with 30, swept a ball from Lock, split his chin and disappeared covered in blood. Frank Tyson, bowling with off cutters off a short run, finished with a masterly 6-40 in South Africa's 134.

The last day of the series dawned cool and cloudy. When England took the heavy roller, it bumped over the craters as if they were the surface of the moon. They needed 189, the highest score of the match, to win, or to bat through the day for a draw. Adcock bowled Richardson for three, then May and Bailey hung on until a creeper from Goddard did for May. Tayfield, with his disintegrating left knee heavily strapped, bowled 24.3 overs off the reel. The wicket was no paradise for a spinner. Lock and Laker had taken four wickets between them, but Tayfield plugged away with absolute accuracy and subtle variations. Thrilling catching by Goddard, Van Ryneveld, Duckworth and McLean did the rest. The latter took a diving ankle-high catch at midwicket to dismiss 'Barnacle' Bailey. Insole smashed Tayfield to square leg, and Duckworth ran in to take a superlative diving catch.

Insole was inconsolable. He had thwarted Tayfield throughout the series until the last innings. Jim Laker had taught him to play off spin bowling, relying on his eye to sweep it with the spin off the stumps or to slice it behind point. He had watched from the other end as Tayfield worked his way through the rest of the team in the third Test and started the slide when Tayfield caught him off Goddard in the fourth. But Hugh had the last laugh.

At 129/9, Loader joined Laker with 60 to win or around 40 overs to bat. Loader aimed a mighty blow at his third ball from Tayfield and it went high and deep. It floated over McLean's head, but he grabbed it in two hands leaning backwards. He shouted to a spectator, 'I told you we'd make it this time.' The crowd erupted. Jim Laker pocketed his fiver from Richardson, with six and three not out. Tayfield's superb 6-78 brought his tally for the series to a record 37 wickets at 17.18. This edged out Ernie Vogler's 36 wickets in 1909/10 and remains a record for South Africa.

England's early victories owed much to the rustiness of South Africa's batsmen and mismanagement by the selectors and the spiky McGlew. Clive van Ryneveld took over in the third Test and built the confidence of his players. Wardle won the second Test with his sublime wrist spin, but a distrustful May failed to back him in the third and surrendered England's major advantage. Bailey was the outstanding England player. His batting technique set the tone for a defiant series. With the ball he took on responsibility and adapted to conditions. Compton was a shadow in a world of riddles, unable to find himself.

13.8 Peter May's failure

May was encouraged to see his failures as bad luck rather than a failure of technique. But luck on its own is never a sufficient explanation. The South Africans figured out his weaknesses. Harry Pichanick's flapping duck encouraged May to see his dismissals as unlikely or unlucky and he sailed on confidently playing shots and finding fielders.

This arrogance betrayed May's insecurities as a batsman and as captain. As a leader, he failed to build momentum or get the best out of his team with either bat or ball. He rarely sought advice. Doug Insole was almost never consulted on the field. Johnny Wardle, England's match-winner from the start, was seldom allowed to bowl his wrist-spin.

Laker too received no encouragement and a couple of boundaries in an over would inevitably mean a long spell in the outfield. May's failure to encourage Wardle and Laker once they were 2-0 up almost

---

certainly deprived a marginally superior England of a series win. After the tour, Wardle wrote to vice-captain Insole thanking him for what had been 'a very happy tour'. Insole was delighted. Wardle did not write to May.[412]

After the McGlew fiasco, Van Ryneveld backed his players to the hilt, with one exception. In the third Test, with South Africa six wickets down and himself and John Waite at the wicket, he abandoned a run chase that could have given South Africa a chance of winning the series. Apart from that, he gave Tayfield his head and encouraged Trevor Goddard as an essential foil. Goddard's performance as batsman and bowler matched that of Bailey.

13.9 Spin

The career statistics of the four spinners in the series compared with the 22 spinners taking more than 100 Test wickets between 1946 and 1982 (rankings in brackets by category). That Wardle bowled around half as many balls as the others emphasises the waste to English cricket.[413]

	Balls bowled	Wickets	Runs per 100 ball	Balls per wicket	Runs per wicket
Wardle	6597	102	31.53 (1)	64.68 (2)	20.39 (1)
Laker	12027	193	34.10 (10)	62.32 (1)	21.25 (2)
Lock	13147	174	33.86 (8)	75.56 (4)	25.58 (3)
Tayfield	13568	170	32.47 (3)	79.81 (9)	25.91 (6)

This was a tour of missed opportunities. The consigning of Trevor Huddleston's book to the Bay of Biscay was only the first of these, but even for those who read it, it had little practical impact. Cowdrey said he had visited black townships in Johannesburg and Kimberley and come across Africans playing cricket. He asked if he should join

---

412 Insole, 15/6/2017

413 Figures based on Appendix E 'More than 100 Wickets in Post War tests by Spin Bowlers' by Robert Brooke in Patrick Murphy, *The Spinner's Turn*, (London: J.M. Dent, 1982) 202

in the game. He was told that they would love it, but decided not to do so with an eye on possible newspaper headlines.[414]

Jim Laker coached in South Africa after the war and was invited by a friend to conduct a clinic at a mine. Two hundred Africans dressed in cricket whites greeted him 'like an oriental prince'. He showed one talented player how to use his feet and was told that the following week his protégé had made 140 coming down the wicket to everything. Writing in 1958, Jim Laker believed there was 'any amount of talent' among the 'coloured' folk. At big matches, he described how they are crowded into a special compound of their own and invariably they shout for the opposition. Given some decent coaching the 'coloured' communities of South Africa could raise a side good enough to play against a touring side.

'I think', said Laker, 'most English cricketers would welcome this idea; it would provide variety and the chance to do something positive for the game. But I can't see it happening. The South African government's views on such a revolutionary idea as a cricket match between blacks and whites can be guessed at and MCC would never suggest such a thing, even if the idea appealed to them. South Africa's racial politics have worked to the disadvantage of all – South Africans have never seen Weekes, Worrell, and Walcott, for example. No coloured side can visit the Union, nor can South Africa visit a "coloured" country.'

In a ghostly foreshadowing of the D'Oliveira affair to come, Laker thought, 'If Raman Subba Row demanded selection for 1964/65, after a quiet word with MCC, I imagine he would tactfully find himself unable to go for business reasons.'[415]

The Treason Trials, which gave farce a bad name, rumbled on for another four years. The combative Jackie McGlew was to stand unsuccessfully as an MP for the ruling apartheid government. The tour shaped the views of Doug Insole (as chairman of selectors) and Colin Cowdrey (as captain) in the Basil D'Oliveira affair. As the

---

414 Cowdrey, *MCC*, 193
415 Laker, *Over to Me*, 92-93

tourists sailed, the bus boycott was still under way. The footsore but
determined residents continued their principled stand. This time they
would win. As Alan Ross described it in 'Bus Boycott':

Two hours there and two hours back.
Buses idle in their hangars,
Illustrate their only right,
To withhold custom from the white.
A penny bus fare raise has proved
The straw upon the camel's back.

At check points passes are demanded,
Holding them up along the track.
Of this ballooning dream that severs
Economic links that bind
The victim to his servile grind.
Today will never be countermanded,
There cannot be a journey back.[416]

---

416 Alan Ross, extract from 'Bus Boycott', *Coastwise Lights*, (London: Collins
Harvill, 1988) 137-138

14

A Woman's Place: Helen Sharpe 1960/61

'NO CHUCKERS in *this* cricket team … you won't find chuckers and draggers in women's cricket,' insisted Elspeth Jackson, manager of the 1960/61 women's tour to South Africa, which was captained by Helen Sharpe.[417] It was a neat way of connecting the women's and men's games, while distancing women's cricket from the controversy obsessing South African cricket and deflecting attention from the politics.

South Africa had blundered into the England-Australia throwing furore in 1960. On the previous Ashes tour, there had been plenty of acrimony over Australian 'chuckers' (bent-arm bowlers) and 'draggers' (who exploited the back-foot no-ball rule to deliver from well in front of the batting crease). With an Australian tour due in England in 1961, the South Africans found themselves sandwiched by the ongoing debate. They also had a potential victim. Geoff Griffin had broken his arm as a child, it had been badly set and it was apparently impossible for him to straighten it normally. He had been called for throwing in domestic South African cricket, but SACA gambled that English umpires would accept his action as fair.

There was no technology available to analyse bowlers' actions. Chuckers were divided into three categories: bowlers who threw their fastest balls but were able to bowl with a normal action the rest

---

417 *Rand Daily Mail*, 11/11/1960

of the time; those whose actions always deliberately transgressed the law; and those, like Griffin, who were for medical reasons unable to bowl with a straight arm. Responsibility was left with the umpires to decide on each ball bowled.

Before the second Test at Lord's, Alf Gover's cricket school straightened Griffin's approach, bringing him closer to the stumps and making it harder to throw. Sensationally, Griffin had Mike Smith caught behind off the last ball of an over and bowled Fred Trueman and Peter Walker with the first two balls of the next, South Africa's first and only Test hat-trick until Keshav Maharaj took one against the West Indies in June 2021 – and the first at Lord's. But this was lost in the smoke when Frank Lee called Griffin 11 times. No player has ever plummeted from a career high to a career-ending low in a single Test.

In the aftermath of the Lord's Test, Don Bradman strapped an aluminium splint on Griffin's arm in the nets. 'I saw him bowl many really fast balls which must have been fair,' the Don conceded, 'but how a bowler bowled one day did not necessarily govern how he bowled on another.'[418] Bradman saw the throwing crisis as potentially 'the greatest catastrophe in cricket history'. He sympathised with umpires forced to decide on the issue in a fraction of a second.

Given Bradman's concerns, it is more than surprising that the Don, MCC's Gubby Allen, who believed Griffin threw every ball, and the South African authorities failed to review the issue and provide guidance to the umpires and players. Instead, they left them to face the full glare of the media. Griffin played on as a batsman and his fate was a huge sadness in a series won 3-0 by England.

The 1960 English women's tour began soon after the massacre at Sharpeville had flashed across the headlines. Several hundred anti-apartheid campaigners had met McGlew's team at the airport carrying 'Apartheid Isn't Cricket', and 'Sharpeville Was Murder' placards. They dogged the whole of the tour. John Waite, the Springboks' wicketkeeper (while not supporting the Sharpeville

---

418 *Ibid*

massacre), put the white South African view, 'The black and coloured public of South Africa is not equipped or ready for multi-racial sport any more than the black and coloured public of the Union is ready to govern South Africa or manage its industries.'[419]

Elspeth Jackson's opening interview found her sheltering behind a car from the south-easter which howled across the exposed Green Point ground. Male and female cricket were separate and unequal. Jackson was confident but emphasised that many of the players were unable to afford £250 required to meet the costs. Rachael Heyhoe was funded by her parents who gave up their new car. Of the current party, only Helen Sharpe, Ruth Westbrook and Polly Marshall had been to Australia on the 1957/58 tour.

Middle-class women and girls had limited sporting opportunities before the late 1920s when sport became an aspect of modernity and this encouraged widespread girls' cricket in public or grammar schools. The England-based Women's Cricket Association was set up in 1926, but by the late 1950s, the earlier generation had lost touch with a new modernity focused on fashion, music and coffee bars. The WCA leadership continued to defend 1930s amateur values, including an obsession with uniform regulations. WCA secretary Netta Rheinberg wrote in *Women's Cricket*, 'Cricket was a way to escape from daily life. The sound of ball on bat is better than any pop music.'[420]

The tourists were required to wear a hat on departure and some, such as Heyhoe, posed in jumble sale bargains. On board, they quickly disabused any passengers who might have surmised that WCA stood for the Women's Christian Association. Unlike the men they travelled tourist class, but when they beat the officers at deck cricket, they were rewarded by champagne on the upper deck which led to further fixtures.[421]

The *Cape Times* reported in 1889, 'Women's cricket is not a novelty but in fact a daily occurrence and has now become stale. It is

419 Johnny Waite, *Perchance to Bowl*, (London: Nicholas Kaye, 1961) 47
420 Rafaelle Nicholson, *Ladies and Lords*, (Oxford: Peter Lang, 2019) 162
421 Rachael Heyhoe-Flint, *Heyhoe!*, (London: Pelham, 1978) 64-65

now admitted, if it were ever questioned, that ladies are not naturally incapable of playing cricket or any other game played by men ... lawn tennis has already paved the way for the admission of women to other sports.'[422]

But an ability to play the game did not confer shared status with males. An 1893 proposal to admit women members to Western Province Cricket Club was ruled out of order.[423] Was female annoyance at this chauvinist response to membership perhaps a reason why the popular fast bowler 'Krom' Hendricks, like them ruled persona non grata by the committee, was invited to play in a women's match in 1895?[424]

But while the gender fault line discriminated against women, it was not comparable to the widening chasm of race. White women cricketers employed black South Africans of both genders as domestic workers subject to increasing poverty and oppression. Unlike black cricket fans at Newlands (or women at Lord's), white women were allowed in the pavilion and not isolated in a fenced-off tin-roofed shed along the railway line.

Women's cricket was a game for whites only. Competitive women's teams were formed soon after the Anglo-Boer War, and in 1902 the Port Elizabeth's Pioneer Club XI took on male and female teams.

14.1 Winifred Kingswell

In the Transvaal, the redoubtable Winifred Kingswell joined the Wanderers in 1911, and created a ladies' cricket team which played against female touring teams such as the Bloemfontein Ramblers and against the men. She resigned following a dispute with the men over women's access to practice facilities.[425] She moved to Cape Town and formed the Peninsula Ladies Cricket Club on a pitch in her back garden in Newlands. Hamiltons Rugby Football Club

---

422 *Cape Times*, 11/1/1889

423 Jonty Winch, *Cricket in Southern Africa*, (Windsor: Windsor Publications, 1998) 270

424 Winch and Parry, *Too Black*, 101

425 Gutsche, *Old Gold*, 148, 153

were one of many men's teams humiliated by the six-hitting batter, Betty Blair.[426]

Kingswell fostered inter-school women's cricket and in 1934 the Peninsula club affiliated to England's Women's Cricket Association. Kingswell was a fearsome fast bowler and energetic organiser. According to legend, she once knocked out the front teeth of Springbok batsman Percy Jones.[427] In 1902, Jones achieved the rare feat of recording a pair in his only Test. Winifred Jeffries and Clarrie Pierce took over from Kingswell in the 1930s and restarted women's cricket again after the Second World War.

The progress of women's cricket in Johannesburg was watched with interest by the WCA, head of what Rafaelle Nicholson calls a 'female cricketing Commonwealth'. Netta Rheinberg encouraged them to set up a national organisation and join the international stage. The decline of the empire post-Indian independence encouraged enhanced sporting contacts from the Dominions. 'I have been interviewed several times by representatives of the South African press,' explained Rheinberg, 'who wish to know when a South African touring side will visit England or England tour South Africa.'[428]

The Johannesburg club structure included some outstanding performers such as Eileen Hurly who had made a hundred on her club debut at the age of 14 in 1947. Similar organisation in other urban centres encouraged the beginnings of annual interprovincial cricket in 1951. Sheelagh Nefdt (nee Charlton), a leg-spinning all-rounder, was the star of the early tournaments. She had been educated at the University of Cape Town where she started a women's team. In 1954, she performed the rare feat of hat-tricks in both innings, ending up with 12-48 for Western Province against Transvaal in the women's Simon Cup. In the final match, she made 100 not out and took 4-5, while Eileen Hurly smashed 106 not out for Southern Transvaal against Natal

426 Odendaal et al., *Divided Country*, 128

427 Winch, *Cricket in Southern Africa*, 271

428 Rafaelle Nicholson, 'Who are We…To Tell the South Africans How to Run their Country' in Murray, Parry and Winch (eds.), *Cricket and Society*, 327-329

Western Province won a hat-trick of interprovincial titles under Valerie Valentine-Brown, who was educated at Cheltenham Ladies College. Opposition in the 1950s was provided by men's teams. The navy in Simonstown were inevitably popular opponents and Cape Town women also played regularly on Robben Island, before it was reinvented as a political prison. By 1956, there were 400 female cricketers in South Africa and about 70 took part in interprovincial tournaments. These were lively affairs. A manager complained that no rules were laid down 'on the erroneous assumption that each member will act in a reasonable and adult manner'.[429]

Western Province were dethroned as champions in 1955 at the end of the first ever women's cricket match in Durban. The poignancy of the game was beautifully captured in the diary of Oenone Gradwell at Kingsmead, 'The game was won, and chatter and clatter had died … there was little to indicate that the tranquility had been disturbed; the only clue a cigarette end reddened by lipstick – a patch of powder on the floor. I walked downstairs and somehow I think the ghosts were smiling.'[430]

In 1952, Springbok Eric Rowan was elected as chairman of the South African and Rhodesian Women's Cricket Association (SARWCA). Rowan had recently retired after a career which plunged him regularly into hot water. He would bring dynamism and independence as well as occasional incoherence to the women's game. The presidents of SARWCA fiercely defended their place at the wicket. As second-class citizens in a man's world, women fought to play cricket on their own terms and not simply provide domestic support to the men. The first secretary, Beverley Lang, had captained Cambridge University before settling in Cape Town. Marjorie Robison, president from 1957, headed the International Women's Cricket Council (IWCC) in the 1960s. She also managed the South African Test team against the tourists.

---

429 Odendaal et al., *Divided Country*, 212
430 Odendaal et al., *Divided Country*, 213

The WCA, borrowing MCC's clothes, demanded a say in the micromanagement of the South African game. Only when SARWCA dress regulations conformed to WCA standards was affiliation agreed in 1955. Women playing cricket was potentially subversive in 1950s South Africa, engaging in a sphere reflecting, but closed to and without being dedicated to, the interests of men. A female reporter at the 1955 tournament said they spurned the use of makeup and clean-bowled glamour on the field. She likened them to the suffragettes half a century previously, feminists who believe that anything men can do they can do better, saying, 'They are tall and striking and many are brilliant intellectuals.' She was right. The provincial captains were Dr Pat Klesser, an ex-captain of Cambridge University and South Africa's only virologist, and Dr Muriel Ritchie, a noted scientist.

South African males in the 1950s repeatedly attacked female cricketers as 'unladylike'. 'Any man who has observed the ungainly and grotesque appearance of a female batsman (or is it batswoman) or wicketkeeper, must certainly agree that there is nothing graceful or photogenic about them,' complained one sclerotic male correspondent. SARWCA followed the WCA in refusing to allow women to wear cricket shirts and trousers, which itself encouraged sexism. Split skirts (no more than four inches from the ground when kneeling) and white three-quarter length socks were used until the 1980s, although wicketkeepers could wear slacks.

Women's cricket reflected institutional values inculcated at Cheltenham Ladies and Roedean. Politically conservative women cricketers romanticised the protocols of the game steeped in a classist and patriarchal culture. Racially exclusive and urban in culture, cricket in South Africa was linked to high status and male-controlled clubs like Wanderers, Ramblers and Alma. It was overwhelmingly played by single women. Only three of 70 participants in the 1956 interprovincial tournament were married.

In male eyes, women represented domesticity itself. The struggle for women between cricket and marriage was perfectly illustrated by Mollie Buckland (nee Hunt), who was selected for the 1960 tour in her early 20s. Her personal diary, quoted by Rafaelle Nicholson, explains that she told Gerry, her boyfriend, that she was going despite the potential risk to her new relationship. On her return, Gerry proposed and she accepted. She 'knew that she would lose her cricket, but she didn't care – she had done it'.[431]

14.2 The Black Sash and the abolition of the Cape franchise

White South African women were not all fervent supporters of the apartheid state. In 1955, Hans Strydom finally succeeded in getting the two-thirds vote necessary to amend the constitution and abolish residual property based (and therefore non-racial) voting rights in the Cape.

White women demonstrated silently with black sashes over their shoulders as a sign of mourning for the death of the constitution. After Strydom's victory, members of the Black Sash fought the erosion of civil liberties, apartheid and the policy of migrant labour. They challenged the arrest and imprisonment of African women under the pass laws, set up a bail fund and advice offices dealing with housing, unemployment, pensions, influx control, farm labour and detention without trial. However, until 1963, membership in the Black Sash was only open to female voters resident in South Africa. In other words, it was middle-class 'whites only'. No Africans.[432]

Only white women played organised cricket in South Africa. Black women did play some cricket in the rural areas but did not form associations. Black society was as strongly patriarchal as white. In his novel *Ingqumbo Yeminyanya* (*The Wrath of the Ancestors*) published in Xhosa in 1944, A.C. Jordan described how cricket was an integral part of the mission school education for young black men. Women and girls faced a similar class contradiction to men. Girls were socialised as 'ladies' absorbing the mores of the patriarchy, while the curriculum prepared them for a life of servitude and domestic labour reinforcing colonial values and gender stereotypes. They transferred some of

---

431 Nicholson, *Ladies*, 220-221
432 Roux, *Time Longer than Rope*, 397

these values to the townships. Milase Majola, wife of double 'black Springbok' Eric Majola, helped form ladies' sections of cricket and rugby clubs in New Brighton (near Port Elizabeth) with their own committees and specially tailored blazers. Women set up netball teams, which proved popular in part because they were not seen as an inferior version of a male game. For most black women, sport reflected the dynamics of community life, of their race, class and social status. Cricket was a matter of cooking, serving, washing, cheering and being the glue that maintained social and community cohesion.[433]

Most women did not have even this luxury. The story of Lilian Ngoyi, born in 1917 in Bloed (Blood) Street, Pretoria, illustrates the brutality of apartheid shared by black South African women beyond the imaginings of South African and English women cricketers. She trained as a seamstress and, after her husband was killed in a car accident, lived as a young single mother in the 'Orlando Shelters' in Johannesburg with her ailing parents. Whole families lived, ate, and slept without water, sanitation or electricity in windowless 12ft by 12ft rooms, under a tin roof weighted down by stones. Thirty families shared a tap, and the nearest latrine was three streets away in a district where to venture out at night was to risk one's life.

Lilian worked in a garment factory where she met the trade unionist Solly Sachs. In 1952, she took part in the Defiance Campaign, which by breaking apartheid prohibitions on a mass scale sought to swamp the jails and stretch the resources of the state to breaking point. She was arrested in Johannesburg Main Post Office while queueing to send a telegram to prime minister Johannes Gerhardus Strydom. It would be inappropriate, she explained, to send a message to the prime minister from the non-white counter.

On her release she joined the ANC Women's League. A young Winnie Madikizela (the future Winnie Mandela) said Lilian 'spoke the language of the ordinary factory worker. When she said what she stood for she evoked emotions no other person could evoke.' Ngoyi joined the Federation of South African Women when Hendrik

---

433 Odendaal et al, *Divided Country*, 216

Verwoerd announced that passes would be compulsory for African women.[434] The extension of the pass laws made African women the targets of white police savagery and deprived them of the right to live with their husbands and raise their children in family units. African women fought the system of migrant workers which isolated most women in the dusty and infertile 'native reserves'. By 1951, one fifth of African women lived in the cities. The militancy, level of organisation and the ease with which women discarded their subordinate role came as a shock to the white authorities.

14.3 The largest gathering of women in the country's history

Lilian Ngoyi campaigned for female anti-pass action in 1956. In the first half of the year some 50,000 women attended 38 demonstrations. Enforcement of regulations meant bitter resistance. Pass books were burned and officials distributing them were stoned. The wave of protests culminated in the Women's March on 9 August when 20,000 women from different racial groups marched to the Union Buildings in Pretoria. They chanted slogans ('when you strike a woman, you have struck a rock'), and carried banners demanding the abolition of the pass system. Ngoyi entered PM Strydom's office, but he refused to see her. She announced to the crowd that 'the cowardly Strydom had run away' and called for a silent protest. The huge crowd stood in silence their arms raised in the congress salute before singing 'Nkosi Sikelel' iAfrika'. The march demonstrated discipline, dignity and unity. Even the police, fearful for once of the consequences of attacking women, arrested no one and the *Cape Times* suggested it was 'the largest gathering of women in the country's history'.[435]

Before the women's march, the 1955 Congress of the People at Kliptown produced the Freedom Charter which shook the South African state. Five months after the women's protest in late 1956,

---

434 Martha Evans, 'Lilian Ngoyi: Flying with Clipped Wings', in Bill Nasson and Vivian Bickford Smith (eds.) *Illuminating Lives*, (Cape Town: Penguin, 2016) 109-123

435 *Cape Times*, 11/8/1956

Lilian Ngoyi, Helen Joseph, Ida Mntwana and 153 other dissidents were charged with high treason. In 1959, the Treason Trial moved to Pretoria and the defendants were whittled down to 30, which included Ngoyi. The long hours spent in court and riding the 'treason bus' from Soweto cost Lilian her job. She worked instead sewing black and green Women's League blouses for supporters attending the trial. The state submitted her statement, 'Ten reasons why I refuse to carry a pass,' in evidence against her. Finally, in November 1961, after the women cricketers had headed for home, the trial collapsed. It had been the longest trial in the country's history and all 156 charged were acquitted. The state had kept the leadership out of circulation for a considerable time, but they had also created a courtroom university of resistance.

Lilian was detained again without charge for five months, much of the time in solitary confinement. On release, her life turned into a litany of harassment, random arrests, raids and banning orders, which not only banished her from politics but condemned her to penury. Two decades later as an elderly and destitute woman in Soweto, she was in urgent need of a pair of glasses, a bed, wardrobe and a coal stove.[436]

In November 1958, a group of dissident members under Robert Sobukwe walked out of the ANC Congress to form the Pan-African Congress (PAC).

While the PAC rejected co-operation with non-Africans it shared the goal of a non-racial South Africa. As with the women's pass issue, the strongest resistance to the implementation of apartheid structures took place in rural areas. In Pondoland, rebels boycotted mine recruiters and formed a 'mountain committee' in opposition to government appointed 'chiefs'. The rebels burned the huts of informers and boycotted uncooperative white storekeepers. The insurrection continued into late 1960 when the rebellion was subdued by the air force bombers.

---

436 Martha Evans in Bill Nasson, *Illuminating Lives*

14.4 Sharpeville

The ANC called for a new anti-pass campaign on 31 March 1960, but the PAC brought forward the date by ten days. On 21 March, a large crowd gathered outside Sharpeville police station intending to destroy their passes and court arrest. The police panicked and opened fire on the unarmed demonstrators. Most of the 69 people killed were shot in the back as they scattered, and a further 180 people were wounded.

On 30 March 1960, a state of emergency was announced and in the next few days the police made 18,000 arrests. A week later, the ANC and PAC were banned.

Former ANC president Albert Luthuli burnt his pass and called for a stay-at-home protest. There was a large capital outflow until South Africa introduced exchange controls. The massacre marked a major turning point in international attitudes to South Africa and triggered anti-apartheid action against the South African cricket and rugby teams in the UK in the same year.

This was a long way from the world of white women's cricket. In 1956, SARWCA had invited the WCA to send an English team to South Africa. Marjorie Robison represented South Africa at the formation of the International Woman's Cricket Council (IWCC) in Australia in 1958 and was acutely aware of the political pitfalls. 'We must avoid in the future any awkward situations that may arise in connection with our racial problems,' Robison wrote, 'and private discussions may avoid future difficulties and the personal touch [will] go a long way to better understanding.'

When the issue of future tours arose, Robison explained that the South African team would be unable to visit Pakistan owing to political drawbacks 'which all sporting bodies in South Africa very much regretted'.

New Zealand feared embarrassment should a Maori woman be included in any team to South Africa. Netta Rheinberg, at her most magisterial, decreed, 'Politics should not enter a council such as IWCC.' Australia agreed and said that a dignified attitude had to be maintained and players had to bear with the country that had these laws.[437]

Rheinberg was more anxious than she let on. A split began to emerge in the men's game from the late 1950s, with India, Pakistan and the West Indies all questioning the position of white South Africa. The IWCC deliberately sought to maintain white racial exclusivity. Canada and Ireland were encouraged to join despite women's cricket in both countries being almost non-existent.[438] Robison was elected vice president and South Africa enthusiastically joined the Test circuit in 1960/61. The WCA co-operated with MCC, making sure that the right political messages were transferred and even allowing women the use of the men's nets at Lord's. Before the team arrived in Cape Town, it was briefed by Elspeth Jackson, based on 'information from a friend in South Africa'.

Mollie Buckland (nee Hunt) explained, 'We were given a little lecture at the beginning ... you had to know if you went into the park for instance that there were seats blacks were allowed to sit in, and those that the whites were expected to sit in ... we had to understand entrances into shops ... and we stuck to the rules because we were guests. And although we didn't like this at all, it was totally foreign to us, we did as we were told.'[439]

The team arrived in the middle of a South African political storm, once again relating to a quarrelsome cleric. Ambrose Reeves, bishop of Johannesburg, had written a book with his account of the Sharpeville shootings, entitled *Agony of South Africa*. He was arrested and forcibly deported without warning, charge or trial. Verwoerd rejected protests from his congregation as 'mere propaganda'.[440] White South Africans had their eyes mainly on the rugby team wallowing in the mud in the middle of an appalling British winter. The Boks lost only one tour game, against the Barbarians at Cardiff Arms Park. Following the anti-apartheid cricket activists, the international

---

437 Rafaelle Nicholson, 'Who Are We...', 333

438 *Ibid*

439 Nicholson, 'Who are We...', 332

440 *Rand Daily Mail*, 12/11/1960

impact of Sharpeville began to be felt by the Springbok rugby team. In Dublin, for example, the South African players were roused from their sleep at 4am by two policemen who, acting on an anonymous call, thoroughly searched the hotel for a bomb.[441]

Developments in black cricket provided an important context for Helen Sharpe's tour. The Kenyan Asians had toured simultaneously with Peter May's MCC tour in 1956/57, completely ignored by the cricket establishment. Two years later, Basil D'Oliveira led a reciprocal visit to Kenya by the SACBOC team. None of the travellers had left South Africa before. They anticipated that the tour would be the start of a series of trips spelling the emancipation of black cricketers. The attack was led by the giant but unruly Eric Petersen who had been excluded from Cape Town's (coloured) Central League apparently because of his too-dark skin. Petersen was irresistible with the ball and in a normal world should have been playing Test cricket.[442]

The SACBOC team won all three unofficial Tests. Prime minister Strydom died during one of the matches and the team were forced to observe two minutes of silence in his memory. Every member of the team must have reflected on the personal trials that Strydom and the apartheid state had inflicted on them and their families. But they returned as heroes to the black cricket community and *Wisden* immortalised D'Oliveira and his fellow players.

14.5 Owen Williams

Owen Williams bowled left-arm spin modelled on the successful Springbok, 'Tufty' Mann. Williams had suffered a peculiarly South African agony caused by the Population Registration Act. The act took effect soon after his 12th birthday. His mother, a brother and a sister were classified as white. Owen, another sister and brother were categorised as coloured. He was separated from and could not legally visit his mother, who had to live in a white area. It is hard to imagine a greater trauma created by a racist state.[443]

---

441 *Rand Daily Mail*, 19/12/1960
442 Peter Oborne, *D'Oliveira*, (London: Little, Brown, 2004) 51-54
443 Oborne, *D'Oliveira*, 50

The obvious next step was a tour from a Test-playing country and SACBOC arranged a tour by Worrell's West Indians in December 1959. As only matches against black players were allowed, the Trinidadian ambassador and West Indies hero Sir Learie Constantine, canon John Collins and Dennis Brutus and his tiny South African Sports Association (SASA) argued that the tour by operating within the rules would reinforce and consolidate apartheid. It was a complex debate with both sides genuinely committed to opposing the system. C.L.R. James, author of *Beyond A Boundary*, argued in favour of a tour which would have cemented Worrell's case as the first black player to officially captain the West Indies. In his view it would have shone a spotlight on black sport and the apartheid system itself. In the end, the coalition against the tour forced its cancellation.[444]

C.L.R. James was a strong supporter of the British feminist movement, which sought to address head-on the WCA ideology of South African-supporting, anti-feminist and class-based postwar conservatism. Selma James (nee Deitch), who co-founded the radical and influential International Wages for Housework, came to England to write *A Woman's Place* before marrying James, who had been deported during the McCarthy period for un-American activities. The couple worked together as political activists for 25 years.

Although the South African regime would probably have banned the West Indies tour anyway, the job was done for them. After 60 years of isolation from representative cricket, followed by a brief venture into the limelight, it was a cruel sacrifice by the SACBOC players, already victims of state oppression and discrimination. D'Oliveira and others followed the only path open to them and looked abroad. Dolly's resurrection began with Middleton in 1960 in the Central Lancashire League. He was followed by Cec Abrahams, Coetie Neethling, Desmond February, Rushdie Magiet, Owen Williams and Dik and Goolam Abed, the latter playing professional rugby league and cricket for Rochdale.

---

444 Jonty Winch, 'C.L.R. James versus Learie Constantine', in Murray, Parry, Winch (eds.), *Cricket and Society*, 275-306

Manager Jackson thought her team would develop into a seasoned combination. In the nets, the *Cape Times* reporter was impressed by new-ball bowlers Esme Irwin and Margaret Rutherford and the accuracy of their spinners. But the South Africans were the real unknown. How would the home side's talent perform given its non-existent first-class experience?

After a one-day run-out in Paarl, Sharpe's team took on Western Province at Newlands as the crowd chewed over the announcement of Marilyn Monroe's divorce from Arthur Miller. England were bowled out for 189 thanks to an astonishing performance from young slow left-armer Maureen Payne. She took all nine wickets to fall (Ann Jago retired hurt) for 56 runs in 22.4 overs. The experienced Polly Marshall hit a stylish 84 not out in 107 minutes, including a straight six and her drives off the back foot through the covers 'could not have been bettered' according to a rapturous *Cape Times*. Mollie Hunt, the England off-spinner, then scythed through the Western Province with 6-27 in 23 overs in the first innings, while the Cape Town veteran Clarrie Peirce contributed a watchful 37. The locals were left with two hours to score 153 but collapsed dramatically for 32. Hunt did even better in the second innings, returning executioner's figures of 7-12 in 7.2 overs. Western Province's last six wickets fell in 21 minutes for one run amid blind panic in the changing room.[445]

Then it was on to Bloemfontein, to take on a South African XI at the Ramblers Club which had fielded a strong women's team between the wars. Ruth Westbrook's half century enabled England to declare on 205/7 and Eileen Hurly hit a bright 52 in a drawn match. The next four games leading up to the first Test showed that the manager's faith in the England batting on the harder pitches of the Highveld was not misplaced. Helen Sharpe made 103 not out and Polly Marshall added 53 against Southern Transvaal. For South Africa, Yvonne van Mentz, Bev Lang, Barbara Cairncross and Shelagh Nefdt all made significant contributions in the provincial games.

---

445 *Rand Daily Mail*, 16/11/1960

Given the patriarchal condescension of the era, it was remarkable how professional the press reporting on the tour was. Media commentators took the cricket seriously and on its own terms. There were few references to the physical characteristics of the players, unflattering comparisons with the men's game or snide allusions to gender politics. Speaking before the first Test, Ann Jago praised the high standard of South African women's cricket given the lack of international competition. Eric Rowan, the convenor of selectors, thought the women's 'attractive and stylish batting was a joy to watch'. [446]

South African selection processes had been embarrassingly exposed on previous England tours and the women's selectors rivalled the ability of the men to shoot themselves in the feet. Led by Rowan, who had himself been dropped in the middle of a Test in which he then made a hundred, the South African team to play in the first Test was selected before any of the provincial games against the tourists in which form could be assessed had taken place. To make matters worse, none of the South African women selected had even played first-class cricket. The Newlands match-winner, Maureen Payne, was not chosen, nor was Bev Lang or any of the Western Province players.

All four women's Tests were played on the main Test grounds. The first was played on the same St George's Park venue where the first men's Test had taken place 70 years previously. Port Elizabeth, known for being both windy and friendly, has always benefited from enthusiastic, knowledgeable (and musical) crowds. South Africa clinched a memorable win on a minefield to draw the series against May's MCC in 1957. A year later, against Ian Craig's Australians, South Africa performed dismally with the bat. Neil Adcock fizzed three consecutive bouncers past Colin McDonald's nose. Adcock was told to pitch it up, but the next ball flew from short of a length and McDonald was able to get a nick and march off. It was a rare positive moment for South Africa in another easy victory for Australia who sealed the series 3-0.

---

446 *Rand Daily Mail*, 25/11/1960

South Africa's women made a strong start in front of around 1,000 spectators. Their 211 relied heavily on Hurly's brilliant 96 not out. The South African disease of running like headless chickens robbed Hurly of a debut hundred. First, Yvonne van Mentz found herself at the same end as Hurly, then Jean McNaughton and Lorna Ward were run out. Ward made up for it in England's innings by taking 4-47, but 16-year-old local fast bowler Audrey Jackson, who had first played provincial cricket as a 12-year-old, had the distinction of taking South Africa's first international wicket. Ruth Westbrook ground out a fighting 58 but England were 24 behind on the first innings.[447]

South African captain Sheelagh Nefdt hit an unbeaten 62 before selflessly declaring on 260/8 in their second innings, leaving England to chase 285 in 160 minutes. England attacked the bowling from the start but ran out of time on 202/4. It had been an excellent Test match with plenty for South Africa to savour.

14.6 The 'Tied Test', 1961

Shortly before the second women's Test was due to begin at Wanderers Stadium, news filtered through of the 'Tied Test' between Australia and the West Indies immediately described as 'the greatest Test of all time'.

The heroes of countless previous Tests shouted themselves hoarse at the Gabba as the last ball of the Brisbane Test saw an arrow-like throw from the West Indies' Joe Solomon at square leg race Australia's Ian Meckiff towards the stumps. The throw won. Meckiff was run out and after 501 previous matches, a Test was tied for the first time. Solomon had somehow managed two direct hits in Wes Hall's final over to leave both Meckiff and Alan Davidson stranded short of their ground and created this most sensational of Test endings.

Even in this moment of high drama, the controversy over throwing was not forgotten. 'Well thrown, Joe,' said the laconic Slasher Mackay, Australia's premier stonewaller, 'but I thought your action was a little suspect.'

---

447 *Rand Daily Mail*, 3/12/1960, 6/12/1960

> The Tied Test provided a much needed boost in global interest in cricket and presaged a new decade of brighter cricket after the often torpid struggles of the 1950s.

In Benoni, the 21-year-old Rachael Heyhoe showcased the team's stylish and attractive batting with 102 not out in 91 minutes to set up an innings victory in a day. Women's cricket was not merely about survival, unlike the stultifying batting prevalent in much of the men's game. Heyhoe, the press commented, showed the men how to use their feet against spin. The English, according to the *Rand Daily Mail*, also excelled in the field and it was top-class fielding that won matches.[448]

A mood of positivity suffused the cricketing world. Outstanding performances by Sharpe, Westbrook, Heyhoe and Marshall meant the English went into the second Test high on confidence and with good form behind them. South Africa strengthened their XI with left-arm Maureen Payne, who had annihilated England in Cape Town, and Bev Lang. Eric Rowan provided some intensive coaching on fielding and gave a talk on tactics.

Helen Sharpe won the toss at Wanderers Stadium. Polly Marshall made a brisk 81 at the top of the order, Alison Ratcliffe a painstaking 95 and Rachael Heyhoe (51) cashed in against a tired attack. Sharpe declared on 351/6. Yvonne van Mentz's leg breaks snared four of the six wickets to fall. Speed merchant Esme Irwin wrecked the South African top order, bowling namesake Joy Irwin for a duck, Eleanor Lambert for two and trapping Barbara Cairncross in front for four. Bev Lang fell to a brilliant catch in the slips by Margaret Rutherford diving high and wide to her right. A fighting 37 from Eileen Hurly, mysteriously relegated to seven in the order, dragged South Africa to 134 in 95 funereal overs, but despite the tedium Hurly executed some switch hits outside the off stump which would have given credit to Roy McLean or even the modern game. Irwin finished with 4-46 in 33 overs, and Polly Marshall took 3-14.

---

448 *Rand Daily Mail*, 17/12/1960

South Africa followed on 217 behind with the sole goal of batting through 82 overs on the last day to force a draw. Western Province left-hander Bev Lang made a half century in under two hours, but when she lost her off stump to Irwin it triggered a minor collapse. Cairncross and Nefdt defended dourly against Alison Ratcliffe's tantalising leg spin. When Nefdt was caught by Ratcliffe for 13, England were into the South African tail. Jenny Gove hung on for 28 minutes without scoring, while England threw the kitchen sink, cooker and toaster at them using all ten bowlers. South Africa hung on by their fingertips finishing on 140/8. It was still 0-0 in the series and the next Test was scheduled for Durban in the New Year.

Between the Tests two black rugby players – Duncan Pikoli from the Eastern Cape, a lightning-fast winger, and Nat Daniels, who represented the SA Coloured side – were signed by the Barrow rugby league club following trials in East London. Pikoli was later to become a political activist. Overseas professional sports clubs had attracted talented South Africans since the 1940s. Robert Priday, for example, grandson of 'Krom' Hendricks, played for Liverpool and Blackburn Rovers immediately after the war. By the late 1950s, the professional northern leagues were beginning to look at black South African talent in rugby as well as cricket. In 1961, Albert Johanneson was signed by Leeds United, and played in English football's First Division for ten years, becoming the first black player of any nationality to play in an FA Cup Final. He was subjected to relentless and cruel racist bigotry and given minimal protection by the club or the football authorities. It was almost unendurable, and he died tragically, destitute and alone, at the age of 55.

In the wider political sphere, the apartheid state's game plan was coming to fruition. White voters voted in a referendum for a republic, which threw off the last cobwebs of imperial control on 31 May 1961. Having achieved the abolition of the tiny minority of black voters in the Cape, the nationalists announced plans for a 'Coloured Affairs Department', defining 'coloureds' as a specific racial grouping under apartheid. This ended some soul-searching among Afrikaners as to whether the population group which shared their language, religion and culture should always be imprisoned in poverty by the colour bar. The diminishing parliamentary opposition called this initiative 'uneconomic, cruel and stupid'.

The third Test began in Durban on New Year's Eve. Sheelagh Nefdt won the toss and batted. Six batsmen got a start, and Lang, Irwin, and Nefdt all got into the 20s, but none went beyond Hurley's 29. Accurate bowling from Alison Ratcliffe and Anne Sanders, who took four wickets each, and a remarkable spell of 16-10-10-1 from Polly Marshall, backed by pressure in the field, preyed on their opponents' inexperience. South Africa crawled to a turgid total of 151 in 102.4 overs.

For England, Helen Sharpe transformed the game with 126 in 225 minutes. It was her only Test hundred, and she joined generations of male Test centurions in proudly planting a commemorative tree behind the Kingsmead stands. The England captain had stamped her authority on the series. Sharpe was supported by Marshall (47) and Ratcliffe (36), and she declared on 269/8. South African medium-pacer Jean McNaughton hadn't played in the previous Test and came on as fourth change this time. Visibly growing in confidence, she took 6-39 in 19 overs. A battling 68 from South African skipper Nefdt forced England to bat again, but there was no late twist and the 49 needed to win was quickly knocked off to give England a 1-0 series lead.

SOUTH AFRICAN WOMEN v ENGLAND WOMEN
Third Test, Kingsmead, 2–3 January 1961

SOUTH AFRICA

B. Lang	c Rutherford b Sanders	22	c Pont b Rutherford	6
J. Irwin	c Rutherford b Ratcliffe	20	c Westbrook b Sanders	2
P. Hollett	st Westbrook b Ratcliffe	6	lbw b Rutherford	0
S.M. Nefdt*	c Sharpe b Sanders	25	run out	68
E.M.A. Hurly	lbw b Marshall	29	c Sanders b Ratcliffe	11
B. Cairncross	c Ratcliffe b Sanders	0	b Irwin	20
Y. van Mentz	run out	3	c Westbrook b Irwin	3
J.A. Gove	not out	18	b Sanders	17

L.G. Ward	c and b Ratcliffe	1	c Rutherford b Sanders	6
J.E. McNaughton	c Sanders b Ratcliffe	15	b Marshall	1
P. Klesser	c and b Sanders	4	not out	0
Extras		8	Extras	32
Total		**151**		**166**

Irwin	22-16-12-0	27-14-32-2
Jago	19-7-27-0	16-8-15-0
Sanders	27.4-9-41-4	28.3-15-28-3
Marshall	16-10-10-1	7-2-6-1
Ratcliffe	16-4-50-4	13-2-31-1
Plant	2-0-3-0	2-2-0-0
Heyhoe		7-2-9-0
Rutherford		27-19-13-2
Fall of wickets	38, 50, 51, 106, 107, 110, 113, 119, 138, 151	10, 10, 14, 35, 118, 128, 134, 155, 166, 166

ENGLAND

O.M. Marshall	run out	47	c Klesser b Gove	15
H.M. Sharpe*	c Lang b McNaughton	126	b Gove	2
R.E. Westbrook	c Gove b McNaughton	15	not out	22
A.B. Ratcliffe	c Gove b McNaughton	36	not out	8
R. Heyhoe	b McNaughton	2		
S.M. Rutherford	c Gove b McNaughton	3		
E.A. Saunders	c Ward b Gove	14		
S.M. Plant	c Lang b McNaughton	0		
A. Jago	not out	1		
B.G. Pont				
E.R. Irwin				
Extras		25		2
Total	**8 wickets declared**	**269**	**2 wickets**	**49**

| Ward | 26-4-74-0 | |
| Lang | 10-3-13-0 | 2-1-1-0 |

Van Mentz	9-1-29-0	
Gove	25.5-5-70-1	8-0-22-2
Nefdt	3-0-13-0	
McNaughton	19-3-39-6	5-1-15-0
Irwin	3-0-6-0	
Hollett		4-1-9-0
Fall of Wickets	101, 153, 232, 240, 244, 268, 268, 269	7, 26

England won by eight wickets

14.7 The early deaths of Dag Hammarskjold and Albert Luthuli

The day before the final Test began in Cape Town, Dag Hammarskjold, the UN secretary-general who was to die in a mysterious plane crash flying to Ndola in September 1961, met three South African leaders – Dr William Nkomo from ANC youth, Dr A.B. Xuma, former ANC president, and K.T. Masemola, secretary of the Pretoria African Advisory Board. The delegation rejected recognition of African traditional chiefs, condemned the nationalist policy of using 'bantustans' – territories set aside for black people – to divide the country on racial/tribal lines, and called for the unbanning of Chief Albert Luthuli and the ANC.[449]

Since 1950, Luthuli had been gagged by the Suppression of Communism Act and had had his movements severely restricted. He won the 1960 Nobel Peace Prize for his peaceful resistance to apartheid and travelled to Stockholm to accept the award. He spent the rest of his life under house arrest in Groutville, Natal, before he died at night on a railway line in 1967, several miles from home. It was hard not to suspect another political assassination.

The final Test began at Newlands in front of an enthusiastic crowd with South Africa needing a win to tie the rubber. England were supported by the *Edinburgh Castle* officers with whom they would

---

449 *Rand Daily Mail*, 13/1/1961

soon be sailing home. The hard-hitting Polly Marshall and Ruth Westbrook put on 133 in 118 minutes before Marshall was caught brilliantly by McNaughton at mid-on for 56 and Westbrook bowled by Jenny Gove for 87. At tea England were unassailable on 187/4, but speedy fast bowler Lorna Ward destroyed the lower order. She took 5-8 (all bowled) in 9.3 overs as England collapsed to 223 all out.

In reply, Yvonne van Mentz demonstrated her quality with a brilliant 105 not out in 228 minutes out of a total of 266/8. Nefdt declared 43 ahead in a bid to force the win, but Ward couldn't repeat her first-innings heroics. An opening partnership of 147 between Marshall (63) and Sharpe (70) put England back in the driver's seat and when Sharpe declared on 236/4, South Africa required 194 in 90 minutes. Despite a quickfire 58 from the reliable Bev Lang and aggressive knocks from Van Mentz and Hurly, the task was beyond them and they finished on 126/4, losing the series 1-0.

Helen Sharpe's team had deservedly won the rubber. It had failed to win at Wanderers Stadium despite a commanding advantage, but had fought back with bat and in the field in the last two Tests. South Africa had proved surprisingly resilient opponents and a little more experience might have seen a home victory in the first Test. Van Mentz and Sharpe were the players of the series. Neither was to play another Test. Ruth Westbrook, who had played an important role with the bat, would marry Roger Prideaux, the man whose withdrawal gave Basil D'Oliveira a chance to play a match-winning innings in that famous fifth Test at The Oval and ultimately bring about the isolation of South African cricket.

Off the field, the England team were kept in cotton wool. The black population were prohibited from entering the ground when women's matches were taking place. But there were no qualms about servants. Mollie Hunt said, 'After a late night neither Ann Jago nor I were anxious to get up early. We woke around 9am, rang down and ordered breakfast in bed. There we were like two titled ladies, waiting for the coloured waiter to bring up the menu so we could order.'[450]

---

450 Nicholson, *Ladies*, 112

These privileges were appreciated. Women's cricket took place in the context of gender discrimination in Britain and South Africa and provided a vehicle for expression. But female cricketers were led by a complacent and reactionary organisation and, as the lives of Lilian Ngoyi and her contemporaries indicated, the gender gap rested on and reinforced the South African racial chasm.

This series would encompass one-third of the total of 12 Tests that South African women played in 60 years. England were prevented from touring in 1968/69 when the Labour government threatened the withdrawal of their funding. But while the D'Oliveira fallout shut down men's cricket, a weak Netherlands team stepped up to fill the gap left by the cancelled English tour. The New Zealand women's team toured in 1971/72, playing three Tests before the curtain finally fell on the women's game. Seven Tests had been played by 1972, but only five more have been played by South Africa in 30 years since isolation. Women's cricket is now a one-day event in South Africa. While the English game has suffered a similar refocus, England have at least played almost 70 Tests.

On 31 May 1961, South Africa became a republic and left the Commonwealth. Any last vestiges of imperial control vanished, and the apartheid regime controlled all facets of South African life. Legally speaking, South Africa left the ICC and future Tests were 'unofficial'. But England, Australia and New Zealand continued their Test-playing relationship as though nothing had changed.

The WCA was even more reactionary and conservative than the crusty MCC. The International Women's Cricket Council provided a bastion of empire, supporting South African exceptionalism and fighting to keep it a white institution. The lack of racial awareness of the WCA, which eventually merged with the England and Wales Cricket Board (ECB), is indicated by the fact that it was not until 2001, 40 years after the South African tour, that Ebony Rainford-Brent became the first black woman to play for England.

15

Last Rites: Mike Smith 1964/65

ON 15 October 1964, the last MCC team to tour South Africa left for Salisbury, some travelling direct, others via Nairobi. Mike Brearley and Tom Cartwright waited for a lift outside the Grace Gates at Lord's when Quintin Hogg, the Tory candidate for Marylebone, drove past, squawking out slogans. Cartwright, car worker and consummate professional, waved his fist. So did the 22-year-old Brearley, Cambridge captain and Classics scholar, who had played for the Gentlemen v the Players in the penultimate year of the fixture's existence.[451] Both men would shape and be shaped by the relationship between South Africa and the UK.

The Oxford-educated J.P. Fellows-Smith, who had been a Springbok on the miserable Griffin tour in 1960, wrote an unusual piece in *The Cricketer* in April 1961. Referencing Conservative prime minister Harold Macmillan's 'winds of change' speech in Cape Town in February 1960 on the global significance of African nationalism, Fellows-Smith argued that South Africa would have to reverse her apartheid policy to retain her position within the cricketing communities of the Commonwealth. He called on SACA to use cricket to unite conflicting racial groups and build a multi-racial team which could hold its own in any company.[452] But the rubric

---

451 Mike Brealey in conversation with Richard Parry, 4 and 11 August 2020
452 J.P. Fellows-Smith, 'Whither SA Cricket?' in *The Cricketer*, 29/4/1961

of 'no normal sport in an abnormal society' was a statement of fact. Non-racial sport was simply impossible on every level in a society whose central organising principle entrenched racial inequality and oppression from birth to death.

The MCC team, under the leadership of Mike – M.J.K. – Smith and managed by MCC's assistant secretary Donald Carr, entered the South African political maelstrom for what would be the last time. They had their instructions. At the beginning of 1964, SACA's president Arthur Coy wrote to Carr, 'Because of political events and decisions made by the British government concerning African states and affecting the European population, there has been a most noticeable deterioration in the prestige, integrity and respect generally associated with Britain … rightly or wrongly the belief among Europeans that they have been let down by the British government is shared by most Europeans in South Africa and I feel everything should be done to correct or alleviate this impression.'[453]

It was a political dilemma – should MCC try to reinforce their relationship with white South Africans or was it MCC's responsibility to support the British government's decolonisation strategy?

The interests of MCC were self-evident and clearly aligned with SACA. Carr was a carefully chosen manager at a crucial moment in the relationship. In his role as assistant secretary, he was at the heart of its strategy and operations. He was also a good speaker, well liked, sociable and supportive of his players. As for the captaincy, the incumbent, Ted Dexter, was standing for the Tories in Jim Callaghan's Cardiff seat and Colin Cowdrey was unavailable. The de facto replacement, M.J.K. Smith, was a taciturn and modest man. He was first and foremost a cricketer, expressed no interest in politics, said little and was content to leave Carr to spin the MCC message.

MCC had failed to loosen Bobby Simpson's grip on the Ashes in 1964. With Boycott, Barber, Barrington, Dexter, Parfitt, Smith and

---

453 Arthur Coy to Donald Carr, 1/9/1964, MCC papers MCC/CRI/5/1/94

Parks, it was a batting line-up strong enough to exclude Tom Graveney and Micky Stewart. The tour selectors also omitted John Edrich in favour of the 22-year-old Mike Brearley, who had broken batting records at Cambridge with 2,179 first-class runs in the summer.

The bowling was another matter. In the Test before the tour, Fred Trueman took his 300th Test wicket. He celebrated at *The Black and White Minstrel Show* that evening and was invited up on stage.[454] It was an odd echo of Aubrey Smith's *Garth Castle* Minstrels blacked up and performing on the first tour 70 years previously. The selectors felt he was not worth his place, but Fred had set his heart on this South African trip after being unjustly excluded in 1956/57. He neither forgot nor forgave. Years later, Warwickshire invited him to a tribute to the popular Smith. 'No, I won't be there,' he said. 'I'll be at home. Just like I was in 1964.'[455]

Without Trueman and Fred Rumsey, who was ignored, the bowling was less than terrifying. John Price and the 35-year-old Ian Thomson, a late replacement for Tony Nicholson, had to carry the seam attack. Tom Cartwright was first change and the raw David Brown on the bench. Smith would rely heavily on the two off-spinners, Fred Titmus and David Allen, backed up by leg-spinner Robin Hobbs. Sending an attack this thin against South Africa's batting power reflected complacency as well as a paucity of bowling resources.

Geoff Boycott was the opener in possession. He sat next to his understudy and potential rival Brearley on the flight from Nairobi to Salisbury and asked him about apartheid. Brearley felt he should have studied the political issues in more detail, but explained the basics. Boycott was moved by the injustice, but characteristically put himself in the middle of the action. 'If I see a white man beating an African,' he said, 'I won't be able to stop hitting the white man myself.'[456] Sadly this early idealism was not consistent with Boycott's

---

454 Stephen Chalke, *The Flame Still Burns*, (Bath: Fairfield Books, 2007) 109-110

455 John Murray quoted in Colin Schindler, *Bob Barber, the Professional Amateur* (Nantwich: Max Books, 2015) 159

456 Mike Brearley, conversations with Richard Parry

future support for SACA/SACU and apartheid sport in the decades that followed.

Aside from Brearley, Cartwright and Barber, there appeared to be few discussions about apartheid. They may have felt some guilt or distaste, but the tourists were determined to enjoy their 'safari by Rolls-Royce'. The history of colonialism is embedded deeply in English culture and cricket is a conservative institution.

15.1 MCC, Kenya and the control of history

MCC had toured East Africa in 1963. It had been a jolly affair, captained by Mike Smith and overseen by Willie Watson and included Tom Cartwright. MCC were there to reassure the white community of their close ties in the aftermath of independence. The team stayed on fortified farms looking over their shoulders at the local Kikuyu who a decade before had sworn bloodcurdling oaths to rid the country of white settlers. The Kenyans eventually achieved this with the pen. As the cricketers enjoyed the local hospitality, Jomo Kenyatta negotiated Kenyan independence with Commonwealth secretary Duncan Sandys. Independence Day would be 12 December 1963.

Colonialism had turned the rural Kikuyu into a landless agricultural proletariat which fuelled the Mau Mau Uprising after 1952. The British imprisoned 1.5 million Kenyans in a network of concentration camps and heavily guarded villages. Official figures reported 11,503 Kenyans and 32 whites killed. Decolonisation was accompanied by the widescale burning of historical records by the local colonial authorities before leaving and any remaining records in the UK remained closed until recently. Kenya's own history had been systematically destroyed.[457]

The tour began in Rhodesia amid a deepening political crisis between Britain and Rhodesian prime minister Ian Smith's government. British insistence on 'no independence before majority rule' on the

---

457 'Uncovering the Brutal Truth about the British Empire', *The Guardian*, 6 June 2020

continent was anathema to Smith and he gambled that his white Rhodesia Front regime could resist ZAPU and ZANU, the African liberation movements, without direct British assistance. When MCC touched down, Salisbury was in uproar. Labour, whose sympathies were with the black majority, had just won a wafer-thin electoral victory and Smith was threatening a Unilateral Declaration of Independence.

MCC's flag-waving exercise was provocative rather than reassuring. Brearley, who put on a century partnership for the second wicket with Bob Barber in the opening first-class match, was surprised by the extent to which the crowd demonstrated a raw edge that was as much political as it was about cricket.[458]

Mike Smith made no unrealistic promises to play bright and entertaining cricket. The performances, he said, prosaic as Peter Sellars' Chance the gardener in *Being There*, would be down to the form of the players and the opposition. He hoped younger players would fulfil their potential and made no predictions regarding the Tests.[459]

A week later, across the border at Zambia's Independence Stadium, 100,000 celebrated as the Union Jack was lowered for the last time. Kenya's minister of justice, Tom Mboya, welcomed Zambia's president Kenneth Kaunda to the community of independent nations and was cheered when he called for the same freedom in Southern Rhodesia and South Africa.[460]

The world was shifting on its axis. Khrushchev had been mysteriously removed in Moscow and China had detonated an atomic bomb, becoming the fifth nuclear power. 'Lord Ted' Dexter, described in the press as 'sometimes aloof and austere', had failed to win a Cardiff seat for the Tories and was warmly welcomed on tour despite his late arrival.

---

458 Mike Brearley, conversations with Richard Parry
459 *Rand Daily Mail*, 17/10/1964
460 *Rand Daily Mail*, 25/10/1964

15.2 Tom Cartwright at Wanderers Stadium

Wanderers Stadium was familiar territory for Tom Cartwright. In 1961/62, Tom spent a season coaching there and learning to live with apartheid. His flat was 'serviced' by a Zulu cleaner called Franz and his cousin Sophie. Tom, like many expats, felt uncomfortable at the paltry wages paid by the club and handed over a bit extra. A Wanderers member caught him. 'We have to live here when you've gone,' the member said. It was a familiar story.

At dinner parties, Tom wife's Joan enquired about treatment of servants while he kicked her under the table. 'For God's sake we're here. Whether we agree with it or not I've got a contract to fulfil,' he argued. But he was not comfortable, 'You could see this empty look … the acceptance of the inevitable, that they had no rights, that they had no way they could complain.'[461]

Cartwright was not aware of the bigger picture. Following the massacre at Sharpeville on 21 March 1960, protest hardened into active resistance. The declaration of a state of emergency signalled a brutal and intensive phase of state repression which was an inescapable step towards armed insurgency. In a final attempt at mass defiance, Nelson Mandela announced a three-day strike to coincide with the Republic Day celebrations on 31 May 1961.

Mandela visited Nigeria, Ethiopia, Tunisia and Algeria, establishing military programmes, and hundreds of recruits were sent for training. On his return to South Africa in August 1962 he was arrested for sabotage.

The ANC called for an international economic boycott to discourage investment and shake white confidence. Its military wing, Umkhonto we Sizwe (Spear of the Nation, known as MK), was born on the Day of the Covenant (the 'holy' day for the white volk) in 1961. Over the next 18 months, MK launched 200 attacks against government buildings, railway and transport systems and electrical installations.[462]

---

461 Chalke, *Flame*, 87-88

462 Tom Lodge, *Black Politics in South Africa since 1945*, (Johannesburg: Raven Press, 1983) 231

The Pan African Congress inspired a parallel movement, Poqo (Pure), which encouraged spontaneous popular uprising. It reflected the reality of the dispossessed who had been forced off the land, suffered acute economic deprivation, administrative harassment and had nowhere to turn. It used the killing of whites as a terror tactic, murdering policemen and informers, and assassinated traditional leaders. In 1964, the minister of justice reported that 202 Poqo members had been convicted of murder, 393 of sabotage and 946 of other related offences. Cells were developed within places of employment. For whites, the infiltration of terrorist activity into vulnerable environments was particularly frightening.[463]

By the time the MCC tourists arrived, African internal resistance had been significantly stifled by police informers, detention without trial (the 90 Days Act) and long periods of isolation and torture. Mandela's arrest relied on informers, as did the capture of the ANC internal leadership at Liliesleaf Farm in Rivonia a year later. The ANC set out its position to the world in the subsequent Rivonia Trial. By imprisoning the leaders of MK, the government temporarily broke the strength of resistance inside South Africa and the leadership passed to the ANC in exile who encouraged economic sanctions and started infiltrating MK cadres across the border.

15.3 Mandela on trial

All ten Rivonia defendants pleaded not guilty, and the prosecution demanded the death penalty. On 20 April 1964, Nelson Mandela made his last public statement from the dock of the Pretoria Supreme Court. He condemned white domination, the illegitimate court in which he found himself and the draconian racist laws which it upheld. Defiance was not just justified it was an obligation.

He said, 'I have dedicated my life to this struggle of the African people. I have fought against white domination, and I have fought against black domination. I have cherished the ideal of a democratic and free society in which all people will live together in harmony and with equal opportunities. It is an ideal for which I hope to live

---

463 Lodge, *Black Politics*, 241-249

and to see realised. But ... if needs be, it is an ideal for which I am prepared to die.'

His defence team led by Bram Fischer, including George Bizos and Vernon Berrange, added the three words 'if needs be' to Mandela's statement, which gave the judge the opportunity to pass a life sentence rather than the death penalty as international protests escalated.

On 30 October, MCC took on a strong South African Colts XI at Benoni. Barry Richards, SA Schools captain in 1963, stroked 63 in his second first-class match. Jackie Botten and Mike Macaulay added 106 in 47 minutes for the tenth wicket. MCC could not catch a cold. Fred Titmus was the main sufferer, but still took four wickets in 41 overs. Brearley found him having an early morning net the next day. Titmus explained that he could not control how well the batsmen played or the catching, but he could control how the ball came out of the hand, his length and accuracy. Brearley made an impressive 68, his top first-class score of the tour, and led a rearguard action for a draw with England 51 runs behind and only two wickets in hand.[464]

MCC hit their stride against Transvaal with an innings victory and defeated Currie Cup champions Natal by ten wickets, as Thomson and Cartwright capitalised in seamer-friendly conditions. The game against Eastern Province introduced them to the Pollock brothers and Barlow. Peter Pollock was at his quickest, but, frustrated by Boycott's unbeaten 193, the highest score of the tour, he bowled deliberate beamers and laughed. The imposing Bob Barber warned Peter that if he bowled another beamer he would be coming after him with the bat.[465] The loss by an innings and 150 runs shook the confidence of South Africa's young stars.

A draw against Western Province with hundreds for Barrington and Boycott meant that England were unbeaten before the first Test in Durban.

---

464 *Rand Daily Mail*, 2/11/1964
465 Schindler, *Barber*, 162

15.4 Barlow and Pollock in Australia

South Africa's new and dynamic team relied on the brilliance of the Pollock brothers, Eddie Barlow, Colin Bland and the reliability of Trevor Goddard. Barlow was a key factor. His pugnacity married psychological intensity to improved technical skills and an appetite for risk. He made hundreds in each of his first two Tests against Australia in 1963/64 – the first during the dramatic no-balling of Ian Meckiff which ended his career. In the fourth Test, Barlow hit a double hundred in a partnership of 341 with Graeme Pollock in 283 minutes. Flying on adrenaline, Barlow then demanded the ball and dismissed Barry Shepherd, Richie Benaud and Graham McKenzie in five overs at a cost of six runs. Just for good measure, he finished off a ten-wicket win with 47 not out.

Graeme Pollock was still only 19 and his 175 followed on from his 122 in the third Test. A new talent had emerged which would light up the cricketing world and define the era. His effortless ability to dominate, his power and his timing had even Bradman in raptures.

Bob Barber, who tended to exaggerate, told Colin Schindler that he had broken two toes tackling Brian Johnston in a game of beach football and the night before the first Test drank an entire bottle of scotch.[466] He played, but Tom Cartwright, who fractured a metatarsal, would not be fit until the fourth Test. England included both off-spinners, Fred Titmus and David Allen.

Charlie (surname unknown – in South Africa, assistant groundsmen were generally black; in Durban this meant of Indian origin, and sadly their surnames were not publicly recorded), Kingsmead assistant groundsman for four decades, thought the wicket would be hard and fast, but on the eve of the Test, all the grass was shaved off. Mike Smith won the toss and in a bit of sharp, but then legal, practice arranged for seven minutes of the heavy roller to the consternation of the South Africans. Peter Pollock began like

---

466 Schindler, *Barber*, 163

a man possessed. His first two balls were no-balls and by the time he finally completed the over, there had been a third no-ball and a wild overthrow from Barlow. This was no slow burner.

Barber caught the mood and batted like a man late for his own wedding. While the pitch defanged the quicks, Barber was on a mission to destroy South Africa's off-spinner. Kelly Seymour's second ball disappeared into the grandstand and a drive and sweep for boundaries did much to demolish South Africa's spin prospects for the series. With his score on 74, and the partnership with Boycott worth 120, scotch-induced exhaustion may have induced him to miss Goddard's slow yorker.

With his dismissal, the fire went out and there were few shots on a pitch which helped neither bowlers nor batsmen. 'You deserve a Labour government', someone shouted at Boycott, who scored 73 in 268 minutes.[467] At tea, Ken Barrington announced that they were 1-0 up. His 148 in 432 minutes and Jim Parks's 108 put on an unbeaten 206 for the sixth wicket. Both planted their commemorative trees behind the main stand. Ken became the first player to have made centuries in all seven Test-playing countries. Smith declared late on the second day on 485/5, with Joe Partridge contributing a wholehearted 3-85 off 45 overs. Smith came under fire for negative tactics but blamed the pitch, the slow outfield and the superlative fielding of Colin Bland, the tobacco auctioneer from Salisbury. He thought Bland saved at least 50 runs in the field. His anticipation, speed and accuracy were so intimidating that no one would run when the ball was hit in anywhere near his direction.[468]

The much-vaunted South African batting line-up, bolstered by the return of Roy McLean, appeared undercooked. A puff of dust rose when Barlow took guard, but the pitch was not to blame for what followed. Goddard turned a catch to short leg, Barlow played for non-existent in-swing with the total on ten and nine runs later Graeme Pollock went for a big hit against Titmus and dragged the

467 Graham Short, *The Trevor Goddard Story*, (London: Bailey Bros, 1965)
468 *Rand Daily Mail*, 7/12/1964

ball into his stumps. The crowd fell silent. From 19/3, David Allen (5-41) and Bob Barber methodically worked their way through the order. The shocked South Africans were 155 all out, 330 runs behind.

In the follow-on, their inadequacies were further exposed by Titmus and Allen on a deteriorating pitch. Barlow and Pollock made ducks, the latter caught first ball by Smith at slip and, at 28/3, Colin Bland came in to his second crisis of the match. He put on a defiant 95 with Tony Pithey, hit Allen out of the attack with three huge sixes and his 68 countered spin with controlled aggression. Alternating between over and round the wicket, Titmus mesmerised the batsmen with his angles and posted figures of 5-66 in 45.5 overs as South Africa were crushed by an innings and 104 runs.

The calm and measured Goddard raged that it was the worst pitch he had ever played on and not fit for Test cricket. M.J.K. said it was the best toss he had ever won. In his usual spare style, he summed up the difference between the sides, 'We had a high-class spin attack, and they didn't.'[469]

Wally Hammond found Mike Brearley batting in the Kingsmead nets. He told him to relax his arms and loosen his left hand. Brearley listened politely but did not take his advice seriously. A decade later Mike sought advice from Tiger Smith, then in his 90s. Tiger showed him how tense he was by asking him if frowning helped him hit the ball harder and he thought back to Hammond's tip to relax the hands.[470]

15.5 Wally

Hammond had lived in Durban since the 1950s with Sybil, his South African wife, but a succession of ill-advised investments and a friendship with chancellor Owen Horwood, the future National Party minister of finance, found him working as a coach and groundsman at Natal University.

Wally played on three MCC tours from 1927/28 and followed the next three as a spectator. In 1964/65, he put on his flannels for one final outing with a Press XI.

---

469 *Rand Daily Mail*, 8 and 9/12/1964
470 Mike Brearley, conversations with the authors

Gubby Allen invited him to the fourth Test and the team had a whip-round for his plane fare and hotel. He hung his coat in the dressing room and shook hands with everyone every day. England's best player and their captain in the timeless Test bridged the three quarters of a century between the first and last tours. He had socialised in Hollywood with Aubrey Smith, eccentric epitome of screen Englishness and captain of the first English tourists to South Africa. And he coached the Durban High School pupil Barry Richards in Barry's Durban backyard. He died of a heart attack in July 1965 at the early age of 62.[471]

'Springboks at the Cricket Crossroads' blared the headlines before the second Test. A single drubbing brought South Africa's insecurities to the surface. No longer members of the ICC, South Africa's Tests were now unofficial. Perform or be ignored. No one mentioned that the issue was less how South Africa performed on the field and more about how her politicians performed off it.

On the other hand, South Africa were not averse to manipulating MCC's insecurities. SACA president Arthur Coy told Donald Carr, 'I consider that you must visit schools … There would be no objection from cricket officials or anyone else if you visited coloured or [African] schools.'[472] It was a remarkable suggestion, legally and politically impossible. Coy knew that Carr would not risk a political incident. As an exercise in blame shifting, it was a dry run for SACA's later approach to the D'Oliveira issue.

In between the Tests, Mike Brearley played against South African Universities in Pietermaritzburg, and met Alan Paton, author of *Cry the Beloved Country*, and de facto leader of the Liberal Party. The meeting had been arranged by lawyer Ernie Wentzel, who was married to Jill, sister of Ray White, a team-mate at Cambridge. Brearley asked Paton whether a sports boycott was an appropriate response to the South African regime given the impossibility of

471 David Foot, *Hammond*, 262
472 MCC/CRI/5/1/94

knowing the outcome. 'Sometimes,' said Paton, 'we shouldn't make sophisticated arguments about the uncertainties of this course of action or that, we should simply do what is right – or because you think it's wrong to do the other thing.' His advice stayed with Mike who would later challenge MCC over their policy on South Africa.[473]

15.6 Geoffrey, the nationalist golfer's brother, and the rhino

Geoffrey Boycott narrowly survived an entanglement at Umfolozi Game Park, a rhino sanctuary founded by Ian Player, brother of golfer Gary Player. Gary was then a rightwing National Party supporter. Bob Barber tells the story of how Ian got a rhino to charge at an angle, so he and Geoffrey could get action pictures. The rhino seemingly didn't like batsmen and veered directly towards them at speed. A rhino can run faster than a horse, but Geoffrey moved quickly too and was a better climber.

Geoffrey had a different take on it. Ian had told them that rhinos were blind and couldn't distinguish you from a tree if you stood still, so he did not move a muscle until the rhino lost interest and wandered off. Barber, not Geoffrey, was apparently the player sweating halfway up a tree.[474]

M.J.K. Smith won the toss and again put England into pole position in the second Test at Wanderers Stadium. Peter Pollock steamed in with his usual menace, Geoff Boycott got a thin edge through to Denis Lindsay and at 10/1 Ted Dexter joined Bob Barber. Barber continued his feud with Pollock. When Pollock bounced him, he turned his cap round and went down on one knee pretending to sweep him. With the total on 146 and Barber's own score on 97, Kelly Seymour had the ball and Barber told Dexter that it was six or out. 'Don't be daft,' said Ted. The left-handed Barber launched an enormous cross-batted heave to a long hop outside leg, missed by a distance and the ball turned across him to hit the stumps. He didn't look back. Dexter conducted a masterclass in batsmanship. In the

473 Mike Brearley, conversations with Richard Parry
474 Schindler, *Barber*, 166

final session, he treated the attempts at a defensive field sardonically, piercing the cordon at will and scoring 82 while Barrington managed 23. The close of play score was 329/2. 'Worse than Durban' howled the headline.[475]

Dexter was eventually caught for 172 off Graeme Pollock, giving the part-time leggie his first Test wicket. Barrington moved sedately towards another Test hundred. In the 90s, the mischievous Ken looked up at Bob Barber on the team balcony. Then he smashed a huge six into the delighted 'non-European' enclosure for his century. A fifty from Parfitt was the prelude to a grand comeback from Peter Pollock, who ended the English innings of 531 with figures of 5-129 in 38.3 overs.

Mike Brearley's education continued over the Christmas period. An Indian hotel worker invited him home to the 'Indian' township of Lenasia on Christmas Eve. He accepted and was struck by the sheer distance that black workers had to travel every day. Despite the warmth of the family's welcome, he was left with an overwhelming sense of the bleakness of the townships.

Brearley, Tom Cartwright, Geoff Boycott and David Brown spent Christmas Day with Ray White, Mike's Cambridge team-mate, and his family. A toast for absent friends brought a dramatic moment when Jill Wentzel proposed a moving toast to John Harris on death row in Pretoria Central. Her husband, Ernie Wentzel, was his lawyer. Harris was convicted of the murder of 77-year-old Ethel Rhys, who, on 24 July 1964, had been killed by a bomb left on a 'whites only' platform of Johannesburg station.

15.7 John Harris

The Oxford-educated Harris was a teacher and had been chairman of the South African Non-Racial Olympic Committee (SANROC), founded by Dennis Brutus in 1962. SANROC played a key role in lobbying the IOC to withdraw South Africa's invitation to the 1964 Tokyo Olympics. Brutus was driven into exile and Harris joined the small, mainly white, African Resistance Movement (ARM) which,

---

475 *Rand Daily Mail*, 24/12/1964

like the ANC's MK, concentrated on dynamiting installations – pylons, radio masts and railway signalling systems.[476] The ARM was infiltrated by the security police and destroyed by torture.

Harris testified that, while he had planted the bomb and timer, he had done all he could to avoid injury. He phoned warnings of the location and time of the bomb to the Johannesburg railway police, the security services and the press. His warnings were ignored and there was no evacuation. At the age of 27, he was hanged on 1 April 1965, singing 'We Shall Overcome' on the scaffold. Out of 134 patriots hanged for political offences before the end of apartheid, he was the only white. The 15-year-old Peter Hain, in his Pretoria Boys High School uniform, standing in for his banned father, read the eulogy at the early morning cremation ceremony soon after the hanging, before being dropped off at school with a note to explain his late arrival.

The second Test resumed on Boxing Day. A patient 85 from Tony Pithey and 71 from Eddie Barlow formed the backbone of South Africa's 317. South Africa followed on and Allen and Titmus bowled 94 overs between them in the second innings. There were signs of a batting revival. Goddard and Barlow put on their 8th half-century opening partnership in nine Tests, Graeme Pollock stroked a fluent fifty before being deceived by Allen and Colin Bland again demonstrated how to play spin. He secured the draw with a magnificent undefeated hundred, which proved that footwork and strokeplay could break the stranglehold. South Africa ended on 336/6, more than a hundred runs ahead when the rains came after tea on the last day.

The game had been drawn, but the momentum had shifted towards South Africa as they headed to Cape Town for the New Year's Test. Dusty Springfield, who had been performing in a Cape Town theatre, flew home immediately before the Test in protest at being told that she could no longer play to mixed audiences. A week later, the police invaded an Adam Faith concert, dragged two

---

476 Tom Lodge, *Black Politics*, 240-241

coloured girls from their seats and manhandled them out of the theatre to the applause of many of the white audience.[477] The realities of apartheid tended to spill out into the aisles.

The commentary box was not free of politics. Clive van Ryneveld, Springbok captain against Peter May's tourists, was a founder member of the Progressive Party, a tiny liberal opposition in parliament. Van Ryneveld had been invited to provide expert opinion but was gruffly informed by Charles Fortune, doyen of South African commentators and apartheid sympathiser, that the deal had not been confirmed and that he had no desire to see Van Ryneveld in the commentary box.[478] The South African experience required a strong stomach. John Arlott had refused to return after his trip in 1948. He described his encounters with African living conditions and their 'appallingly brave' efforts to make their lives bearable. 'The conscience, he said, cannot throw it off'.'[479]

Even the conservative E.W. Swanton, a strong supporter of the 'no politics in sport' lobby, had had enough after the 1956/57 tour.

In the third Test, Goddard won the toss for the first time and Eddie Barlow (138) and Tony Pithey (154) enabled him to declare on a commanding 501/7. The simmering discontent over umpiring, which had been a contentious issue since Aubrey Smith, took the headlines. On 41, Barlow may or may not have edged Titmus on to his boot and been caught by Parfitt at slip. Umpire Jack Warner, officiating in his eighth first-class game in six years, gave it not out and Barlow stood there. Titmus called him an 'effing cheat' and Barlow responded in kind. MCC pointedly ignored Barlow's subsequent hundred.

Howard Kidson, umpire in the previous Test, blamed a conspiracy by the English press to discredit the umpires.[480] On the eve of the Test, E.M. Wellings wrote a critical article, 'harping on'

---

477 A Sengupta, *Apartheid: A Point to Cover*, (Amsterdam: Amstelveen, 2020) 191. For Bill Nasson's recollection of these events see *History Matters*, 19

478 Sengupta, *Apartheid*

479 John Arlott, *Gone with the Cricketers*, 105-106

480 Howard Kidson, *Over and Time*, (Cape Town: Howard Timmins, 1983)

in Kidson's view, about the 'immunity' of South African batsmen on the front foot as evidenced by the failure of Titmus and Allen to gain a single lbw decision so far. As far as edges were concerned, the South Africans, Wellings continued, knew the umpiring was poor and stood their ground while the English precluded miscarriages of justice by walking promptly. The South African (and Australian) counter view was that English batsmen gamed the system, walking on big nicks but cashing in their credit as 'walkers' to survive finer edges.

The timing was bad. MCC royalty, including treasurer Gubby Allen and president Richard Twining, had arrived to survey their dominion. Donald Carr scrambled to manage the incident. He told the press that in the MCC view the umpiring had been fair and unbiased and although there had probably been a mistake or two, they had no complaints. Twining called it a storm in a tea cup and Allen startled the members by pronouncing that in his day the custom was not to walk until you were given out.

Behind closed doors, Carr threatened to send Titmus home unless he apologised. According to Ken Barrington's MCC version, Titmus caught up with Barlow, "'I've been ordered to apologise to you," said Fred, "so I'm doing so." Barlow, to his eternal credit, replied, "I understand, Fred, I'm sorry it all blew up."[481] An alternative and more believable account was that Barlow asked Titmus if he had been ordered to apologise. Titmus nodded. 'I wouldn't have,' said Barlow and walked off.[482]

15.8 Verwoerd and MCC

On the third day, prime minister Hendrik Verwoerd, the Dutch-educated architect of apartheid, chose to watch some of the cricket, which reflected the significance of international sport for whites, and Verwoerd's desire to build closer cultural linkages across the white community in support of grand apartheid. After a chat with Gubby Allen and the dignitaries in the pavilion, he visited the

---

481 Ken Barrington, *Playing it Straight*, (London: Stanley Paul, 1968) 72
482 Schindler, *Barber*, 170

English dressing room at tea. With his snow-white hair, he looked like everyone's favourite grandfather, but his fangs were discernible.

Donald Carr went into diplomatic overdrive, 'The prime minister found the players in various states of undress, but he was very charming.'[483] Carr might have been referring to Mike Brearley's appearance in a crumpled t-shirt, in his own personal protest. Mike became known within the team as 'the refugee'.

After tea, and with England on 170/2, Ken Barrington on 49 got a hard edge to an out-swinger from Peter Pollock. The hapless Warner again stood frozen in the face of a concerted appeal. Barrington waited for five or six seconds, but Warner made no decision. 'I just felt I couldn't stay; it was a matter of principle and sportsmanship,' he said. Barrington deliberately tucked his bat under his arm, turned and walked. The whole South African team applauded him as did the crowd. He did not consider how his 'gesture' might be misinterpreted. 'You've done 'em, you've *done* 'em,' said one wild-eyed chap.[484] The English press supported Barrington's 'sporting' action, but the *Daily Mail* thought it 'too ostentatious … it smacked of we chaps know how to play the game, even if you lot don't.'

Jack Warner had, according to Kidson, been ridiculed. Barrington had made players into final arbiters, waiting until after the umpire had given his decision before walking. Barrington explained and Goddard accepted that his delay was the result of his own confusion. Mike Brearley, for one, had little doubt as to Ken's intentions. He saw him look directly at Barlow before he turned around and left the pitch. But a deliberate effort by Ken to show up Barlow does appear out of character. This was Warner's last Test.

15.9 Ken Barrington

This was not Ken Barrington's only entanglement with the walking issue. In his benefit match shortly before the tour, he had walked when Fred Trueman claimed a low catch at short leg. A photographer later showed the catch had not been taken and an

483 Sengupta, *Apartheid*, 190
484 Barrington, *Playing it Straight*, 75

enraged Ken confronted Fred. Fred refused to concede. The next day Ken woke up feeling dreadful, saying later, 'I had no go in my legs; no life in my mind.' He withdrew from the remainder of his own benefit despite being captain.

Journalist Gideon Haigh has suggested that this was not an isolated incident. Ken's mental health was severely tested by the demands of professional cricket. His nervousness before going out to bat was a necessary corollary to his success. In 1966, he knew it was over when he trudged to the wicket, 'I felt absolutely nothing … and if things went wrong and I got into a bad patch of poor scores I scarcely bothered.'[485]

But the clouds lifted and Ken regained his appetite. In 1967 and 1968 he played a further 14 Tests, scoring 1,208 runs with four hundreds, including 143 at Port of Spain (against Charlie Griffith who had been his principal antagonist in 1966), and five fifties at an average for the period of 67.11. A mild heart attack forced his premature retirement, but he had sealed his reputation as one of England's all-time best and most reliable performers.

International umpiring always suffered from a confusion of incompetence and bias. England automatically believed their umpires were better, given their vastly greater umpiring and often first-class playing experience. The English 'tradition' of walking may have been partly a matter of fashion, as Gubby Allen suggested, less universal than was commonly believed.

Walking was a matter of context: of opponent, form, pressure, mood, scoreboard and inclination as much as natural justice. But there may have been different 'rules' or customs in county and Test cricket.[486] County cricket was played under conventions grooved by the familiarity between players, and between players and umpires, and in circumstances where dismissals may have been of less significance. In Tests, where conditions were less familiar, more uncomfortable, more public, and outcomes determined individual careers, players may have taken a different view on walking. In addition, as Barrington

485 Gideon Haigh, *The Cricket Monthly*, April 2020
486 Mike Brearley, correspondence, 27/09/2020

admitted, 'walkers' did so against some opponents but not others.[487] When umpiring decisions were made in the wide area encompassing caution, error, incompetence and outright bias it was not surprising that it all boiled over.

In South Africa, umpires inevitably suffered from the paucity of first-class cricket. A cautious approach was understandable and provided naivety or suspicion were avoided players were inclined to accept umpires as final arbiters. But, as the previous MCC tours demonstrated, perceived bias threatened the edifice of trust on which the international game rested. It took Imran Khan to cut the gordian knot by using neutral umpires.

Both teams were relieved when the game moved on. Mike Smith got his third Test hundred and after three years in the international wilderness, off-spinner Harry Bromfield returned figures of 57.2-26-88-5. After the controversies of days one and three, the game turned into a snore-fest. South Africa were 59 runs on with seven hours to play and a Test to win. Barlow, Varnals and Pollock smashed the ball around, but how much was needed on a wicket which looked good for another 1,000 runs?

Goddard ducked the challenge. South Africa batted on and on against a succession of trundlers. All 20 outfield players bowled for the first time ever in a Test. Geoff Boycott bowled 20 overs of 'seam-up' to take 3-47 and Barrington's leg breaks cleaned up the tail with 3-4. England had dug themselves out of a hole. 'A farce and a circus,' said Jackie McGlew. The press called for an end to five-day Tests and for the last day to be expunged from the records.[488]

Trevor Goddard was summoned by the selectors. They suggested that his form as captain had suffered and asked him to agree a press release saying he wanted to be relieved of the captaincy. Goddard was shocked. He disagreed that his form had suffered. The team were finding their feet and he had been appointed for five Tests. The selectors asked him to continue and

487 Barrington, *Playing it Straight*, 69
488 *Rand Daily Mail*, 7/1/1965

he agreed but told them during the fourth Test that he would retire at the end of the series.[489]

Back in Johannesburg for the fourth Test, M.J.K. Smith called correctly, but inexplicably he, Donald Carr, Barrington and Dexter, completely misread the pitch. Spotting a bit of extra grass, they picked the now fit Tom Cartwright in place of David Allen, leading wicket-taker in the series so far. Following the logic, Smith put their hosts in for the first time in 34 years in South Africa. With seamer Joe Partridge feeling unwell, South Africa were delighted. Had there been a chance of Smith's strategy working, rain delays put paid to it.

When play finally got under way, the ever-reliable partnership of Goddard and Barlow put on 134 for the first wicket on a shirtfront. Cartwright induced a caught and bowled from Barlow on 96. He was Tom's only wicket in a marathon 55 overs for 97 runs. South Africa declared on 390/6 with 95 from Pithey and fifties from Goddard, Bland and Waite.

The reply began after a minute's silence had been observed in honour of the death of Winston Churchill. Mike Brearley, distracted by his 12th man duties, somehow found himself in the South African line-up. Boycott fell cheaply, but Barber hit his fourth successive half century. The aggressive style he brought to the English batting had a huge impact on the series. He allowed Boycott to bat without scoreboard pressure. Bob Barber called Brearley on to the field to inform him that his next chess move was Queen's Pawn to QB4. It was typical of his approach to the stresses of Test cricket.[490]

South Africa unaccountably dropped catch after catch. Barber was missed on 29 (Partridge), 44 (Waite), 59 (Goddard); Barrington survived chances on five (Waite), nine (Bland, an astonishing but futile effort at square leg), and 13, and Waite dropped Peter Parfitt on 38 on his way to an undefeated hundred. Peter Pollock had tweaked a hamstring and once the Barrington run machine warmed up, he

489 Graham Short, *Trevor Goddard*, 186-187

490 Mike Brearley, *Art of Captaincy*, (London: Hodder and Stoughton, 1985) 134

cruised to 93 and met constant shouts of 'walk' with a toothy grin and a waving bat, inviting the crowd to have a go.[491]

Then came further drama. Partridge to Smith, John Waite collected and in a single movement flicked the ball to Peter van der Merwe at leg slip. M.J.K. had moved out of his crease for a spot of gardening and Van der Merwe threw the stumps down and appealed. Kidson raised a finger and Smith hesitated before heading for the pavilion. Trevor Goddard ran to Kidson and withdrew the appeal. Had the ball settled in the hands of the wicketkeeper before being flicked in a single motion to short leg? If so, it was dead. Smith, Waite and Goddard thought so, Kidson and Van der Merwe did not. Goddard's resolution of this incident, given the nightmare run of missed chances and the pressure to level the series, demonstrated his integrity.

South Africa were 177 runs ahead with nine wickets standing at the end of the fourth day. Goddard agonised overnight, not only over the 11 runs he needed for his first century in 41 Tests but, given his timidity in the previous appearance, over the target he should set MCC. The next morning, Cartwright almost ran him out on 99, missing the stumps by a whisker with Goddard well out of his ground. 'I've forever been glad I didn't,' said Tom. 'He was such a nice man.'[492] It was an emotional hundred after 62 Test innings and must have given him huge personal satisfaction. It was a fitting riposte to the selectors. Goddard had been an unsung hero in South Africa's success for more than a decade. By the time Barber caught him on the square leg fence for 112, Goddard had become the eighth South African to score 2,000 Test runs and in statistical terms displaced the legendary Aubrey Faulkner as South Africa's leading all-rounder.

A funereal over rate killed the game. Carr offered the usual defence that seamers needed time to recover in the thin atmosphere. Despite this, Pollock and Bland flayed 96 runs in 73 minutes off the exhausted Cartwright and Titmus. Goddard set England 314 to win

---

491 *Rand Daily Mail*, 26/1/1965
492 Chalke, *Flame*, 117

in 260 minutes on a perfect pitch. But Barber had fractured his finger in catching Goddard and could take no further part in the series. Peter Pollock came out with his hamstring strain forgotten. Boycott was dropped in the gully off Pollock's first ball, and he knocked over emergency opener Fred Titmus and Ted Dexter for a duck. When Atholl McKinnon trapped Barrington lbw for 11, England were 33/3. There could only be one winner. But England's Horatio, Boycott (76), was unmoved and unmoving and with Tom Cartwright steered England to 153/6 at the close. The three hours lost at the start had proved crucial and South Africa's chance to win the series had gone.

15.10 Bram Fischer

Big matches at Wanderers Stadium often coincided with political drama in the city. Bram Fischer was the grandson of the prime minister of the Orange River Colony (a key mover in the Union negotiations) and a Rhodes scholar. He led the South African Communist Party and the team which defended Nelson Mandela at the Rivonia trial. He had only just missed being arrested himself at Rivonia and was charged under anti-communist legislation in 1964.

On the third day of the Test, Bram went underground saying that no one should submit to the barbaric laws and monstrous regime of apartheid. His Oaklands house swarmed with security police and his son-in-law was taken away for questioning. Grim-faced white housewives gathered in the street, speculating on whether, in the middle of a severe housing shortage, they might buy his house on the cheap.[493] Bram was captured in November 1965, tried and sentenced to life. He was not sent to Robben Island, which was for black prisoners only. The struggle continued.

The injury to Barber was a massive blow. In four innings, he had struck 74 out of 120; 97 out of 146; 58 out of 80; and 61 out of 78. He averaged 72.50 and scored 68 per cent of the runs when he was at the wicket. He had led from the front and his attitude as well as his runs gave England a significant advantage. He had previously

---

493 *Rand Daily Mail*, 27/1/1965

metamorphosed from a dogged amateur batsman with Lancashire to a dashing opener with Warwickshire. On the tour, he revealed a 'satirical attitude to authority. He was reborn a different kind of creature.'[494]

Like Brearley, Barber had seen the tour as a chance to see apartheid up close. He told Colin Schindler that a driver twice took them both into the townships at night. Mike Brearley doesn't recall these visits, but according to Barber they stopped at a house and had a chat with the occupants. It would have been a culture shock for all, a reminder of Plum Warner's 1906 evening visit to huts in the Eastern Cape. Neither Carr nor Smith seemed aware of these expeditions.

Barber's injury had left Boycott without an opening partner. Brearley and reserve wicketkeeper John Murray opened in a shootout for Barber's place in the two games before the last Test. Against Griqualand West in Kimberley, Murray went for two and Brearley spent 158 minutes top-scoring with 43, showing what the *South African Cricket Annual* described as 'honest endeavour'. In the next match, against an experienced SA Invitation XI at Newlands, Brearley and Murray failed to get out of single figures in both innings.

15.11 Carr and black cricketers in Kimberley

While they were in Kimberley, MCC were invited by a group of black cricketers to a sundowner after close of play. As usual, the politics were complicated. The group, who had previously belonged to the South African Coloured Cricket Association (SACCA), broke away when SACCA and other racially based bodies decided to merge into SACBOC and play non-racial cricket. The secretary, C.J. Jacobs, extended a warm welcome to the tourists in a letter passed on by SACA's Algy Frames to Carr. Jacobs was a prominent batsman, hitting the record SACCA score of 209 not out for Griqualand West against Natal in 1956/57.[495]

The proposal was 'approved' by the white Griqualand West Cricket Union. One wonders if their resistance to SACBOC, who

---

494 Mike Brearley, *On Form*, (London: Little, Brown, 2017) 261
495 Odendaal et al, *Divided Country*, 316-17

represented non-ethnic cricket, might have encouraged Frame's apparent willingness to engage. Carr told Jacobs that he hoped that he, Mike Smith and one or two of the players would join them. There is no record of MCC attending.[496]

England went into the fifth Test at Port Elizabeth having survived a potentially disastrous misjudgement in the previous match. But they were scraping the bottom of the barrel. 'England with their backs to the wall' was the headline.

The opening conundrum was still unresolved. With the bowling in near meltdown and a draw needed to retain the series, they decided to go for experience and John Murray, who had played 14 Tests, was selected as an emergency opener. John Edrich, who was coaching in the Transvaal, might have been the better option. Brearley had no complaints; he was not confident that he had the mental resilience or technical competence to play Test cricket at this stage. Scrabbling to cobble together an attack in the absence of Barber, Cartwright, Price and Brown, they called up Somerset seamer Ken Palmer for a first cap. Geoff Boycott would have to fill in as third seamer.

SACA appointed Les Baxter and Kidson as umpires. MCC made an official objection to Baxter. In Carr's view, he had shown no partiality or bias, but was hesitant in making decisions and too inclined to give a batsman not out, as great a fault, according to Carr, as giving a decision against a batsman. Carr was prepared to 'invoke examples known to your committee'. He was ignored.[497]

Goddard and Barlow put together yet another century opening stand, then Graeme Pollock had a triumphant homecoming. His composed 137 characterised by silky yet thunderous off-driving drove South Africa to an unbeatable 502 in their first innings. The local hero became the second batsman after George Headley to score three Test hundreds before the age of 21. Boycott sent down 26 overs, picking up the wicket of Barlow, caught without incident by Parfitt

---

496 MCC/CRI/5/1/93
497 MCC/CRI/5/1/94

at slip. Could South Africa, who had clawed their way back from 2-0 down in 1956/57 and from 1-0 down in Australia, force another drawn series?

In reply, Geoff Boycott played the anchor role with which he was already synonymous. The Murray opening experiment failed, but Boycott (117) and Barrington (72) defended dourly, runs came down the order and England were all out for 435, 67 behind with four sessions to play. Smith deployed his full go-slow kit, with Thomson and Palmer bowling short of a length to defensive fields. Graeme Pollock crashed a quickfire 77, batting as if he was facing his mum in his backyard. For the third Test in a row, Goddard was forced to time a declaration. Only a win would draw the series, so he had to risk losing. England were set 246 in 233 minutes on a deteriorating wicket. It was soon irrelevant; the rains brought the series to a watery close with England on 29/1.

Mike Smith was more a draughts than a chess player, a man of tactical counters rather than long-term strategy, but he prevailed through streetwise captaincy and consistent performances from key players. He gave nothing away. Almost all the batsmen enhanced their reputations. Barber grabbed the momentum in every innings he played, Barrington, a relentless if dour run machine, averaged 101.60, Dexter batted imperiously and Boycott was the glue that held it together when the team began to fray at the edges. Parfitt, Parks and Smith all averaged over 40. For South Africa, Colin Bland hit 822 runs in 14 innings, averaging 71.5 in the Tests in addition to his brilliant fielding (but strangely no catches). Barlow, Graeme Pollock, and Tony Pithey all averaged over 50.

Barber neutralised the threat from the hostile Peter Pollock (12 wickets at 37 each). Joe Partridge (six at 48) had a fitful influence, Goddard's form (six at 51) was not up to his usual standards and Barlow (five at 39) might have been underused. England's David Allen (17 at 26) and Fred Titmus (18 at 38) were the difference between the sides and, while the latter faded after the shenanigans in the third Test, Allen was a constant threat. His exclusion in the fourth Test could have been catastrophic.

But numbers don't always tell the story. South Africa's record of six opening partnerships over 50 (two at more than 100) dwarfed England's two (with one century), but England's 120-run partnership in the first innings of the first Test proved the key moment behind the only win of the series against an undercooked opposition. On universally good batting wickets, winning the toss usually meant controlling the rest of the game and Barrington's breezy prediction that it was 'our series, boys' at tea on day one of the first Test proved accurate. Smith had some luck, his bizarre decision to field in the fourth Test might have swung the series back had Goddard not batted on for too long. But Smith's captaincy, slowing over rates, defensive fields and encouraging crease occupancy enabled England to cling on for three Tests in a row. They may not have been pretty, but they were hard to beat. Smith's reputation rested on his complete support of his players however they performed.

It was a lesson in Test captaincy. Result is king. Focus on the task at hand, subordinate means to ends. The game is played on the pitch, ignore the cacophony from media and crowds. Make no promises, tell no lies.

Epilogue

The Sixteenth Tour: 1968/69

IN 1965, Mike Brearley continued his education. He arranged a visit to the Ford Motors plant on the outskirts of Port Elizabeth and asked Tom Cartwright along. As a former Rootes car worker in Coventry, Tom was a knowledgeable visitor, and they grilled the manager on the application of the job colour bar in the car industry. The law set out the percentage and nature of jobs, supervisory and control work, and skilled functions such as welding, reserved for whites. Tom was a bit embarrassed at Mike scribbling down wage scales and comparisons. I was probably a bit earnest then, conceded Mike. It was indicative of his seriousness of purpose.

It kicked off Mike's post-series adventure. The chairman of Standard Bank, Sir Cyril Hawker, an alumnus of Brearley's City of London school (where Mike's father taught maths and cricket) and future MCC president, provided a car and driver and Mike spent three weeks touring the country and talking to the locals. Two meetings stood out. Knowledge Guzana, an opposition leader in the Transkei Bantustan, spelt out 'grand apartheid' – the political significance of South Africa's 'separate development' policy. The Transkei was one of ten so-called 'Homelands' or Bantustans, which were supposedly independent countries but were simply puppet regimes appointed and controlled by South Africa. They stripped Africans of their South African citizenship and, for other than licensed migrant workers, the right to enter South Africa at all. The second was a conversation with a (white) Transkeian magistrate with 40 years' experience. In a sing song voice, as if talking about children, he told Mike, 'The only thing that Africans understand is corporal punishment.'[498]

No one knew it then, but England had played their last match in South Africa for 31 years. As the tourists flew home, county champions Worcestershire landed in Salisbury on their 'world tour'. They had just played in Nairobi against Kenya. Basil D'Oliveira, back at the scene of his triumphs with the SACBOC tourists in 1958, didn't let the locals down. He hit a scintillating 162 out of Worcestershire's 353 all out. But Kenya savaged the Worcester attack, scoring 354/4 declared in reply.

Three days after the end of M.J.K. Smith's series, D'Oliveira was in Rhodesia for two games in which he played against six current or future Springboks (Colin Bland, Tony and David Pithey, Joe Partridge, Goofy Lawrence and Jackie du Preez). No Rhodesians appeared to notice or care and the 1965 edition of the *South African Cricket Annual* simply described Basil as 'South African-born'.

The political environment was overheating. The Ian Smith regime extended the state of emergency in the African townships and filled its jails with 1,165 political detainees. Smith refused to meet the commonwealth secretary to resolve the deadlock. ZANU and ZAPU demanded a constitutional conference to pave the way for majority rule. It would take a 15-year armed struggle to achieve this at Lancaster House.

Back in the UK in the summer of 1965, Peter van der Merwe's South Africans squelched through a three-Test series. South Africa won the second Test and the series thanks to Graeme Pollock's 125 and 59 confirming him as the world's most exciting batsman. His brother Peter took 10/87 in the match. Peter van der Merwe had his revenge on Mike Smith. It was yet another ending, the last South African tour to England for 29 years.

Protests at South African participation in international cricket gathered momentum and MCC were alarmed enough to draft a

---

498 Mike Brearley, conversations with Richard Parry, 4 and 11 August 2020

response to anti-apartheid campaigners to be used by all county clubs.[499] The upcoming 1968/69 tour came under the spotlight as soon as D'Oliveira, the high-profile cricketing refugee from apartheid who had captained the so-called 'South African non-European XI', made a successful debut for England against the West Indies in 1966. Basil's rise to global cricketing prominence and his possible return as part of an England team taking on the cricketing representatives of the apartheid regime was an irresistible but politically unfeasible story.

It was rugby, the South African apartheid regime at play, that first muddied the political waters. While Basil was taking on the West Indies, South Africa in uncompromising mood declared Maori players unwelcome. New Zealand cancelled the tour. It was a huge shock to white South Africa's fanatical rugby supporters. B.J. Vorster, who had taken over from the caretaker prime minister Dr Eben Donges after Hendrik Verwoerd's assassination, had his own political balancing act. In the end he recognised that it was politically preferable to avoid alienating rugby fans although this did risk upsetting far right apartheid purists. He announced a 'liberalisation' of the regime's sports policy in 1967 to allow the possible inclusion of black players in visiting international sports teams. Internally, this sparked a breakaway, resulting in the formation of the ultra-right Hersigte (Purified) National Party but with only a couple of MPs lost the damage was containable.

MCC in their naivety failed to grasp that this 'liberalisation' did not necessarily mean what they might have hoped. First, since the days of Cecil Rhodes and 'Krom' Hendricks, sports policy had been central to the operation and inner logic of the South African state, a status reinforced under apartheid. Developing a potential special foreign exemption from apartheid on the rugby field to support apartheid's national game did not necessarily transfer to cricket tours, a game already viewed with suspicion by the apartheid regime.

---

499 MCC Minute Books 1962–'65, MCC/SEC/1/14

However MCC saw it, for South Africa the D'Oliveira affair was not a legal issue around foreigners, but whether they should exempt a rightless black South African, already a cause celebre for black South Africans and international forces ranged against South Africa to return as a member of a foreign sports team and take on his white fellow countrymen in front of South African crowds.

If MCC wanted a tour, South Africa expected them to fix the problem – as they had done previously with the non-selection of Ranji and Duleep. Politically, South Africa would not cancel the tour and deliberately increase their own isolation but given the unusual circumstances effective cancellation by MCC action might have been preferable to the political frenzy, which the D'Oliveira factor, whether he was playing or not, might cause within the country.

The MCC wanted to believe that South Africa valued their position within world cricket highly enough to find a political fix and that their position on black sportsmen might soften by the time of the tour. But they had far more to lose; they either risked their credibility and independence, or a cricketing relationship which was critical to MCC's continued dominance over world cricket.

In the end, either South Africa would have to accept Basil or MCC would have to find a way of leaving him out. The MCC's naivety turned this simple premise into a fully-fledged Shakespearean tragedy.

D'Oliveira was a symbol of a new kind of society in England and in South Africa, but neither side in this diplomatic snarl up supported what he stood for. It was almost inevitable that this most steadfast and principled of men never got on the plane to Johannesburg despite an MCC tour contract in his name signed by the secretary Billy Griffith.

Papers in the MCC archives throw new light on the affair. As we have seen, MCC spent eight decades doing all they could to support the South African state and British investment in the mining industry. It was no surprise, therefore, that when an issue arose which posed a real risk to its objectives, MCC was unable to shake off its complacency and even try to understand the political dynamics of the country. When the South African regime boasted in 1966 that, in the period since 1948, they had spent four million rand on housing South Africa's 16.3 million Africans, coloureds and Indians, and 216 million rand on housing for 3.3 million whites, MCC and the British establishment chose not to hear or to care.

At the end of 1966, Griffith visited South Africa. He expressed the support of Lord's for South Africa's readmission to the ICC (when the timing was right) and in return looked for movement on D'Oliveira. The MCC papers later noted that a meeting with a senior unnamed government official (identified privately as acting prime minister Eben Donges) told them what they wanted to hear. He gave the 'impression' that the attitude to multi-racial sport might well have changed for the better by the time the team was selected.[500] Two things were clear. South Africa took the issue seriously enough for direct involvement at prime ministerial level, and they were going to keep their powder dry.

Further down the food chain, and with a domestic audience in mind, Piet le Roux, South African minister for the interior, categorically stated that D'Oliveira would not be allowed in. The British minister for sport, Denis Howell, told parliament that if any selected player was rejected, MCC would find the condition wholly unacceptable, and the tour abandoned. The MCC committee had been bounced and had to support the statement. Treasurer Gubby Allen muttered darkly that Howell should not have been 'so definite or strong without the MCC having first considered it'. If it was likely that D'Oliveira would be selected it was essential to make a definite decision before the 1968 season.[501]

The South African ambassador met with officials at Lord's and the MCC committee empowered the president (former Conservative prime minister Sir Alec Douglas-Home), the treasurer and secretary to take decisions 'in exceptional circumstances' without the approval of committee meetings.[502] This traditional power structure was based

---

500 MCC Minute Books, 1965-67, MCC/SEC/1/15; Drafts of Statement for Special General Meeting, December 1968, MCC/CRI/5/1/105

501 Minutes of Special Meeting, 1/2/1967, MCC/SEC/1/15

502 MCC Minute Book, 1965–67, Minutes of Committee meeting, 15/2/1967

on the Lord Harris model, with the treasurer at the apex, supported by the president (nominated by his predecessor) and the secretary 'advised' as needed by the members of the MCC committee and its sub-committees.[503] In fact, Douglas-Home's status as a former prime minister meant he appears to have led this official cabal with the strong support of Allen as treasurer.

D'Oliveira played five out of six of the Tests versus India and Pakistan in the 1967 season and would play in all five Tests against the West Indies in the winter. It was highly likely that he would be selected for a tour of his home country. The MCC committee agreed to ask SACA to provide assurances that there were no preconditions on selection in January 1968.[504] Receipt was acknowledged by SACA, but no substantial response made.

Aware that SACA were messengers for the prime minister's office, MCC grandees beat a path to Vorster's door. On 22 February, Douglas-Home met Vorster and concluded that no assurances would be forthcoming. Three weeks later, Vorster told Lord Cobham, the next former MCC president to arrive, 'quite categorically' that D'Oliveira would not be acceptable.

But instead of going public and cancelling the tour at this critical point, the inner cabal led by Douglas-Home decided not to report Vorster's position and advised the committee to drop the request for assurances and wait until the party was selected.[505] At the same time, the South Africans also wanted the question of the itinerary and notably the vexed question of the MCC visit to Rhodesia, to be

---

503 The general primacy of the treasurer over the president is best indicated by the fact that presidents of MCC, who served for one year only, were only appointed treasurer later in their career. Lord Harris was president in 1895, and treasurer between 1916 and 1932; Lord Hawke was president between 1914-18 and treasurer from 1933; Gubby Allen was president in 1963 and treasurer from 1965 to 1976. Tony Lewis, *Double Century, the Story of the MCC and Cricket*, (London: Hodder and Stoughton, 1987) 362

504 South African Tour Sub-Committee, 8/11/1967 in MCC Committee Minutes, MCC Library, MCC/CRI/5/1/105/1

505 MCC Minute Book, 1965–'67, MCC/SEC/1/15; Drafts of Statement for Special General Meeting, December 1968, MCC/CRI/5/1/105; MCC Minute Book, 1967-68, MCC/SEC/1/16

deferred. Here there was no possibility of manoeuvre. The MCC decided the itinerary should be announced as soon as possible with a statement that they would not be playing in Rhodesia.[506]

The D'Oliveira deferral reflected a key change in strategy. It was now obvious that the tour could only survive without D'Oliveira, and the MCC cabal gambled on his apparently inadequate performances on and off the field in the West Indies, or a poor domestic season removing him from contention. Failing that, they relied on the success of South African efforts to bully, bribe and browbeat him into making himself unavailable. In June, D'Oliveira played in the first Ashes Test of the summer at Old Trafford and top-scored with 87 not out, the only English player to pass 50.

With the second Test at Lord's starting just over a week later and Basil in the 13-man squad, Vorster immediately sent SACA president Arthur Coy to Lord's to warn MCC of the impact of selecting him. In the week preceding the Test, Coy, journalist E.W. Swanton and Billy Griffith all separately approached D'Oliveira, arguing that the tour could only be saved if he declared himself 'unavailable for England but available for selection for South Africa'. They were putting the responsibility for saving the tour on him.[507]

The proposal was fantastical and without any possible logical or even legal basis. Coming from three sources – MCC, SACA and the press – and building on earlier efforts to bribe Basil to remove himself from selection, it was a breathtakingly cynical and cruel attack on a man who was playing for England because he had been categorically excluded on grounds of colour from representing his country. Basil treated these overtures with the contempt they deserved.

---

506 MCC Committee Minutes MCC/CRI/5/1/105. In response to a question from committee member D.B. Clark, the SA tour committee agreed that it might be possible to add two or three matches in Rhodesia at the start of the tour should the politics change. South African Tour Sub-Committee, 20/5/1968, in MCC Committee Minutes, MCC Library, MCC/CRI/5/1/105/1

507 Bruce Murray, 'The D'Oliveira Affair' in Murray, Parry and Winch (eds.), *Cricket and Society*, 311

If Basil wasn't prepared to go quietly, even more desperate measures were needed. Despite top-scoring in the first Test and taking 1-38 in 25 overs and 1-7 in five overs, D'Oliveira found himself left out of the 13 on the day of the Test and facing the likelihood that he would not be selected for the tour. He was replaced, not by Tom Cartwright who had been in the 13 before pulling out injured, but by Barry Knight who was brought into the squad at the last minute. Colin Cowdrey, presumably acting on instructions, was forced to blather on about Basil's lack of penetration as a bowler.

This was the end of the first act as the blameless and loyal D'Oliveira had to endure the duplicitous and hypocritical destruction of his life-long ambition. MCC's inner cabal, represented by Griffith and Swanton, far from supporting their player, worked with Vorster's henchman, Arthur Coy, in a three-pronged approach using the outrageous argument given Basil's entire cricketing history, that he should play for South Africa.

The rest of the summer was agonising for Basil. While Barry Knight did well in the second Test, he had an undistinguished third Test (six and one, and 1-34) and just before the fourth Test a lurid article appeared in which Barry said his marriage was broken, his business bankrupt and he had contemplated suicide.[508] Knight disappeared and, instead of D'Oliveira, was replaced by debutant batsman, Keith Fletcher. The tour pool of 30 players was released in July and Basil was not included. It confirmed that his dream was dead. But fate had some extraordinary twists in store.

In the second act, Colin Cowdrey, who had played at The Oval the previous week, decided he needed medium-pace cover for the fifth Test. Cartwright's long-standing shoulder injury had not responded to treatment and Knight was 'unfit'. Despite his miserable season with the bat, D'Oliveira was in fine form with the ball. He was seventh in the national averages with 55 wickets at 15.36 and Cowdrey picked him as a medium pace bowling standby despite having 'dropped' him for his lack of penetration with the ball after the first Test.

---

508 Lewis, *Double Century*, 314

Did Cowdrey deliberately decide to give D'Oliveira a chance? Maybe not, but Basil had at least made the subs' bench. Then opener Roger Prideaux pulled out with a virus on the eve of the match. Suddenly Basil was required as a replacement batsman rather than a bowler and held his ambition in his own hands. Other players might have been overwhelmed, but not Basil. His legendary fixity of purpose and a summer's anguish fuelled a match-winning 158.

This improbable sequence of events was to turn the cricketing world on its head. Businessman Tienie, who had previously offered Basil a ten-year coaching contract for £40,000 to make himself unavailable, called the Surrey secretary. Geoffrey Howard passed on his message to Doug Insole, chairman of selectors, that 'if today's centurion is picked, the tour will be off'.[509] Insole ignored it. South Africa and the MCC cabal had somehow failed to derail D'Oliveira, Cowdrey was off-message and Basil had displayed his class under pressure. Would MCC obey the South African diktat or stand up for their player and risk the tour?

As Peter Oborne suggests, the selection of the tour party remains one of the best-kept secrets of the 20th century.[510] But thanks to recent work by Oborne, Stephen Chalke, Bruce Murray and Mike Brearley, a confession and further analysis of the MCC Archive, it is possible to get closer to untangling this knottiest of cricketing controversies.

On 27 August, after a long rain delay and a heroic mopping up operation, Australia looked like holding out for a draw until at 5.15pm D'Oliveira clipped Barry Jarman's off bail, and within ten overs it was all over. Derek Underwood mopped up the tail in 33 balls.

Two hours after the players wearily left the field at the end of an exhausting Ashes series, and as the celebrations were just beginning, the selectors – having driven from The Oval – began discussions at Lord's to select a touring party which would not leave for South Africa until November. The curtain rose on Act III.

---

509 Stephen Chalke, *At the Heart of English Cricket*, (Bath: Fairfield Books 2001) 206

510 Oborne, *Basil D'Oliveira*, 189

It is hard not to discern the panic which drove the MCC cabal to seek an immediate decision on D'Oliveira. An emotionally and physically exhausted Cowdrey changed out of his whites and gave Jack Bailey a lift to Lord's in his Jaguar, registration plate MCC 307. Virtually Cowdrey's first words to Bailey were 'We shall have trouble with South Africa ... They can't leave Basil out of the team. Not now.'[511] Cowdrey had been vindicated in selecting Basil, even if it was as a bowler, and would have recalled his embarrassing justification for dropping him for the second Test. As he said, 'they' – tellingly not 'we' – 'can't leave Basil out.'

The formal minute of the MCC selection sub-committee meeting for Tuesday 27 August names those present: Doug Insole (chairman); Arthur Gilligan (president); Gubby Allen (treasurer); Billy Griffith (secretary); Les Ames (tour manager); Colin Cowdrey (captain); Alec Bedser; Don Kenyon; Peter May; Donald Carr (assistant secretary). All except Kenyon, D'Oliveira's county captain, had direct South African experience.[512]

The minutes for this meeting are not signed and dated unlike other meeting notes in the files. The note summarised the outcomes of a six-hour discussion of the most complex and sensitive issue the selectors had ever faced in one page. It listed the unavailable players and named the 15 selected (plus a fast bowler, probably Jeff Jones, to be added subject to fitness). There was no mention of fitness checks on any of the other players' although Tom Cartwright had not been fit for the fifth Test or played a Test match in the summer. The chairman and captain would decide on reserves in due course. No mention of the name D'Oliveira.

Bruce Murray, having interviewed Doug Insole in 2000, reported that Gilligan and Allen began by speculating on whether there was any point in selecting a team at all given the political issues. Presumably, they intended to spook any selectors who hoped to select Basil and still have a tour. The meeting went nowhere until Insole

---

511 Jack Bailey, *Conflicts in Cricket*, (London: Kingswood Press, 1989) 52

512 Gubby Allen had not actually played in South Africa but had watched three Tests in 1965 and met the South African prime minister, Hendrik Verwoerd

encouraged his fellow selectors to pick a team 'as if it were going to Australia'.[513]

Insole claimed for 50 years that D'Oliveira had not been selected 'on cricketing grounds'. He put it tartly in his article on 'Selectors' in E.W. Swanton's *Barclays World of Cricket*, 'The original outcry arose because … D'Oliveira scored 158 and was considered by many people to be an automatic choice for the tour. The selectors thought otherwise.'[514]

Peter Oborne argues that the 'cricketing grounds' must have included a close discussion of the merits of two all-rounders – Cartwright, a front-line bowler, and D'Oliveira, primarily a prolific batsman, but in fact there was little point of comparison. Cartwright, an outstanding medium-pace seamer at county level with exceptional control and movement, played five Tests in four series, the last in 1965. He had toured South Africa in 1964/65, but injury prevented him from playing in more than a single Test, in which he took 1/97 and 1/99. He had 15 Test wickets with a best of 6/94 against South Africa at Nottingham in 1965 and did not make double figures with the bat. But his Test figures do him little justice compared with his first-class return of 1,536 wickets at 19.11 and 13,710 runs at 21.32. Although at the height of his powers, he had suffered from injuries bowling only half the overs of the previous summer but still captured 71 wickets at 16 each. When Insole asked him if he was fit to tour, Cartwright said he wasn't, but Insole said it didn't matter and hoped he would respond to treatment.

Despite starting his first-class career in his 30s, Basil D'Oliveira had played 16 Tests since 1966, averaging a 48.6 with seven fifties and two hundreds, second only to Barrington among contemporary England batsmen. In his five series, only once – in the West Indies – did he average below 40, and in three out of five series he averaged over 50. With the ball, his medium-pace seamers were described

---

513 Murray, 'D'Oliveira Affair', 316. This is based on Murray's interview with Doug Insole, Cape Town, 4 January 2000

514 E.W. Swanton (ed.), *Barclays World of Cricket*, 3rd edition, (London: Guild Publishing, 1986) 367

by scorer and statistician Bill Frindall as 'an effortless masterpiece of deception', but his Test figures at the time of the meeting were underwhelming. He had taken 18 wickets, the vast majority top-order batsmen, but at 46.94 (which he was to improve to 47 wickets at 39.55 by the end of his Test career). He ended up with 551 wickets at 27.45 in first-class cricket.

Any discussion of South African conditions would also have been inconclusive given that the wickets had not suited Cartwright on the previous tour. But the emergence of Mike Procter to partner Peter Pollock meant a move to harder, faster wickets.

D'Oliveira had had a quiet season with the bat but excellent returns with the ball. More importantly, he had shown a priceless ability to rise to the occasion driven by his unique blend of talent and hunger. Given his achievements in the fifth Test, it was plainly unreasonable to omit D'Oliveira on cricketing grounds unless the definition included off-field behaviour.

The puzzle of what really happened deepened when Mike Brearley, in *On Cricket*, reported a different account from Doug Insole from an anonymous source.[515] Mike's source was Professor David Allison, who had attended a Cricket Society meeting at which writer Rob Steen discussed the affair. Allison was a friend of fellow jazz buff Insole, and both regularly attended the MCC carol services.

At one of the services, he raised the Cricket Society meeting with Insole, who in an unguarded moment, told him that the selectors had picked D'Oliveira, but that the MCC officials had 'rescinded' the decision 'within 24 hours'. Allison then told the story to Mike Brearley in 2018.[516]

But even then, Insole was careful not to give too much away. If true, there were three possible explanations. The 'de-selection' may have happened during the marathon selection meeting; or in the 13 hours before the start of the committee meeting (and the minutes

515 Mike Brearley, *On Cricket*, 135-145

516 Interview by Richard Parry with Prof David Allison and Maurice Nettley, 26 May 2021

fabricated); or 'rescinded' during the committee meeting that same afternoon, immediately before the press conference.

A six-hour meeting was not a rubber stamp for D'Oliveira's omission, hence the extended preliminary discussion followed by Insole's proposal to select a team as if it were going to Australia. At this stage, there must have been several supporters of D'Oliveira in the room. Don Kenyon was one, Cowdrey had made his position clear in the car with Bailey and Insole himself said he had supported Basil. The committee meeting the following day indicates that there was at least one vote. Even if the other two selectors (Bedser and May) and the tour manager (Ames) supported his omission, this would still have split the initial vote 3-3 with Insole having the casting voice as chair. This would have fitted with Insole's volte-face as told to Allison.

It is conceivable that Allen called for a break around this point and on their return stressed the need for further discussion. The officials may have focused on Basil's alleged drinking in the West Indies when Cowdrey was captain and Ames manager in the light of the enormous pressure which D'Oliveira would face in the minefield of South Africa's racist system and in the full glare of the international media. But D'Oliveira and Cowdrey had already discussed how Basil might cope. Basil described it as his crowning ambition and had given his absolute assurance regarding his behaviour. Colin believed him and said he would support him.

The question of culture and drinking is an important one in the cricketing context, with recent revelations surrounding the racial abuse suffered by Azeem Rafiq and others in county cricket. D'Oliveira had been a teetotaller but had come under huge pressure to fit into cultural norms on his first England tour. Drinking was encouraged but behaviour had to fit within the constraints of class and a very particular culture. It was a difficult skill to master when coming from a community where alcohol consumption implied alcohol abuse. Get it wrong and a player might be subject to 'othering', left outside the dominant group encouraging a vicious circle of alienation, self-doubt and poor performance followed by more drinking as a refuge for loneliness and despair.

But around 2am, as our third act draws to its conclusion, it is likely that under pressure from Gubby Allen, an exhausted Cowdrey facing a tour with such off-field risk finally caved in and a decisive vote left D'Oliveira out in the cold, the ultimate in 'othering' by the committee.

The second possibility based on Insole's account was that he was selected in the initial meeting but that the decision was 'rescinded' prior to the committee meeting. For this to be true, the decision would have to be ignored by Allen's cabal and the minutes falsified, with an incorrect statement read to the committee and minuted. But there is no evidence beyond Insole's language in his 'confession' to Allison that this might have happened, and it appears unlikely.

Which leaves the third possibility, that the decision was made at the committee meeting which started at 3.45pm on 28 August. The press conference to announce the side began at 5pm, so there was little more than an hour available for discussion. The minutes show that 19 committee members covered 16 agenda items in this time.[517] Item four confirmed the selection sub-committee minutes of the previous day. Discussion took place 'on the selection of MCC team … and on possible ways in which press and other observations on the composition of the team should be met', which took up the bulk of the item.[518] They agreed that Insole, as chairman of selectors, should act as spokesman with the media for 24 hours until he went on holiday, and that 'no voting figures regarding the selection of the team should be given to the press'.

What are we to make of this terse bureaucratese? On process, Insole would have summarised the previous evening's discussions and read the selected team. It was presumably agreed with little discussion. Once the committee knew the team, the issue simply became how to manage the inevitable media outcry. Insole himself may have insisted that explicit agreement was recorded in the minutes that no 'voting

---

517 The 19 committee members included Maurice Allom, George Mann, Aidan Crawley, Peter May, Sir Cyril Hawker, Freddie Brown, Sir Alec Douglas-Home and Raman Subba Row

518 MCC Committee Minutes, 28/8/1968

figures' regarding selection the previous evening would be divulged. Clearly the voting had been other than unanimous.

In the end, logic and Occam's razor suggest that the decision was taken at the selectors' meeting, even if the officials needed six hours to get their way. Insole announced the party to the press at 5pm. The names were read in alphabetical order and a collective gasp came as John Edrich followed Bob Cottam. Insole told the world that D'Oliveira was not picked because 'we have various players who are rather better'.[519] He may have been summarising the arguments at the selection meeting, but it was a further monstrous injustice which must have cut D'Oliveira to the heart. It was a callous dismissal unworthy of a decent man.

Basil explained his feelings after his innings in the *Daily Telegraph*, 'I can at this moment still see the ball going off the bat as I turned Gleeson for a single to get my Test century at The Oval last Friday. I can't lie about that innings. I played it with only one thought in mind. It was the one great chance; the one opportunity and I was going to take it. I knew that not even 99 would be enough.

'As I scored that 100th run I kept saying to myself, "I've done it. I've done it. I have had my chance and I've done it."'Going back to South Africa was a dream … just to walk on the grounds at Newlands … and know I was there chosen as a cricketer.'[520]

This poignant account illustrated how rejection by his adopted country was even sharper and more painful than the discrimination he had suffered all his life, particularly a few hours after an English triumph for which he had been responsible. Billy Griffith assured a disbelieving press that Basil had been omitted not because of 'political preconditions' but because he had had a 'poor tour' of the West Indies and 'although he made a century yesterday', he had had a moderate season. Moreover, he was not rated as a Test bowler overseas and was an 'indifferent fielder'.[521]

519 *Daily Telegraph*, 29/8/1968
520 *Daily Telegraph*, 30/8/1968
521 *The Times*, 29/8/1968

After persistent questioning, Insole said that D'Oliveira and Don Wilson were going to be in South Africa and might be called on in case of emergency. This would have been news to Basil who was still expecting to be part of the MCC squad. Basil was told the news as he came off after scoring 128 for Worcestershire.

As Duncan Fearnley told Mike Brearley years later while Middlesex were playing Worcestershire and D'Oliveira was the visitors' coach, Gubby Allen was in his usual seat by the Long Room window when Basil stormed in and poked him in the chest with his finger, saying, 'You stuffed me, you [expletive deleted].' The next day, when Basil was said to be heading for the Long Room, Allen placed his Tio Pepe aperitif in the drinks cabinet for safety and fled.[522]

There was no formal or informal acceptance of guilt or apology by Allen, Griffith, Gilligan, Douglas-Home or the MCC committee for the pain caused to D'Oliveira by this farrago of obfuscation, innuendo and lies over an entire season. MCC's cruelty and inhumanity towards D'Oliveira and its craven approach to the South African regime were the culmination of the racist logic and dynamics of the cricketing relationship over 80 years and the maintenance of imperial control over international cricket.

Surely now there was no way back for Basil?

But the perfect storm of D'Oliveira's non-selection was not over. Tom Cartwright's fitness remained uncertain. MCC relied on an increasingly redundant, class-based confidence in their ability to command the adherence of professionals. 'You're our property now,' said assistant secretary Donald Carr, semi-jovially, when he took Cartwright to see orthopaedic surgeon Bill Tucker on 11 September.

Tucker's medical report suggested that he had a long-standing rotator cuff injury in his right shoulder which had restricted his movements for a decade and a new injury dating back to June was causing pain and stiffness. It was possible that with a fortnight's graduated exercises, Cartwright would lose his symptoms. But it was

---

522 Brearley, *On Cricket*, 143. Prof Allison also spoke to Duncan Fearnley who confirmed the story. Email to author, 14 September 2021

difficult to guarantee that he would be free of recurrences given the wear and tear in the shoulder joint and neck.[523]

The MCC committee met the next day. Insole introduced the 'element of doubt' about Cartwright's fitness and asked pointedly, 'If there were any players whom, for any reason, the committee did not wish to see considered.'[524] As it turned out there was one. It was decided, after discussion, that B.R. Knight from Insole's home county, Essex, 'should not be available' to tour South Africa. Moreover, if 'the need arose it would be made clear that this had been decided by the committee and not the selectors' taking Insole out of the firing line.

This decision, astonishing in the light of the unfolding D'Oliveira affair, was presumably related to his messy move from Insole's Essex to Leicestershire and a newspaper article in July in which Knight spoke about his bankruptcy and the collapse of his marriage. MCC had decided that Knight's demons made him unselectable. Like Basil, he didn't receive an availability letter in July, and he was dropped for Fletcher in the fourth Test, forcing a reluctant Dexter to take on the third seamer role. Knight later told Rob Steen that he had been available for the tour and hoped to be selected. Neither he, nor anyone else, was aware of MCC's self-imposed prohibition against him. In any event, MCC had painted themselves into a corner. Cartwright's recovery was the only escape route.

Basil D'Oliveira's name came up in the minutes for the first time. Vorster had made it clear in the media that Basil would not be welcome as a journalist for the *News of the World*. George Mann, captain in South Africa for the 1948/49 tour, suggested that the committee had a responsibility towards Basil. Mann thought MCC should clarify the position if he was picked as a cricketer.

Eventually it was agreed that if they needed to replace Cartwright and if D'Oliveira was not picked to replace him, then the following would be sent to the South Africans, 'D'Oliveira is a reserve for the

---

523 Report from W.E. Tucker on Tom Cartwright, 12 September 1968. MCC/CRI/5/1/105/1

524 MCC Committee Minutes, 12/9/1968. Item 10. MCC Library, MCC/CRI/5/1/105/1. The Minutes were signed off by Ronnie Aird on 20/11/1968

England XI. We have always assumed that purely as a cricketer, he will be acceptable. In view of recent doubts which have arisen about his eligibility to enter South Africa, would you please confirm his acceptance as a cricketer. For obvious reasons, it is imperative that we have your assurance by the end of the month.'[525]

The game was up. D'Oliveira would either go as a replacement for Cartwright or if not, be selected as a reserve. If he went as a replacement, the ball would be in the South African court. If not, his position as one among the reserves was a compromise which the South Africans might buy, postponing, possibly forever, the key question of whether he would appear on the field. It was the last roll of the dice and MCC knew it. South Africa would have to concede or take the blame.

On Monday, 16 August, the morning of the selectors' meeting, Cartwright had a further examination. Bill Tucker thought there was some 'considerable doubt as to his fitness for the tour', although an improvement might be accelerated by 'manipulation under anaesthetic'. But it would take at least three more weeks before his fitness could be established.[526]

Carr and Cartwright hurried back to Lord's, where they met Insole and Griffith. Bill Tucker had failed to provide adequate reassurance. It was a grave risk, and Tom's young family were against him going.[527] After extensive persuasion failed, Carr, Insole and Griffith had to accept Tom's decision to withdraw on medical grounds. Tom had also had a change of heart, 'At the time I was picked ... I still thought it was the right thing to go out there and try to influence the right people and make it clear to Africans that there were whites elsewhere who had different ideas. But I read a little article that when the tour party was announced [omitting

525 *Ibid*, item 11

526 MCC Sub-Committee on SA Tour Selection Minutes, 16/9/1968. MCC Library, MCC/CRI/5/1/105

527 Chalke, *Flame*, 150. The cheering in South Africa when the non-selection was announced was not actually in parliament but when it was announced by Louwrens Muller, minister of police, at a National Party rally in Potchefstroom. *Daily Express*, 30/8/1968

D'Oliveira] in parliament in Cape Town, the whole assembly stood up and cheered. When I read that I went cold.'

Cartwright caught the train home to Birmingham as the selectors began the meeting. When he got to his front door, the phone was ringing, and Colin Cowdrey was on the other end of the line. 'Will you at least start the tour?' Cowdrey asked. 'If you break down, we could bring in someone like Don Wilson who is coaching in Johannesburg.' Basil was not mentioned. Tom just said no, and Colin accepted that response.[528]

The selectors met at 4pm. Cartwright's medical report was submitted. Doug Insole reported the discussion with Cartwright, and it was agreed to tell the press that Cartwright had not responded to treatment and had expressed doubts to the selectors about his fitness for the tour. There was 'no direct replacement for a bowler of Cartwright's specialist abilities and the balance of the touring party has inevitably to be altered. Basil D'Oliveira is being invited to join the touring party.'[529] Four reserves were selected – Bob Taylor, Fred Titmus, Don Wilson and Ken Shuttleworth.

The MCC committee ratified the replacement and the reserves in ten minutes the following day.[530] The usual formal touring agreements between MCC and the players, including one with Basil D'Oliveira, awarding him the standard sum of £700 plus £25, were drawn up and signed by Billy Griffith.[531] Basil never saw his.

The newspaper headlines confirmed Basil's selection. Why, after fighting so hard to keep Basil out, did MCC simply select him in the end? The committee may have hoped that with the the anti-apartheid movement circling ever closer, and the lessons of the cancelled All Blacks rugby tour in mind, South Africa might decide to preserve a cricketing relationship that was too useful to lose.

---

528 Chalke, *Flame*, 153

529 MCC Sub-Committee on SA Tour Selection Minutes, 16/9/1968. MCC/CRI/5/1/105

530 MCC Committee Minutes, 17/9/1968. MCC Library, MCC/CRI/5/1/105

531 MCC Library, MCC/CRI/5/1/105

Gubby Allen had travelled with the 1964/65 tour and met prime minister Hendrik Verwoerd, the grand architect of apartheid, at the Cape Town Test. Verwoerd would have told him that he supported MCC's important role in bringing the Afrikaner and English communities together and Allen must have hoped that a vestige of that rapprochement thinking might save the tour. But Verwoerd was dead, assassinated by Dimitri Tsafendas. Verwoerd's temporary replacement Dr Eben Donges may have been equivocal, but new PM J.B. Vorster, a veteran activist in the neo-Nazi Ossewabrandwag, which had supported Germany in the war, was not. Just how many times did he have to tell the 'Engelse' (English) that D'Oliveira was the tool of the enemy? The new 'team of the anti-apartheid movement' was rejected.[532]

The MCC had run out of options. The pro-D'Oliveira media storm had been a PR disaster. The cabal decided that the tour had to be sacrificed if the cricketing relationship with South Africa was to be maintained when Basil was no longer around to muddy the waters.

Within a week of the cancellation announcement, MCC had called a special committee meeting (on 24 September), which SACA's Arthur Coy and Jack Cheetham attended fresh off the plane. Arthur Gilligan explained that Colin Cowdrey had asked that he and Billy Griffith travel immediately to South Africa to persuade Vorster to change his view. The meeting told Cowdrey to stay in the UK and made a hollow-sounding pledge to advance 'coloured' cricket in South Africa 'within the laws of the country'.

A few weeks later, MCC formally cancelled the tour. But it would take direct government intervention in 1970 to end formal cricketing links.

The MCC replaced South Africa with a short tour to Pakistan. Basil played in all three Tests and made an undefeated hundred in the second. A political protest, unrelated to MCC, forced the abandonment of the third Test shortly before lunch on the third day.

---

532 Chalke, *Flame*, 146-154

It was a reminder that the rest of the world no longer behaved as the MCC establishment decreed.

MCC was a bastion of race, class and gender privilege and political and social conservatism run by a tiny oligarchy. South African historian Colin Bundy described the closed shop character of MCC between the wars.

'MCC presidents held office for a year – and between 1919 and 1939 only six were not aristocrats: they compensated for this inadequacy by including a Tory MP who became governor of Bengal[533]; the chairman of Midland Bank; the proprietor of the *Times* newspaper, and a baronet who became Lord Mayor of London. Of the 67 Committee members in the period, all had been to public school, 23 to Eton alone. Twenty were MPs, including the Prime Minister Baldwin, the Home secretary, a Governor-General of Australia …'[534]

Viscount Monckton, simultaneously MCC president and minister of war in Anthony Eden's administration, told Doug Insole that in comparison to the MCC committee the Conservative cabinet were a bunch of 'liberal pinkos'. By the mid-1960s, the members of this pillar of the British establishment were incapable of recognising, let alone understanding, the implications of the political and cultural revolutions – from decolonisation and flower power to the Paris Spring and Tommie Smith and John Carlos's raised fist protest at the Mexican Olympics – that swirled around the receding island of establishment values.

After 15 English tours and 80 years of cosy contacts with the white South African Cricket Association, MCC had ended up with no tour, seriously damaged credibility and a reputation for political connivance, but they hoped that they had maintained the relationship,

---

533 F.S. Jackson, often described as the epitome of cricket's Golden Age

534 Colin Bundy, 'On a sticky wicket: English cricket from the golden age to the IPL', UCT summer school lecture series with Andre Odendaal, 2019. For a more detailed discussion see Jack Williams, *Cricket and England: A Cultural and Social History of the Interwar Years*, (London: Taylor and Francis, 1999) 22-25.

which was fundamental to the global structure of cricket and to MCC's own power base.

For the first time, the MCC monolith began to come under challenge from a group of members who saw its support for the South African regime as unacceptable. On 5 December, a group of MCC members led by Charles Barr, a lecturer in film studies, called a special general meeting expressing no confidence in MCC's handling of the D'Oliveira affair and the ongoing relationship with South Africa. The Reverend David Sheppard proposed, and Mike Brearley seconded, the resolution that regretted the mishandling of the events leading to the selection of the team for the 1968/69 tour; required that no further tours be undertaken to South Africa until practical progress is made towards non-racial cricket and proposed setting up a committee to monitor SACA's proposals.

Sheppard introduced the motion. 'We need a full debate and a just policy regarding cricket ties with South Africa,' he said. 'South Africa has brought politics into cricket and not the other way round.' He demolished the MCCs case regarding its retreat from its efforts in January to get a straight answer on the 'no preconditions' question.

Brearley seconded the first resolution, 'When I left South Africa after playing cricket there, I left hesitant and somewhat pessimistic about the country. I thought there was a context of increasing extremism but that liberal influences which can be spread to some extent by cricket teams might possibly be of some value. Since then I have partly changed my views. We should be very hesitant about the rightness of undertaking tours there. It is impossible for the selectors to choose and be seen to choose objectively and freely. Our responsibility to the increasing number of [black] cricketers [in England] is surely greater than our responsibility to white South Africa.'[535]

It was a thoughtful and courageous statement from a principled young cricketer, reminding MCC of their responsibilities. It was met by what John Arlott called a four-hour parade of prejudice.

---

535 MCC Library, Minutes of the Special General Meeting, MCC/CRI/5/1/95

Supporters of the motion were unprepared for the intensity of personal hostility. Even the official history of MCC admitted, 'The defenders of the MCC debated as emotionally as the Sheppard group had been clinical stumbling into personal attacks on Sheppard and losing the day in all but the final vote,' where postal votes counted in their favour.[536]

MCC failed fundamentally, not only in their duty to D'Oliveira and to other black players, but in their inability to question their own politically inspired mishandling of the affair in support of an odious and vicious regime. Moreover, they failed themselves, ignoring the inadequacies of their 19th-century thinking in a post-colonial world, driving their own institution further into a cul-de-sac. By missing this opportunity to recognise, let alone right the wrongs of their long relationship with the South Africa state and the mining industry, they betrayed their self-appointed mandate to speak for the cricket world at large.

In cricket, resistance to sporting ties with South Africa was the culmination of a decade-long struggle, on university campuses, by trade unions, in churches, schools, on the streets and on cricket fields, as MCC fought to maintain its South African connections. The cancellation of the 1968/69 tour to South Africa had been a battle lost, but MCC had no intention of losing the war and invited South Africa to tour the UK in 1970. An uprising led by Peter Hain, which resulted in the sensational anti-apartheid protests on the rugby field did not shake MCC resolve. They planned to create defensive encampments to protect the Springboks and play cricket behind barbed wire. Even then, the absurdity of their stance did not register, and it took a direct order from the Labour government to bring 80 years of cricket between England and South Africa to a formal close on 22 May 1970.[537]

The world had changed, and cricket followed miles behind, dragging its feet. It would soon be a global game both on and off the

---

536 Tony Lewis, *Double Century*, 315

537 See Peter Hain and Andre Odendaal, *Pitch Battles*, (London, 2020) chapter one

field. The West Indies were asserting their dominance on the pitch and were joined by India and Pakistan. Meanwhile, MCC continued to ignore the systematic oppression of the South African state and the barbaric dehumanisation of the majority of South Africa's population.

South African gold fuelled British imperialism while MCC became the cultural arm of empire. The MCC's racism and support for apartheid reflected a cultural continuity intact since the Victorian period and were as much about self-interest as ideology. Racism reflected Victorian values, but put down deep roots by buttressing the operation of the South African political economy. Segregation and its ideological offspring, apartheid, facilitated the cheap labour which produced the gold (a quarter of the world's production) and diamonds which were the 20th-century fruits of empire: providing buccaneering capital, country houses, civic amenities, jobs and even cut-price soldiers for European wars. MCC members shared in the profits generated by forced labour in South Africa's mines and industries.

Not much had changed by the 1980s, when the *Morning Star* revealed that despite economic sanctions against South Africa one in four Tory MPs had interests as 'directors, shareholders, parliamentary consultants or advisers' in 83 companies with a financial stake in apartheid South Africa.

The cosy if sometimes awkward relationship between the cricketing elites of Britain and South Africa came to the messiest of endings. Cricket was changing, as the one-day game achieved a new prominence, the Kerry Packer revolution grudgingly rewarded the players, while passing most of the profits to giant media conglomerates and the MCC private members club ceded its responsibilities to the Test and County Cricket Board and ultimately the England and Wales Cricket Board.

In South Africa, the Soweto uprising in 1976 and the deaths of hundreds of schoolchildren brought new levels of repression and resistance as the apartheid regime acted out its own endgame. It was squeezed by economic and sporting sanctions, threatened by external and internal forces. A popular uprising which made it ungovernable by the end of the 1980s forced the reactionary F.W. de Klerk to come to the negotiating table.

Finally, in the early 1990s an independent and democratic South Africa arose from the wreckage of a fractured, illegitimate state to meet its own complex future. On the pitch, the chaos of a succession of 'rebel' tours from England, Australia, Sri Lanka and the West Indies ended in 1990 when Mike Gatting led an English party under Dr Ali Bacher's guidance in the face of sustained mass protests. Gatting initially described them as a few people singing and dancing, but they forced him and his team to pack their bags and head home, a few days after Nelson Mandela was released. In 2013, Gatting became MCC president.

In October 1995, the first official England tourists for 30 years under Mike Atherton played their opening first-class match at the Soweto Cricket Oval against a South African Invitation XI captained by Hansie Cronje and including Soweto-born batsman Geoffrey Toyana and wicketkeeper Lulama Mazikizana. Both were Xhosa speakers from the Eastern Cape, like the African cricketers who had almost toured England more than a century earlier. Toyana, the urbanised city dweller from Soweto, was to make a name for himself as a coach, mentoring South Africa's first cricket captain of African descent, Tembu Bavuma. Mazikizana, growing up on the east coast, had been one of the first two black players to represent SA Schools in 1991/92. Neither had been born when Smith's MCC had flown home 30 years before.

Nelson Mandela paid an unannounced visit and stopped in front of Devon Malcolm. 'I know you, you're The Destroyer,' he smiled.[538] A new era had begun. But cricket and politics was a no less volatile mix in the new country. There were many false dawns to come, it was not going to be a smooth ride.

Devon Malcolm spoke of the strain of racism which continued to infect English cricket. More than two decades later, the Azeem Rafiq case illustrates how cricket in England is still played within a

---

538 Devon Malcolm, *You Guys are History*, (London, Collins Willow, 1998) 151

discriminatory and exclusionist culture, including institutional blocks to black opportunities, and a victim-blaming discourse. An increasing acknowledgement of black perspectives must be the starting point for ensuring the long-term health of our game.

Eighty years of cricket tours to South Africa have juxtaposed a complex story of heroism on the field and tragedy and farce off it. Ironically, almost all communities of South Africans have shared a common love for this, the most sublime of all games, which presented a primary opportunity to integrate South Africans into a common culture and identity. Yet the class framework and racism of both the South African state and imperialist social institutions sacrificed the integrationist potential of cricket to a brutal and self-serving regime over more than a century.

Now, almost 30 years later, the timeless pilgrimage of the swallows delights the southern skies while cricket is struggling to reflect the changed realities of the 21st century. A democratic and common ownership of the game, led by the daughters and sons of those who had been excluded, has yet to fully emerge. But there is hope that after the trauma of a pandemic that has changed the world, and the accompanying shocks applied by a global sporting movement that insists that black lives matter, this most uplifting of summer games can reflect a new set of values, which counter racism and discrimination on grounds of gender and economic oppression, and provide for an inclusive society and a level playing field.

Sources and Bibliography

Interviews and conversations
Douglas Insole, 15 June 2017
Michael Brearley, 4 and 11 August 2020
David Allison, 26 May 2021

Archives
MCC Library and Archive, Lord's
MCC minute books
MCC minutes of committee meetings

Newspapers and periodicals
British Lion
Cape Times
Cape Argus
Cricket
Cricket Field
Cricket Lore
Cricket Monthly
Daily Express
Daily Independent
Daily Telegraph
Diamond Fields Advertiser
Manchester Guardian
Natal Mercury
The Cricketer
The Cricket Field

The Owl
Rand Daily Mail
South Africa News
The South African Non-European Cricket Almanack 1953–54, 1954–55, 1969 edited by Reddy S.J. and Bansda, D.N.
South African Cricket Annual
The Sportsman
Standard and Diggers News
The Star
The Times

Books and articles

Allen, David Rayvern, *Sir Aubrey* (London: J.M. McKenzie, 2005)

Arlott, John, *Gone with the Cricketers* (London: Longmans, 1950)

Bailey, Jack, *Conflicts in Cricket* (London: Kingswood Press, 1989)

Bailey, Trevor, *Wickets, Catches and the Odd Run* (London: Collins, 1986)

Barrington, Ken, *Playing it Straight* (London: Stanley Paul, 1968)

Bassano, Brian, *Mann's Men* (London: J.M. McKenzie, 2004)

Bedser, Alec and Eric, *Our Cricketing Story* (London: Evans Bros, 1950)

Birley, Derek, *A Social History of English Cricket* (London: Aurum Press, 1999)

Bradford, Helen, *A Taste of Freedom* (London: Yale University Press, 1987)

Brearley Mike, *On Cricket* (London: Constable, 2018)

Brearley, Mike, *On Form* (London: Little, Brown, 2017)

Brearley, Mike, *The Art of Captaincy* (London: Hodder and Stoughton, 1985)

Cape Times, Sports and Sportsmen in South Africa (Cape Town: Cape Times, 1929)

Carr, A.W., *Cricket with the Lid Off* (London: Hutchinson, 1935)

Chalke Stephen, *At the Heart of English Cricket* (Bath: Fairfield Books, 2001)

Chalke, Stephen, *The Flame Still Burns* (Bath: Fairfield Books, 2007)

Cowdrey, Colin, *MCC* (London: Coronet Books, 1977)

Cox, Charles, *The Cricketing Record of Major Warton's Tour* (London: reprinted by J.M. McKenzie, 1987)

Du Preez, Max, *Of Warriors, Lovers and Prophets* (Cape Town: Zebra Press, 2004)

Duffus, Louis, (ed.), *South African Cricket, Volume 3, 1927–1947* (Johannesburg: SACA,1949)

Duffus, Louis, *Cricketers of the Veld* (London: Sampson, Low, Marston and Co, 1947)

Edrich, Bill, *Cricketing Days* (London: Stanley Paul, 1950)

Edrich, Bill, *Cricketing Heritage* (London: Stanley Paul, no date known)

Evans, Godfrey, *Behind the Stumps* (London: Hodder and Stoughton, 1951)

Farnes, Ken, *Tours and Tests* (London: Lutterworth Press, 1940)

Ferguson, W.H., *Mr Cricket* (London: Nicholas Kaye, 1957)

Foot, David, *Wally Hammond, the Reasons Why* (London: Robson Books, 1996)

Fortune, Charles, *The MCC Tour of South Africa 1956–1957* (London: George Harrap and Co, 1957)

Fraser, Maryna and Jeeves, Alan, *All that Glittered* (Cape Town: Oxford University Press, 1977)

Fry, C.B., *Life Worth Living* (London: reprinted by the Pavilion Library, 1986)

Gibson, Alan, *The Cricket Captains of England* (London: Cassell, 1979)

Green, Benny (ed.), *The Wisden Papers, 1888–1946* (London: Stanley Paul, 1989)

Green, Benny (ed.), *Wisden Anthology, 1864–1900* (London: Queen Anne Press, 1979)

Green, Benny, *A History of Cricket* (London: Barrie and Jenkins, 1988)

Greyvenstein, Chris, *Giants of South African Cricket* (Cape Town: Don Nelson, 1971)

Gutsche, Thelma, *Old Gold: The History of the Wanderers Club* (Cape Town: Howard Timmins, 1966)

Hain, Peter, and Odendaal André, *Pitch Battles* (Cape Town: Jonathan Ball, 2020)

Hammond, Walter, *Cricket My Destiny* (London: Stanley Paul, 1948)

Hammond, Walter, *Cricket My World* (London: Stanley Paul, 1949)

Hammond, Walter, *Cricket's Secret History* (London: Stanley Paul, 1952)

Hawke, Lord, *Recollections and Reminiscences* (London: Williams and Norgate, 1924)

Hayhoe-Flint, Rachael, *Heyhoe!* (London: Pelham, 1978)

Hayter, Reg (ed.), *The Best of The Cricketer 1921–1981, The Sixtieth Anniversary Selection* (London: Littlehampton, 1981)

Henderson J.T. (ed.), *South African Cricketers' Annual 1906–07* (Pietermaritzburg: Times Publishing, 1907)

Hill, Alan, *Johnny Wardle, Cricket Conjurer* (London: David and Charles, 1988),

Hobbs, Jack, *My Cricket Memories* (London: Heinemann, 1924)

Hobbs, Jack, *Playing for England* (London: Victor Gollancz, 1931)

Hodgson, Janet and Edelmann, Theresa, *Zonnebloem College and the Genesis of an African Intelligentsia, 1857–1933* (Cape Town: African Lives, 2018)

Howat, Gerald, *Plum Warner* (London: Unwin Hyman, 1987)

Insole, Douglas, *Cricket from the Middle* (London: Heinemann, 1960)

James, C.L.R., *Beyond a Boundary* (London: Serpent's Tail, 1994)

Joseph, Helen, *If this be Treason* (Johannesburg: Contra Press, 1998)

Keppel-Jones, Arthur, *Rhodes and Rhodesia* (Kingston: Queen's University Press, 1983)

Kidson, Howard, *Over and Time* (Cape Town: Howard Timmins, 1983)

Kynaston, David, *Bobby Abel* (London: Secker and Warburg, 1982)

Laker, Jim, *Over to Me* (London: Frederick Muller, 1960)

Lee, H.W., *Forty Years of English Cricket* (London: Clerke and Cockeran, 1948)

Lemmon, David, *Johnny Won't Hit Today* (London: Allen and Unwin, 1983)

Leveson Gower, Henry, *Cricket Personalities* (London: Williams and Norgate, 1925)

Lewis, Tony, *Double Century, the Story of the MCC and Cricket* (London: Hodder and Stoughton, 1987)

Lodge, Tom, *Black Politics in South Africa since 1945* (Johannesburg: Raven, 1983)

Luckin, M.W., *South African Cricket, 1919–1927* (Johannesburg: published by the author, 1929)

Luckin, M.W., *The History of South African Cricket* (Johannesburg: W.E. Hortor and Co, 1915)

Malcolm, Devon, *You Guys Are History* (London: Collins Willow, 1998)

May, Peter, *A Game Enjoyed* (London: Stanley Paul, 1985)

Maylam, Paul, *South Africa's Racial Past* (Aldershot: Ashgate, 2001)

McGlew, Jackie, *Cricket for South Africa* (London: Hodder and Stoughton, 1961)

Moodie, T. Dunbar, *Going for Gold* (Berkeley: UCLA, 1994),

Mostert, Noel, *Frontiers* (London: Jonathan Cape, 1992)

Murphy, Patrick, *The Spinner's Turn* (London: J.M. Dent, 1982)

Murray, Bruce and Vahed, Goolam (eds.), *Empire and Cricket* (Pretoria: UNISA, 2009)

Murray, Bruce, Parry, Richard, and Winch Jonty (eds.), *Cricket and Society in South Africa, 1910–1971* (London: Palgrave Macmillan, 2018)

Nasson, Bill and Bickford Smith, Vivian (eds.) *Illuminated Lives* (Cape Town: Penguin, 2019)

Nasson, Bill, *History Matters: Selected Writings 1970–2016* (Cape Town: Penguin, 2016)

Nicholson, Rafaelle, *Ladies and Lords* (Oxford: Peter Lang, 2019)

Oborne, Peter, *Basil D'Oliveira* (London: Little, Brown, 2004)

Odendaal, André, *Vukani Bantu! The Beginnings of Black Protest Politics in South Africa to 1912* (Cape Town: David Philip, 1984)

Odendaal André, *The Founders* (Cape Town: Jacana Media, 2012)

Odendaal, André, Reddy, Krish, Merrett, Christopher, and Winch, Jonty, *Cricket and Conquest, 1795–1914* (Cape Town: HSRC, 2016)

Odendaal, André, Reddy, Krish and Merrett, Christopher, *Divided Country: The History of South African Cricket Retold 1914–1950s* (Cape Town: HSRC, 2018),

Omer Cooper J.D., *History of South Africa* (London: James Currey, second edition, 1994)

Pakenham, Thomas, *The Boer War* (London: George Weidenfield and Nicholson, 1979)

Parry, Richard, 'African Cricket on the Rand: Piet Gwele, Frank Roro and the Shaping of a Community', in Murray, Parry and Winch (eds.) *Cricket and Society in South Africa* (London: Palgrave Macmillan, 2018)

Parry, Richard, 'Black Cricketers, White Politicians and the Origins of Segregation at the Cape' in Bruce Murray and Goolam Vahed (eds), *Empire and Cricket* (Pretoria: UNISA, 2009)

Paynter, Eddie, *Cricket All the Way* (Leeds: A. Richardson, 1962)

Peebles, I.A.R., *Batter's Castle* (London: Pavilion Books, 1986)

Plaatje Sol. T., *Native Life in South Africa* (London: King and Sons, 1916)

Ranger, T.O., *Revolt in Southern Rhodesia* (London: Heinemann, 1978)

Read, W.W., *Annals of Cricket* (London: Sampson, Low, Marston and Co, 1896)

Rendell, Brian, *Frank and George Mann* (Cardiff: ACS Publications, 2015)

Ross, Alan, *Cape Summer* (London: Constable, 1957)

Ross, Alan, *Coastwise Lights* (London: Collins Harvill, 1988)

Roux, Edward, *Time Longer than Rope* (Madison: University of Wisconsin Press, 1964)

Schindler, Colin, *Bob Barber, the Professional Amateur* (Nantwich: Max Books, 2015),

Sengupta, Arunabha, *Apartheid: A Point to Cover* (Amsterdam: Amstelveen, 2020)

Short, Graham, *The Trevor Goddard Story* (London: Bailey Bros, 1965)

Simons, Jack and Ray, *Class and Colour in South Africa* (London: IDAF, 1983)

Spinney, Laura, *Pale Rider: The Spanish Flu and How it Changed the World* (London: Vintage, 2017)

Stone, Duncan, *Different Class* (London: Repeater, 2022)

Strudwick, Herbert, *25 Years Behind the Stumps* (London: Hutchinson, 1926)

Swanton, E.W, *With P.B.F. May's MCC Team 1956–57* (London: Robert Hale, 1957)

Swanton, E.W. (ed.), *Barclays World of Cricket* 3rd Edition (London: Guild Publishing, 1986)

Tate, Maurice, *My Cricketing Reminiscences* (London: Stanley Paul, 1934)

Tennyson, Lionel Lord, *From Verse to Worse* (London: Christopher Johnson, 1936)

Tharoor, Shashi, *Inglorious Empire* (London: Penguin, 2018)

Turnbull, Maurice and Allom, Maurice, *The Two Maurices Again* (London: E. Allom and Co, 1931)

Waite, John, *Perchance to Bowl* (London: Nicholas Kaye, 1961)

Walmsley, Kevin, 'A.C. Skinner Revealed', *The Cricket Statistician*, issue 180, 2017, 27-31

Wardle, Johnny, *Happy Go Johnny* (London: Hale, 1957)

Warner, P.F., *Cricket in Many Climes* (London: Heinemann, 1900)

Warner, P.F., *The MCC in South Africa 1905–06* (London: Chapman and Hall, 1906)

Warner, P.F., *My Cricketing Life* (London: Hodder and Stoughton, 1924)

Williams, Jack, *Cricket and England: A Cultural and Social History of the Interwar Years* (London: Taylor and Francis, 2003)

Winch, Jonty and Parry, Richard, *Too Black to Wear Whites* (Cape Town: Penguin, 2020)

Winch, Jonty, 'C.L.R. James versus Learie Constantine', in Murray, Parry, and Winch (eds.), *Cricket and Society in South Africa* (London: Palgrave Macmillan, 2018)

Winch, Jonty, *Cricket in Southern Africa* (Windsor: Windsor Publications, 1998)

Winch, Jonty, *England's Youngest Captain* (Windsor: Windsor Publishers, 2003)

Woods, Sammy, *My Reminiscences* (London: Chapman and Hall, 1925)

Wyatt, Bob, *Three Straight Sticks* (London: Stanley Paul, 1951)

Index

437

Also available at all good book stores

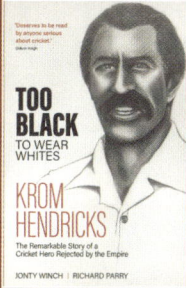

9781785318252

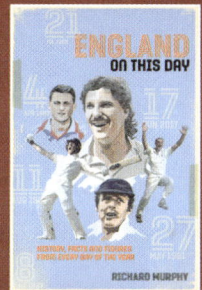

9781785317224

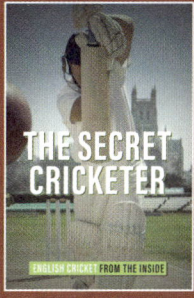

9781785319860

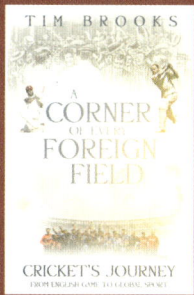

9781785316395

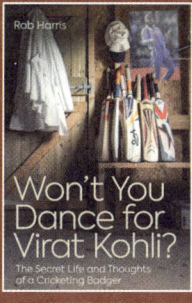

9781785317798

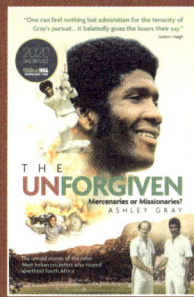

9781785315329

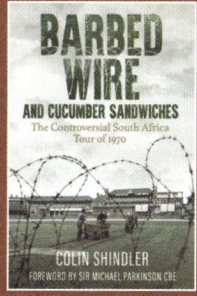

9781785316340

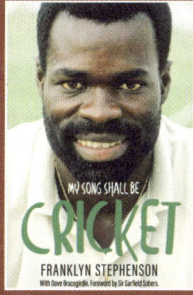

9781785316920

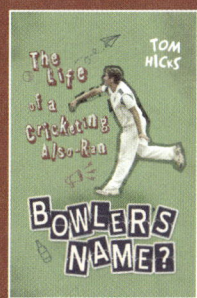

9781785318412